IMAGINARY
EMPIRES

IMAGINARY EMPIRES

WOMEN

WRITERS

and

ALTERNATIVE

FUTURES

in

EARLY

US LITERATURE

MARIA O'MALLEY

LOUISIANA STATE
UNIVERSITY
PRESS

BATON ROUGE

Published by Louisiana State University Press
lsupress.org

DESIGNER: Andrew Shurtz
TYPEFACE: Monotype Fournier

Cover illustration from *Studies on Twilight Phenomena*
by Johannes Kiessling, 1888.

Grateful acknowledgment to the journals where the following
chapters first appeared in slightly altered forms:

Chapter 1 first appeared as "Dangerous Domestic Spaces in
The Female American" in *Women's Studies: An Interdisciplinary Journal* 45.8
(2016). Chapter 5 first appeared as "Imagining Massachusetts: Political
Geography and Sexual Control in Harriet Jacobs's *Incidents in the Life
of a Slave Girl*" in *Journal of Narrative Theory*, 46.1 (2016).

Library of Congress Cataloging-in-Publication Data
Names: O'Malley, Maria, 1976– author.
Title: Imaginary empires : women writers and alternative futures in early
 US literature / Maria O'Malley.
Description: Baton Rouge : Louisiana State University Press, [2023] |
 Includes bibliographical references and index.
Identifiers: LCCN 2022023291 (print) | LCCN 2022023292 (ebook) |
 ISBN 978-0-8071-7848-5 (cloth) | ISBN 978-0-8071-7926-0 (pdf) |
 ISBN 978-0-8071-7925-3 (epub)
Subjects: LCSH: American fiction—Women authors—18th century—History
 and criticism. | American fiction—Women authors—19th century—History
 and criticism. | Alternative histories (Fiction), American—History and
 criticism. | Women in literature | United States—In literature.
Classification: LCC PS374.W6 O63 2023 (print) | LCC PS374.W6 (ebook) |
 DDC 813/.6—dc23
LC record available at https://lccn.loc.gov/2022023291
LC ebook record available at https://lccn.loc.gov/2022023292

To Elizabeth

Contents

Acknowledgments

I have the "unearnèd luck" to have too many people to thank for their personal and professional contributions to my efforts to complete this book over several years. It is a pleasure, though, to single out a few individuals and institutions who have been particularly generous in offering help during the research and writing process. Several universities provided support through research grants, travel funds, and release from teaching, including the University of Nebraska at Kearney, Eureka College, and Briar Cliff University. The Research Services Council at UNK made it possible for me to travel to the Library of Congress to conduct research. I especially thank Sam Umland, Bill Jurma, and Kenya Taylor for helping me secure funding and for their sound counsel.

Thank you to the *Journal of Narrative Theory* and *Women Studies: An Interdisciplinary Journal* for permission to reprint parts of articles previously published. Part of chapter 1 on *The Female American* was published in *Women Studies*, vol. 45, no. 8 (2016) at https://www.tandfonline.com. I thank Denise MacNeil for her feedback on that essay and for connecting me with other scholars writing on the same text. An earlier version of chapter 5 on Harriet Jacobs's 1861 slave narrative appeared as "Imagining Massachusetts: Political Geography and Sexual Control in Harriet Jacobs's *Incidents in the Life of a Slave Girl*" in the *Journal of Narrative Theory,* vol. 46, no. 1 (2016).

Thanks as well to the American Studies Association, the American Society for Eighteenth-Century Studies, the American Literature Association, and the Society for the Study of American Women Writers at whose conferences I presented the first iterations of these arguments. At Louisiana State University Press, James Long has been a consummate professional throughout the peer review and the book production process. I also appreciate the expertise of Tammy Oberhausen Rastoder and Neal Novak in preparing the final manuscript. Many thanks to the anonymous peer reviewers whose careful reading and constructive comments improved the book. In particular, I thank Jillian Sayre for her discernment, insightful suggestions, and generosity in revealing her role as a reader. Several early readers of individual chapters offered helpful feedback, including Theresa Gaul, Julie Husband, and Laura Laffrado. Of course, all "accidents, mistakes, and errors" are my own.

Many people have enabled me to navigate the travel involved in researching material and presenting at conferences as well as offered intellectual stimulation, including those from the "256," Karen, Erin, Eileen, Deirdre, John, Elizabeth, Martin, Kevin, and Gabriel who all taught me that the imaginary could be more real than "this world, this life." I am grateful as well to my aunts, Margaret Wynne, Noreen Colgan, and Sr. Carmel O'Malley; my in-laws, Denys and Ellen; and my late parents, John and Betty. My parents, especially in the years leading up to tenure, made sure that "the wind was always at my back." Above all, my oldest debt lies with my sister Elizabeth whose influence on my academic career stretches all the way back to when we moved into our first apartment on Gregory Street in Champaign, Illinois, my freshman year of college. Since then, she has been a steadfast champion for my career and a model for living an ethical life of meaning, purpose, and service.

My greatest and luckiest debt is to Denys, office suitemate, colleague, sometimes coeditor and cowriter, and foxhole partner. Although life has led us on some unexpected circuits across the continent and the Atlantic, I have found that, as Michael tells Eve in Milton's *Paradise Lost,* "where he abides, think there thy native soil." My daughter, Kate, and sons, Henry and George, deserve thanks as well for contributing to a life brimming with the arts, history, nature, and justice or, in other words, truth and beauty.

IMAGINARY

EMPIRES

INTRODUCTION

Imaginary Empires EXAMINES STORIES OF NATIONAL BEGINNINGS
or renewal that place the lives of American women characters at their center.
Read closely, the texts under discussion here, published between 1767 and
1867, recognize the multiple histories that women, indigenous, and Black
people experience within larger and monolithic historical narratives. These
authors attempt to inscribe these coincident histories through the form of
the novel or autobiography in order to shape future social and political formations. Ultimately, the women writers and characters studied here imagine
different sociopolitical trajectories for empire, or in some texts, they seize
on repressions empires foster to put forth alternative assemblages rather
than ignoring marginalized others or elegizing their oppression. Their texts,
in short, work against a cultural amnesia. It is common, for instance, for
scholars to cite Jacques Derrida's metaphor about the founding of nations as
involving "l'amnésie." In his *On Cosmopolitanism and Forgiveness*, Derrida
writes, "All Nation-States are born and found themselves in violence. The
foundation is made in order to hide it; by its essence it tends to organize amnesia, sometimes under the celebration and sublimation of the grand beginnings" (*On Cosmopolitanism* 57). The evocative oxymoron of an "organizing
amnesia" has led literary scholars to find aporias in texts that omit references
to foundational acts steeped in violence or that occlude displaced others.[1]
But the metaphor of amnesia, as an involuntary physiological condition, implies a passive rather than overt response to nation building, especially as
nation building in the United States is entangled with its imperial ambitions.
This study follows Ed Larkin's and others' lead in understanding the United
States' imperial ambitions as reaching back to the late eighteenth century
even before the American Revolution: "[T]he United States was conceived
as an empire from the outset" (Larkin 7).[2]

Just as metaphors of amnesia undergird studies of empire in literary studies, so do metaphors of ghosts, hauntings, and revenants to describe textual
traces that hint at unacknowledged violence or injustice toward racialized
others. Some critics also note silences, omissions, or obfuscation toward colonial violence in literary texts.[3] These studies are often masterful at foregrounding aspects of a text that have barely registered for generations of
readers: for example, Deborah L. Madsen, who analyzed the silence about
slavery in Nathaniel Hawthorne's *The Scarlet Letter* in 1991 in *Journal of
American Studies,* Saidiya Hartman's 1997 book *Scenes of Subjection,* or Edward Watts's 1998 book on *Writing and Postcolonialism in the Early Republic.*
In drawing attention to silences in literary texts from the early United States,
like *The Scarlet Letter,* critics seem to not only recognize marginalized others
but also seek a semblance of justice by identifying how authors were com-
plicit with the marginalization of indigenous people and people held in slavery. However, I am interested in authors who highlight acts of foundational
violence rather than repress them and who imagine different possibilities for
the future of the United States without relying on characters who are scape-
goated, sacrificed, or, at the other end of a power spectrum, omnipotent.[4] In
particular, these texts' shed light on political undercurrents, as they intersect
with constructions of gender, in the formation of empire.[5] This book puts
in conversation texts in which ghost-like figures refuse to die, leave, or stay
silent. Instead, they demonstrate the imbrications of violence in the public
sphere as emanating from the domestic.

At the same time, each text engages with futurity, bringing to the fore
what Paul Armstrong refers to as the "third horizon" of a literary text. Armstrong makes a convincing case that literary critics focus on only two of the
three "horizons" that texts set forth: their portrayal of the present and past.
He explains how "[c]ontextual historical studies that take into account only
two of those three horizons—the text's relation to its contemporaneous situation and the traces of the past in its originating circumstances—but those
that neglect futurity, the third horizon, are fatally incomplete" ("In Defense"
94). By drawing attention to future readers, a text presents itself as a measure
to gauge progress toward a more equitable America. Although new historicism continues to inform us about the variety of late eighteenth- and early
nineteenth- century US literary cultures, relying solely on new historicist
methodologies undercuts how some texts represent tension about unresolved

racial injustice under imperialism and slavery for future readers to witness, condemn, or even ameliorate. As Armstrong maintains, "To reduce meaning to 'meaning then' by privileging the contexts governing the moment of production is to rob the situation of writing of its historicity by suppressing its futurity" ("In Defense" 94). This study seeks to reaffirm the place of the imaginary in shaping, or at least measuring, the future. It follows the work of Jeffrey Insko, who questions the hold that new historicism exerts on literary studies.[6] He ultimately finds a place for the much-maligned "anachronism" in literary history because "history is not either a unique and distinct past or our present-day reconstructions of it, but a negotiation, a contact zone, an imagined experience born of the interaction between the two" (Insko, *History* 70).

In imagining different kinds of futures, the writers studied here reckon with the various power loci within empires and the ambivalent role of women who negotiate between their own subordinate position and sovereignty over others. Critics have long noted how the discourses surrounding European incursions into new territories made direct comparisons between the land and woman's bodies. As scholars, like John Carlos Rowe and others, sought to demarcate the organizing principle of empire in American studies, women's roles were often neglected except as they offered symbolic registers for the land or as bodies on which sexual conquest figured as imperial conquest. Myra Jehlen, Annette Kolodny, Amy Kaplan, Lauren Berlant, Elizabeth Maddock Dillon, Jenny Sharp, Laura Wexler, and Gretchen Murphy have filled this gap. Building upon their work, new studies have emerged in the past decade that articulate women's role in shaping, contesting, and bolstering empire. Yet most scholarship on empire and women focus on late nineteenth-century American literature when US imperial ambitions became more explicit. Renewed interest in the colonial period in understanding women's role in empire is evidenced by scholarship such as the volume of essays, *Women's Narratives of the Early Americas and the Formation of Empire* (2016), edited by Mary Balkun and Susan Imbarrato, that focuses specifically on early America. Marion Rust, in the introduction to that volume, observes how examining women's role in empire presents challenges because as "both agents and objects of empire, they simultaneously shaped and unsettled the way expansion unfolded" (2). These scholars and others provide new ways with which to understand some of the dynamism within empire-building.[7] Adria Imada, for instance, in looking at the history and appropriation of hula on the Hawaiian archipelago, studies women who, through "unpredictable and occasionally insurgent disruptions—while not necessarily oppositional to colonialism— nonetheless disorganize empire" (17).

The idea of "disorganizing empire" runs through my analysis of these women authors as well. For the underlying syntactical framing in the literary works examined in the following chapters lies the subjunctive—the *what if.*[8] In particular, when women insert themselves into the cultural imaginary, they overturn some assumptions on which historicism rest. More specifically, when an event is filtered through nation, period, genre, and maleness, the assessment of it can be limited. The first four chapters describe how these narratives not only depend on the subjunctive but also seem to rest on a subordinate clause, as they follow characters alienated from geography, family, language, culture, history, and citizenship. The last chapter on Harriet Jacobs's *Incidents in the Life of a Slave Girl* (1861), though, offers a point of contrast. Unlike the other fictional works studied in the first four chapters, Jacobs's text is part of the genre of life writing. Yet within her text, she writes letters offering a fictional account of her whereabouts to evade those who wish to keep her in bondage against her will. In chapter 5, I highlight how she seized upon contested sociopolitical spaces within the United States to harness conflicting definitions of US identity from within that challenge a coherent, monolithic construction of the nation.

Scholars have produced substantial evidence on how literary works codify the operations of empire.[9] As some critics point out, the relationship between empire and the imagination is reciprocal. Discussing the influence of imaginative literature on the asymmetrical power relations that arose in the eighteenth century among nation-states, Delmot Ryan asserts, "The imagination contributes to the constitution of imperial constellations rather than simply reflecting them" (151).[10] Yet I posit that works of the imagination, whether or not they contribute to the operations of actual empires, still influence the ontology of the modern subject as it relies on the imagination in its negotiation with the state apparatus. By looking at fiction by or about women, we not only find alternative ways to respond to contact, exchange, and cohabitation in the early United States, but we also observe the possibilities inherent in the literary to foster participation, resignification, and even rapprochement.

The term "women writers" is an inexact description of the authors discussed over the following chapters because the authorship of *The Female*

American is unknown. The other four chapters look at three white women and one Black writer. Karen Sánchez-Eppler's term "feminist-abolitionist" might provide a more accurate description of these writers, even if some of the authors' commitment to the abolition of slavery or the slave trade are unknown. Yet Sánchez-Eppler's term takes into account "the degree to which domestic and sentimental antislavery writings are implicated in the very oppressions they seek to reform" (Sánchez-Eppler 16). On the whole, though, these white women writers use racialized others to represent the boundaries of American identity, gender norms, and geopolitical spaces in ways that sometimes undercut their alterity. Yet the writers' representations underscore how violence was enacted on racialized others. The last chapter examines Harriet Jacobs, who as a Black woman writer puts the discussion of the US as an empire into relief. As Laura Doyle explains, Jacobs, along with other African and African American writers "do more than ventriloquize the dominant liberty narrative with a subversive différance. They implicitly generate an African-Atlantic archeology of it, installing themselves as its absent origin" (6).[11]

Readers may note the undisguised politics through which these women writers summon a community of readers to reinterpret the past; these texts evince a deep ambivalence, too, about the modern subject to effect change. As Christopher Castiglia and Russ Castronovo posit, literature, among others uses, "reveals that aesthetics disrupt the individual subject and provide the groundwork for an alternative, post–identity collectivism" (433). Some of the disruptions the authors studied here foster include de-essentializing identity. Even if the texts put forth myriad cultural traces over which the authors have little control, the fictional worlds the authors usher in and the methods that they employ to direct the attention of their reader to collective problems deserve more scholarly examination, for these authors write not only about imaginary events but also to an imagined public at some futurity.

GHOSTBUSTING
THROUGH THE ARCHIVES

In surveying criticism of early American culture and postcolonial literature, as mentioned above, one finds literary critics relying on the imagery of ghosts, hauntings, erasures, silences, and amnesia to analyze how works of literature omit certain figures.[12] For instance, the language of haunting infuses

Toni Morrison's 1992 *Playing in the Dark*, her study of how Black characters are, paradoxically, central and yet sidelined in major works of American literature. Writing about Morrison in 1999, Jennifer DeVere Brody observes how "[s]uch racialized absent presences and disappearing traces have been the focus of many recently published books, both popular and academic" (Brody 737). The metaphor of ghosts seems particularly apt to reproduce itself as critics who mention unnamed "ghosts" in literary works are then likewise accused of ghosting others in their own scholarship. By 2008, Leslie Bow revisits Morrison's book, looking for "ghosts [that] haunt this seminal text"; she concedes, though, "while there may be ghosts in the machinery of her own text, [Morrison] has nonetheless given us the tools to see them" (Bow 564). Bow's article appeared in a special issue of *American Literary History* alongside an essay in which Russ Castronovo revisits Amy Kaplan and Donald E. Pease's edited collection *Cultures of United States Imperialism* (1992). The language of ghosts also appears throughout Castronovo's essay as he suggests the editors and contributors to the volume ignore "present-day ghosts" (432); he concludes that Kaplan and Pease's whole volume is "haunted by the present" (430). Castronovo's point is that footnotes by subsequent scholars referencing Kaplan and Pease are an empty genuflection. Still, he admits "it is safe to say that the amassing of references to this collection provides evidence of a paradigm shift to correct for the *amnesia* that effectively decouples imperialism and culture in the historical and literary registers of 'America'" (Castronovo 428, emphasis mine). In other words, the language of ghosts, haunting, and amnesia recenters the critic as ghostbuster and herald of repressed memories even if at times the critic ends up an unwitting accomplice to ghosting other marginalized characters, critics, or historical figures.[13]

Yet certain texts in the American literary canon not only seem to run counter to instituting such amnesia but also flout textual practices that ignore marginalized others. Edward Watts provides a useful correction about the trope of amnesia in early American studies by historicizing the turn to forgetting: "the amnesia [. . .] set in only after ideas of romantic nationalism—in which all nations are immemorial—emerged after 1820, on the heels of European Romanticism and Sir Walter Scott. Early republic *literary* nationalism was functional and republican, matching the founding generation's enlightenment-influenced civic nationalism. . . . Moreover, many texts are poorly suited to the accusation of empire-building amnesia" ("Settler"

460–61). I wish to take Watt's points further by questioning the efficacy of the metaphor of amnesia; for the term does not quite catch the nuance of deleting uncomfortable truths from the historical record or withholding information from subsequent generations. A literary representation of amnesia might explain what I mean. In Helen Hunt Jackson's novel, *Ramona* (1884), an indigenous man named Alessandro experiences amnesia after the trauma of witnessing white Americans destroy his village at Temecula in California.[14] Alessandro's literal amnesia does not enable him to adapt to a new world order. Instead, he reverts to behaviors more conducive to his early life in Temecula as though his amnesia sets him further back in the past, not more firmly in the present. As John M. Gonzalez explains, "Alessandro suffers from never really having left his tribal nation at all" as he starts to treat all property as communal despite private property laws that get him arrested (80).

Another example from a literary work, this one from the genre of life writing, might also complicate to the metaphor of amnesia. It seems that, in texts that represent nation-building, violence is either repressed and therefore resurfaces in scenes of uncanny echoes, or violence traumatizes an individual casting them into an ever-present past. Mary Rowlandson's famous 1682 account of her captivity among an Algonquin tribe during Metacom's War provides an example of the latter.[15] In her written testimony, Rowlandson evidences a sustained bigotry toward her Algonquin captors that leaves them unindividuated in her text, but reading in between the lines of her text, her captors' perspectives seep into her account. At the end of her account, Rowlandson reflects on how the trauma of her captivity in 1676, though now consigned to the distant past, continues to affect her at night when she cannot sleep; she interprets those lingering effects as psychospiritual insight. She writes, "I can remember the time when I used to sleep quietly without workings in my thoughts, whole nights together, but now it is other ways with me. . . . Oh! the wonderful power of God that mine eyes have seen, affording matter enough for my thoughts to run in, that when others are sleeping mine eyes are weeping" (Rowlandson 111). Bryce Traister explains how "Rowlandson's insomnia gestures to a gap between exemplary and extraordinary experience: between her representative role as redeemed sufferer and her unique identity as a traumatized individual whose memories remain, to borrow a term from Cathy Caruth, 'unassimilated'" (324). Traister's analysis considers the trauma of colonial violence without resorting to metaphors of haunting in order to delineate the psychological response that the author experiences and the text records. Those critics who invoke ghosts and silences might add more nuance to their analyses by following Traister's lead by examining the kind of defense mechanisms trauma brings about and how literature shores up those psychological defenses or, in some cases, how testimony manages to break through those defenses to allow readers to bear witness to "foundational violence."

This book surveys a sampling of texts that place the lives of women at their center, published between 1767 and 1867, as they attempt to confront the violence of settlement and slavery rather than cultivate a cultural amnesia. These texts were chosen because their representation of the alterity of the dispossessed other leads them to imagine alternative futures. The primary works under discussion include *The Female American, The Secret History or the Horrors of St. Domingo, Hope Leslie, A Romance of the Republic,* and *Incidents in the Life of a Slave Girl.* The texts neither deny the past nor stay stuck replaying the violence. By launching readers into an imaginary world of their creation, these texts suggest that writing about the constructedness of the past disables and disputes the dominant narratives of culture and therefore serves as the means of demarcating the possible. They stand apart from other books, even those written by some of the same authors.

For instance, compare two texts by Lydia Maria Child that rely on tropes of death and return: *Hobomok* and *Romance of the Republic.* In *Hobomok,* published in 1824, a white male protagonist, Charles Brown, "returns" from the dead after his white fiancée has married the title character, Hobomok, an indigenous man. When Hobomok encounters the living Charles Brown, the narrator reports that "After repeated assurances the Indian timidly approached— and the certainty that Brown was indeed alive was more dreadful to him than all the ghosts that could have been summoned from another world" (Child, *Hobomok* 138). When Hobomok decides to "disappear" to allow the English couple to reunite, he takes on Charles's role as the text's ghost in service to America: in the words of critic Renée Bergland, "Hobomok fosters the 'mighty' [US] nation by voluntarily becoming a ghost" (81). Nancy Sweet observes how even though Mary and Hobomok have a mixed-race child, the text fails to engage in the implications of that representation: "Child breezes over the taboo of his interracial parentage by whitening the half-Indian child. This erasure of Little Hobomok's Indian identity attests even more strongly than his father's exile to Child's inability at the age of twenty-two to envision an America of racial heterogeneity" (Sweet 117). Even Hobomok's mother is seemingly erased from the text: Jillian Sayre, examining the narrator's omission of details about the death of Hobomok's mother, claims, "This silence forecloses the possibility of identification; the haunting Native American described by Renée Bergland might therefore be seen as a product of deep structure, and inability to grieve that girds the subject's fundamental social identification" (127). The language of "ghosts" and "erasure" mark the critical discourse of Child's *Hobomok*. In contrast, Child's post–Civil War novel *A Romance of the Republic* (1867) offers vivid scenes of return and reparation—characters presumed dead who return and gain restitution—rather than abstracted scenes of loss or figurative hauntings, as will be discussed in chapter 4. In *A Romance of the Republic,* reunion does not simply mean a rapprochement among diverse racial and ethnic groups but reparation in the form of economic justice. It also celebrates mixed-race ancestry as the key to American geopolitical power.

It seems that texts that offer scholars an opportunity to identify aporias, erased persons, and projections in forging imperial control, like *Hobomok*, have received disproportionate attention.[16] An emphasis on hauntings in empire studies arises from scholars' investment in bringing to light what powerful figures hid, disavowed, or could not even conceptualize.[17] Two veins within new historicism have emerged that I dub, in a playful and not unironic allusion to Freud, as rooted in mourning and melancholia.[18] In the former, scholars sort through data and primary source materials from the past to ascertain ever more nuanced details about the discursive practices and epistemological foundations at the time when an author published. Melissa Ganz's 2013 article in *ECTI* on the relation between the novels of Frances Burney and the 1753 Marriage Act in England would provide an example in this vein, as would Clayton Marsh's 2016 article in *American Literature*, in which he examines Nathaniel Hawthorne's "The Birthmark" in the context of mid-nineteenth-century temperance reform to understand how the metaphor of temperance shapes Hawthorne's engagement with the past.[19] I refer to this vein using the term "mourning," Freud's term for healthy, natural grieving, because these analyses often lament lost opportunities in the past whether in terms of the abuses or uses of power, in terms of past scholarly omissions, or in their efforts to present more nuanced understandings of the conditions of literary production by employing a new historicist approach.

The second vein of new historicism, which I refer to as "melancholia," Freud's term for severe and long lasting grief, marked by doubling and substitution, is infused not only with the methodology of new historicism and cultural studies but also seems informed by Derrida's "hauntology."[20] New historicism in this line has provided some beautifully written scholarship, as it employs uncanny ghost metaphors to demystify neglected and oppressed actors from the past while further elucidating literary history.[21] Diana Taylor, in proposing that scholars look to "scenarios" that repeat across texts, offers an analysis firmly rooted in ghosts and magician-like tricks (28). She writes, "The scenario structures our understanding. It also haunts our present, a form of hauntology…that resuscitates and reactivates old dramas. We've seen it all before. The framework allows for occlusions; by positioning our perspective, it promotes certain views while helping to disappear others" (28). Taylor's work has a two-pronged approach: her substantiating the "repertoire" poses a useful challenge to text-based archives and, moreover, enables scholars to fill in missing archives in hemispheric contexts. It also lends a gothic bent, in tone and substance, to the practice of literary criticism and cultural studies. The stress on melancholia, as part of literary practice, is made explicit in the critical writing of Heather Love. Her scholarship on modernist literature that represents same-sex desire, aims "to create an image repertoire of queer modernist melancholia in order to underline both the losses of queer modernity and the deeply ambivalent negotiation of these losses within the literature of the period" (*Feeling Backward* 5). Much of this vein of criticism, especially from scholars in early modern and queer/sexuality studies, offers its own poignancy as well as an engrossing intellectual precision as critics, like Carla Freccero, attempt "to work through some of the ways we continue to be haunted, at times knowingly, but also in ways we are unable to acknowledge or cannot imagine" ("Figural" 46–47). Yet the language of ghosts recurs even in the digital humanities and those who advocate for "surface reading": Stephen Best and Sharon Marcus cannot get away from the figuration of ghosts when trying to back away from historicist practices to advance what they term "surface reading": "Just [surface] reading sees ghosts as presences, not absences, and lets ghosts be ghosts, instead of saying what they are ghosts *of*" (13).

One learns a great deal from the ways in which this scholarship, much of it derived from queer historiography, stretches the boundaries of the archive;

however, my study, though informed by these critics, seeks to mark out a different approach.[22] What connects the texts studied in the following chapters is a tacit refusal to treat others as ghosts and instead to use the literary as a way to engage with possible futures. Scholars working from within hauntology identify gothicism in unexpected texts as they seek to name that which "Memory can step / Around—across—upon it," to quote Emily Dickinson (Fr515);[23] my work, in contrast, aims to delineate attitudes that seemingly hide in plain sight. Instead, the strangeness they cultivate reverberates to raise questions about the normative and the processes through which people naturalize certain habits, thoughts, and experiences in narrative form.[24]

The conclusion of Harriet Jacobs's life writing, *Incidents in the Life of a Slave Girl* (1861), best encapsulates the oscillation among the past, present, and future with which these authors engage. In *Incidents,* Jacobs recounts her life story from when she was born into slavery in North Carolina in 1813 to her manumission in New York in the 1850s. The last chapter of her text describes Jacobs's transition from slavery to freedom. Her northern employer puts a stop to the harassment Jacobs faces from a slave-owning family in the South, in effect "purchasing" her. Her friends happily report that they have seen the "bill of sale" for the transaction granting Jacobs her freedom. Jacobs recalls her mixed feelings about her legally guaranteed freedom: "'The bill of sale!' Those words struck me like a blow. So I was sold at last! A human being sold in the free city of New York! The bill of sale is on record, and future generations will learn from it that women were articles of traffic in New York, late in the nineteenth century of the Christian religion. It may hereafter prove a useful document to antiquaries, who are seeking to measure the progress of civilization in the United States" (200). Jacobs reiterates how the terms of her personhood—as an article of traffic—can overwrite geographic concerns (New York City) and religiosity (Christianity) because of the overdetermined significance of the material (the bill of sale). Rather than celebrating that she is "free at last" she must contend with how she is "sold at last!" But she undercuts all these terms (the institution of slavery, capitalism, free/slave states, market transactions) by redirecting her attention to future readers and historians. She asserts her agency by relegating her bill of sale to a testimonial to injustice and barbarity ("civilization") in contemporary nineteenth-century United States from the perspective of some future time ("hereafter"). By engaging with futurity, she stakes a claim that the constructedness of experience and thus history are open to interpretation and even reinterpretation.[25] To me, the most important word in the passage is "measure." Literary works not only reflect the times in which they were published but also serve to gauge "progress." Notice how Jacobs refers to herself as "a human being" and never as a slave. By using the phrase "article of traffic" she does not allow the institution of slavery to define her sense of being but rather puts the emphasis on those who profit from such inhumane traffic. Her passage illustrates Jennifer Fleissner's take on how feminist readings disrupt normative temporalities. Drawing upon the work of Diane Elam, Fleissner comments how women's writing leads to paradoxical time constructs such as the "'future anterior': the still unknown past as contained within the future" ("Is Feminism" 58). Jacobs's ironic disdain, however, undercuts the need for any such futurity even as she invokes it.[26] She recognizes the absurdity of the transaction as it occurs.

THE THIRD HORIZON
OF LITERARY TEXTS

This book contributes to two current scholarly conversations in early American studies. First, the study takes seriously the third horizon of literary texts: how they engage with futurity. My methodology seeks to explain how facets of social and political experience become fodder for the imagination, especially as the authors attempt to forge a compensatory realm. They all deal with "real-world" problems not by creating "imaginary solutions" but by launching readers into an imaginary to confront the restitutions, whether cultural or material, required as recompense for colonial violence. The writers suggest that literature, which foregrounds the constructedness of the past, disables and disputes the dominant narratives of culture and therefore serves as the means of repair. Texts like *The Female American* (1767) and *Hope Leslie* (1827) are set in colonial times and reanimate accounts of Euro-indigenous relations through their portrayals of contact. Others, like *Secret History* (1808) or *Incidents in the Life of a Slave Girl* (1861), depict contemporary events but cast race and interracial conflict as mutable through the act of storytelling.

In fact, some of these texts may inadvertently promote the racism the authors attempt to upend; however, they still offer an alternative to the other representations, in particular, the trope of the "Vanishing American" imposed on indigenous characters. Jillian Sayre sums up a prevailing argument on that trope within early American studies: "The Vanishing American discourse aggressively excludes the Native American from contemporary participation in the national community even as, at the same time, this figuration, circulated in history, poetry, and prose, is elevated as the legitimizing claim to a national culture" (76). Moreover, Sayre explains, "Effacing the issue of racial toleration, the marginalized death of the Indian allows both the community within and the one without the novel to focus on the consolidation of a white, Christian, American subject" (128). She is correct, but the language and metaphors that some scholars use muddle the issue because they collapse literary representation and federal policy that removed indigenous people from their land; moreover, they conflate the lack of literary representation with actual vanishing. Lisa Brooks offers a useful reminder: "Most important, we cannot repress or replace the stories of Indigenous survival. We must join with tribal scholars and community-engaged historians in recovering the stories of Indigenous persistence and *adaptation* in the wake of the impacts of colonization, including these many wars" (Brooks 346).

Second, the book further questions the efficacy of literary periodization. The chapters cover a one-hundred-year period from 1767 to 1867. The dates present an almost paradoxical symmetry; these hundred years neither match disciplinary periodization nor suggest chronotopic significance (like 1776–1865, for example), for 1767 signifies the period between the Seven Years' War and the American Revolution, and 1867 the short interval between the end of the Civil War and the start of Congressional Reconstruction. As such, these texts provide what Adria Imada refers to as "'counter-memories' that contest sedimented histories of settler colonialism and sustain decolonizing processes" (15). "Sedimented histories" offers a vivid figuration for the intractability of context that these fiction and nonfiction texts trouble. Even though the texts examined are often historicized, they also produce "counter-memories" of *what might have been* in terms of attitudes toward colonialism or other asymmetrical relations in the United States.[27]

While "altern*ate* history" suggests a sensational accounting of what might have happened if some major event had turned out differently, its danger lies in thinking of binary options for worldwide reverberations, as though one configures outcomes of the US Civil War as pivoting between two distinct realities: either the Union or the Confederacy wins the war, a line of thinking Herman Melville dubs the "might-have-been" in *Billy Budd* (57). In this study, "alterna*tive* history" implies multitudinous modes for configuring the subject while rearticulating the origins and permutations of contact and community in the New World. As Susan Gillman and Forrest Robinson explain, "new historicism . . . refers broadly both to a field of study which foregrounds the issues of race, class, and gender, *and* to the production of an alternative cultural realm in which those issues can be addressed adequately" (ix–x). The following chapters revivify the concentration on "alternative cultural realms" in new historicism as those realms illuminate social and political constructions. Catherine Gallagher's 2018 book on counterfactual histories notes how she was surprised to find that counterfactual narratives include "histories that are simply fictional or even mendacious; 'secret' histories that purport to explain the hidden private stories behind the official explanations of historical events; 'counterhistories' stressing the forgotten struggles or viewpoints of those outside of the mainstream; or imaginary histories that are 'counterfactual' in the sense that they envision states of the world, usually utopias and dystopias, that might be, but have not yet been, realized" (2). The authors studied here fall under the first two subcategories. Rather than indulging in the extremes of utopic or dystopic worlds, they give insight into the role art plays in shaping meaning and, therefore, attitudes toward empire, capital, and others.[28] They also feature what Gallagher identifies as a primary feature of counterfactual narratives: a tendency to "scale up" or move away from the novel's identification with individual characters to "scale up into larger collectivities, stretching our normal view of what can count as a character" (14). The language of the imaginary, rather than "fantasy," distinguishes the narratives I study that proffer alternative worlds, not counterfactual narratives, because the latter, especially those that involve alternative resolutions to wars, indulge in cataclysmic formulations of history.[29]

The book demonstrates how certain narratives rewrite the past to accommodate the contributions of traditionally marginalized groups to foster Americas, or countries receptive to multiple and competing pasts. The simulated worlds put forth by imaginative literature—the networks of characters, the sensorium of visual, aural, olfactory, and tactile imagery, the language employed that both constructs and reverberates with old meanings—constitute their own value as an object of study separate from the study of history and separate from the study of aggregate texts in the digital humanities. Early

American women writers who projected a future that never materialized allow us to consider "new historicisms," a plural sense of different, multiple historical exigencies that emerge side by side.

Thinking in terms of alternative history avoids the diction of "fantasy" in favor of "imagination." Many scholars in sorting through the politics of imagination have turned to the psychoanalytic theories of D. W. Winnicott, who articulates the clearest distinction between fantasy and imagination: fantasy usually involves an untested omnipotence, and imagination involves a transitional space between self and other.[30] In particular, scholars invoke his diction of "transitional space" and "play." The poet Joan Retallack prefers Winnicott's vocabulary for understanding the imaginary because "play as the imaginative activity . . . constructs a meaningful reality in conversation with the world as one finds it" (Retallack 7). Although the words "play" and "a space apart" provide useful language for creative thinking or negotiations between inner consciousness and external world "as one finds it," the prominence of "play" fails to convey the projection involved in acts of the imagination. Sometimes play is just play and sometimes playing involves trying out the parameters for the enactment of power. In fact, the key word in Winnicott's formulation of play is often overlooked: the verb "expands." Winnicott writes, "I have tried to draw attention to the importance both in theory and in practice of a third area, that of play, which expands into creative living and into the whole cultural life of man . . . [this] intermediate area of experiencing is an area that exists as a resting-place for the individual engaged in the perpetual human task of keeping inner and outer reality separate yet interrelated" ("Location" 102–3). Although "play" might take place in an "intermediate area of experiencing," the person does so in order to "expand into creative living." The histories unfolded in literature about women characters not only command a space apart but create these worlds to put forth new ways of living and, more important, new ways of thinking about social, economic, and political power.

Each of the following chapters examines texts that assert an imagined world in an attempt to wrest power from the prerogatives of empire-building to provide an imagined ontology of power for women as they escape patriarchal systems. These imaginings are rooted in language and narrative as these women come to understand the stakes of their emancipation discursively. But it does not mean that some of these women characters forge power without resorting to violence or aggression toward (racialized) others; these authors make explicit white women's complicity in empire and overturn the conceptual framework for white, middle-class women's public participation as rooted in "republican motherhood."[31] Some of these literary works, nonetheless, imagine the anxiety produced when women take charge and how that anxiety is allayed by defense mechanisms that lead one to perceive powerful women as possessed or haunted by malignant, otherworldly forces. As an alternative to reading these texts as a conduit to the period in which they were published, readers should look to see what they could teach about the operations of empire and the ambiguous responses to women's agency. These women characters do not die like other radical types, such as Little Eva in *Uncle Tom's Cabin* (1851) or Zenobia in *The Blithedale Romance* (1852); nor do they capitulate to the community, like Gertie in *The Lamplighter* (1854), Ellen in *Wide, Wide World* (1850), or Hester in *The Scarlet Letter* (1850). Instead, they grasp the precariousness of power and, at times, relish in the domination they exert over others. Marriage serves as the tissue that connects these texts, in part because they present main characters who are single women of marriageable age, and because they all raise thorny political questions about consent and economic ones about property transmission. They each embrace the familial position of daughter, one that suggests a liminal figure and shifts the emphasis away from regeneration and reproduction.

The study begins with *The Female American* (1767), whose authorship is still unknown. The text, usually interpreted through its intertextual traces, especially as a Robinsonade, or works that riff upon Defoe's *Robinson Crusoe*, rewrites colonial Christian encounters in the New World. Like the other texts studied here, it engages with marginalized figures who refuse to stay sidelined. Two minor figures loom large in shaping the fate of the title character, the mixed-race Unca Eliza Winkfield, who finds herself a castaway on a semideserted island. One is her deceased aunt, the Indian Queen, who, coveting Unca Eliza's father, assassinates her mother. The other is a hermit who occupies Unca Eliza's island before her arrival. These two figures revise the literary-cultural canon and shape Unca Eliza's venture to convert the indigenous people of a nearby island. *The Female American* operates as the Ur-text for the rest of the study because it directly represents the anxieties that attend women's ascendent economic and political power and frankly addresses the devastation wrought upon indigenous people by European settlers. Even if one accepts the theory that the history of the novel, as put forth by Nancy Armstrong and others, is rooted in its disguises of the politicization of the domestic sphere, *The Female American* stands apart, for it forthrightly presents the entanglement of the domestic and the political. The text, therefore, reterritorializes women's role in empire building while simultaneously charting the fears women's agency inspires.

While chapter 1 looks backward to colonial Virginia, the subject of chapter 2 examines the Haitian revolution as represented in Leonora Sansay's novel *Secret History: or The Horrors of St. Domingo*. Published anonymously in 1808 before Sainte-Dominque was even named Haiti, the epistolary novel centers on two American sisters seeking to reestablish a colonial plantation in the hopes that Napoleon's Army will retake the island for France. The narrator, Mary, might daydream about a day when whites will resume control; however, the text overturns that dream by highlighting how the Black revolutionaries maintain control, not merely through the threat of violence, but by usurping discursive control over the how the revolution is portrayed. Try as she might to silence Black people, Mary unwittingly gives them a voice. Instead, her narrative depicts how France lost control of Saint-Domingue, because it forfeited rhetorical and sexual dominance to the free and enslaved Black population on the island. When the text was revised and republished in 1820 after the end of the hostilities by an unknown author, the narrator Mary is the one erased from the text in order to place at its center the eponymous mixed-raced Black woman: *Zelica*. The new version of the text not only discards Mary but also the frame story involving a public figure: Aaron Burr, to whom Mary addresses the text. The transformation from *Secret History* to *Zelica* signifies *Secret History*'s complicated effort to establish the "third horizon" of a text. Even as Mary sides with the French, the text ultimately underscores the heroic achievements of Black liberators, especially when contrasted with the humiliation and scandals surrounding Colonel Burr.

Like *The Female American*, Catharine Maria Sedgwick's *Hope Leslie: A Tale of Massachusetts* (1827) attempts to retell the stories of colonial America. Based on Sedgwick's archival research, the novel follows the resourceful Hope Leslie as she resists some of the strictures of Puritan culture in the Massachusetts Bay Colony while also drawing upon scenarios (in Diana Taylor's sense of the word) like the encounter between Pocahontas and John Smith from colonial Virginia. Yet many critics lament that the text is not titled

"Magawisca" after the indigenous woman who begins the text as a captive among the Puritans. Yet, unlike other early American authors, Sedgwick does not erase or discard Magawisca; instead, she reenters the narrative with a maimed arm. Rather than being treated as a ghost—safely out of sight and no longer a threat—Magawisca remains part of the narrative even as characters attempt to forget her. Sedgwick enacts the loss of local indigenous cultures and reminds Americans, just prior to the advent of the Indian Removal Act, of the price paid by marginalized others as white settlers build their towns and open their shops. Sedgwick's refusal to consign indigenous characters to sacrificial death involves representing the colonial space as heavily militarized.[32] *Hope Leslie* highlights some of the problems with fictional works engaging with the historicity and futurity. Like *The Female American*, it looks backward, and, like *Secret History*, it looks toward future political formations. Nonetheless, the removal of indigenous tribes out of the South, along with the notorious Trail of Tears, followed the book's publication and thus nullifies the text's inclusive vision. The social and political shifts after its publication cast a different shadow back upon the text even as it attempts to sort through early indigenous and European antagonisms.

Sedgwick's *Hope Leslie* is often read alongside Lydia Maria Child's *Hobomok* (1824). But, in chapter 4, I examine Child's later work, *A Romance of the Republic* (1867), because of the way it directly tries to participate in political conversations about the legality of interracial marriage. Published after the passage of the Thirteenth Amendment but before the start of Congressional Reconstruction and the passage of the Fourteenth and Fifteenth Amendments, the novel offers an alternative cultural imaginary for a post-Civil War United States that presents a mixed-race, amalgamated people as a force for driving American hegemony abroad. Other texts might hint at the unacknowledged parentage of mixed-race peoples in the United States, but Child's text offers an explicit engagement with the implications of emancipation and people's right to inherit the wealth of their white fathers. Rather than safely consigning Black or mixed-race people to a ghost-like presence, Child has them emerge as central to unifying the nation after the war. Child depicts how some white characters pay reparations whereas some seek to deny Black people their very being in an effort to prevent the transmission of wealth. Although the language of ghosts recurs in the novel, it does so ironically, for those characters who seem sacrificed to maintain the status quo or reaffirm the cohesion of the community, or even the nation, return and make demands upon those who profited from their oppression. Thus, Child's text forces white northerners to apprehend how they might recompense people formerly held in bondage despite the resistance that stems from their supposed lack of culpability regarding slavery. The text unveils histories' discarded others, especially the secreted paternal lines of those forced to live in slavery, who must confront the force of capitalism that runs roughshod over attempts at reparations. Child outlines how attempts to project a multicultural or heterogeneous sense of belonging in the United States are undercut by the ways in which liberal capitalism easily discards its ties to the nation-state.

The study in its first four chapters looks at fiction, but the last chapter examines a work of life writing: Harriet Jacobs's 1861 *Incidents in the Life of a Slave Girl*. Though Jacobs's life writing offers a wealth of firsthand accounting of slavery's daily degradations, the imaginary that Jacobs marshals to evade her enslaver is the topic of this chapter. The imaginary she employs cuts through monolithic conceptions of the United States and its multifarious positions on race, slavery, sexuality, and emancipation. Surveying criticism on the text, the central image of the text remains the one of Linda Brent (Jacobs's pseudonym) prostrate in the garret of her grandmother's house to escape life in bondage, a tableau that seems to evoke death. In many ways, "Linda" is characterized as a ghost or not quite dead by critics. Sánchez-Eppler describes how "while [Linda] haunts these houses [in the South], she cannot occupy them" (87), and Doyle, too, invokes ghost imagery: Jacobs's "voice in this sense is a ghostly one, speaking doubly and from nowhere [in the garret], expressing an illicit freedom" (259).

However, I look at the fictional letters "Linda" sends to the man who relentlessly pursues her. The fiction within *Incidents* reveals how Jacobs relies on sociopolitical space, principally the Commonwealth of Massachusetts, to gain agency and speak to and create a futurity in which her story is shared, not as exceptional case within slavery but as its terrifying norm. Her representation of a divided United States troubles the notion of a coherent nation that aspires to imperial might. For Jacobs, the political, which hinges on an imagined spatial ontology, can shape the personal in order to overturn structures of power.

Imaginary Empires concludes with a brief coda on Hester Prynne in contradistinction to the other women characters. The heroine of Nathanial Hawthorne's *The Scarlet Letter* (1850) concludes the romance as a treasured counselor to her community and a political futurist. Her vision of a later era mollifies her listeners while foreclosing the radical vision of gender equality that she had entertained during her years as an outcast in seventeen-century Boston. Hawthorne's 1850 text, a cornerstone of American letters, counters the more unpredictable, uneasy modes of affiliations represented by the women authors presented here. A renewed interest in these women writers leads to alternative ways to conceive of the political work of stories.

The

"FANTASY"

of a

WOMAN

IN CHARGE

in

The Female American

SCHOLARS TEND TO INTERPRET THE ANONYMOUSLY PUBLISHED
The Female American (1767), set in early seventeenth-century Virginia and
then on a remote West Indian island, through its intertextual traces, especially
as a Robinsonade, or a work that adapts Daniel Defoe's *Robinson Crusoe*.[1] The
story presents the quintessential "female American" as a mixed-race proselytizer who single-handedly converts an indigenous tribe to Christianity.
Yet based on scholars' assessment of the text, it seems to exceed the formal
boundaries to which Robinsonades adhere for they frequently invoke the
word "fantasy" in their arguments about the text. The word "fantasy" recurs
in a way that differs from other texts that adapt Defoe's novel. Scholars, for
example, do not describe *The Female American*'s plot twists or marvelous
features as fantastical; instead, they identify the central "fantasy" as Unca
Eliza's usurpation of power as a woman.[2] Rather than engaging with the
modes of power the text makes available to women, readers seem to recenter
the book's more fantastical elements and its borrowings from other texts, as
though seeing these same tropes elsewhere (and composed by men) defuses
the text's troubling portraits of powerful women. By focusing on borrowed

source material, critics ignore a feature of the text that seems solely the property of the anonymous author: the subplot of the murderous Indian Queen and the text's refusal to divert questions about the appropriation of Unca Eliza's mother's wealth by her English father.

Reading scholarship on the text, one comes away with the impression that if John Smith, Daniel Defoe, Samson Occum, or Quakers or Anglican clergymen are the real source of the text, then one need not feel unsettled by Unca Eliza's usurpation of colonial control. The critical emphasis on Unca Eliza, in short, as enacting a fantasy of women's agential power undercuts how the text de-naturalizes white male hegemony. A scene toward the end of the text includes its own allegory of reading when Unca Eliza sees a British ship sail onto her island and a group of men disembark. She does not approach them directly; instead, she decides to meet them "drest in my priestly habits, and with my staff and crown. . . . As they stood, it would be impossible for them to see me ascend form the earth. I pleased myself much with the surprise they would be in, to see me in a dress of which they could form no expectation, nor conceive the meaning of" (124). Her plan backfires because the men on the ship run away from her. They assume she is a witch because they have no paradigms ("could form no expectation") with which to process the sight of her in her costume. Likewise, readers have to cut through the strange garb the text accumulates to confront anxieties about women and power and to address the abuses of New World settlement. The book in some ways cuts across the history of colonial development and the history of the novel. Catherine Gallagher in her recent study on counterfactual narratives observes how the "tendency of counterfactualism to stop the forward movement of time . . . is one of its most useful features, for it helps recover and explore history's cul-de-sacs and unfinished projects, aspects of 'the way it was' that are often overlooked in unilinear histories" (47). *The Female American* not only explores "history's cul-de-sacs" but has also inspired literary criticism that underscores how scholars conceive of historical development and how women complicate our formulations of it.

Scholars have not determined whether the author was a man or a woman or British or American. Because they cannot reliably ascertain the gender or nationality of the author, the text offers an interesting site to work through anxiety about both gender and print publication. I include it in a study on women writers because of the way in which the main character's gender and the book's "mobile anonymity" ("Indian Slave Trade" 115), as Anna Brick-house dubs it, shape critical commentary on the text; furthermore, the author chose for a pseudonym the name of the heroine, at the very least presenting the pseudofactual illusion of a text authored by a woman. Repeatedly, the text models how extenuating circumstances or manipulation within the domestic sphere—subtle modes of coercion—are obscured insofar that one's submission to more powerful agents is characterized as an individual preference. Marriage operates in the text as the ultimate site for this exercise of power. The narrative reveals how domestic coercion undergirds colonial projects. As Ann Laura Stoler argues, the intimate, despite appearances, serves as the locus for colonial control: "To study the intimate [in colonial contexts] is not to turn away from structures of dominance but to relocate their conditions of possibility and relations and forces of production" ("Intimidations" 13). Rather than impose separate spheres to discuss sexuality and colonial control, this novel illuminates how the intimate and the political inform one another. Indeed, *The Female American*, with its backward glance to the early 1600s, represents the dispersal of indigenous people as rooted in rivalries within the domestic sphere of the family. In interactions across the text—between Unca Eliza's father and mother, between her parents and the aunt, between her and the Hermit, between Unca Eliza and the indigenous people she converts, between Unca Eliza and her cousin who becomes her husband—one sees how power is naturalized and subtended by the claims of heteronormativity. Thus, acts of coercion are either exposed or misrepresented as involving choice and consent. Although the text may assert more rights for women within marriage and for colonized people in the New World, these groups are only granted alternatives in order to refuse them.

The text, ultimately, elucidates how coercion undergirds the expansion of liberal democracy and representative government against the backdrop of colonial ventures and slavery through its plot involving Unca Eliza's reluctance to marry. As historian Kathleen Brown explains, "The English state ultimately gained strength from the conjunction of domestic interventions and imperial projects. Discourses about female subordination, which explained and justified the expansion of royal authority at home, also proved highly useful abroad, allowing the English to depict indigenous peoples, whose lands they wished to claim, as conquerable 'others'" (17). Brown's analysis hinges on how these discourses "naturalize power." *The Female American*, though, disrupts the naturalization of power. At times, the title character either renounces power or, when she grasps it, men maneuver it out of her hands. The novel unmasks how men who usurp power away from Unca Eliza, like the ship captain who does so aggressively or like her cousin who wears her down with an ultimatum, undermine this "natural order" of men's supremacy over colonial others and women. If the power deferential between men and women were natural either in the domestic or political spheres, then these men would not feel as threatened by her agency or her wealth.

DOMESTIC INTERVENTIONS

AND COLONIAL CONTROL

Scholarship on *The Female American* frequently cites a line from the first page when the heroine declares that "the lives of women being commonly domestic, the occurrences of them are generally pretty nearly of the same kind; whilst those of men, frequently more vagrant, subject them often to experience greater vicissitudes, many times wonderful and strange" (35). While her statement attempts to make the narrator's actions palatable to a wider audience—her life does, after all, resemble a man's—the text contradicts the sentiment that the domestic sphere lacks that which is "wonderful and strange" (35). Colonial exchange begins in Unca Eliza's mother's hut when she seduces her father; later, after Unca Eliza is born, their home becomes the center of bloodshed as the Indian Queen's men assassinate her mother (the queen's sister). Unca Eliza's mischaracterization of the domestic sphere as "generally pretty nearly of the same kind" is reinforced by a text like *Robinson Crusoe*, whose hero leaves home without alerting his parents at the beginning of the story to define himself in opposition to domestic and filial obligations. He, in fact, "mak[es] an Elopement" by going to sea (Defoe 7). Yet the domestic in England differs greatly from the domestic in Virginia in the days of early settlements. Unca Eliza's home is marked by domestic attachments that cannot withstand brutal acts of violence. Later, at the end of Defoe's novel, when he returns to England, Crusoe reports that he married, had children, and was widowed in three sentences. On his marriage, he concedes that he "marry'd and that not either to my Disadvantage or Dissatisfaction" (Defoe 219). The use of the double negative reveals Crusoe's expectation that marriage leads to "disadvantage" and "dissatisfaction." Defoe underscores how men cannot be subjected to (and do not need) women's influence to maintain their position. Yet for Unca Eliza in *The Female American*, evading marriage requires heroics that she cannot sustain: if she wishes to secure her position among the tribe and have her evangelical work validated by Christian rites of communion, she needs to marry her cousin in the narrative's conclusion. She describes how "through his constant importunity, I was at last obliged to give my hand" (140–41). He convinces her "for though the Indians, I believed would not entertain any ill suspicions of my conduct, yet I could not satisfy myself with the reflection of being much alone with a man, as it hurt my modesty" (139). Within marriage, the man then appropriates her ministry among the tribe, an act of usurpation that mirrors Unca Eliza's exploitation of the indigenous people who "choose" to convert based on threats issuing from their idol via Unca Eliza's disguised voice.

In this chapter, I argue that *The Female American* is not a Robinsonade; moreover, reading it as another telling of Defoe's *Crusoe* shifts the focus away from the text's engagement with the anxiety that attends when a woman is in charge. Rebecca Weaver-Hightower argues that the absence of women is a defining feature of Robinsonades. When authors feature a woman protagonist in the castaway role, the genre shifts.[3] By 1767, the first great rush of Defoe imitators had abated. Rousseau's use of Crusoe in his 1762 text *Emile, or On Education* seems to provide a dividing line between mere imitations that highlighted the sensational aspects and those that used the castaway narrative to offer edification.[4] In particular, the anonymous author of *The Female American* speculates how a colonial settlement might have differed if a woman of mixed English and indigenous ancestry were to convert and colonize the tribe she encounters on a remote island. That speculation has less to do with surviving in the wild or away from others and more about how to negotiate with others, seize resources, and maintain that control while protecting one's person from violation.[5] Rather than consigning a woman to the margins, this strange text places Unca Eliza's story of maturation and usurpation of power at its center.

The Female American draws not only from *Robinson Crusoe* but also, as critics have noted, from American sources. The overwhelming number of familiar tableaux or scenarios that the text draws upon—Pocahontas saving John Smith, the marooned islander, contact and conversion, the excavation of Egyptian ruins—gesture beyond the text. According to Diana Taylor, "scenarios" refer to "meaning-making paradigms that structure social environments, behaviors, and potential outcomes" (28). For Taylor, these repeated scenarios gain significance because "[t]he framework allows for occlusions; by positioning our perspective, it promotes certain views while helping to disappear others" (28). The anonymous author, however, through an excess of allusions, hinders occlusions. Instead, the text redirects attention to the causes and repercussions of colonial violence. Some characterize the text's exaggerations as satire, but its hyperbole, rather than gesturing toward a condemnation of familiar practices or behaviors, brings to the fore otherwise ignored practices within colonization. Its premise, in short, highlights the interventions of historical marginalized groups. Still, if we must label the text as something, then it is better referred to as a bildungsroman than a Robinsonade.

At bottom, the critical reception to *The Female American* reiterates that, unlike the character Robinson Crusoe who approaches verisimilitude, a *woman* Crusoe seems purely an exercise in authorial creativity or serves an allegorical purpose. Many critics seem to concur with Eve Tavor Bannet, who argues that *The Female American* was out of touch with the zeitgeist of late eighteenth-century literature about indigenous people: by the time of its publication, "[s]ensational accounts of wonders and illustrious providences, which readers of all ranks in England and New England had one once shared, were now ridiculed in Britain as superstitious tales that were only fit for the ignorant and lower orders or for pagans" (Bannet 181). Moreover, as Laura Stevens observes, by the latter half of the eighteenth century, there was "a growing tendency on the part of Anglo-Americans and Britons to regard Indians as doomed to vanish because of their unwillingness to accept civilization or Christianity," even if "missionary efforts did continue" (197). The text's engagement with sensationalism (through its women heroine, its account of elaborate ruins holding "immense treasures" [79], and an untouched indigenous tribe) exposes how European interlopers distorted experiential reality to fit their dominant narratives. By referring to the text as an out-of-date fantasy, readers could avoid its central question about whether contact and conversion could not occur without destroying indigenous cultures. As opposed to reading *The Female American* as an addendum or whimsical sequel to European encroachment on indigenous cultures, we might read the text as inviting alternative renderings of New World settlements even as it establishes the corrosive effects, and perhaps the inevitability, of exploitation of European contact.

In the end, its pseudofactual framing lies in tension with the "fantasy" element of the text, a fantasy that appears rooted in the main character's gender rather than any fantastical plot devices.[6] Nicholas Paige observes how, with most pseudofactual texts, "No one believes in all these 'real people,' of course, but everyone agrees to *pretend*" (30). In *The Female American*, however, despite its pseudofactual framing, no one seems willing to pretend she's real. Even other characters are more inclined to find her a supernatural figure just as critics anxiously reassert the text's fictionality.[7] In this instance, a willingness to pretend would mean relinquishing or even admitting to beliefs about the incommensurability of women and power or the limitation on women's roles within empires. Despite its attempts to analog itself to the real, the text seems to require readers to label it a fantasy to assuage the anxiety it inspires about women's command over others.

Nonetheless, in breaking through the "scenarios" or familiar tableaux from other texts, the author refuses to allow the past to haunt. The text's tendency to refuse to repress history's ghosts appears most pointedly when Unca Eliza builds an elaborate mausoleum in England for her mother, an indigenous woman from Virginia, with memorials written in three different languages—her indigenous language, English, and Latin—to ensure she is not forgotten (50). Furthermore, the marginalized woman, in the form of Alluca, the Indian Queen and aunt of Unca Eliza, literally attacks and reasserts her centrality rather than haunts. The appearance of another figure, usually occluded, occurs again with the departed hermit. At first, Unca Eliza assumes the hermit, who set up the island's living spaces and leaves her a handwritten tome describing its features, must be dead, but then he appears and speaks to her even if he dies shortly thereafter. Instead of haunted by unrecognized forbears, the text repeatedly stages confrontation or contact with those other texts represented as safely consigned to the past to press all facets of imperial encroachments into memory. Indeed, the text memorializes the dead who were marginalized or forgotten in the shadow of settlements. In the case of her mother, Unca Eliza uses English land to commemorate her mother.

Unca Eliza's unsettling exhibition of power as a solitary woman indoctrinating an entire people (what Turley refers to as "ethnocide") puts into relief how the text in its opening chapter represents marriage as the ultimate institutional form through which Europeans exercise power. *The Female American*, in sharp contrast to works of domestic realism in the eighteenth and nineteenth century, directly links sexuality and political history. It serves as a counter to the novels of Samuel Richardson and Jane Austen, which Nancy Armstrong uses to build her case that the novel reifies the domestic sphere. Armstrong argues that the novel "no longer constituted a form of resistance but distinguished itself from political matters to establish a specialized domain of culture where apolitical truths could be told" (21). *The Female American* stands out for not doing the subtle work of apoliticizing the domestic sphere. Like many of the texts under discussion in this study, it acknowledges the losses incurred by colonialism and acknowledges those sacrificed by it.

The narrative encourages readers to reconsider New World exploration because it demarcates how imperialism and the domestic sphere are mutually constitutive. This tale of a female castaway frankly acknowledges the very real threat of subsequent European invasions to agency of the indigenous tribes, but, despite her prescience, Unca Eliza lays the groundwork for further exploitation. The tension between reimagining the settlement of the New World and its actual unfolding breaks toward the end of the text when Englishmen arrive on the deserted island seeking to rescue Unca Eliza. She decides to hide in case they are pirates. She explains, "My next fear was for the poor Indians, who would come in the evening, . . . and be taken for slaves. Nor might the evil stop thus; their country might be discovered, and probably invaded, and numbers of the people be carried away into slavery, and other injuries committed" (121). She casts herself as the preserver of indigenous peoples even as she ushers in European practices and dominance. Nonetheless, the character thinks her presence and her conversion of an indigenous tribe can occur separately from other European models of contact, but the text, as a whole, paints her as naive. Contact even in this fictional story leads to oppression and widespread loss even if it occurs in what Unca Eliza describes as her "busy imagination," (121), despite the character's use of passive voice ("be taken for slaves," "be discovered," "be . . . invaded," "be carried away") to hide the agent of all this "evil." The novel presents a belief in separate spheres of power as illusory, whether domestic, religious, cultural, or political.

The text confronts the destruction Europeans dealt to indigenous peoples in explicit terms as it reimagines the first contact among them. Her frank admission of cultural decimation contrasts with the way in which critics continue to stamp the work a "fantasy" as though there were a danger of forgetting its fantastical premise. The first pages relate a strong warning from

Unca Eliza's uncle, who remains in England instead of joining her father and grandfather as they depart for Virginia: "We have no right to invade the country of another and I fear invaders will always meet a curse" (37). The Indian King proffers a similar line of the thought in one of the most quoted lines from the text when he asserts the injustice of colonial incursions: "we know you not, and have never offended you; why then have you taken possession of our lands, ate our fruits, and made our countrymen prisoners? Had you no lands of your own?" (38). Although these lines receive a great deal of critical attention, many fail to note that these words are spoken in a language Winkfield cannot understand: "It seems they [the Indians] had no idea that there are more languages than one" (38). The author surprisingly characterizes the indigenous people as exhibiting solipsist behavior because they take for granted that the Europeans should understand their tongue, their sensible condemnation of European colonialism then goes unheard. Although someone later translates this message to the Englishman Winkfield, the delayed transmission mirrors the text, which sets its story in early seventeenth century transatlantic sites to question the basis of European colonialism in the New World in the late eighteenth century.

The Female American puts forth a strong condemnation of English colonial practices. The misfortunes that befall the characters can be interpreted as punishment for English intrusions into the New World, intrusions that seem to multiply with each passing calamity, even as Anglo-American hegemony becomes entrenched along the Eastern seaboard. Ultimately, the English reap the advantages of New World wealth and resources. The text's "time drag" allows it to test out how women, if they had been in direct charge, *might* have colonized differently from the way the history of colonial settlement and aggression unfolded. The Englishman Winkfield misappropriates the possibilities that the New World promises because he uses the colony merely to reinforce English wealth. Nonetheless, the exploitative effect of invasions permeates the text, most pointedly in the text's treatment of Unca Eliza's parents, whose love story offers no respite from the brutal conditions of settlement. The costs of settlement are forthrightly assessed. The text also suggests that ethnographic and geographic records of New World sites will set the stage for women to exercise more control over their surroundings. Imposing strategies based on discursive knowledge, such as Unca Eliza's multilingualism and the Hermit's manuscript, will compensate for women's seeming vulnerability. Even as it indulges Unca Eliza's elevation, the text portrays the kinds of anxiety Unca Eliza's competence provokes in others.

Relying on the methodology of new historicism, one might connect the text's concerns with individual choice or consent to the rise of discourses surrounding liberalism and republicanism. Moreover, in interactions across the text, one sees how power is naturalized and subtended by the claims of heteronormativity. Although the text may assert more rights for women within marriage and for colonized people in the New World, these groups are only granted alternatives in order to refuse them. The new vocabularies of liberalism and republicanism legitimate the old order. Yet the text does not allow for such easy points of connection between text and context. Instead, *The Female American* confounds. Its bizarre twisting of more familiar scenarios leaves a general impression of the uncanny rather than leveling a satiric punch. More frustrating, the text reemerged (2001) during the height of cultural studies but remains difficult to connect to its historical milieu because its indeterminate author, unfortunately, confuses recent forays into the new disciplinary categories of the transatlantic or the transnational.[8] Thus, one cannot vacillate between text and context. This difficulty is, perhaps, best exemplified by a strange dog-like animal Unca Eliza encounters when on her deserted island (101–2). Despite the detailed imagery of the creature's body and of its ability to trap prey, no actual animal seems to fit the description, even as it provides an aptly disturbing analogy for colonial aggression in the benign way it traps its prey. Many readers lament that, despite its mixed-race heroine, the text promotes the same patriarchal chauvinism toward indigenous tribes as other texts from the era by or about men. Unca Eliza claims to ameliorate the conditions under which Europeans took control of the new world, but she furthers the colonial project for her own sake even as she indicts the practices of those who exploited indigenous peoples during conquest. She does not balk from using exploitative means to force indigenous people to convert to Christianity while fostering her own sense of power.

THE INDIAN PRINCESS
AND HER DANGEROUS DOUBLE

The text focuses on individuals as they think through the terms of settlement and how they adapt to them or use them discursively to maintain a semblance, or in some cases an illusion, of autonomy. In several instances, a character under duress cognitively rearranges the impetus for the situation to make it his/her choice. The entry of Unca Eliza's father, an Englishman in Virginia, permanently upsets the domestic tranquility of the people he encounters. Rather than retelling another Pocahontas-inspired tale, the text doubles the Indian princess, Unca, by portraying her sister Alluca, a dangerous woman who brutalizes the Englishman after he rejects her advances. Eventually, Alluca has her sister Unca assassinated, which is followed by a bloodbath between the household servants and the perpetrators. The source of conflict was the Englishman who inspired sexual possession in each sister. The sisters' mutual fascination with Winkfield stems from physical attraction, a plot point that redirects the metaphorical allure of the indigenous body onto the English man. In this way, the novel subverts the usual pattern in colonial texts of using individual sexual desire (for a woman) to cloak colonial incursions. The sisters' rivalry over the man prefigures the violence that will permanently upset the indigenous communities.

The text gently mocks the sisters' desire for the foreign white man. Winkfield, despite his ability to attract the two indigenous women, comes across as befuddled and inept, not unlike John Smith in *The Generall Historie of Virginia*. Gary Nash posits that few marriages arose between Englishmen and indigenous women in colonial America because, "As for Indian women, they had little reason to admire white men, who could hardly keep themselves alive in the early years and who launched attacks on Indian villages once they had gathered strength" (254). Unca Eliza's parents' meeting does not downplay the brutality involved in settling the colony. Following Unca Eliza's grandfather's death in a massacre, the tribe takes the father prisoner, humiliating and then terrorizing him: he is stripped of clothes and placed in circle with other naked Englishmen, who then are decapitated in front of him.[9] They spare Unca Eliza's father the same fate because of her mother's interference, *a la* Pocahontas and John Smith. Instead of laying her body upon his, she marks her possession of him by touching him with a wand held at distance. After saving his life, Unca Eliza's mother treats him like an exotic animal whom she must take home, feed, and keep for herself; the text, in short, dehumanizes and infantilizes the Englishman. Indeed, Unca Eliza describes "his black deliverer [her mother], who, smiling, gently pulled him by his chain, and led him, now willing and fearless, to a neighboring cabin" (40). The "black deliverer" distracts readers from recognizing the real "savage," the father who provides a pattern for the novel's readers by learning to overcome his initial distaste for her mother's dark coloring.[10] Again, while the domestic sphere enables cross-cultural relations, the father begins to assert a strange and undeserved power. Unca Eliza adds as an aside that her father is "now willing and fearless" to submit to her mother. Moreover, his willingness is difficult to define, because he has no means of escaping Unca Eliza's mother. To be "fearless" strikes an odd note for someone so passive. The mother's "smiles" and her "gentle" pulling do not detract from the father's presence in chains and the power relation they imply. He remains at the mercy of this woman who arbitrarily saved his life and might just as arbitrarily end it.

Although Unca Eliza describes the father as "willing," his humiliation continues. This pattern of events wherein the distinction between coercion and consent dissolves recurs throughout the text. The Indian princess hands over William Winkfield in chains to her father, the Indian King: "while his patroness [her mother] presented the end of the chain she held to her father, who with much seeming affability returned it to his daughter. By this act my father understood he gave him as a captive to his daughter, who, immediately breaking the chain from around his neck, threw it at his feet" (40). And while the Englishman may not understand all that transpires, he sees that the Indian princess and her father find delight in the transaction with "seeming affability," even as it leaves him vulnerable to their games. In a reversal of English practices, Unca Eliza's mother woos the father and proposes their marriage. She also changes his name from William Winkfield to the more indigenous sounding "Winka." According to John D'Emilio and Estelle Freedman, "In certain tribes, women, like men, could exercise considerable choice in their selection of sexual partners" (7). Unca Eliza never suggests what would happen if Winka recoiled from the mother's treatment. Instead, she narrates that her father "now loved Unca as much as she did him, and was therefore willing to make her and her country his for ever" (42). Once the father moves toward consent, the power dynamics switch whereby this woman, as his wife, becomes "his" and, furthermore, her wealth ("her country") becomes his wealth to send back to his family in England. By portraying Unca Eliza's mother as the aggressive pursuer, the text downplays how her possession of William Winkfield, ultimately, undoes her family and tribe. All of the violent potential of this relationship is projected onto Unca's sister Alluca.

Yet, the possibilities and dangers of women exerting choice yield the same result as violent colonial practices; the English assert cultural hegemony and accumulate wealth and property in the colony. Indeed, Unca and Alluca may express their sexuality, but they are both dead by the middle of the story. The heroine Unca Eliza, in contrast, renounces any sexuality to accrue power. Inevitably, these choices all lead to an Englishman amassing control over the colony either in Virginia or on the remote island.

The character of Alluca allows the author to imagine an alternative relationship between European men and indigenous women characterized by the unrequited love of a ruthless, vengeful woman. In his dealings with Alluca, William Winkfield has no recourse to the weapon of choice, the language of intimacy to placate her, as he does with her sister. When Alluca traps the father in the forest, she presents him with a poison, "I offer you love or death; make your choice" (44). As usual, she couches a threat, really an ultimatum, in the language of choice. This kind of undisguised coercion hangs over the text, rendering the rhetoric of choice meaningless. Winka, at first, does not take Alluca seriously because, as Unca Eliza reports, "my father was not greatly alarmed, as [her words] were uttered by an unarmed woman" (43). Her father smiles at her threats, but then the aunt summons nine henchmen whom she brought to enforce her plan. A woman's power, despite her position as queen, seems unthreatening, and yet Alluca causes considerable mayhem not only within the domestic sphere but also to the entire tribe. However, the author clearly differentiates female power—which aligns love with the military and social might of the tribe from male power. After all, William Winkfield expresses love but gradually depletes the (economic) power of the tribe. Yet the novel seems to depict, at least in the case of Alluca's potential marriage to the father, cross-cultural encounters as failing to change the tribe; Alluca's love for Winkfield, therefore, may have offered an alternative to the seemingly inevitable transformation caused by European settlements. Instead, it might have buoyed the indigenous tribe's power.

His refusal, in fact, to love the aunt leads to more violence. Unca Eliza's mother appears again to save William Winkfield's life after her sister forces the poison on him. When this same aunt later becomes queen, she continues to inspire dread because she is, as the text reports, "still single," as though her unmarried state makes her a source of disruption and leaves her mind unhinged (47). Because she has no intimate ties to the Englishman, she cannot be coaxed into submission. While Alluca's behavior remains untenable in the face of European social codes, *The Female American* shows that both Alluca and the father miss opportunities to draw on the potential of cross-cultural encounters. On the one hand, William Winkfield opts to transmit the wealth he gains from the Indian King and from the other English settlers to England (46, 52). On the other, Alluca demands unquestioned allegiance.

By presenting the women as two extremes of moral behavior (angel mother, demon aunt), the text portrays the repercussions from the father's rejection of an alliance with the mother's people. Despite their marriage, Unca (la mère) must conform to the father's cultural practices, and her wealth is appropriated by the English and sent abroad. Whenever Unca doubts the husband's intentions, he subdues her with talk of love, exploiting and renegotiating the terms of their relationship. After living together for six months, the mother proposes marriage, and when the father hesitates, she demands, "What, . . . does not my Winka . . . love me?" an exclamation that can be interpreted as a threat (41). Perhaps not just the irrational Alluca poses a danger to him; the mother also expresses a possessive jealousy of Winkfield. But when he explains that Unca, the mother, must convert to Christianity, the mother immediately accedes to his demands. The narrator explains, because "we readily believe those whom we love, he was more successful [in converting her] than he expected, and in a little time the princess became convinced of her errors" (41). Despite the mother's power as the father's "deliverer" and his "patroness," once she depends on his affection, she proves susceptible to coerced conversion to his belief system. The daughter explicitly notes that the intimacy between the mother and father then requires little work on the father's part to convert the mother. Furthermore, the act of conversion involves not just spreading Christianity but also demeaning prior belief systems: "she became convinced of her errors."

The novel laments the erosion of Unca's power following her marriage and unveils how patriarchy obtains its power. The novel's indigenous society vests power in women, though this power peaks during courtship. Before he marries her, Winkfield has Unca convert to Christianity; he then coaxes her to change her appearance, even as he sends her dowry to England; he neither shares this wealth with fellow English colonists nor uses it to forge stronger ties to the tribe. Stripping her of identity, he has rendered her vulnerable to other women. In fact, years later, she dies, because her husband cannot protect her. As Roxann Wheeler argues, "Native conversion to Christianity validates English cultural superiority and is signified by Unca donning European dress at her husband's insistence" (169). The two sisters' loss of power proves mutually destructive while the Englishman thrives. The novel expresses what Stoler terms "structures of dominance"; these emerge in colonial domestic spheres and shape attitudes toward indigenous peoples ("Intimidations" 13). More telling, the Englishman continues to send his wealth home despite assurances to his wife that he plans to stay in Virginia. His daughter reports, "He took every opportunity that offered to send part of the riches over to England privately, to be there disposed of, and such goods in return to be sent as he wanted" (46). Interracial love functions as a veneer that conceals the intimate metropole-colonial relationship of capital accumulation. This "privat[e]" relationship offers ironic commentary to expose the pretense of enclosed and sentimental domestic spheres.

While the father practices undisguised looting, Alluca presents an interesting dilemma in the text. The text seems to suggest that a woman's power is dangerous and therefore must be co-opted because it undermines the naturalization of patriarchy. For instance, the novel exaggerates the aunt's violent behavior, but, nevertheless, it demonstrates one possible mode to resist colonization. Her violence shapes subsequent scenes, especially as the adult Unca Eliza eschews marrying. Unca Eliza seems to learn from the excesses and foibles of the older generation. Her resistance to marriage makes her public pronouncements that she will not assume power suspect: if she will not marry, then her wealth remains under her control. Unlike her mother, who loved her inept and hapless English father, Unca Eliza declares that she will not marry anyone who cannot match her skills with a bow and arrow. Even though the text begins by referring to Queen Elizabeth I (as the namesake of Virginia [36]), a female ruler, like Alluca, without a husband, remains dangerous. Alluca, obsessed, eventually dies of grief from her unrequited love for the Englishman. Her odd behavior culminates in having her heart extracted and delivered to William Winkfield following her death. The trope of a broken heart literally delivered to the beloved draws into relief the father's rapacious hoarding of jewels and resources that he can turn into material wealth. It also gestures at her and the other indigenous women in the text, like Unca and Unca Eliza, who refuse to be turned into undifferentiated bodies: Alluca's heart is metonymic for her love, not a synecdoche for her body. The father as a source of conflict between the sisters represents the scarcity that the "choice" of marriage partner veils, for indigenous women have only one choice, submission, and with it comes an array of cultural subjections that are nonnegotiable.

Unca Eliza and Marriage

Because of the violence at the heart of the domestic order, it is not unreasonable that the author portrays Unca Eliza as reticent to marry. She seems keenly aware that in English culture women hold power during courtship, and then it dissipates in marriage when coverture laws transfer power onto the husband. Elizabeth Barnes notes, "The ideological shift from a coercive to a consensual view of paternal rule informs my reading of sentimental family narratives as well, but I argue that the move from coercion to consent ultimately bolsters patriarchal claims to domestic authority" (10). Elizabeth Maddock Dillon also argues how consent and heterosexuality in the courtship narrative give shape to the ways in which "[w]omen's consent to the marriage contract and to the structuring force of gender division thus both grants women the status of subjects . . . and locates them firmly on the private side of the public/private divide" (Dillon, *Gender* 46). While her mother and aunt attempt to claim the father, Unca Eliza, back in England, listens but does not respond to proposals from men, whom she assumes are attracted to her fortune. She, however, enjoys exerting this meager power over men: "I yet had my admirers, or such they pretended to be; though perhaps my fortune tempted them more than my person, at least I thought so, and accordingly diverted myself at their expense; for none touched my heart" (50). She admits to tormenting her well-meaning cousin, who loves her. Whenever he proposes, "I always laugh at him, and answered in the Indian language, of which he was entirely ignorant; and so by degrees wearied him into silence on that head" (51). Unlike her mother and aunt, her treatment of men remains passive. She uses her multilingual skills to befuddle her cousin, but she refrains from exerting any real power over him. By answering in the native language, she seemingly reasserts cultural differences between them, the same cultural differences that her father successfully brushed aside with Unca Eliza's mother. Still, she remains apprehensive about matrimony, especially as she reflects on her parents' marriage: "What is human felicity? How often our greatest pleasures procure us the greatest misery! This moment behold a happy couple mutually endearing themselves to each other, whilst the infant offspring of their loves beholds their joys, partakes of, and adds to them. The next—but let the scene sink into darkness! 'tis too affecting for a daughter's pen to draw" (47). The dash that seeks to cover up the murder of her mother appears as an affectation, for the text is forthright with the violence that propagated colonial settlements.

As an adult, Unca Eliza attempts to stay *feme sole,* but, even unencumbered by domestic strife, she remains just as vulnerable to the men who prey upon her. *The Female American* underscores how a woman cannot seek relief from domestic entanglements, unlike Robinson Crusoe, just as the colonized other cannot maintain unadulterated contact with Europeans without ushering in religious and capitalistic exploitation. Women, like New World lands, represent unprotected and therefore exploitable resources. A woman of resources not only unsettles others but also finds herself susceptible to abuse. The Indian Queen's violent acts of coercion are mirrored by men, like the ship captain, who try to force Unca Eliza to marry. But, once married, someone like Unca Eliza's mother cannot find protection in a husband, nor does William Winkfield have any real power to protect his wife from the vengeance of the Indian Queen. Domestic power relations indeed structure every facet of colonial life.

The text creates an illusion of separate spheres, but the political continues to lurk and emerge from the domestic. While critics herald Unca Eliza as a mixed-race heroine, she disappoints because she fails to embody productive collaboration between Europeans and the local tribes, a collaboration that seemingly hinges on her choice of spouse. Instead, her mixed-race identity renders her strangely inert. Unca Eliza as the heir apparent attempts to evade her parents' fate by refusing to take on the role of queen after her aunt dies and by refusing to marry. Political power and domestic tranquility intertwine. Nonetheless, Unca Eliza's renunciation of power is ambiguous. She observes how in England, people treat her like a princess: "[I]ndeed I might have been a queen, if my father had pleased, for on the death of my aunt, the Indians made me a formal tender of the crown to me; but I declined it" (49). While her diction gives her agency ("I declined it"), the subjunctive ("if my father had pleased") re-empowers the father. This odd logic again signifies the illusion of choice that the novel both offers and denies. Jeannine Blackwell argues about women castaways in general, "In order to be a sympathetic heroine, she cannot willfully desert duty for desire and therefore must be driven to it. Her act of escape ceases to be personal choice and becomes unavoidable" (10–11). By having Unca Eliza cast ashore, the narrative absolves her from responsibility for her failure to serve England or Virginia. Blackwell's analysis further explicates Unca Eliza's resistance to marriage: "[I]t is hinted that [the Robinsonade heroine] accomplishes her adventure through passive resistance in refusing marriage. That is her revolt" (10–11). In this case, Unca Eliza exercises power only after she is abandoned on a deserted island, but unlike these heroines who pose "passive resistance" to marriage, Unca Eliza is forthright in her refusal to marry, and the text demonstrates how her inflexibility provokes aggression from men, like the ship captain who casts her ashore or the English sailors who later leave her stranded.

Still, the same domestic disagreements that plagued the father follow her. Rather than capitalizing on her freedom and selecting her family like Robinson Crusoe, she is assailed with marriage offers. The deal the ship captain offers Unca Eliza, either to promise to marry his son back in England or to be cast ashore to be eaten by wild animals, is a reductive form of coverture—it again uncovers the inanity of "choices" which permeate the rest of the text. Michael McKeon identifies "what seems truly innovative about [eighteenth-century England] is its extraordinary concentration upon the question of the marriage choice, and upon the paradigm of a basic opposition—embodied in typical familial (or simply human) personages—between love and money" (131). Yet *The Female American* reconsiders this opposition between love matches (disregarding money) and marriages (in which money is paramount) to reveal how even romantic attachments prioritize socioeconomic mobility. The ship captain, moreover, illuminates the ruse of courtship as the most powerful stage in a woman's life. Indeed, he even troubles the much-touted superiority of English monogamy. Unca Eliza reports that he would have married her himself but he was already married. Instead, he settles for the role of father-in-law to have at least some claim on her wealth. Later Unca Eliza reconsiders her actions in response to the captain's proposition: she declares she should have agreed to his terms and then later, when safe on land in England, rescinded her acceptance, but she claims that "I did not know law enough then" (54). This is a major refutation of love as a fantasy zone. It upends Armstrong's observation about the *apoliticalizing* of desire as offering relief from the political. For Unca Eliza needs to know "law enough" in order to decline and accept offers of marriage.

The text, therefore, exposes how the violence and coercion that inheres in the domestic supersedes and subtends the state.[11] Marriage is founded upon leveraging power; as an unmarried woman (a resource unattended by men) Unca Eliza represents resources vulnerable to exploitation. She must consistently renounce power; yet it does not prove sufficient to protect her. To assuage fear, she seizes upon the act of renunciation. But renunciation itself confers power: the ability and means to refuse as when she declines the mantle of Indian Queen and then marriage. The first allows her to forestall any threat to the power system, but her wealth remains a powerful inducement to scoundrels. The consolidation of resources undermines agency and opportunities to explore other modes. The transition of power from Alluca to Unca Eliza, however, constrains female power for Unca Eliza's power hinges on the property she can transfer into English hands. The captain knows the extent of Unca Eliza's wealth because she has already promised to give him the ship on which they sail once they reach England. Her act of generosity, giving her ship away, marks her as powerful but vulnerable. Once her wealth dissipates, Unca Eliza remains a sympathetic heroine on the island, but her power to transform cross-cultural alliances evaporates. The novel seems fascinated by what Alluca represents and the ways in which Unca Eliza manages the transition of wealth and symbolic power but cannot figure out a way to perpetuate female power within the socioaesthetic matrices it inherits.

STRANGE MENTORS

In refusing the path of her father or aunt the Indian Queen, Unca Eliza ends up a castaway on a deserted island, but the narrative's plotting resists leaving her to herself; instead, the character gets help from unlikely sources even if her seclusion narrows her influences. Unca Eliza's ability to constitute herself as a subject, despite her grave circumstances, depends on aid she receives from three sources. First, the island's previous inhabitant, a hermit, provides a model for her. Second, the handwritten manuscript that the hermit bequeaths her based on his long study of the island further helps her conceptualize her surroundings and take command over them. And third, Unca Eliza's English uncle with whom she holds imagined discourses when she self-reflects also influences her behavior. Each of these mentors enables her to turn happenstance or even suffering into a choice. The text in tracing her moment-to-moment thinking uncovers the epistemic paradigms that undergird colonial enterprises, as it depicts Unca Eliza alone on the island from which she will launch a full-scale attempt with overblown theatricality to convert a nearby tribe to Christianity.

If Unca Eliza's father represents one extreme of the dangers of marriage, then the hermit who preceded Unca Eliza on the island represents the other extreme of social isolation as one totally removed from positions of power or community. The hermit, like the father, comes across as a safe male figure (in contrast to ship captain). All alone, he has begun a lengthy, handwritten manuscript which details the island's habitat, its ruins, and the customs of the nearby communities who visit the island. Like the father, the hermit's role seems thrust upon him by extenuating circumstances even as he claims to have chosen it. Stranded on the island, Unca Eliza at once identifies his dwellings as something she has heard about in the past: "I now concluded that this was the habitation of some human being: but this gave me no alarm; for as I had read of hermits, who frequently retire from public life to enjoy their devotions in private, I imagined, from what I saw, that this must be the habitation of such a one, from whom I did not doubt but I should meet with protection and spiritual consolation" (58). In her mind, a hermit "retires" to "enjoy" greater vicissitudes of prayer in private. But this perspective on the hermit, paradoxically, elides and confronts the mishaps that landed him on the island against his will. *The Female American* in this instance, as in so many others, offers a totalizing vision of European encounters along the Atlantic. Texts, like this one, though, refuse to obscure the lived experience of Europeans in the New World; it later makes explicit that the hermit did not choose to live there. Kathleen Donegan, writing about the actual period of settlements, argues, "colonial settlement can be more fully understood if we try to see it as a cluster of unassimilated events rather than as an established body of forward-leaning facts" (7). Even as the text rushes past the "unassimilated events" it gestures toward anomalous fact. The manuscript he writes makes it plain that he was a castaway on the island and then "chose" his life as a hermit.[12] Again the text models how to conceptualize one's inescapable situation as selected among other alternatives. When she has a sudden and brief encounter with the hermit right before he dies, he explains to her, "Have I then . . . been so happy as to have my misfortunes prove the means of affording assistance to an innocent and unhappy sufferer" (76). He continues to lament his life as "my misfortunes" even as he did nothing to seek help from the peoples who came to the island year after year. Unca Eliza not only takes advantage of the hermit's lengthy manuscript on how to survive island-living but she also proves more daring than him by initiating contact with the tribe who visit, whereas the hermit hid whenever they made their annual pilgrimage to the island's sacred ruins. Yet the book situates Unca Eliza's ability to capitalize on the island's wealth as bound up with the hermit's conceptualization of the island; through his text, she takes a command over that which he himself could not. Without the hermit's hand-written guide, Unca Eliza could not beguile or intimidate the tribe that pays a yearly visit.

Unca Eliza continues to waver between understanding her situation as a personal choice and as a condition beyond her control. After an earthquake, she finds the hermit's dwellings toppled. Realizing she will have to reside in the underground apartments attached to the sacred oracle, she reflects that the last time she visited the underground rooms, she was "not thinking I should ever have made it the voluntary place of my residence, if indeed I may say voluntary; for it was a necessity, not a free choice, that led me thither" (90). At this point in the narrative, she lapses into the language of voluntarism even if she corrects her diction to assert that it is "not a free choice." The text again poses external circumstances as a matter of personal volition. Her self-correction reveals the ways in which Unca Eliza conforms to the ideal behavior of proper young women even as she lives isolated from society and how word choice (such as "voluntary") can color one's predicament.

Despite her boasts about her natural resourcefulness, such as her adept-ness with a bow and arrow and with multiple languages and dialects, she depends on the work of the hermit and the ancient buildings on the island to survive. Unlike Crusoe, she need not build any habitation or do much work on the island. The text, moreover, also offers wry commentary on how print culture acclimates young women readers into middle-class life. The hermit's manuscript, totaling more than four hundred pages, functions at first as a mediator between Unca Eliza and the island; as such, it seems to operate in much the same way as books that were used to inculcate middle-class values into English women readers. The text is introduced to the reader through its excessive detail; Unca Eliza explains how she learns on the first page: "[T]here are no wild beasts or noxious animals to injure thee; nor savages, except once a year, on one day, see page of this book 397" (58). The size of the volume seems to mock the use of written sources and, indeed, Unca Eliza has some difficulty getting through it. Using the book, however, Unca Eliza reestablishes the historicity of the island and its relationship to the indigenous, information that allows her to manipulate them into submission. Even as the title character receives direct instruction from the male hermit, suggesting the necessity of a male guide, *The Female American* ironically suggests the unreadability and inutility of these instruction manuals. As Julia Crick and Alexandra Walsham have argued, "the tendency to align written culture with privacy and individualism belies the way in which, either verbally rehearsed or silently perused, books forged links between scattered individuals and groups of people" (18). The manuscript encapsulates the hermit's commitment to others even amid his extended isolation on the island.

Imagination is key to Unca Eliza's conceptualization of new world challenges, but, when she over relies on it, it becomes hard to disentangle the real and imagined. Unca Eliza has created a system of self-instruction that she learned from her uncle: meditation and speaking aloud to oneself. When soliloquizing, she explains, "on these occasions, it was always my custom to imagine to myself that my uncle was speaking to me; this I thought, as it were, inspired me, and gave me energy to my words, strength to my arguments, and commanded my attention. I have sometimes indulged this reverie to such a degree that I have really imagined, at last, that my uncle was speaking to me" (69). These lines evoke the ways in which the imagination can take hold of the person who creates and thus controls the fantasy. For using the power of her own imagination, her uncle "commands her attention." The character easily slides between the fictional and the real. Yet the subject of her talk with her imagined uncle is how to acclimate to one's condition and avoid self-pity. She imagines the uncle would teach her to compare her condition, however lamentable, to those who suffer more: "How preferable is your condition to that of those consigned to slavery for life!'" (70). Although the text avoids the question of slavery, it emerges here as a readily identifiable way to define freedom. This imagined lecture successfully changes her point of view on her abandoned state: "Submission or hope, one or both, were ever in a less or greater degrees my solace" (71). That conjunction "or," repeated three times in the sentence, carries great importance because submission, on the one hand, and hope, on the other, do not function as opposites. *The Female American* conflates them by portraying submission as a choice, which implies greater individual autonomy.

Unca Eliza uses the handwritten manuscript to colonize (convert) the tribe. Instead of asserting power as Indian Queen, Unca Eliza presents herself as a Christian woman, a role that involves elaborate subterfuge. Her proselytizing aligns with acceptable female behavior, for religion in the eighteenth century offered a realm for women's agency within English and American Protestantism. In this way, the novel functions, as Michelle Burnham characterizes it, as a "fantasy of female power exercised within and by means of a Christian colonialist utopia" (Introduction 19). Within the context of the story, when Unca Eliza renounces the position as Indian Queen and later as queen of the neighboring tribe she encounters on the island, her power of proselytizing remains a safe zone for her as a woman to exercise power. Nancy Cott explains how women's role in ministry "preserved conventional appearances but gave them a new direction. Evangelical activity fostered women's emergence as social actors whose roles were based on female responsibilities rather than on human rights" (156). As Cott further explains, "re-creating" the kinds of religious institutions gave women, as they moved, "a continuing sense of belonging to a female Christian community" (154–55). By taking on this role, Unca Eliza both asserts and disavows her individuality.

Converting the tribe not only gives her renewed purpose but also gives her the means to create boundaries to maintain her privacy. When deciding whether to convert them, she indulges in shared fantasies: "This moment I imagined hundreds of Indians prostrate before me with reverence and attention, inculcated them with a voice magnified almost to the loudness of thunder" (86). Once she "imagines," she creates a new reality that acts upon her, for she thereafter renounces responsibility for taking the decisive step. After her initial meeting with them, she tells them to come back to the island in a week: "Besides, I had some domestick cares upon my hands" (101). It little matters in the text how she will serve the public if she fails to manage the private sphere. In her case, the "domestick" refers to exploiting the ancient relics and jewels that she has found. These treasures prove crucial to dominating the indigenous people and, eventually, frightening away her European deliverers. The domestic, again, directly enables colonial oppression.

In her role as a preacher of the Word, she manipulates the tribe whose religious practices are tied to the island. She speaks through their idols, while hiding her identity, to transmit Christian ideology. She further obscures her identity to the point that the people think she is a kind of god, while appropriating their ancestors' wealth—vestments and jewels to costume herself.[13] She undercuts the authority of the priests while building up her own through the amplified voice of the idol. When the tribal leaders think she may be some type of devil, she quells their fears by telling them, "Return, I am not the evil being whom ye dread; return and provoke me not, to destroy you, before you can reach your own shore" (96). When they return, she promises, "Fear not, I am not the evil being; and if you will hearken to me, he shall never hurt you" (96). Her verbal manipulation (she has no actual means to destroy them) obfuscates the choice she frequently lays before them. Unca Eliza gives the people the illusion of choosing Christianity and her role among them as an "instructor." Under the guise of the idol, she reiterates to the people, not just the priests, "But I do not want to force her among you: if you do not choose she should come, speak, and she shall not come; I will be dumb for ever" (112). The tribe willingly obliges her: "Our countrymen rejoiced to hear the good news, and all desire you will come and live among them; they will love you, obey all your commands, and will make you their queen, for our king is lately dead, and as he had no children, we have not as yet chosen a new king. Will you therefore go home with us, and be our queen?" (115). The tribe has pivoted from their conception of her as prophet to her as a ruler in a way that corresponds with Unca Eliza's usurpation of their idols and sacred traditions, even as she renounces any such title as queen. She explains, "[B]ut I will not be your queen, therefore you may choose whom you please. But, as you desire it, I will come and live among you, and will be only your instructor" (115). The lines again double back upon themselves. While she demonstrates a generosity of spirit—"choose whom you please" as your king—she reiterates that she "will be only your instructor" and indeed their *only* instructor. She remains more powerful than any king or the priests while disavowing any titles.

She exalts in her life among the tribe in a way that blurs concerted action and happenstance: "How greatly was my situation changed! From a solitary being, obliged to seek my own food from day to day, I was attended by a whole nation, all ready to serve me; and no care upon me but how to discharge the important business of an apostle, which I had now taken upon me"

(118). Unca Eliza's language in this instance disavows responsibility as though her "situation" merely altered, whereas she calculated each step toward placing herself in this position with the tribe. Her last words reinforce her responsibility and her deliberate choice: "I had now taken upon me" the role of proselytizer. She, however, continues to situate herself as a solitary being, because the people around her remain aggregated as a "nation." She refrains from intimacy with individuals; instead, she forges ties with the priests and with the "public" in general. This language draws attention away from Unca Eliza's repeated claims that she fears the power of the priests and how she subdues any resentment or factionalism. Stoler argues that studies in colonialism often neglect the "epistemic politics" of colonial projects. She suggests that one needs to understand "the conditions of epistemic choice and chance, of inculcation and innovation, how people charged with large-scale management and local situations imagined they might identify what they knew they could not see and what common sense they used to assess racial belonging or political desires unavailable to ocular evidence" ("Epistemic Politics" 351). *The Female American* closely follows Unca Eliza's thoughts as she adapts herself to their sensibilities. At first, she cannot understand why they run from her until she infers that they perceive her as a devil. She must also infer how the priests interpret her intrusions and thus construct ways to diminish their power over the people. Her elevated position removes her from close contact with the indigenous people in a way that her father could not manage.

The text presents Unca Eliza as living undisturbed among the tribe for two years until the arrival of Europeans, one of whom is her cousin who wants to marry her. His persistence in pursuing Unca Eliza further illustrates the repeated slippage of choice. The tribe is forced to convert to Christianity, and Unca Eliza is forced to marry. "This is not a peaceful accommodation; it is a take-over," as Eve Tavor Bannet argues (184). Bannet continues, "This 'marriage' which subordinates the Indian missionary to the white minister, and the woman to the man, and forces Unca—as American Indian, Indian missionary, and wife all rolled into one—into obedience to her English lord and master" (184). Bannet provides a fine summation of the ways in which race and gender intersect in the text, but "marriage" in the scare quotes misses how incendiary marriage is throughout the first part of the text as well.

Unca Eliza's reliance on the hermit, his book, and her advisor in the imaginary form of her uncle do not enable a sustained command over others because of her gender and perhaps, too, because of her wealth. Her cousin continues to seek her, and, when he finds her, he appropriates her religious role among the local tribe and invites more Europeans into these remote sites. Whatever "fantasy" of just a little colonialism Unca Eliza wants to spread based on her commitment to Christianity or her desire to interact minimally with other people, the text will not indulge. Colonial encounters lead to fundamental changes beyond the epistemes available to those who usher in European-Christian domination. Unca Eliza attempts to see all, while hidden in her idol, but this elevated position cannot be sustained once she enters colonized space.

Perhaps, the last page of the text offers the most unsettling image for Unca Eliza's total usurpation of power: she relates how "we first determined to go upon my island, to collect all the gold treasure there, to blow up subterraneous passage, and the statue, that the Indians might never be tempted to their former idolatry" (154). Instead of promoting collectivity, Unca Eliza seizes on the codes of empire to hoard wealth and knowledge from others. She frames her destruction of the ruins not as a tactical move to secure her power over indigenous people but as benevolent gesture to ensure they "might never be tempted." By destroying the points of entry into the idol on her otherwise unoccupied island, she obliterates the indigenous people's cultural practices, heritage, and any other (European) attempts to use the idol to exploit them. The text traces which fantasies of colonial power are tenable and which untenable.

Rather than interpret the text as ambiguous in its attitude toward colonization and conversion, I read it as drawing attention to the constructedness of the stories we tell about conquest. The book enacts the process by which we *retell* the story of settlement and fits into what Mary Louis Pratt calls "anti-conquest narratives."[14] Pratt observes how those narratives offer "strategies of representation whereby European bourgeois subjects seek to secure their innocence in the same moment as they assert European hegemony" (7). By representing the interiority of the title character, Unca Eliza, the reader follows the retroactive formulation of desire. This explains the text's strangeness; it does not portray mimetic desire, to use Rene Girard's term for mediated desires, but instead how individuals learn to desire what they have already received. In the text, for example, attitudes toward empire and colonialism—its violence, aggression, and exploitation of others—seem to hinge on how an individual rejects large-scale hegemonic processes even as she enacts them. Unca Eliza notes the impending collision between the tribe and Europeans, but her management of these encounters exacerbates them. The novel achieves this slanted telling by relying on a woman as its colonizing agent. As an alternative to providing historical insight into the development of successful or unsuccessful settlements, the text focuses on the attitudes toward development that take shape and how those attitudes can transmute an incident of misfortune into an experience that was initiated by calculated agency. Moreover, the text flirts with the possibility of condemning exploitative religious conversion, but instead it traces the processes by which Europeans feel entitled to co-opt the religious and cultural practices of "others" and the pleasure of exercising this power over them.

As in works of domestic realism, this one, too, ends in marriage. Commentators lament the breakdown in point of view toward the end of the text as the narration turns to one Englishman after another, as Unca Eliza listens to reports about what happened to the ship captain who abandoned her and how her cousin found her. The usurpation in point of view recapitulates the inauguration of coverture as Unca Eliza transitions from *feme sole* to *feme covert* to her cousin. As Hendrik Hartog explains, "An unmarried woman was not subject to the disabilities of coverture; single women possessed all of the rights married women lost. A single woman's legal status was, for the most part, indistinguishable from the legal status of many men. A single woman could contract, own, dispose, write wills, engage in most forms of business, testify, demand the obedience and the guardianship of her children" (Hartog 24). Just as her mother's power diminished following her marriage, the end of Unca Eliza's autonomy is marked by her marriage to her cousin. When her cousin proposes again, she goes silent; "[Y]et I declined a direct answer; for though I loved him as a friend and relation, I had never considered him as a lover; nor any other person" (139). Marriage begins a declension in Unca Eliza's power. Here she does not "decline" her cousin's proposal but "declined a direct answer."[15]

In an ironic turn, Unca Eliza's pretense of terrifying the Englishmen leads to her marriage to her cousin. Like Alluca, her outward show of power leads to her undoing. While she plays a trick upon the English sailors who come to rescue her by speaking with the amplified voice and by dressing in a costume, she fails to anticipate the extent of the men's fear. She even toys with them when they hang back, chiding them that they do not act as men should: "[H]ave you forgot all your gallantry, and must I make the first advance?" (126). The

sight of a woman so powerful incites such great fear, even among these experienced sailors, that the men abandon her cousin on the shore, effectively
leaving him stranded with a monstrous woman. After Unca Eliza refuses her
cousin's marriage proposal, they find a handwritten farewell note from his
friends who have left him behind. Unca Eliza, for her part, "was heartily sorry
at reading of this; but my cousin smiled, and said he should now live with me
whether I would, or not" (138). The cousin ignores Unca Eliza's wish that he
return to England without her, because he claims her costume has frightened
away his friends, even as he invited this turn of events. He tells her, "[I]t is in
your power, my dear Unca Eliza, greatly to add to [my parents'] pleasure, by
enabling me to acquaint them, that you have become their daughter. Let us
then be united" (138). While he reiterates that she has "power," he admits,
"One motive for my seeking you was, that, if we should meet, we might be
for ever united. Consider one thing more, but if you refuse me, we cannot
enjoy those hours of privacy together, I at least you wish for, without an
offense to those around us; at least I know your delicacies would be hurt by
them" (138). He manipulates her by alluding to her affection for her aunt and
uncle back in England (his parents) but then pivots to a threat: he is prepared
to renounce any private intercourse with her. If his proposal began by noting
her "power" it morphs into an ultimatum: "consider one thing more, if you
refuse me." Unca Eliza for her part remains silent. However, she eventually
succumbs because she worries about maintaining propriety, imbibing what
he refers to as "her delicacies."

The Female American refuses to ignore the multivalent repercussions of a
marriage that depletes Unca Eliza's power. With her cousin on the island, her
central role as instructor of the tribe recedes: "I had now the great pleasure of
once more enjoying all the ordinances of the church, and the constant company of a religious and sensible companion, to whom, through his constant
importunity, I was at last obliged to give my hand, about two months after
his arrival" (140–41). Her final capitulation hardly evidences a strong desire
for the match as she oscillates from describing "his constant importunity" to
"at last obliged." Her reticence demonstrates Boe and Coykendall's claims
that heterosexual marriage's dominance lies in its "reconfiguration of male/
female sexes as an interlocked set whose conjugal union sublated otherwise
troubling incongruities in the economic, geopolitical, or religious complexion
of the espoused families" (9).

Subtle modes of social control concerning sexual propriety permeate beyond European sites to circumscribe a woman's volition. Her cousin's presence necessitates her marriage because she fears, after her cousin has insinuated it, that their relationship as an unmarried man and woman would violate social dictums of behavior, even though the people do not seem inclined to censure her for it (139). Moreover, her marriage enables her to finish her conversion of the tribe, because through her husband, an ordained minister, they could be "properly baptized, married, and many of them, at their earnest desire, admitted to the Lord's supper" (141). Although Unca Eliza's hesitation about and eventual acceptance of marriage undergird the last pages of the text, she emphasizes that the tribe sought to take communion "at their earnest desire." Yet the whole text has portrayed people's desire as forced compliance. Unequivocally, her marriage seems to inaugurate more European incursions even as she renounces Europe by permanently settling on the island. She and her husband plan to live among them, but then a ship captain asks to join them. They also need supplies from England and thus continue to publicize their whereabouts. To preserve the island from European intruders, they request that the sailors land only so far inland as to keep their distance, but that plan has faltered before. Even so, she explains that she writes the text and sends it back to England for the sake of her in-laws: "As we never intended to have any more to do with Europe, [C]aptain Shore and my husband ordered a person who came for that purpose, to return to Europe with the ship, by whom, for [his] father and mother's satisfaction, I sent over these adventures" (154–55). Yet this publication will alert others to their situation and the islands she seeks to protect. Appeasing her husband's family leaves Unca Eliza and these new world domains open to more exploitation. Paul Armstrong makes a strong case that textual ambiguities are a "strategy of transforming dilemmas . . . into provocations to future readers to struggle with them and perhaps do a better job than [an author] could" ("In Defense" 103). *The Female American*'s ambiguities, its mixed-race heroine who defies feminine conventions, on the one hand, and its objectification of indigenous people and the religious conversion imposed upon them, on the other, have led to many critical takes that struggle to reconcile what seems progressive and simultaneously regressive about the text. In re-reading the text, we struggle again to identify the forces shaping the possibility, rather than the fantasy, of women's role in shaping imperial power.

To contrast the seizure of power in *The Female American* through the colonization of an island in the West Indies, I turn to Leonora Sansay's 1808 secret history of the Haitian Revolution. Unlike *The Female American*, Sansay's text draws upon an eyewitness account of an actual West Indian island. However, despite its claims to testimony, Sansay's account emerges as exceptional, because its telling does not align with contemporaneous accounts of the Haitian Revolution. Whereas for Unca Eliza Winkfield, the people remain unnamed and docile, Sansay's narrator finds that the people of Saint-Domingue are not as easily subordinated. Thus, *Secret History* reads like an antidote to *The Female American:* whereas Unca Eliza remains in the West Indies, Mary, the narrator of Sansay's text, has to return to Philadelphia; whereas Unca Eliza exerts discursive control over the local tribe, Mary find the leaders of the Haitian revolution and other Black Haitians dominate discursive realms, giving them inordinate powers over the whites; whereas Unca Eliza weds, even if unwillingly, Mary remains unwed and joined in partnership with her sister (unlike the rivalrous portrait of sisters in *The Female American*). Nonetheless, each text demarcates the limits to new historicist readings of texts by incorporating people like the Indian Queen, Unca Eliza's father and mother, her dead uncle, the hermit, and her persistent fiancé, who each chip away at Unca Eliza's claims to self-direction.

2

TALKING SEX

AND REVOLUTION

in

SAINT-DOMINGUE

in

SANSAY'S *Secret History*

The Female American MIGHT BE CONSIDERED A LITERARY TEXT WITH-
out a country because of how little we know about its author or even the island
where the narrator purports to have lived. Contemporary readers have much
more information on another anonymous text, *Secret History: or The Horrors
of St. Domingo,* published in 1808: the author's name (Leonora Sansay, aka
Mary Hassel), her place of birth (Philadelphia), and information that she spent
time in Saint-Domingue following her marriage to Louis Sansay, a displaced
French merchant.[1] Despite their differences, both *The Female American* and
Secret History represent the political violence that extends out from the domestic sphere, not merely intrudes upon it. While *The Female American* may
be characterized as historical fiction about indigenous-European relations
during the early seventeenth century, Sansay's novel entered the literary marketplace alongside many firsthand testimonies about the revolution written by
white men that sought to undermine the significance of Haiti's liberation from
France even as it unfolded. In some ways, *Secret History*'s idiosyncrasies offer
a counternarrative to the ones circulated through newspapers or other first-
person accounts of the Haitian Revolution. Rather than demonizing the Black
liberators or emphasizing their physical strength, Sansay portrays them as
strategic in their use of rhetoric to usurp and maintain control of the country.[2]

Those very idiosyncrasies that mark it as different from other texts make it amenable to new evaluations of Haiti's revolution. I argue that Sansay's text provides a much more varied account of the revolution that surveys the multiple perspectives of participants and participant-observers. The ultimate effect of her text is to demarcate the slow, difficult work of trying to transform a colonized site. Its epistolary form highlights that sense of contingency. By providing a one-sided correspondence between the fictional Mary and the former vice president Aaron Burr, the author further emphasizes the linkages between private and public spheres that other novels obscure. For the past twenty years, scholars have brought about a major reevaluation of the causes, significance, and implications of the Haitian Revolution. Scholars Doris Garraway, Deborah Jensen, Laurent Dubois, and Jean Casimir, among others, have sifted through some of the sensationalism of the primary source materials and brought to light information about its leaders that had been elided in previous decades of scholarship. Their work coincided with greater attention in literary studies to transnational literature and hemispheric studies. These studies demonstrate how characterizations of the revolution (1791–1804) in the nineteenth century and for much of the twentieth century failed to reflect the contingency of the revolutionaries' aims or how those aims shifted in response to geopolitical interference. The very name, Haitian Revolution, is a retroactive construction of the conflict; for the island was only named Haiti after the hostilities subsided. Yet its overlap with the French Revolution and then the rise of Napoleon only further muddied the revolutionaries' objectives and how France and the United States responded to them.

Several literary works, like the novels by Fanny Reybaud, Pierre Faubert, and Dumas set during the period, have helped scholars sort through competing claims and interpretations about the turbulent period. Among them, Sansay's epistolary novel actively captures the contingency of living in the midst of national conflicts, while depicting the alluring dreams of colonial authority, and the concomitant rebellion it stokes among people who are rendered abject under that authority. *Secret History,* dismissed upon publication, is somewhat awkwardly constructed in term of its genre, frame story, plot, and character development. Indeed, according to Michael Dexler's introduction to the Broadview edition, shortly after her next novel, *Laura,* appeared in print in 1809, Sansay gave up writing and started what developed into a more financially rewarding venture as the owner of a flower shop. Yet, despite its flaws, the text showcases the rhetorical power, rather than the sensationalized violence, of the leaders of the Haitian Revolution. Studies of the revolution in Saint-Domingue bring to the fore problems with language about cultural amnesia that do not quite hold up to scrutiny. Many historians agree that a surfeit of texts circulated about the revolution and its aftermath in the nineteenth century even as its implications seem absent from studies about the Age of Revolutions. Yet for many literary historians, the insurrection and its aftermath have not made the same imprint on the US cultural imagination as the American or French Revolutions. Marlene Daut has brought greater nuance to understanding how the revolution is characterized as at once too "silent" and too loud by explaining how discourses on "the formation of the first black republic in the Western Hemisphere. . . . were perhaps less 'silenced' in literal terms than they were incessantly narrated in a particularly 'racialized' way that had the ultimate effect of subordinating the position of the Haitian Revolution to the French and American revolutions" (3). Daut makes a convincing case that too often the revolution was characterized in terms of "vengeance" rather than liberty or equality, in what she terms the "mulatto/a vengeance narrative" (4). However, the varying and contradictory narratives about the Haitian Revolution—whether understanding the revolution in terms of the "mulatto/a vengeance narrative" (Daut 4) or the Enlightenment ideals of equality and liberty, among others—offer an opportunity to destabilize monolithic narratives about other revolutions. Sansay's text, rather than silencing the revolution's consequences, demystifies how Black revolutionaries' discursive control enabled them—even if only temporarily—to set the terms for understanding what a sovereign Haiti might represent.

In the first part of the chapter, I survey new historical interpretations of the conflict to highlight how discursive power partly enabled the Revolutionaries' success in wresting control from France. This section draws upon recent historical work, which overturns long-standing misinterpretations of the Haitian Revolution. It illuminates how Sansay can both identify the Revolutionaries as deft politicians and undercut their accomplishments by claiming that circumstance rather than strategy gave them an advantage. At one point, the narrator explains how the black rebels overwhelm the French military because "the climate itself combats for them," as though it is happenstance that enables their victory over the French officers (73). In the second part, I trace

Sansay's frustration with the French military's inability to forge a viable public sphere when they attempt to retake the colony. Sansay equates eloquence with sexual appeal. Indeed, the French people attempt to silence others on the island to ward off sexual intrusions and further incursions on their power. The French officers use their waning political power to claim sexual partners rather than strengthen their colonial foothold on the island; nonetheless, their inept maneuverings render themselves less sexually appealing.

In the third part, I demonstrate how Black women are endowed with both verbal and sexual power as Sansay recalibrates ethnosexuality as enabling political domination in Saint-Domingue, although not in the United States. In the last section, I argue that Sansay's depiction of a sexualized public sphere in Haiti creates a space for her to address her personal relationship with Aaron Burr: these letters addressed to the American Revolutionary hero titillate her readers about political scandal in the United States even as they refocus attention on America's neighbors. She appropriates "black" sexual appeal in order to assert hemispheric control. Sansay's repeated attention to men and their attractiveness leads me to take issue with critical readings that laud the text's treatment of an all-women community as an idealized world without belligerent men. While these critical readings try to locate feminist undercurrents in Sansay's work, they ignore the text's ambivalence with the foibles and attractions of white men. Though Sansay's novel failed to create a new and longstanding image of Haiti in the American collective imaginary, the text still offers an alternative understanding of the relationship between the United States and Haiti. Sansay forces us to reevaluate how sexual behavior, undergirded by militaristic campaigns, shapes public participation in colonial sites for both men and women.

VERBAL ACUITY, SEX APPEAL, AND MILITARY MIGHT

The Secret History also marks a transition between the flowering of literary texts that appeared in the 1790s, like *The Coquette, Charlotte Temple,* and Charles Brockden Brown's novels, and the emergence in the 1820s of a concerted effort to create an American literature by Irving, Cooper, Sedgwick, and Child. Like *The Female American,* discussed in the previous chapter, *Secret History* was published in a period that usually draws minimal attention to literary works from America. It also seems to frustrate critics' ability to articulate clear claims about the era and the text's claims to historicity. Overall, the text seems to tease contemporary critics who seek more information about the "horrors" of revolts to which the title hints, about the conspirator Burr, and about the genre of the secret history. On all fronts, the novel disappoints. But rather than reading the text for what it fails to reveal, one should read it for the way in which it elucidates the processes by which episodes are turned into "history." The narrator at first seems to cast the Revolution as a temporary inconvenience for her; she hopes the returning French will regain colonial control and some inhabitants will resume their subordinate positions that she imagines them occupying as nameless, silent background figures. Her mindset indicates how colonizers' authority erodes: they, on some level, recognize the source of their decline but prove unable to adjust because of their fixed attitudes about the relationships among language, race, and (sexual) power. Paradoxically, even as the narrator seems to long for conquered Haiti, her text unfurls why the revolutionaries successfully kept Napoleon's army away because of their ability to shape public perception.

As one of the only eyewitness accounts by a woman of the Haitian Revolution, Sansay's novel traces the methods of control and domination either obscured or normalized in subsequent texts that touch upon the Revolution. By focusing on the French military, she elucidates the imbrications between landed gentry and the military in fostering Saint-Domingue as an island paradise. That imbrication yokes together the text's seemingly incongruous focus on the personal and the political, specifically the troubled marriages of the creolized French landowners. Upon their arrival in Cape Francois, the French officers seem positioned not only to curtail potential unrest but also to shift the imbalance in the sexual economy on the island in which white women compete with Black women for white men's sexual attention.

Sansay's *Secret History* depicts US interests in the Atlantic world of the eighteenth century, foregrounding the importance of Haiti to its nascent imperial designs.[3] The text begins in Saint-Domingue but follows the sisters, Mary and Clara, into the Spanish-controlled San Domingo and into Cuba and Jamaica, leading readers to reinterpret the early US republic in hemispheric terms. One must keep in mind Ralph Bauer's indictment of early American literary scholars who continue to centralize the role of the continental United States when reading texts from Latin and South America. As Bauer asserts, scholars "run the risk of subsuming the hemisphere within the literary history of the United States, rather than the U.S. within the literary history of the hemisphere," creating what he terms a "U.S.-centric metanarrative of hemispheric literary history" (255). By analyzing Sansay's text, one continues to look at the Caribbean through the lens of a US writer and US concerns about liberation, terror, and revolution. Yet Sansay's text, despite its limited scope, provides a larger context for understanding how Haiti operates in the social imaginary of the US and even how her text might protect the United States from undergoing a similar rebellion by identifying the French military's inadequacy and the Haitian leaders' strategic superiority.[4]

The United States marginalized the history of Haiti, in particular its revolution, because of fears in the early years of the republic that insurrections would spread. *Secret History* appeared in print just as Jefferson's policy of denying Haiti's independence from France cemented itself.[5] Indeed, Sansay's text is part of an explosion of printed texts that provided American and European audiences with an eyewitness report of Haiti's Revolution (Clavin 29). As such, the text creates a shared history between the United States and Haiti, one that seems laden with power struggles over the center and periphery.[6] Meanwhile, Sansay has her narrator simultaneously espouse sympathy for the Revolutionaries and regret for the French military officers' incompetence at keeping the colony under its control, principally because their failures curtail her enjoyment of the island.

As the Revolutionary leaders shaped and reshaped the narrative of the causes and aims of the Revolution and shifted it to suit the expediencies of the moment, the French continued to struggle to articulate their claims to power. In *Secret History*, Sansay highlights a power vacuum among the French landowners and military. In Saint-Domingue, the French Creoles are portrayed as listless, dull, and unwilling to exert themselves. Mary describes the Creole women on the island as "[a]lmost too indolent to pronounce the words they speak with a drawling accent" (71). While the French military commanders obsess over their sexual entanglements—a losing battle because they possess little sexual appeal—they jeopardize their object of recapturing the island. When the text opens, the two American sisters at the center of the text, along with the rest of the returning French population, occupy the margins of the island in the hopes of reclaiming their vast estate. These women insist that the Revolution will be quickly stamped out by Napoleon's forces so they can reoccupy Clara's husband's plantation. Mary whines, "I wish [the negroes] were reduced to order that I might see the so much vaunted habitations" (73). Her attitude belies the ways in which the military would have to be expanded even if it crushed the insurrection in order to maintain French control to sustain their indolent lifestyle. The French underestimate their task. "Indeed," reports the narrator, "the professed intention of those who have come with the army, is to make a fortune, and return to France with all possible speed, to enjoy it" (66). Their geographic insularity at Cape Francois reinforces their isolation from others on the island. Sansay shows that the French have not forged a vibrant public sphere in Haiti. Moreover, the narrator Mary condemns the French general, Le Clerc, because instead of arresting the Black chiefs, he believes everything they say and "relies on their good faith, has them continually in his house, at this table, and wastes the time in conference" with them (65). His lack of diplomacy or military strategy proves a disaster. While the French Creoles object to the commanders' methods, they merely "murmur" their opposition rather than publicly assert themselves (65). The Black population, however, controls the conversation. As Tessie Liu summarizes, "throughout the novel it is the black population that initiates the movement of other groups; in so doing, blacks propel the story forward" (397). Sansay, though, highlights how linguistic acuity precedes and solidifies military might and how each contributes to sexual dominance.

The allure of Saint-Domingue for white visitors is not just the indolent lifestyle supported by the work of those held in slavery but also the sexual pleasure visitors experience just by looking upon the Black women on the island. Sansay's text suggests that Napoleon wants to reclaim the territory for France, not just for the valuable commodities, like sugar, it exports throughout the world but also for the sexual permissiveness the place inspires. As Joane Nagel observes, "[A]lthough our discussion of the commercial expansion of ethnosexuality has focused mainly on the second half of the twentieth century, depictions of distant lands as libidinous locales run through centuries of travel narratives, such as those of Columbus and Vespucci or Lewis and Clark" (200). This libidinous label proves particularly apt for colonial Saint-Domingue. Although crimes committed during war are often whitewashed, Sansay highlights the strategies involved in using the military to create sites for indolent whites; as such, threats of sexual violence are central rather than obscured or erased. Sansay, therefore, never obscures the role the military plays in allowing her to enjoy her tour of Santo Domingo. Rather than portraying the Revolutionaries as vengeful, unrestrained people who had been held in slavery, Sansay, despite herself, reveals the complex politico-social systems of the Black liberators, admitting, in a sense, her own woeful inadequacy in promoting her own nascent career as a lady novelist, for her aims—to advance European power in its colonies—undermine what the novel depicts: Black leaders who create superior political-economic systems. She allows readers to glimpse the two-pronged approach of Europeans in their peripheral settlements.

Yet Sansay's little-known text did not shape attitudes toward revolution, Haiti, slavery, or even Aaron Burr when it appeared in print. Burr himself was erased from political memory after his public disgrace following his killing of Alexander Hamilton in a duel and his trial for treason for attempting to lead a separatist movement in Louisiana. The United States also refused to recognize Haiti independence until 1865. *Secret History*'s anomalous fashioning of American attitudes toward Haiti offers insight into a geopolitical stance that *might* have codified, especially since the book appears in print just as Great Britain and the United States abolished the importation of people as slaves.

Secret History reveals how sex and war, politics and marriage are not merely interconnected but ontologically cohesive. Sansay uses the site of the Haitian Revolution to sustain a prolonged—and farcical—intimate relationship with American Revolutionary hero and former vice president Aaron Burr in epistolary form. By doing so, Sansay suggests that scandal stitches together a community in ways that other discourses cannot; she insists that people who talk about sex constitute the strongest national assemblage and thus talk also provides a way for women to contribute to the formation of empire. Mary often remarks on speech as an indicator of a person's character. On General Le Clerc's reputation, Mary shares how: "He has the reputation of being very eloquent, but he has shocked everybody by having ordered a superb service of plate" using funds intended to feed the French soldiers (Sansay 66). The General's indulgence in fine dinnerware overshadows his ability to speak eloquently, a reputation he fails to import with him as he moves from France to the colony. His indulgence in luxury consumes him and diminishes his conversational abilities; his dinner guests will marvel at opulence rather than at his conversational skills. Instead of being the facilitator of a salon, the General has established a museum.

Sansay portrays identity as tied to and given shape by a person's ability to speak, more so than identity categories such as race, gender, or class. One's behavior in the drawing room then indicates military power or weakness. As noted, the French Creoles are portrayed as lacking conversational skills and thus useless. She portrays the French as notably lacking any interest in debate; they will not even begin a rudimentary discussion of the moral dilemma of slavery as they attempt to reenslave self-emancipated men and women. They are eager to move past the work of fighting the Revolutionaries. When a new general is brought in, the Creoles immediately consider the battle won: "Every proprietor feels himself already on his habitation and I have even heard some of them disputing the quality of the coffee they expect to gather" (71). Rather than confront the trouble in front of them, the Creole indulge in distracting disagreements about what they conjecture their crops will be like in their imaginary reestablished plantations. In contrast, Sansay portrays the rebelling Black factions as monopolizing rhetorical power. In Haiti, when the colonized "ventriloquize," filling the silence of the mute, stammering French subject, they have usurped power. Eventually, this ventriloquism develops into a unique discourse for the rebels, supplanting a colonial one. However, in Sansay's text, verbal power also indexes sexual appeal, not just political dominance.[7] According to historians, the Haitian revolution seemingly lacked a clear trajectory or line of dissent. Carolyn Fick explains, "Independence for Haiti was therefore an unfolding process, subject to the contingencies of a world being reshaped and redefined in ways that neither the slaves nor the slave owners, nor even the French revolutionary governments, could have predicted" (Fick 177–78). Sansay focuses less on the specifics of what the Revolutionaries declare as their demands changed over time and more on their ability to be heard at each turn.

The power of speech indicates control and strength in the text. The text is rife with the violent response wrought by jealousy, including the threat by Clara's husband to throw acid in her face for merely speaking to another man, and a story about a white woman who had a beautiful woman she held in bondage beheaded because she feared her husband was in love with her (125, 70). These actions seek to "silence" the desire they inspire in others. Mary, lamenting that St. Louis, her French brother-in-law, is "vain, illiterate, talkative" (63), uses him as a proxy to suggest the French's incompetence in maintaining and regaining control in Haiti. Indeed, Mary wonders how her sister can suffer through his conversation: "How painful must her intercourse with him be; and how infinitely must that pain be augmented by the idea of being his forever" (63–64). Mary's horror at her brother-in-law's poor conversation leads her to lament her sister's marriage. Because his obtuseness renders him unappealing and he cannot engross interlocutors, the text delegitimizes his capacity to rule and, by extension, France's capacity to govern Haiti. As the text unfolds, though, the reader learns that St. Louis has been terrorizing her sister: raping her, threatening to disfigure her, imprisoning her; this violent behavior overshadows Mary's concerns over his stupidity. When Clara hears her husband threaten to rub her face with acid, "This last menace deprived me of the power of utterance; to kill me would have been a trifling evil" (138). To further explain her agitation, Clara states, "I passed the night in speechless agony" (138). Indeed, utterances operate as a form of "power" in the text. At one point, Mary proves her disdain for a friend's husband by declaring, "To the husband I have never uttered a word" (115). The power to silence is portrayed as the exercise of brute strength, and to be silenced epitomizes one's powerlessness. Even so, the power to reduce others to speechlessness is temporary; it offers no permanent hold over those it seeks to repress into submission. Historian Laurent Dubois observes how depictions of the Revolution focus on its most brutal violence; he wonders if the excessive violence reported, if not actually witnessed, testifies to "individuals haunted by something quite different from what they represented—not an onslaught of atavistic barbarism, but an organized and strategic revolution of slaves" (Dubois 112). In Sansay's *Secret History,* her portrayal of St. Louis provides a counternarrative to the usual portrayals of the Revolution. In Sansay, the words "organized and strategic" do characterize the people formerly held in slavery, whereas "atavistic barbarism" marks the behavior of the French.

Hence, Sansay tries to resubstantiate white authority that has been weakened by the insurrection and the French troops' malaise through her novel. The most devastating setback for the "natives," as Mary calls them—the French Creoles—is that "they offer advice, which is not listened to" (65). The overlap between the reception of French Creoles and the reception of her novel demonstrates the urgency of establishing a network rooted in print and oral discourse. In fact, Sansay herself expresses this anxiety: the phrase "I fear" opens the text. But the author refers not to her fears regarding the

Revolution or the horrors it engendered but to her trepidation regarding the public reception of her novel. The novel is a test case to reaffirm her friends' praise and widen her audience to share and reinforce her ideas: her friends admire her writing and "it was chiefly with a view to ascertain what confidence I might place in their kind assurances on this subject" that she publishes *Secret History* (60). Thus, print will verify her friends' affinity for her while it offers her an alternative community in print.[8] Publication also makes visible the similarities between the two cultures: Haiti and the United States; and while it asserts her cosmopolitanism, it makes the case that what succeeded in Haiti can burnish a wider American agenda. She forges, then, not only a salon culture but also an alternative community in place of the French military's inertia. This community allows her to reassert a position of power even as a white American woman.

The text plays upon meanings of "conversation," especially its denotation for sexual intercourse, a meaning that precedes the use of the word to mean engaging in talk. The public sphere in Sansay's *Secret History* bears little resemblance to the coffeehouse roundtables extolled by Jürgen Habermas in his idealized portraits of public life in the eighteenth century anchored by rational discourse. Rather, conversation produces a sexual will to power among participants. Talk, indeed, serves as a provocation or even a proxy for sex. Yet Habermas's theories are not as restrictive as my brief summation implies. Historian Sara Maza reminds readers that for Habermas, private scandal, and the talk that ensued, provided the foundation for the public sphere; as she explains, the bourgeoisie "derived its first identity from the common experiences of human beings within the intimate sphere of marriage and the family" (Maza 13).[9] These "common experiences" give Mary, the narrator, the authority to weigh in on geopolitical conflict. Her authority cuts across the private and public spheres, enabling Mary to use her text to strengthen the US position with its own enslaved Black population. That is, rather than obscure or displace sexuality onto US Black people in the United States, she claims it to strengthen the United States. Through the text, Sansay attempts to compensate for the white population's inability to sustain a public sphere. Through her text, she constitutes a sexualized, sensationalist, colonizing public sphere to revitalize the United States as offering a public sphere and thus a less vulnerable state.

LETTERS OF THE

HAITIAN REVOLUTION

The shifting leadership and political goals of the Haitian Revolution, as it spanned fourteen years, along with the decision of the United States and other world powers to deny Haitian nationhood from 1804 to 1865 have led to competing narratives about the Revolution's origins, legitimacy, and success. Until recently, historians focused on the island's demographics to explain the impetus and opportunity for revolution. Because Saint-Domingue's population was dominated by individuals recently kidnapped from Africa for chattel slavery, scholars argued that they did not have generational ties to either the institution of slavery or Saint-Domingue and thus were more likely to rebel against their forced enslavement. At the beginning of the revolution in 1791, the enslaved population "made up roughly two-thirds of the total labor force of the colony" (Casimir xiii).[10] Just prior to the start of the Revolution, a new influx of enslaved people directly from Africa arrived on the shore, seemingly to replace the overworked and dying population.

Yet these theories based on demographic numbers have lost ground as scholars focus on how the Black revolutionary leaders shaped public opinion through the distribution and manipulation of printed documents and other media. Notably, they cite how the demands for more rights from free people of color preceded demands for the emancipation of enslaved laborers. David Geggus, in particular, has brought more attention to the different factions who precipitated the Haitian Revolution. Among them he identifies the white plantation holders, who were dissatisfied with the French colonial administration; free people of color, who agitated for more rights; and those held in slavery, who experienced some of the worst working conditions in the hemisphere. All together, they created the "explosive potential" in the wake of the French Revolution (Geggus 14). Bryan Edwards, an early-nineteenth-century chronicler of the British West Indies, notes that "the free men of colour in all the French islands were still considered as the property of the public, and *as public property* they were obnoxious to the caprice and tyranny of all those whom the accident of birth had placed above them" (Edwards 10, emphasis added). Edwards describes how the law circumscribed free men's lives: these men were forced into mandatory (and unpaid) military service, restricted from holding public office, and excluded from many professional jobs. When the leaders of the French Revolution issued a decree on 15 May 1791 lifting these bans and granting citizenship to free Blacks who owned property, the rancor and backlash from the white population led to the formation of Black militia groups. Moreover, the initial demands by the hostile Black factions for the return of King Louis XVI to the French throne, a move that would seemingly keep slavery legal, reiterates how the rebellion originally focused on securing rights for free Blacks rather than emancipating people held in slavery (Benot 103–5).

By focusing on demographic disparities, scholars have obfuscated how the Revolution was initiated by free people of color and how the conflict was sustained and spread through a heavy reliance on manifestos, decrees, press releases, and speeches. For years, scholars seemed to imbibe mischaracterizations of the Haitian Revolution as ungraspable. As Michael Drexler and Ed White explain: "[A] major challenge we face today is not just the (historical) *thinking* about the moment [of the Haitian Revolution] but a better understanding of its distorted *articulation*" (*Traumatic Colonel* 12). Until recently, historical analysis of the Revolution downplayed the rational discourses used by revolutionaries about which Sansay reports and laments. The tendency of Europeans to underestimate the linguistic formidability appears in the revised version of *Secret History* published by an anonymous author in 1820, titled *Zelica: A Creole*. The revised story includes an anecdote at the beginning of volume 2, in which the French general Le Clerc writes a letter to Revolutionary hero Henri Christophe to intimidate him. But this letter backfires: it is Le Clerc who is outmaneuvered when he receives Christophe's reply as it displays his command of writing, history, and literature. The anonymous author uses this exchange to explain how Napoleon's army can conquer much of Europe and Egypt but cannot overcome Haitian Revolutionaries.

The Revolutionaries' skillful manipulation of public opinion through written and spoken discourses has received greater attention of late as well. Deborah Jenson's scholarship on the island's literary culture during the Revolution (rather than before or after) reveals how the Revolutionaries were saturated in print, including poetry, dramatic dialogues, letters, and pamphlets. She maintains that Toussaint Louverture and Jean-Jacques Dessalines "are literary in the degree to which they harnessed poetics to persuade large audiences, represent the stake of freedom and domination, and engage in political construction of themselves and their constituencies" (Jenson 9).[11]

Furthermore, Jenson claims that "without his communicative diplomacy in literary form, it is not clear that the Haitian Revolution would have 'translated' from paradigms of class and race upheaval to a paradigm of black historical/national genesis" (47). Indeed, Jenson uses the contemporary colloquial expression "spin" to discuss how Toussaint manipulated the international media regarding the fight for Haiti's independence.

In addition to Jenson, scholars such as Yves Benot, Malick Ghachem, and Laurent Dubois have demonstrated the centrality of print in shaping the Revolution. Benot has studied the layers of meaning in decrees issued by the leaders of the Revolution; they reveal, he argues, an adroit manipulation of public perception to appease different factions and spread assent. At first, in 1792, the leaders called for the return of the recently deposed King Louis XVI. Despite the leaders' initial demands for the return of the French king, "Underneath this, the plan of campaign, with its killing of white masters and burning of plantations, reveals a quite different vision. It can be summed up in the slogan that was recorded on several occasions: take over the country" (Benot 106). Indeed, by 1792 the insurrection leaders were drafting a constitution. According to Malick Ghachem, by the time of the Revolution, free peoples of color reconfigured the legal definition of slavery. Ghachem describes how the official Code Noir of 1685, a legal guide to slaveholding composed under Louis XIV, was appropriated by the Revolutionaries. In an unprecedented turn during the Revolution, "free people of color and slave insurgents now took control of these interpretative activities to serve their own strategic needs and goals" (Ghachem 15). Yet this involved the free Black leaders reinterpreting the Code Noir by omitting parts and emphasizing others. Ghachem explains, "In a time of revolution, they invoked the letter or spirit of those provisions of the Code Noir that best suited what they believed was their rightful place in the new colonial order to come" (15). While Sansay hints at the outsize power the Black revolutionaries exercised to control how the revolt was characterized in public and in the press, the publication of official documents demonstrates how thoroughly Blacks co-opted government decrees and discourses. In doing so, the Haitian revolutionaries legitimated the fear that the whites were losing the battle.

The rebelling leadership in Haiti, in fact, adapted to the constant oscillation of granting and rescinding rights to Black peoples during the ongoing French Revolution. They responded to new laws issued from Paris as well as wrote their own when they exercised control over the island. For instance, during the French Revolution in 1794 Robespierre emancipated all people held in slavery in French dominions, only to have the new leaders of the Directory backtrack on that edict after his execution. Enshrining the rights of emancipation required careful political maneuvering by freed people and their leadership amid the chaos back in Paris. Laurent Dubois argues that the threat of counterrevolution loomed large with Haiti surrounded by slave-holding empires. Therefore, Toussaint Louverture maintained the plantation system with Black labor to show the world that the colony exported the same levels of coffee, sugar, and indigo as when the colonial French administration was in charge. Despite this capitulation to global market demands, when Napoleon came to power, he sent the French military to oust Toussaint, regain control of the colony, and reenslave the Black population. This aggressive move led to unity among the different classes of Black peoples on the island; free and enslaved mulattos and newly arrived Africans sought to eliminate any lingering French presence on the island (Dubois 121). Once the whites were finally ousted in 1804 and Toussaint had died and was replaced by Dessalines, the Black revolutionaries again issued new edicts.

After 1804, the colony's separation from France was presented as a triumph over oppressive European powers. In renaming the island "Haiti," the leaders capitalized on the tumult as well as responded to the waves of revolutions that swept across the continent, reflecting an awareness of their opportunity to forge larger assemblages of colonized peoples: "Dessalines's answer was to portray the expulsion of the French as an act of vengeance not only for their recent brutality but for all the violence of the European colonizers in the Americas" (Dubois 122). Despite Dessalines's efforts to portray the Revolution in one light as the ouster of tyrants, he was still at the mercy of the global press. In this way, Dubois claims, "In claiming the mantle of the long-defeated indigenous peoples of the island, [the revolutionaries] infused their own struggle against the French with a broader historical significance, adding to their list of grievances those of the inhabitants brutalized by the Spanish centuries before and presenting themselves as their avengers of a violent history" (Dubois 122).[12] Yet following the Revolution, neither France nor the United States would recognize Haiti's sovereignty, and thus its national story never took coherent shape globally.[13] Sansay allows readers to glimpse the inner workings of this period before the United States and

Haitian leaders produced competing narratives about the end of French rule. Readers can witness the underlying factors that led to Black leadership on the island, namely their verbal prowess; in *Secret History*, Sansay attempts to appropriate it for the US.

CONTAINING ETHNOSEXUALITY
AND REVOLUTION ABROAD

By analyzing how Sansay portrays the rebelling Black factions as adroit at manipulating public discourses and print media, I draw attention to Sansay's interpretation of the root causes of France's military and colonial vulnerability in Haiti—their inability to maintain rhetorical dominance, while the Blacks present formidable linguistic powers. Moreover, Sansay explicitly connects the failure to offer a robust public sphere and the French colonials' ineptness at flirting to regaining control of the island. For her, a strong public sphere animated by sexual desire confers political power. Once she sets the stakes for political viability as tied to a sexualized public sphere, she provides an alternative framework for understanding post-Revolutionary Haiti as a former colony and a site for sexual libertinism; for Sansay those are not mutually exclusive terms but rather mutually reinforcing modes of agency. France's failure in both spheres is more pointed because military intervention must be erased by leaving behind only a sexualized space. In her text, neither the military presence nor the sexualization of space is erased, nor do they completely converge.

Although hypersexualization of Saint-Domingue may seem unsurprising in light of the post-Revolutionary propaganda that sought to portray Haiti as the locus of unbridled sexuality and unprecedented violence, Sansay not only participates in this discourse but also draws attention to the root causes of French colonial vulnerability in Haiti: their inability to control public discourse. The explicit ties she identifies between sexuality and state security contrast with the way in which powerful interests usually deploy discourses of sexuality. Michel Foucault, in his *History of Sexuality*, argues that state power organizes control by policing and politicizing sexuality. Foucault's analysis focuses on late-nineteenth-century Western cultures, noting how "one also sees [discourses of sexuality] becoming the theme of political operations, economic interventions (through incitements or curbs on procreation), and ideological campaigns for raising standards of morality and responsibility: it was put forward as the index of a society's strength, revealing of both its political energy and its biological vigor" (*History* 146). Indeed, by the mid-nineteenth century, Haiti became metonymically linked to pathological hypersexuality in the rhetoric of US writers. This characterization provided a way to maintain sexual control of the US population by displacing an unhealthy, libidinous sexuality onto the disenfranchised Haiti, then an unrecognized nation led by a free Black population. By then, the Black Revolutionaries' commitment to Enlightenment discourse is repressed. However, during the conflict, Sansay represents how sexual attraction is exploited to capture and direct people's attention. The white colonizers have lost control, and Sansay shows them how to reassert it, while suggesting that white colonizers lack sexual power and thus cannot assert military dominance.

The sexual lives of the people on the island dominate Sansay's coverage of the Revolution, in part, because the colonists have more to fear from violent responses to sexual jealousy than they do from the Revolutionaries or the French military. More important, though, before the insurrections began, Mary explains, tensions between women in Saint-Domingue were exacerbated by sexual competition. Mary even remarks on the "rage of white ladies," asking, "for what is so violent as female jealousy?" (96). The first horror she records is an act of beheading by a white French Creole woman upon a Black woman whom she fears has attracted her husband's attention (70). Creole women had called for laws to govern the dress of mulatto beauties to diminish their appeal; specifically, the women had to cover their heads: "No woman of colour was to wear silk, which was then universally worn, nor to appear in public without a handkerchief on her head" (95). Yet the Black women chose handkerchiefs from India to wear as headdresses and thus exhibit a fashion for madras. By focusing on clothes, the whites attempt to place the attraction of the Black women on physical objects; in the case of Haiti, the scene that depicts white women's focus on madras encapsulates the attempt to govern Black women's sexuality and the failure to do so, while also relegating Black women to the object of male desire rather than ascribing desire to them. But in *Secret History,* the madras is first introduced when describing Napoleon's sister Pauline, who came to Saint-Domingue as the wife of General Le Clerc (65). By focusing on clothing, Europeans police the sexual dynamism and turn Black women's appeal into a material object that can be contained or appropriated.[14] These laws did not, nevertheless, deter the French Creoles from desiring or pursuing the mulatto women. Sansay conveys how covering these women's heads fails to diminish their physical appeal. Mary describes the "voluptuousness" of the mulatto women whose "very feet speak" because their look and manners combine to attract men (95). Speech is a metaphor for instilling desire. As the book exposes the "horrors" of Saint-Domingue—its violence and sexual transgressions—Mary details conversation's powers and limitations in solidifying colonial rule, because she understands political and social efficacy as rooted in conversational power, a power that overlaps with the speaker's sexual appeal.

Mary's faith in the power of words is encapsulated in a story she tells about the final assault on Saint-Domingue's white population. As an alternative to brute strength, Sansay offers a portrait of restrained but effective power through conversation, specifically a Black woman who combines fluency and sex appeal. Even so, this power hinges on the sexual appeal of the speaker. When she recounts secondhand the triumphant story of a Black woman who dissuades a mulatto revolutionary from arbitrarily murdering a Frenchman, the episode is rife with racial violence that is subdued through the power of persuasive reasoning. As the massacre throughout Port-au-Prince mounts, a Frenchman finds himself hostage to a "ruthless mulatto," as Mary describes him, who demands a high ransom. The Frenchman asks to visit an American friend who can lend him money. Once the two arrive, the American balks at the deal, refusing to hand over the money until the Frenchman boards a ship to safety. The scene represents a microcosm of international conflict as it plays out in Haiti: one finds the passive Frenchman, the determined Black revolutionary, and the paralyzed American who offers liquidity but not safety to the Frenchman by offering to pay the ransom.[15] An argument ensues until a Black woman, the lover of the American, enters the scene. Ultimately, the American can offer the Frenchman passage back to the US or Europe, not a solution that keeps the French colonials on the island.

In a failed colonial site, the desires inspired by ethnosexuality spur action while the military retreats into inaction. Sansay describes how the conflict among these men reaches an impasse: "The mulatto refused. The unfortunate Frenchman wept, and the American kept firm. While they were disputing, a girl of colour, who lived with the American, entered, and having learned the story, employed all her eloquence to make the mulatto relent" (131). The Frenchman does not engage; he cries instead, and the American lacks the flexibility to negotiate with the mulatto. Into this entanglement "a girl of colour" enters and through her adept use of reason persuades the mulatto to let the Frenchman live. It takes some time, through words and gestures, for this "girl of colour" to convince the man to give up his scheme and free the white Frenchman. When the mulatto finally consents, he tells the woman, "He shall be concealed, and guarded by myself till the moment of embarking for the U.S.; but, when he is out of danger, you must listen to me in your turn. She heard him with horror; but, dissembling, said there would be always time enough" (132). His request to be heard fills the woman with "horror" because "listening" becomes a code for sexual subservience. She never learns what the mulatto man had to say because the American's influence with the Black revolutionary leaders later convinces the mulatto to give up his demands. As frequently happens in the text, a Black man's desires are blocked.

The scene illustrates how power manifests through speaking and the "attention" she must later give him. Being heard confers and demonstrates one's power, control, and advantage. The episode, as a microcosm of conflict, not only represents how violent threats can be resolved through talking but also hinges on a Black woman who is eloquent, appealing, and, ultimately, convincing. Marlen Daut has characterized this character as a "tropical temptress" (259–60). Daut explains how this literary figure serves "as an agent of non-compliance and rebellion" (264). Yet the character does seem reduced to her sex appeal, and the scene does seem part of a shadow or sublimated scene. Mary, the narrator, is direct in her admiration for her and even acknowledged her other triumphs. Instead, Jenny Sharpe's ideas about representations of Black women better elucidate the figure's importance. Rather than focus on "equating black female subjectivity with individual consciousness or modes of self-expression like songs and testimonies," Sharpe advocates for finding depictions in which "the unspoken narratives of everyday life intersect with the known stories of slavery" (xxvi). The unnamed woman answers Sharpe's call. In this passage, the woman of color eases geopolitical tensions through intersubjective exchange based on reason and persuasion; she is not represented as just an "individual consciousness" or through "modes of self-expression." The anecdote occupies only a short section of the text, but when *A Secret History* was revised, presumably not by Sansay, into *Zelica: A*

Creole (1820), this woman becomes a main character of the text while Mary is eliminated from the narrative and Clara's role recedes. In fact, in *Zelica*, Clara's character dies an untimely death while the woman of color triumphs.

Despite Sansay's observation that the Revolutionaries maintain power through their ability to control conversation, she portrays this sphere of influence as tied only to a specific geographic space of Saint-Domingue. Mary longs to return to the "peaceful security" of the US without commenting on the dispossessed population of people living in slavery there (92). In fact, the text is at pains to gloss over disagreements among Americans. In one scene, she recounts giving a gift to General Le Clerc's wife (the sister of Napoleon) of a silver medal featuring George Washington's face. According to the Michael Drexler, those silver medals did not exist until Thomas Jefferson became president. He speculates that the change from Jefferson to Washington was made so as not to offend anti-Jeffersonian readers (Drexler, Introduction 65n2). Through the figure of George Washington, however, Sansay reasserts America's founding—as the true revolution in the hemisphere while Sansay takes care not to provoke political factions within the US. Still, Mary is forthright about the unjustified treatment of humans used as slaves, going so far to blame the colonials: "More than five hundred thousand broke the yoke imposed on them by a few thousand men of a different colour, and claimed the rights of which they had been so cruelly deprived. . . . Dearly have [landowners] paid for the luxurious ease in which they reveled at the expense of these oppressed creatures" (77). Her language exposes the arbitrariness of race-based slavery ("men of a different colour") and she interprets the insurrection as payback for the "luxurious ease" of the white population. Indeed, for Mary, this seems like the chief indiscretion of the enslavers: they have created a lax, indulgent culture she herself sometimes exemplifies, enjoying leisure before the military has instituted stability.

Master and slave relations extend beyond labor into sexual subjection, a point frequently alluded to in the text. At one point when Mary parodies the voice of the French elites who are lulled into inaction by seemingly supplicant Blacks, she muses on how she will spend her days once the military has subdued the Black population. She describes how "I should repose beneath the shade of orange groves, walk on carpets of rose leaves and frenchipone; be fanned to sleep by *silent* slaves, or have my feet tickled into ecstasy by the soft hand of a female attendant" (73, emphasis mine). Despite the text's foregrounding of heteronormativity among the French Creoles, Mary often highlights the sexual appeal of Black women on the island, while portraying Black male sexuality, in contrast, as forbidding. Mary's fantasy involves an enslaved population that is "silent" but continues to offer sexual gratification to whites. In this way, she attempts to disentangle two ontologies—one related to speech ("silent slaves") and one related to sexuality ("soft hand") that she elsewhere understands as imbricated. It seems white sexual gratification depends on suppressing Black speech and sexual desire, for, in her imagination, their sexual services reinforce white power. Mary's own failure to see the connection between sexual and verbal power in this instance underlines the vulnerability of whites. As Marianne Noble reminds us, "The refusal to acknowledge the ways that masochism may have served women as a mode of power derives from a limited and limiting understanding of women's relationship to power, which is not simply a force wielded by men against women but instead is available for people in all social positions to wield for their own ends" (Noble 9). The masochism of the women pervades Sansay's text. Sansay also ridicules the lives of the Creole ladies prior to the Revolution. The very next paragraph reads in its entirety: "Such were the pleasures of the Creole ladies whose time was divided between the bath, the table, the toilette and the lover" (73), as though Mary simultaneously ironizes and indulges in fantasies of their lives. The word "divided" proves ironic, for these women, who have no interest outside the home, are portrayed as having divisible time even as her list suggests movement between narrow confines. Moreover, the spaces of privacy include "lover" not as a person but as yet another site that further taxes their time and as a routine task that has to be completed.

Sansay's uneven treatment of the Revolution emphasizes the book as a transitional text, one that occupies a liminal space before the Haitian nation is founded or US policy toward it took shape. Eventually, Mary concedes the impossibility of depriving people formerly held in slavery of their freedom again. She plans to return to the United States because "[t]he [Saint-Domingue] negroes have felt during ten years the blessing of liberty, for a blessing it certainly is, however acquired, and they will not be easily deprived of it" (73). Despite her concession, Mary does not extend her progressive ideas of equality to the Black population living in slavery in the United States. According to Michael Dash, the early 1800s witnessed various responses to the Haitian Revolution before US policy mandated an attitude of disdain and condemnation of Haiti's leaders. In such literature as Thomas Branagan's *Avenia* and the poetry of John Greenleaf Whittier celebrating Toussaint, "Haitians are depicted as responsible and rational" (Dash 6). This attitude, Dash claims, could not be maintained when the United States had to subdue a Black population—free and enslaved—from rebelling and declaring their freedom within its own borders (Dash 6–7).[16] Sansay's text registers the threat that a democratic Haiti poses six hundred miles off the US coast; if it becomes an autonomous state, the country offers Black people not only a haven but also legitimation because it upends proslavery propaganda about self-government. Sansay, despite her wavering support for the revolutionary impulse, attempts to thwart these developments within the United States by rebinding Caribbean whites through a militarized and sexualized public sphere.

The demand for sensational literature on Haiti's revolution seemed to draw upon the violence and sex that underscored these narratives. Matt Clavin notes, "Authors insisted that they performed vital public service when they satisfied readers' demands for sensationalistic descriptions of unimaginable acts of violence. Nevertheless, the telegraphing of the disturbing language they employed indicates that these cautions served to whet readers' appetites for the unseemly" (Clavin 25). *The Horrors of St. Domingo,* then, not only chronicles the racialized violence but also interests whites easily captivated by sensationalist literature. The politics of Haiti's founding are not *intertwined* but rather *known* through sexualized violence. Haiti, though, might be too close to the United States even if it is not close enough for France. Its proximity leaves the Pacific as a distant, more pliable site for American ethnosexual fantasies that undergird colonial ventures.[17]

Empire studies have made explicit how imperial ventures require women both as figurations for land, as objects of desire, and as consumers of resources from those sites. For Sansay, sexualizing the public sphere enables women's participation. The silence of women in American culture has long been a topic among feminist literary critics. Within these debates about the efficacy of voice in American culture, Carla Kaplan offers a valuable model for understanding intersubjective discourse through her concept of an "erotics of talk": "Taking desire as a privileged entry point into cultural conversation, my trope of an erotics of talk can be used to map the textual inscription of those forms of intimacy, reciprocity, equality, recognition, and respect for difference which do not find realization under the prevailing conditions of modern social organization" (C. Kaplan 16). Sansay's text operates in much the same way as an alternative means of understanding the Haitian Revolution and the powerful role of white and Black women when they have a chance to speak and attempt to gain recognition. In fact, the narrator remarks on the Black woman who saves the French man, "The same girl was the means of saving others" (132). Sansay, however, silences the black man: "she heard of him no more" (132).[18] It represents the limits of Sansay's vision as it begins to participate in an ideology that, in order to elevate white women by equating power with sexuality, excludes Black men, whose sexuality is depicted in menacing terms.

In contrast to the ways in which Mary depicts Black men's menacing sexuality or Frenchmen's inadequacy as lovers, Mary describes Don Alonzo, a Spaniard the sisters meet in Cuba after having fled Santo Domingo, as possessing a forthright sexual appeal manifested through his ability to converse with Clara. Frequently, his physical body is characterized as "eloquent": "his large black eyes seem to speak every emotion of his soul, . . . Clara listens to him, and looks at him as if she was fully sensible of his advantages, and frequently holds long conversations with him in his own language, which, if gestures deceive not, are on no uninteresting subject" (125–26). The man's very eyes "speak," and he has bewitched Mary's sister, Clara, through his powers of conversation, especially since Clara can communicate in his native language of Spanish. The sites opened by imperial ventures confer more power on women even as they buffer patriarchy. She mocks how her husband had forced her to learn the Spanish language: "He had insisted on my learning the Spanish language, yet if I spoke in that language it was to express sentiments I sought to conceal from him" (138). Clara's dexterity with language allows her to have affairs, not through a sexual dalliance but through her ability to talk behind his back in a language he does not understand. Later she admits that Don Alonso's speaking has almost seduced her: "You know my dear Mary, how eloquent are his eyes! you know the insinuating softness of his voice! Sometimes, when listening to him, I forget for a moment all I have suffered, and almost persuade myself that a man can be sincere" (148). Shortly after meeting this captivating figure, Clara flees her husband. All signs point to Don Alonso as her lover and her means of escape. Clara, though, protests her innocence: "It is true, the eloquent eyes of Don Alonzo often spoke volumes, but I never appeared to understand their language, nor did a look of encouragement ever escape me" (138). Here a woman retains her power over a man by pretending not to understand the man's "language." Yet Mary's cloying descriptions of Don Alonso provide the prototype for the way a man should attract and even control through the power of expression. Instead of Black violence, Spanish eloquence combines with softness, eliciting the willful submission of subjects through the deployment of unsatisfied desire.

Similarly, Mary outwits others with verbal fluency, proving herself capable of using language to her advantage when conversing with men. She meets a sixty-year-old officer and declares that she would prefer him as a lover, because "his conversation is sprightly" (76). Meanwhile, she presents verbal dexterity as a means of protection among strangers. Mary disguises herself verbally when she encounters a group of men from a Spanish ship by allowing them to believe that she is French and cannot speak Spanish or English. She refuses to converse with them, but once she is exposed as American and fluent in Spanish and English, she embarrasses these sailors because she has comprehended all they said even when they openly debated her attractiveness. In withholding her conversation and then revealing herself as a polyglot, she asserts a position of power over men through her mastery of languages. Sansay suggests that travel gives women an advantage over the very military men who open up access to colonial sites.

. . .

Mary's correspondence with a man frames the entire text, even if that man, Aaron Burr, never physically appears; furthermore, Burr remains effectively silenced since Sansay only includes a one-sided correspondence from Mary to him. Some critics surmise that Burr's name serves as an unfulfilled tease that the text will provide titillating information about US politicos. The original title page announces itself in large type as written "to Colonel Burr, Late Vice-President of the United States" (59).[19] All but four of the letters that constitute this epistolary novel are addressed to him. Burr remains an undeveloped personage in accounts of the early US republic. In some ways, his disgrace has been used to put the other founders' accomplishments into relief. Drexler and White offer a new analysis of Burr in American culture as a cultural trace "to explore the coded racialization of US cultural discourse"

(13). Yet the context of the early nineteenth century might explain why he looms large if invisibly over Sansay's text. Putting aside the disastrous turns of his vice-presidency, Burr, in contrast to other Founding Fathers, achieved his fame for his military valor during the Revolution. He did not participate in politics until after the war. During the contested presidential election of 1800, the Washington Federalists advocated for Burr to assume the presidency because even though he "never penned a declaration of independence, I admit,—but he has done much more—he has engraved *that declaration in capitals* with the point of his sword" (qtd. in Isenberg 211). Furthermore, Burr is closely associated with his advocacy for individual women. It is as if Sansay acknowledges that men can participate in the expansion of the United States, but only if they lay the groundwork for women's exertions. Historian Nancy Isenberg refers to Burr as feminist, not in nineteenth-century terms but in present-day ones.[20] Even among the politically innovative founders, he stood out for his unorthodox ideas. Alexander Hamilton was shocked by Burr's political views, noting "he has talked perfect *Godwinism*," referring to William Godwin (qtd. in Cayton 189). Hamilton was probably not exaggerating for we have it recorded that Burr considered Mary Wollstonecraft a genius (qtd. in Cayton 251). For Sansay, he encapsulates military valor and sexually inflected intellectualism.

Her inclusion of Burr reinforces the interplay between print and oral culture. While the text is framed around letters, assembled by Sansay for print publication, the text shapes its plot around verbal conversations. She describes a productive tension between print and orality, because characters themselves are described formally, particularly by *how* they speak, rather than *what* they speak. One finds this same dynamic in some of the few extant notes by Aaron Burr on Leonora Sansay. Burr writes a letter of introduction for Sansay to Pierpont Edwards: "She speaks and & writes french [sic] & has more sense & information than all the women to be found in St. Dom" (Burr 702). His letter of introduction has everything to do with her capability as a speaker. Burr even writes to William Eustis, "why did you not tell me whether [Sansay] had left Boston or when she would leave it. . . . How could such an Animal be Months in my Vicinity & I not even hear of her?" (Burr 317n3). Conversing and being the object of conversation evoke her identity for Burr; thus, a buzz about her presence in the city should alert him to her proximity. Likewise, the characters in Sansay's text are understood as talkers and the subject of talk. As Michael Drexler comments, "While [Sansay] certainly traded on the public's appetite for descriptions of racialized violence, she also capitalized on its hunger for news about the scandalous Aaron Burr, converting what for her had become a potentless patronage into something of value" (Introduction 33). Drexler believes Sansay wants to commercialize the horrors to provoke her white audience's interest, and legitimize her voice in the public sphere. Yet in writing the text to Burr, she shapes her text around an ongoing public conversation about him by printing an imagined private conversation between former lovers who write about public affairs and the private lives of the Creoles. The implication is that print culture, like the oral culture depicted in the text, gains power when the author sexualizes it.

Just as the text hinges on this sexual relationship, critical analyses of the text always reference the sexual relationship between Burr and Sansay, perhaps to give the novel more weight as a trace of early American life and politics. Sansay, even publishing her text anonymously, would seem to expose herself to derision. Her seemingly flagrant exposure of her sexual entanglement with Burr complicates the text's position and its depiction of sexual license in Haiti and in the United States. Writing on women writers' use of sexuality in late nineteenth-century literature, Dale Bauer finds, "Only when women could use sex as symbolic power—rather than as a commodity to be sold or as an identity to be sold cultivated for emotional capital or influence— could women writers imagine sex power as a liberating possibility" (Bauer 9). Instead Sansay's use of sexuality in the early nineteenth century seems to cultivate *public capital* to trade on sex as a way to establish political voice.

While critics celebrate the world of women that Mary describes in her journey to Cuba and Jamaica after the fall of Saint-Domingue, the text continues to frame its story as letters to Burr undercutting this woman-centered reading.[21] Violence, however, is not categorically connected to men but to jealous Creole women as well. Rather than forging solidarity among women, the text seems focused on adopting means to assert power over others, militarily and sexually; she seeks power that one can carry across spaces because Saint-Domingue falls under French control again. As Lui maintains, if readers interpret the text as creating an analog between marriage and slavery, then Sansay fails to incorporate "the lives of women differently positioned (free Blacks, slaves and former slaves, mulattoes, poor whites)" (Liu 414). Instead of reading the text as an indictment of legal marriage between whites, it offers a portrait of heterosexual coupling across racial divisions as animating public sphere politics. The text is ultimately more concerned with militarization than slavery. Whether Sansay recounts a wife beheading her husband's mistress or a husband imprisoning his wife to keep her from prospective lovers, the inanity of sexual violence springs from both men and women but is a tactic exclusive to the dispossessed whites. Sansay saves her approbation for those who use eloquence to further their position politically or sexually. The latter chapters position Sansay as concerned with power, verbal power in particular, measured by one's ability to provoke (hetero)sexual attraction.

The text abruptly ends with the sisters heading to Philadelphia, where Mary, now reunited with her sister Clara, anticipates a happy reunion with Aaron Burr. Indeed, Mary perceives their future happiness as depending on Burr: "There I hope we shall meet you [in Philadelphia]; and if I can only infuse into your bosom those sentiments for my sister which glow so warmly in my own, she will find in you a friend and a protector, and we may still be happy" (154). This last attempt to draw Aaron Burr into the narrative is ironic since white men throughout the text fail to offer any lasting protection. Yet prior to their departure, a telling moment occurs when Clara, traveling in Cuba, happens upon an Irish Spaniard who keeps a vast library on his estate.[22] He offers great conversation, but his library offers greater treasures for Clara, including the works of Shakespeare. Clara exclaims, "Judge of my delight at meeting with Shakespeare in the wilds of Cuba" (149). Up to this point, the text has sensationalized the world of conversation and print through its depiction of politics fused with sexuality, vengeance, and revolution. The staid works of Shakespeare represent an idealized and perhaps illusory sphere of culture that Sansay's *Secret History* treats as benign. Sansay, however, shows that when print and orality converge, sociability is constructive, illuminating, and cohesive even as it lacks the sexual appeal augmented by militarization. This characterization shows that if the Americas can combine a western tradition with a vibrant orality, the resulting civilization will be a formidable empire.

Sansay's text illuminates how we might approach war propaganda, the sex lives of politicians, and the operations of military without "consuming them," that is commodifying them. After all, the novel's very failure illustrates its inability to resignify its objects of representation. First, she provides a portrait of the public relations campaign by the revolutionaries to establish a sovereign Haiti, one obscured by concerted efforts by the US press to sensationalize the war. In framing the revolution in Haiti as a discursive and sexualized episode, she eroticizes political participation. Second, Sansay frankly addresses the topic of politicians' sex lives in a manner that seems more in line with "scandalmonger" journalists, like her contemporary James Callender, who cavalierly revealed Alexander Hamilton's and Thomas Jefferson's sexual affairs. She, though, connects sexual promiscuity to military might and political efficacy and therefore normalizes it as another dimension of empire. Third, Sansay's narrator explicitly ties together the attempts of the French army to retake Haiti with her own consumption of the island's pleasures. Instead of erasing the mutual construction of Haiti by people like Mary and the military, France's defeat exposes this two-pronged effort. But this paradise for white Westerners never develops and thus was never "masked." The French were forced to withdraw or, as it is commonly described, were "massacred" or "expelled." Indeed, that language (massacred rather than "defeated" the French) further obfuscates the revolutionaries' military victory.[23] Colonial ventures are undergirded by the fantasy of mutual attraction between the native population and the colonial armed forces to draw attention away from the use of sexual violence to control civilian populations during war. But for Mary, the narrator, the military also paves the way for women to exert a political role beyond formulations of domesticity or "republican motherhood."

Nonetheless, the interlinked modes of politics and sexuality might obscure how individual attempts to assert agency are repeatedly thwarted by powerful economic or political stakeholders. Sansay counters this tendency not by exposing how capitalism and politics shape sexuality but by linking the ability to be heard—and therefore participate in the public sphere—to an ability to sexually attract. For Sansay, sexuality is embedded within the public sphere, and therefore its expression can function as a social critique of the institutions that enforce compliance from citizens. In Haiti, she meets the limits of the "(fantasy) zone" of the intimate because the political order crumbles, which not only subtended the economic order but also gave whites unfettered access to the object of their sexual desire: Black women on the island. Sansay's text reveals how the revolution implodes an imaginary that severs the political and the intimate.

In Sansay, the military attempts to lay an invisible foundation on which to proffer white dominance, but in looking at texts that imagine the settlement of the frontier in colonial New England, the collapse of the home into a militarized site becomes more prominent. To examine the novelistic imagination in the lead-up to the Jacksonian era, in the next chapter I look at Catharine Maria Sedgwick's novel *Hope Leslie* (1827). In that novel, powerful men cannot solely be relied upon to negotiate the terms of contact between white settlers and racialized others. Instead, to forge enduring settlements, women will have to take a more active role in claiming territory and shaping politics and, perhaps, in challenging the state to protect nonwhite actors who are most vulnerable to its abuses. The subtext of military aggression proves important for reconsidering the role of women within American imperial sites. The text offers a respite from competing narratives to imagine what *would* happen if we shared our stories of peoplehood and how those very stories, in their multiplicity, might demand a change in gender constructions.

3

The

MILITARIZATION

OF HOME

in

CATHARINE MARIA SEDGWICK'S

Hope Leslie

EDWARD WATTS, WRITING IN *American Literary History* IN 2010, provides compelling evidence that an organizing amnesia about the foundation of colonial settlements and the United States did not take hold until the third decade of the nineteenth century. He pinpoints a year, 1820, in which a shift toward organized forgetting begins. The year 1820 often serves as a disciplinary boundary, because *The Sketch Book* by Washington Irving appeared in print that year and Romanticism made its way across the Atlantic around that time. The date is an intriguing one since 1820 falls in between the end of the US participation in the slave trade (1808) as well as the last wars with Britain (1812–14) and the Indian Removal Act (1830). Watts's claims about cultural amnesia may hold when looking at certain cultural representations.[1] However, the novel, *Hope Leslie*, by Catharine Maria Sedgwick, published in 1827, seems to intercede to stall the turn to cultural forgetting. Sedgwick joins the authors of *The Female American* and *Secret History* by testifying to the violence that subtends imperialism without sublimating it. A refusal to "organize amnesia" emerges in Sedgwick's story of colonial days in the Massachusetts Bay Colony even as she puts forth the story of the English-turned-American title character Hope Leslie to create a telos for the emergence of the United States.

Published in 1827, the text makes indirect connections between the Pequot Wars and debates about the removal of Cherokee, Chickasaw, Creek, Choctaw, and Seminole peoples in the 1820s—debates that led to the passage of the Indian Removal Act of 1830. My take differs from other critics who recognize that Sedgwick's text offers more representation of marginalized others (compared to authors like James Fenimore Cooper) but who still think she fails to give those characters full agency. Doyle makes a bold statement that "Sedgwick helps to generate the story of 'vanishing' Indians, and she does so at the very moment when the question of Indian land rights was being hotly debated, eventually culminating in the Indian Removal Act of 1830" (282). Philip Gura also argues that Sedgwick contributes to a "vanishing" narrative (59) even if he praises Sedgwick because she "was courageous to offer such an alternative history, for the United States was mired in problematic relations with the Native American nations at the time" (58). Nina Baym, too, argues that Sedgwick's text "proposes that. . . . the Indians will be willing or at least acquiescing agents of their own removal" (*Feminism* 35). Furthermore, Baym comments that "Sedgwick's three surviving Pequods and Faith voluntarily 'vanish' into the western forests" (*Feminism* 34). Ashley Reed, too, shares this view: "Sedgwick's narrator acknowledges prior Native presence on the land whites occupy but obscures the process of removal" (96). Dana Nelson, though, offers an equivocal take on Sedgwick. According to Nelson, the text "counters the 'Adamic myth' and its valorization of white, male conquest" ("Sympathy" 193). Nelson even favorably compares the character Magawisca to Frederic Jameson ("Sympathy" 196) to acknowledge Sedgwick's progressive ideas of historicity, but she still condemns Sedgwick for the way she "establishes a metaphor which allows the Indians to peacefully fade from her vision of the text" (201). I disagree that Sedgwick "obscures the process of removal," nor do any the characters "peacefully fade" or "vanish" any more than other characters, some of whom are killed in an explosion and some whose happy endings the narrator refuses to narrate.[2]

The text is ridden with violence like *The Female American* and *Secret History*. Not only do these three texts accentuate rather than hide foundational violence, but they also make clear how arms or military power undergird white women's claims to autonomy. That is, the government exploited families' domestic ambitions to serve as the front line for its military efforts.[3] By perceiving the domestic as also a militarized site, one can challenge familiar modes for interpreting feminized spaces in the early US. Over two decades ago, Amy Kaplan called for a more nationally inflected understanding of "domesticity" because the private is defined in relation to the public sphere and gestures at "foreign" polity. Kaplan, along with Lauren Berlant, Elizabeth Maddock Dillon, and others, articulate how the home, rather than creating a space apart, actually subtended imperial ideology, not just the male-dominated public sphere.[4] Sara Blair takes issue with Kaplan and Berlant, in particular, because their interpretation of domestic space, she claims, "elid[es] the differentiable, microhistorical realities of 'home' as a social process and space, which the literary, in all its contestatory and emergent modern forms, enters into shaping" ("Home Truths" 434n2). Yet in posing the question, Blair sets up another divide not just between domestic and public spaces, but between micro- and macro-histories ("Home Truths" 435n10). To address how these further distinctions of history collapse, I use Sedgwick's 1827 historical romance *Hope Leslie* as representative of early American efforts to deploy English settler households as a militarized space, not just a home, and how she uses the form of the novel to disseminate the many competing stories of peoplehood that emerged out of the Massachusetts Bay Colony.

In *Hope Leslie*, Sedgwick links the virtual history she imagines to the militarization of home and by extension the militarization of women.[5] "Virtual" because Sedgwick attempts to make history a sensual experience of shared participatory discourses even as she concedes that settlers rejected the possibility of affiliation with indigenous peoples. Those rejected affiliations lead some characters to imagine "what might have been," leaving them not just longing for a past that never took place but also lamenting a futurity that was lost. According to Sedgwick, the expansion of the US westward affects the entire body politic. Yet Jacksonian policies of removal of the "Five Civilized Tribes" instituted after the book's publication nullified the text's inclusive vision. The events of the 1830s cast a different shadow back upon the text even as we attempt to sort through early European antagonisms with tribes in the northeast. Relying on Rogers M. Smith's theories of stories of peoplehood, I demonstrate how Sedgwick's novel attempts to shape attitudes toward incorporating the experiences of indigenous peoples into the stories of American peoplehood. Her book does not rewrite the Puritan past; rather, she links the stories we tell about colonial history and violence to the possibilities for political action in early nineteenth-century culture.

To understand the political work of stories upon which Sedgwick attempts to build her tale, it is helpful to look at Smith's theories about stories of peoplehood. His ideal formulation involves listening to as many stories as possible while maintaining democratic principles of fairness and recognition. Toward the end of his study, he explains, "I think Americans are best advised instead to embrace fundamentally historical accounts of their national identity. . . . [T]hose stories should be linked to accounts of humanity more broadly in ways that can and do call for ongoing transformation in American peoplehood" (R. Smith 186-7). Historical accounts, Smith emphasizes, allow citizens to see the past as constructed by real human beings with foibles, successes, and failures (material and ethical). To avoid stories of peoplehood that, ultimately, revivify moral superiority or universalizing claims, a nation's people must maintain "a sustainable politics of robustly contested people-making that chiefly features *varying historical stories*" (R. Smith 194, emphasis mine). Sedgwick indeed features "varying historical" accounts of the Pequot Wars to demonstrate the ways in which subsequent actions influence how one chooses to frame the past; one account comes from Everell, the son of Massachusetts Bay Colony settlers, and the other from Magawisca, the daughter of the Pequot chief. The text offers, to borrow Smith's words again, a "less teleological tale in which progress has come, when it has come, through contingent, ongoing contestation" (196). In this way, Sedgwick's novel contrasts with the antiteleological thrust of *The Female American* that seeks to rewrite colonial settlement entirely.

Dana Luciano explains how Sedgwick's *Hope Leslie* alters our very sense of historical time: when Magawisca relates her version of the Pequot Wars, Sedgwick "enables it at once to suspend time and to alter its flow, turning official history back on itself. . . . [it] also creates space for the actualization of counternational and counterfamilial histories into the novel" (Luciano 104). I appreciate how Luciano coins new terms such as "counternational" and "counterfamilial" because they imply the struggle to differentiate history from cultural imperatives while allowing multiple histories to remain side by side for readers to discern or dismiss how they contradict one another. Yet she, like other critics, interprets the ending as "causing the counternationalist claims of the Pequots to diminish into silence" (Luciano 111). Luciano then quotes a line from the text to substantiate her point: "That which remains untold in their story, is lost in the deep, voiceless obscurity of those unknown regions" (Sedgwick, *Hope Leslie* 339). However, that description of a region: "lost," "voiceless," "obscurity," "unknown" (Sedgwick 339) tantalizes the reader about what is there rather than "framing Indian vanishing" (Luciano 111). Anthropologist Patrick Wolfe's oft-cited theory on the "logic of elimination" in settler colonialism explains how indigenous people were driven out by white settlers, in Australia and other parts of the world, in the settlers' pursuit of controlling more territory. Yet J. Kēhaulani Kauanui, responding to Wolfe, offers an alternative term to consider alongside the logic of elimination: "enduring indigeneity": "first, that indigeneity itself is enduring . . . that indigenous peoples exist, resist, and persist; and second, that settler colonialism is a structure that endures indigeneity, as it holds out against it."[6] Instead of treating the silence as a diminishment, I read it as a provocation, regardless of Sedgwick's intent, especially since the book does not so much "silence" Magawisca as it simply ends, a provocation that hints at "enduring indigenity." What remains is Sedgwick's forthright depiction of the militarization of home, one that echoes through Wolfe's study of colonialism.[7] Through her virtual history shared among the next generation of settlers who reconstruct and compare various versions of the past, Sedgwick paints the growing militarization of the home in early settlements and thus portrays women characters—Magawisca, Esther, Hope, Mrs. Winthrop, and Mrs. Fletcher—as political forces, whether savvy, self-sacrificing, rebellious, distracted, or powerless. Although her virtual history gave way to more uniform, chauvinistic historical accounts of early settlements, ones that have contributed to the critical commentary on the "vanishing narrative" in US culture, *Hope Leslie* stands as a commentary on the kinds of stories of peoplehood available in the first decades of the US.

VIRTUAL

HISTORIES

In a preface, Catharine Maria Sedgwick opens her novel *Hope Leslie* (1827) by anticipating criticism about the realism of her character Magawisca, a seventeenth-century Pequot woman: "The writer is aware that it may be thought that the character of Magawisca has no prototype among the aborigines of this country. Without citing Pocahontas, or any other individual, as authority, it may be sufficient to remark, that in such delineations, we are confined not to the actual, but the possible" (4). The same tension one sees in *The Female American* about stretching the boundaries of the imagination through the portrayal of an indigenous woman resurfaces here in Sedgwick's suggestions to suspend disbelief or embrace "the possible" when reading fiction. However, Sedgwick's first critics found another portrayal more challenging to accept. It is not the fantastical or coincidental scenes that stretched belief, even though the text boasts more than one prison break and, in its conclusion, a ship explosion that kills everyone onboard, including the text's arch villain, a moneygrubbing Royalist.

Instead, critics took issue with the portrait of uncompetitive friendship among women. Following the text's publication, a reviewer in the *North American Review* famously questioned the verisimilitude of the women characters' camaraderie amid their rivalry for the same man. The reviewer considers it "improbable" that "Here are three ladies, who seem to love and admire each other as much as they do Everell Fletcher" (42). Highlighting the text's depiction of women's friendship, though, distracts from how the text advocates for the empowerment of women as aggressive agents in the early US, either in conjunction with or against the state. As opposed to re-creating a fictional world in which the military invisibly bolsters the characters' colonial presence, as in Sansay's *Secret History, Hope Leslie* imagines the empowerment of women to contribute to the explicit show of force required to shape the US into an imperial power.

According to the lore surrounding the novel's publication, other women writers, like Lydia Maria Child, rallied to Sedgwick's defense to contradict not just the chauvinism of the *North American Review* but also as a public show of women writers' solidarity. The reviewer has received sustained critical attention for this slight criticism, but to be fair, he otherwise fawns over Sedgwick's book. He pointedly compares her work as a novelist to the power a mother has over her children. Indeed, the word "power" reverberates throughout the review. As many scholars have noted, his praise of Sedgwick firmly sets her among women novelists who, even if respected, are categorized as performing a culturally specific gendered role.

Child published her own commendatory take on Sedgwick early in her career, writing, "All think *Hope Leslie* is a work of great merit; but all do not prefer it" ("Miss Sedgwick's Novels" 237). She explains, "[I]t has more of the glow and vivacity of genius, and more of its inequality than its predecessors: it is a work of more power" (Child, "Miss Sedgwick's Novels" 238). Child suggests that this very "power" makes it less popular. The anonymous reviewer from the *North American Review*, though, casts the book's power as relegated to the domestic, either as transmitted from mother to children or woman to woman, and thus as nonthreatening. The reviewer claims, "The consciousness of power [in a woman writer] will produce self-respect [in women], and self-respect will lead to improvement" (*North American Review* 404). But because the critic places undo emphasis on how the novel depicts homosocial relations among women, he dismisses the text's central concern with the empowerment of women to advance the needs of the state. He misreads how Esther, the Puritan girl, and Magawisca feel indifferent to, if not dismissive of, each other.

Everell may not seem worthy of the love of these formidable women characters, but their successive pairings (Magawisca and Everell, Esther and Everell, Hope and Everell) have less to do with him than how each possible marriage would allow Sedgwick to tease out different historical trajectories for a colonial settlement *that might have been*.[8] Elizabeth Freeman, analyzing wedding scenes in American novels in general, comments, "Understood as a historically sedimented scene, the wedding has the capacity to suggest alternative futures to the one toward which U.S. culture seems to be moving" (*Wedding Complex* xvi). By imaginings so many pairings between Everell and the women, Sedgwick troubles the notion of the wedding as "historically sedimented." However, the narrator pointedly refuses to portray wedding scenes. Instead, she keeps the focus on how marriage contributes to "alternative futures" while foreclosing others. The text's commitment to heterosexual marriage limits its radical vision of American womanhood. On the one hand, marriage would bolster women's efficacy and, on the other, marriage would stifle some of the characters from finding their proper social role. Yet the text does not shy away from tying nonnormative modalities to the regeneration of the state. Critics, though, continue to categorize the book as one example amid the uniformity that is "women's writing." *Hope Leslie* tends to be read as another *Hobomok*, Lydia Maria Child's 1824 novel, as if women's writing were a series in which each new book replicates the same agenda and the same cast of characters.[9] Late nineteenth-century critics even incorrectly categorized *Hope Leslie* a children's book, as though they could gauge its genre based on Sedgwick's last published books aimed at juvenile audiences.[10]

Yet the novel is best interpreted as a mode of alternative history; indeed, the language of "alternative history" undergirds discussions of its reemergence in the 1980s. Ann Douglas figures *Hope Leslie* as "counter history"; she explains, because the title character "defies the stern edicts of Governor Winthrop and his peers, frees witches and defends Indians, Hope Leslie suggests counter history; she is an *ex post facto* protest against the masculine solidities of the past" (185). And, stated differently, Judith Fetterley playfully argues, "Catharine Sedgwick could never be made up, for she exceeds the imagination" (78). Philip Gould goes further by referring to the text as "metahistory": "By reframing the massacre at Mystic, and constructing parallel massacre scenes, Sedgwick's engagement in gender politics ultimately exposes the metahistorical status of *Hope Leslie*" (82). Jeffrey Insko also posits that the text embraces anachronism to challenge historicism: "By deploying anachronism as both method and trope, *Hope Leslie* challenges fundamental conceptions of the form and shape of history that are as prevalent today as in Sedgwick's time" ("Anachronistic" 183). Luciano "extends" Insko's reading of the text by focusing on Magawisca's "melancholy voice," which enables Segwick's "reimagination of historical time" (Luciano 102). She claims "Magawisca's melancholy speech as at once figuring the suspension of the obscured past within the present and endowing that suspension with a revolutionizing *liveness* that might enable it to rearticulate the range of social possibilities" (Luciano 102–3). These critics highlight the radical vision Sedgwick creates not just of the past but also of the very act of remembering and the "possibilities" she engenders. The text, in fact, opts to promulgate a community founded on cross-cultural relations and points to a counterfactual rise of the United States.

Rather than interpreting the text in terms of "sisterhood" (either between the characters, or between the author and her peers, or even between the author and her women audience), interpreting it in terms of intergenerational transition brings the focus back to the militarization of women and the intersubjective exchange of history. *Hope Leslie* creates a virtual history of the people who lived in colonial times by contrasting the first two generations to settle New England to promote the militarization of women; upon that foundation, she endeavors to build conceptions of American citizenry as emerging from cross-cultural exchange. As a work of historical fiction, the novel does not merely riff upon past figures, real and imagined, but offers commentary on the politics and elisions in the construction of history in what might be termed "a virtual history." I use "virtual history"—what Carried Hyde refers to as the "the peculiar episteme of fiction—virtual histories it both enacts and archives—" ("Novelistic" 29), because, in *Hope Leslie*, it evokes the idea of the "virtual" as a sensuous experience of something vicariously imagined. As a text written to her contemporaries and to later generations (the narrator directly references "future readers" throughout the novel), Sedgwick knows that by inserting her text into a teleological historical frame, she binds it to— and troubles—subsequent stories of American peoplehood. She, then, creates a self-conscious readership about the futurity of American history because of the ways in which *Hope Leslie* offers dire warnings about cultural corrosion.[11]

"Virtual history" returns us to the idea of the virtual as a sensuous experience of something imagined, not just media involving high-tech three-dimensional visual and audio effects. The phrase "virtual history" carries some contradictory tension, for virtual seems to suggest futurity. To be more exact, the word "virtual" rests unanxiously on the subjective ("how it could have been"), while reaffirming the value of the imaginary.[12] It can mean "almost," as in "might as well be"; it can also refer to how something feels as opposed to its actual materiality. The adjective "virtual"—to denote something that almost occurs or appears—is like an asymptote that never intersects with the X-axis on a grid but comes infinitesimally close. The simulated worlds put forth by imaginative literature—the networks of characters, the sensorium of visual, aural, olfactory, and tactile imagery, the language employed that both constructs and reverberates with old meanings—constitute their own value as an object of study separate from the discipline of history and separate from the study of aggregate texts in the digital humanities.

The word "virtual" also attunes a reader into noticing how a text engages with futurity. Literary works are constructed with an eye toward a reader separated by time and place. By gauging the virtuality of a text, scholars would engage with its orientation toward a reader who encounters the text at some indeterminate time in the future. As Wolfgang Iser articulated it, readers activate texts through the act of reading: "The work is more than the text, for the text only takes on life when it is realized, and furthermore, the realization is by no means independent of the individual disposition of the reader. . . . The convergence of text and reader brings the literary work into existence" (*Implied* 274). Indeed, the many reader-text worlds ushered into existence are the subject of this book.

Hope Leslie militarizes its citizens (including the women) and calls upon engaging with "virtual history" as an intersubjective exchange in which the senses are activated through its retelling of the past. In its broad swath of women characters, the text brings incredible pressure to bear on generational fluctuations. It portrays the first women émigrés as unprepared for the ways in which settlement will tax their sensorium. Mrs. Fletcher and Mrs. Winthrop, both born in England, fail to grasp the full weight of their complicity in forging the colony. In contrast, the women of the nascent (rising) generation are called upon to bring full perceptual awareness—a virtual mode, with all the attendant meanings of "virtual."

Its treatment of the virtual complicates its portrait of the budding friendships between the native young woman and the English young man and then the native young woman and the English young woman: plots involving interracial friendship, though crucial to the characters' maturation, prove transitory. In thinking through the similarities between conspiracies and fiction plots, Hyde observes how "[p]lots obtain their persuasive power from the speculative histories they allow us to treat as if they were real—even as their virtuality frees us from the exigent circumstances that would follow the physical enactment of the scenarios they envision" ("Novelistic" 29). Hyde's language helps us sort through what makes readers so uncomfortable in Sedgwick's treatment of the Pequot girl Magawisca: readers rest uneasily in the "virtual freedom" of indulging in a story of cross-cultural contact based on friendship when subsequent events in the 1830s eviscerated indigenous communities through Indian Removal Acts. Magawisca's virtuality rests not in the early conspiracies she engages in against Everell's family or the subsequent ones against the Boston inhabitants but rather in the marriage plot with Everell that the text hints toward and then withdraws from—and even laments.

The text's virtual history ties the empowerment of women to the military arm of the state. As critics have outlined, by using the family as the founding unit of empire, the imperialist project can code certain modes of colonization as natural, familial, and domestic; in the process, it softens the militarization that undergirds the encroachment onto new territories. Moreover, settling families, rather than armed forces, diminishes the seeming threat of "amalgamation." Families imply the continued presence of women, specifically white woman, as readily available marriage partners. But describing the settlement of the colonies as exclusively by *families* distracts from the empire-building of the British and later the United States, and therefore we instead interpret the word "settlements" as synonymous with "home," "domesticity," "the private sphere," or "feminized spaces."

However, in *Hope Leslie*, Sedgwick refuses to code these domesticated processes and instead highlights the advantage it gives to settler communities; she portrays the politicization of Hope and Magawisca as the proper exertion of women's ingenuity. Much of the criticism on the domestic sphere's participation in imperial projects relies on the language of ghosting, specters, revenants, and hauntings as though efforts to "organize amnesia," in Derrida's terms, are not wholly successful, but create fissures for the return of the repressed. In this text, though, Sedgwick does not shy away from showing the actual bloodshed, as in *The Female American* and *Secret History*. She narrates the destruction of settlers and the Pequots. These are not ghosted settlements but ones about which she can catalog the destruction of the lives and habitations of indigenous peoples.[13] The Pequot, Magawisca, who might serve as a figure to haunt the white settlers, reappears after she loses a limb while saving Everell from execution. She remains alive, and the text gives ample attention to the amputated arm that she loses in saving a white Puritan's life. In one scene, while on trial for plotting a massacre against the inhabitants of the Massachusetts Bay Colony, she exposes her "mutilated" arm. Sedgwick stages but does not participate in the act of erasing her when Everell averts his gaze from her injury: "Everell involuntarily closed his eyes, and uttered a cry of agony, lost indeed in the murmurs of the crowd" (309). The novel refuses to allow readers to close their eyes to the destruction of Native peoples.[14] It also renders the thwarted love that *might have* developed between Magawisca and Everell not as repressed but openly discussed and rejected.

To bring the political-military role of women to the forefront, Sedgwick represents women's ability to adapt as wives in a capitalist, imperialist country in which no line of demarcation separates war from the home. In the next section, part 2, I examine Old World models of married women who embody subservient loyalty to their husbands and how their subservience makes them vulnerable in the militarized zone of the frontier. Then, in part 3, I analyze the underdiscussed presence of Mrs. Winthrop in the text; she is the fictionalized wife of the colonial governor John Winthrop, who acts as confidant and even counselor to her husband. Sedgwick uses the figure of Mrs. Winthrop to warn against the perpetuation of separate spheres because the sometimes-superficial interests associated with the women's sphere distract women from the power that constitutes the sphere associated with men. In the part 4, I compare the characters Hope Leslie and Magawisca, as they represent models for women whose attention focuses on the politics of settler-indigenous relations. Although both Hope and Magawisca represent more robust political roles for women, they embody different gradations of engagement. Hope represents a kind of new world woman who can adapt to unfamiliar surroundings and protect herself and others through stratagems and direct confrontation with the state, whereas Magawisca, rather than moving forward based on her own desires, subsumes the self to promote her father's political purposes. Her refusal to turn her back on her family of origin proves incompatible with an American, like Hope, who achieves self-agency through the loss of family and property. In the final section, I discuss how the book encourages various and perhaps incommensurable stories of the founding of New England. The text uses history to cast Hope as a possible role model for nineteenth-century women and to create a virtual history grounded in the possibilities of citizenship that America may promise even if it had not fulfilled them yet.

SPECTACLES
OF HOME

Critics have become more attuned to the ties between domesticity and empire, but they continue to see domesticity as reaching out to empire or empire intruding on the domestic rather than the domestic launching the empire through its role as a thinly disguised militarized site. Philip Gould describes the two massacres in *Hope Leslie* as involving private spheres: "The Puritan attack on Mystic, and Mononotto's revenge against the Fletcher household at Bethel, constitute analogous violations of the home" (76). Instead, the Fletcher household in that unsettled area comes across as a militarized space, not a home. One cannot "violate" a military outpost. Using the word "home" offers the settlers cover. Critics continue to see domestic space as "private, protected" and not the seat of war. Indeed, Gould interprets into the "massacre a particularly dark irony rooted in an emergent antebellum ideology of the home" (77). Gould rightly points out that this ideology at the time was "emergent." Still, the "irony" seems performed to distract us from seeing the home as an arsenal. It can seem as though the Puritans take the ideology of the sacred space of the English home and use it to cover their armed occupation of this Connecticut territory, a covering that *Hope Leslie* exposes to advance a model of citizenship for women that entails recognizing their ability to participate in advancing imperialism.

Sedgwick's language highlights how the family functions to antagonize remaining Pequots. Referring to Mrs. Fletcher at home, she writes, "A mother, encircled by her children, is always a beautiful spectacle" (61). Despite the tableau of mother and children, the word "spectacle" draws our attention to the performative and public aspect of the "home" the Puritans have created, even as they move into contested, isolated territory that will likely invite attack. Given the already frequent use of military terms, "encircled" almost suggests that the children serve to shield the mother from threats. The "spectacle" of the mother and children by the hearthstone is undercut by the attitude of the inhabitants who do not recoil from the activity of men standing ready with muskets which "were not infrequent, and caused no unusual excitement in the house" (40).

The families' vulnerability on the frontier seems compounded at times because of attitudes toward traditional gender roles. Mrs. Fletcher reports to her husband: "We have been advised to remove, for the present to the Fort; but as I feel no apprehension, I shall not disarrange my family by taking a step that would savour more of fear than prudence" (34). Her worries about the perception of her fears as an inconvenience prove sound: when she mentions some concerns to her servant Digby, he does not seek additional help from a nearby fort because it would mean listening to a woman. He tells Everell, "I would have sent to the fort for a guard to-night, but I liked not being driven hither and yon by that old hag's tokens [referring to the Pequot Nelema's warning], nor yet quite to take counsel from your good mother's fears, she being but a woman" (42). Digby's masculinity would feel threatened by heeding the pointed warnings from women, which leaves the family vulnerable to attack.

Sedgwick's narrative strategy puts forth seeming commonplaces but proceeds to undermine them, leading readers to acknowledge that their historical (and present) understanding of early America necessitates interrogation. The death of Mrs. Fletcher and her children during a raid at their home illustrates how a more equitable relationship between men and women should follow the militarization of the family in New World settlements. Mrs. Fletcher accepts "undisputed masculine supremacy" (16) in deferring to her husband. Her devotion, for example, leads her to underplay the anxiety she feels living in a remote area despite "inconveniences and dangers of that outpost" (41). She did not want to build their home in this spot, but she had to acquiesce to her husband's wishes. The bustle at Mrs. Fletcher's house evidences the role of families in operating as a unit of the state. At night, the men of the house stand guard with muskets supplied from their own arsenals. The narrator explains, "[S]uch precautions were not infrequent, and caused no unusual excitement in the house" (40). Military-like duties have become routinized and part of domestic everyday life. Indeed, Sedgwick explains how the house provides nooks to protect oneself from violent encounters. Standing under an extended roof, Everell "could, without being seen, command the whole extent of cleared ground that bordered on the forest, whence the foe would come, if he came at all" (41). The style of warfare between settlers and the indigenous tribes is marked by surprise attacks on both sides; thus boys, like Everell, always guard their homes. Settlers design households in anticipation of attacks.

Women, therefore, also need the authority to safeguard the militarized "home." In an interesting allusion, the narrator invokes Mungo Park (1771–1806), a Scotsman sent to explore the interior of Africa, to compare Mrs. Fletcher's seeming abandonment to claim a frontier without adequate protection (57).[15] Just as Mungo Park was ill-equipped to penetrate the heart of Africa, Mrs. Fletcher was sent with her family to settle new territory, which ultimately served to test its safety for others. The allusion to Park, unlike others that punctuate the text, seems out of context because his trek (his account was published in 1797) is more contemporaneous to Sedgwick's time than to the seventeenth-century characters who populate her story. Moreover, despite the use of epigraphs to connect her work to British and American writers, this allusion to Park appears in the text of a chapter and implies connections between attempts to colonize Boston and Africa, and between colonial American settlers and the Europeans who died in early ventures to scope out the interior of Africa. *Hope Leslie* suggests that if Mrs. Fletcher exercised a more equal relation with her spouse, they may have avoided the death and destruction of Mononotto's attack.

Readings of home as a safe haven in early settlements pervade literary criticism. However, within the narrative, Mr. Fletcher moves into an even more dangerous spot after first attempting to settle in Boston: "in spite of the remonstrances from the proprietors [of a nearby town], he fixed his residence a mile from the village" (16). Lori Merish reads Sedgwick's novella *Home* (1835) as sentimentalizing female attachments to material objects. She interprets, "The house in sentimentalism is sanctified as a privileged object of attachment: as shelter for the individual's most intimate objects of affection as well as a monument to familial love, often remaining in the family's possession for generations" (Merish 121). Yet for Sedgwick, in *Hope Leslie,* the house functions as a military fort. From the colonial home, white settlers launched surprise attacks on indigenous tribes, and they used those same homes to protect themselves from reprisals. When Mrs. Fletcher learns that her husband has decided to settle away from Boston on a new frontier, "the inconveniences and dangers of that outpost were not unknown to her, nor did she underrate them" (16). These homes are easily destroyed and everything in it. Merish wishes to correct historians who interpret the home as outside market forces, or more specifically "as a sanctuary outside market exchange" (134). And she is right not to allude to the home as a sanctuary from capitalism but neither does it serve as a sanctuary from state-sponsored violence.

In *Hope Leslie,* commerce is implicitly inflected by imperial might. Sedgwick breaks the narrative thrust by pausing the story of the Fletchers, on the eve of their deaths, to describe the same region as it has been transformed by the nineteenth century: on this same frontier "now contiguous rows of shops, filled with the merchandise of the east, the manufactures of Europe, the rival fabrics of our own country, and the fruits of the tropics" (17). She uses this break in the story's time frame to provide a contrast between how it looked in the seventeenth century and how it stands in the early nineteenth century when Sedgwick composes the book; back in the time when *Hope Leslie* is set, there "were, as the early period of our history, a few log-houses, planted around a fort, defended by a slight embankment and palisade" (17). Sedgwick highlights the globalized marketplace that undergirds the establishment of North American towns while eliding the aggression or slave labor that facilitates global trade and shipping even as she marvels at "the fruits of the tropics." Furthermore, in this description, she glosses over the military offensives establishing these bustling towns. She claims that the natural environs provided military cover, "defended by a slight embankment and palisade," even as her subsequent chapters detail the personal arsenals and the men, like Everell, who act as "good knight[s]" to protect their settlements. These homes are central to the flows of capital and exploitative labor in far-flung spots.

Because the home is militarized, women will have to be, too, or else they may share Mrs. Fletcher's fate. The text offers Hope as the type of American woman who can navigate the wilderness after she escapes capture by Mononotto.[16] Sedgwick, however, sees women's empowerment as tied to the family and especially bound up with men's explicit public responsibilities. The war between white settlers and local tribes highlights the central drama of the novel: the importance of the heterosexual couple as principal actors, and perhaps even cocombatants, in the colonial sphere. In this case, romantic attachments emphasize aptitudes for adapting to new challenges as the country expands and annexes territories westward. Sedgwick insists that a more robust role for women in marriages underwrites individual settlements.

The militarization of the domestic hearth alters how we think about the separation of private and public spheres in early American literature. First, discussions of public and private realms often leave the idea of "domestic space" uninterrogated. The Fletchers are a public family who share a household with servants, prisoners of war, family members, and adopted orphans.[17] This paradigm of the home as a public site alters English-imported ideas about property. As Elizabeth Maddock Dillon argues, "In narrative terms, private property thus stands as the origin of liberal autonomy: property ownership enables one to move forward into the public sphere" (*Gender of Freedom* 21). Yet this formulation does not describe the ways in which Sedgwick conceptualizes early New England settlements: once one has property, then the public sphere emerges from within it. The idea of "moving forward into" implies some private space one emerges from or retreats to. In Sedgwick's text, she imagines how the public sphere overlaps with all facets of life. Collapsing public and private sphere has important ramifications because Sedgwick starts her narrative with Mrs. Fletcher before introducing her heroine, Hope, who will reinvigorate North American womanhood as an example of a more agential and militarized wife who along with the men will transition the colonies from a theocracy to a democratic republic with imperial ambitions.

Vacant Spaces, Vacant Minds

In sorting through the marriages Sedgwick acknowledges and even apologizes for the subservence she portrays in the attitudes of Puritan wives toward their husbands. According to Sedgwick, the tacit agreement between husbands and wives involves the wife's acceptance of the husband's role as primary agent. But when indulged, this acceptance of man's superiority seemingly leads to a wife's "vacancy." Sedgwick includes several examples of English women whose thinking atrophies because of their dependence on men: Alice Fletcher (Hope's mother), Rosa (the lover of the rake Sir Philip), and Mary (Hope's sister). Alice "had suffered a total alienation of mind" when her father forbids her from marrying the man she loves (14); the narrator repeats "her mind had departed" (14). Love does not affect the heart in *Hope Leslie* but rather one's cognition. In the next generation, this vacancy seems unsustainable within a community as new as the Massachusetts Bay Colony, which faces immanent threats from indigenous peoples, the environment, and rogue members of the congregation and new arrivals. Sedgwick associates the "natural" dependence of women on men with the character Esther, who is briefly engaged to Everell before she realizes he does not reciprocate her love, and she departs back to England (215). In detailing Esther's feelings for Everell, the narrator hedges that "men like to inspire [meekness in women], because—perhaps—it seems to them an instinctive tribute to their natural superiority" (219). In these descriptions, Sedgwick's "perhaps" offsets her more definitive diction: "natural" and "instinctive."

A gap emerges between the ways in which the relations between husband and wife are spoken about and the lived reality of their relations. At one point, Sedgwick switches point of view to describe how the indigenous people interpret gender relations among the European white settlers to defamiliarize the gender categories other novels substantiate. A Pequot scout, observing "English strangers," "returned with the report that the strangers' skin was the colour of cowardice—that they served their women, and spoke an unintelligible language" (86). The scout implies that the English men's subservience to their women will hurt their ability to survive in New England. Sedgwick also playfully alludes to a Scottish proverb, "Ilka man can manage a wife but him that has her," to highlight how people talk about managing women and the difficulties of actually doing it (119). One character refers to a generalizable story, a "fable," to enforce a gender hierarchy: "Importunity, I know, is not beseeming in a wife—it is the instrument of weakness whereby like the mouse in the fable she would gnaw away what she cannot break" (35–36). Sedgwick insists that early Americans had to generate new models to reimagine the relationship between husband and wife. The author, in fact, shows that a wife should "gnaw away" at a husband, no matter how powerful his role in the eyes of the state; because of their intimacy and access to each other, her input might lead to the betterment of the community.

Sedgwick both notes and embellishes the contributions of women in early America. The final pages of the text make clear that this mode of femininity, which seems meek and subservient, will lead to sterility and danger in New England, which requires more daring women to navigate its terrain and enter its power struggles. While omitting any description of the wedding or marriage of Everell and Hope, the novel ends with an involved description of what happened to Esther, the dutiful Puritan girl who is Hope's foil. She breaks her engagement to Everell and leaves the colony so he can have his happy ending by marrying Hope.[18] When she returns years later, the narrator informs readers that she never married: "Her hand was often and eagerly sought, but she appears never to have felt a second engrossing attachment. . . . She illustrated a truth, which, if more generally received by her sex, might save a vast deal of misery: that marriage is not essential to the contentment, the dignity, or the happiness of woman" (349–50). Rather than lament her unmarried state, Esther redefines it. In the context of the narrative, women, like Esther, who acquiesce too readily to authority will not survive or advance the imperial designs of the US.[19] If marriage does not advance US imperial interests, then it should not transpire. Esther heroically withdraws, knowing on some level that her infatuation with Everell would not stabilize the community. Her "happiness" proves self-sustaining, and other women will carry out the civilizing and imperial work of the frontier.

Women's commercial competition reveals the ways in which the authorities underutilize them on the frontier. The focus on fashion and consumption among women in the novel is exemplified by the comic portrait of the less-than-devout aunt Mrs. Grafton, who the narrator describes as "far more ambitious of being leader of fashion, than the leader of a sect" (27). Indeed, "ambition" undergirds the women's efforts at having the best hats and competing at church services with each other based on who wears the newest clothes (168). Women are portrayed as much more amendable to the new economic order of capitalism. While the competition for dress is presented as shallow (neither Magawisca nor Hope Leslie indulge in material concerns), it serves as a metonym for other processes: competition for land, power, and authority. The older generation admonishes the young people repeatedly that "[o]ur individual wishes must be surrendered to the public good" when considering a marriage partner (161). Yet that decision-making process leads to inefficient or undesirable outcomes. Sedgwick, therefore, suggests that the young recognize the ever-changing ideologies and choose a marriage partner to respond to them. An undercurrent to the book lies in the liberal proposition that if everyone followed his or her inclinations rather than place the community's wants before one's own, then advantageous outcomes would result. Sedgwick ends her text on a note both chiding and valorizing contemporary young women for their eager consumption and joy in observing the minute details of wedding ceremonies. Their perceptual power and taste not only evidence the power of their imagination but also imply a community of like-minded readers: "We leave it to that large, and most indulgent class of our readers, the misses in their teens, to adjust, according to their own fancy, the ceremonial of our heroine's wedding" (348). Readers' fascination with the pomp and circumstance of a wedding suggests that Sedgwick endows an even younger generation than the one depicted in the novel ("the misses in their teens") with the capability to plan, "according to their own fancy," public events, events that will determine the next generation of leaders.

THE COLONIAL
MAGISTRATE'S WIFE

Sedgwick frames the book around romantic entanglements and disappointments even as she declares how the Puritan settlers were not "invested with any romantic attractions. It was not assisted by the illusions of chivalry, nor magnified by the spiritual power and renown of crusades. Our fathers neither had nor expected their reward on earth" (11). Yet Sedgwick interweaves "illusions of chivalry" and the "crusades" implying how love and honor stories from the Old World embed imperial aggression (crusades) with romantic love. Nonetheless, the Puritans, in Sedgwick's novel, invest heavily in heterosexual marriage, whether grounded in "romantic attachment" or not. The colonial magistrates, for example, expend considerable time and effort assorting the young people into couples. The right marriages (husbands and wives who promote qualities in each other that enable them to further the best interests of the colony) strengthen the community and legitimize their "errand into the wilderness." Because of the prominence of marriage in the text, Sedgwick's rewriting of history emerges just by imagining different pairings of couples among the characters. The book seeks to illuminate and to rewrite the past while pausing at turns to consider how events might have unfolded if we imagine, for example, Everell married to Magawisca, or to Hope, or Esther, respectively. Marriage, the story implies, drives colonial subjugation and the history of it.

The political order faces internal threats when household members find their attention divided. As Diana Taylor writes, in imperial contexts, "attention is power" (244). Just as Mrs. Fletcher fails to take on an equal role to her husband commiserate with life in the unsettled frontier, Mrs. Winthrop abdicates her spousal role as confidant to the detriment of the colony. The magistrates, no matter how many times they declare that wives are naturally obedient, reveal an anxiety to fix marriages between the young people, because some women might exercise outsize power over their husbands. The governors eagerly wish to attach Everell to Esther so as to circumvent a match between him and Hope. They believe Hope will accentuate different qualities in Everell that would diminish the probability of the colony's survival. Sedgwick's fictional version of John Winthrop explains to Everell's father: "I feel, as you doubtless will, the urgency of coupling him with a member of the congregation, . . . [because] 'the believing wife shall sanctify the unbelieving husband'" (150). Here Winthrop concedes the power a woman holds over her husband as the one who socializes him into faith, morality, and duty. Winthrop attempts to cover his concession by a number of platitudes; he claims a woman's "passiveness," for example, "next to godliness, is a woman's best virtue" (153). Yet the urgency of attaching Everell to someone undercuts his words about women's selfless purposes.

Among these colonial magistrates who seek to arrange marriages in the text, Sedgwick offers an imagined portrait of Mrs. Winthrop (one supposes a fictional version of Margaret Tyndal), wife to the colonial governor John Winthrop. Nowhere in the book does the text's contrary impulses regarding women's behavior become more vexed than in Sedgwick's portrayal of Mrs. Winthrop, which likely explains why this character garners so little critical examination. At some points, she models a new mode of wifely behavior as counselor and confidant; at others, she inculcates subservience, and still at others she promotes superficial indulgence in women's matters, such as wedding plans. Sedgwick's fictional portrait of John Winthrop, the first colonial governor of the Massachusetts Bay Colony, comes across as rife with contradictions, and thus Mrs. Winthrop, too, may operate as an analog to the author's ambivalence about the Massachusetts Bay Colony. Specifically, Mrs. Winthrop's descriptions of love index whether the New World will reimpose Anglo-European ontologies or respond in new ways to place and circumstance. In England, for example, Sedgwick imagines John Winthrop as bored by William Fletcher's love problems. Winthrop fails to sympathize with Will because "he had been long married—and twice married" (11). Winthrop listens "as one listens to a tale he has heard a hundred times" (11); for Winthrop, marriage is a stale story. But in the second half of the book, Sedgwick characterizes Mrs. Winthrop as the governor's closest advisor without whom he makes the grave error of trusting Sir Philip Gardiner, an imposter and Catholic, who seeks to marry Hope for her fortune. Sedgwick seemingly advances the notions that the nation-state has at its disposal a nontransferable private relation between husband and wife, which must be propagated. Couples, not working in tandem, cause repeated crises in the text.

In particular, Sedgwick demonstrates how women's attention must work to advance the colony. In a drawn-out aside about the governor's growing intimacy with the reprobate, Sir Philip, Sedgwick paints a portrait of the Winthrop marriage. The narrator makes a point that Mrs. Winthrop was distracted and inattentive to her husband because she was engrossed in the young people's nuptials. The scene implies that Mrs. Winthrop would have offered a different perspective on the affairs of the colony and that a division in the attention of a married couple endangers the state. Sedgwick reports in a single-sentence paragraph: "The Governor was in the habit of participating with his wife his most secret state-affairs; moved to this confidence, no doubt, by his strict views of her rights as his help-mate; for it cannot be supposed, even for a moment, that one of the superior sex should find pleasure in telling a secret" (205). As in many passages, the narrator employs the high arch of irony to comment on generalizations about the sexes. The substance of the statement, though, contradicts gender binaries. Sedgwick often situates her irony in words that imply absoluteness ("no doubt") or uniformity across time and place: not "even for a moment." She chides the common generalization that men ("superior sex") like to share secrets. Her play of language critiques a mindset that does not consider wives the peers of their husbands.

But even this aside about the pleasures of secret sharing gets more nuanced when she uses the verb "participating" instead of a word like "relating": John Winthrop "was in the habit of participating with his wife." This is a joint conversation, not a one-way communication. Moreover, "habit" allows Sedgwick to imagine the governor as confiding in his wife as an integral and normalized part of his daily life. The sentence's key exchange involves the simple substitution of "secret state-affairs," with all its pomp, for just "secrets," an equation that taps into how discourse cements gender binaries: women gossip; men share state secrets.

If the governor finds a new intimate in the dangerous Sir Philip because his wife is occupied with weddings, then the blame not only falls on Winthrop for breaking his habit but on the subject that has arrested his wife's attention away from him. If a culture perpetuates different spheres for men and women, then men lose a key ally in their struggle to safeguard or amass resources. Sedgwick explains, "Madam Winthrop was happily too much absorbed with the feminine employment of watching the development of her niece's affairs, to have much curiosity in relation to cabinet secrets" (206). Mrs. Winthrop receives condemnation for her lack of "curiosity." The New World woman has to be alert on the frontier and in the city among political machinery. To explain, Sedgwick again employs a number of qualifiers both to jab at culturally constructed gender differences and to gesture at her inability to know the workings of this woman's mind: "[Mrs. Winthrop] naturally concluded that some dangerous adherent of that arch-heretic Gorton, had been discovered; or, perhaps, some new mode of faith had demanded magisterial interference; whatever her mental conclusions were, it is certain her thoughts all ran in another channel. In all ages of the world, in every condition, and at every period of life, a woman's interest in the progress of a love affair, masters every other feeling" (206). In a passage dripping with irony, Sedgwick overdetermines it by starting with the adverb "naturally." Mrs. Winthrop knows something is abreast among the magistrates but instead of lending her husband an ear, she "concludes" whatever relieves her of duty. Yet the narrator does not pin down a reason. She employs a syntactical frame similar to what F. O. Matthiessen dubbed Hawthorne's "device of multiple choice" (276). Maybe Mrs. Winthrop thought it was Gorton or some heretical religious practice. Sedgwick refuses to say and, like Hawthorne, loads the passage with qualifiers: "or," "perhaps," "whatever."[20] Although Mrs. Winthrop surmises multiple reasons for what she assumes troubles her husband about the colony, Sedgwick then adopts an immovable certainty about what occupies Mrs. Winthrop; but here, too, the generalizations about the ubiquity of gender norms undercut this certainty: "In all ages of the world, in every condition, and at every period of life, a woman's interest in the progress of a love affair, masters every other feeling" (204). Not only does the hyperbolic language undercut the substance of the statement, but the text is also awash in women who do not care about the movements of a love affair, most especially Hope, whose chief concern lies with her lost sister, and Magawisca, whose chief concern remains the plight of her people. Sedgwick's hyperbole highlights the constructedness of "interest."[21] The irony does not stop there, for the entire passage indicts Mrs. Winthrop for failing to protect the state by not paying attention to her own marriage. In using the characters of Mrs. Fletcher and Mrs. Winthrop as examples of how not to behave, Sedgwick advocates for the militarization and politicization of women.

To describe the dynamics of power and control between the Winthrops, Sedgwick employs an involved analogy about horses. Sedgwick pays both homage and censure toward the historical John Winthrop, recognizing his skills as a thinker and leader at the same time as she condemns him as part of the Puritan establishment whose narrow-mindedness led them to commit atrocities.[22] Likewise, Sedgwick acknowledges the obedience expected of women in Puritan times is now passé. In one description of Mrs. Winthrop, Sedgwick belabors her obligations to her husband: "the duty of unqualified obedience from the wife to the husband, her appointed lord and master; a duty that it was left to modern heresy to dispute; and which our pious fathers, or even mothers, were so far from questioning, that the only divine right to govern, which they acknowledged, was that vested in the husband over the wife" (141). The gift of the Puritans lies in how they undercut the authority of the monarchy while committing themselves to liberty.[23] Sedgwick implies that questioning the divine right of kings may have led to more equal partnerships between husbands and wives even as her diction ("heresy") implies that Puritans would balk at contemporary marriages. The sentence's easy transversal between time periods and points of view models the unvexed adaptability of the modern subject to political and social transformations.

Sedgwick, who never married herself, seems fascinated by the ways in which individual couples sort through the power dynamics of marriage within a patriarchal culture. The narrative's asides about relations between men and women often include irony or a chiding tone. At one point, she interrupts the narrative to contemplate Mrs. Winthrop's relationship to the famous governor. A wife, like Mrs. Winthrop, Sedgwick describes, is not exactly "servile"; instead, the narrator outlines her compliance with an unusual analogy: "It was prompted by feeling; and, if we may be allowed a coarse comparison, like a horse easy on the bit, she was guided by the slightest intimation from him who held the rein; indeed—to pursue our humble illustration still farther—it sometimes appeared as if the reins were dropped, and the inferior animal were left to the guidance of her own sagacity" (145). Sedgwick does not gloss over the "coarse[ness]" of comparing a wife to a horse, but then she does so to allude to a wife's self-direction: "it sometimes appeared as if the reins were dropped." She implies that the husband-and-wife relation proves subtler and perhaps its dynamism escapes notice. And the passage concludes with a reference to the woman's "own sagacity." This doublehandedness frustrates more than illuminates. "The humble illustration" only barely veils the passage's interest in the "sagacity" and independence exhibited by women. The horse analogy seeks to prop up a husband's power over his wife while simultaneously undercutting it through the author's meta commentary on the analogy's grossness. Mrs. Winthrop is, ultimately, a marginal character whose chief role in the text contrasts with the playful and resourceful Hope. Mrs. Winthrop seems to possess power; therefore, her subservience to her husband seemed performed. Not so, Hope, who having an "independent temper, and careless gaiety of heart, had more than once offended against the strict notions of Madam Winthrop, who was of the opinion that the deferential manners of youth, which were the fashion of the age, had their foundation in immutable principles" (206). The Puritans' commitment to "immutability" is the key characteristic that the younger generation must overcome.

In American literature, if at one extreme stands Dame Van Winkle, badgering her husband until he absconds into the woods, then at the other extreme, we find many more women protagonists in early American literature who find themselves socialized away from girlish impetuosity into respectable, productive Christian wives, such as Gerty in *The Lamplighter* (1854) or Ellen Montgomery in *The Wide Wide World* (1850). In addition to these heroines, feminist critics have traced characters who model the role of the republican mother who molded her children into future citizens.[24] Nancy Sweet points out how those texts (along with Sedgwick's *New-England Tale*): "the disobedient daughter proves an invaluable literary construct for synthesizing a particular blend of progressive and conservative ideologies that dispenses with the hierarchy and intolerance of colonial Calvinism yet maintains the measure and constraint of traditional social order" (Sweet 109). But in *Hope Leslie,* mothers are killed off quickly, and several critics have noted how many of the women in the text are childless: Hope's sister Faith/Mary, Esther, Rosa, and Mrs. Grafton. Although these women characters offer an array of stock types, Sedgwick portrays the mutual maturation of Hope Leslie and Everell Fletcher, who enter responsible and moral adulthood without the cloying obedience of Calvinism and the chauvinism of white settlers. Sedgwick downplays the role of the community and instead insists that the couple socializes each other into right behavior. Her focus underscores the individual's romantic interest as an expression of the aspirational self. As Nancy Armstrong states, "domestic fiction unfolded the operations of human desire as if they were independent of political history. And this helped to create the illusion that desire was entirely subjective and therefore essentially different from the politically encodable forms of behavior of which desire gave rise" (N. Armstrong 9). Yet rather than depoliticizing it, as Armstrong suggests, Sedgwick grants the intimate pair (specifically husbands and wives) overdetermined importance, as they bring together the spheres of politics and sociality, while cautioning individuals not to interfere with the pairs or with those who choose nonnormative modes (such as Faith and Esther) because each serves the community's goal of stability and possibly expansion.[25] In starting the text with the massacre at Bethel and then portraying Sir Phillip's nefarious conspiracy to avenge Thomas Morton, Sedgwick casts women as central in the formation of the state and its imperial designs.

POLITICAL RECOGNITION
AND THE AMERICAN ANTIGONE

Hope Leslie has long invited interest for the way in which its plotting seems to recapitulate the marginalization of indigenous peoples in the US as an object of fascination and then erasure. The first hundred pages of the novel are devoted to cultivating a love story between Everell, the oldest son of white settlers from England, and Magawisca, the daughter of the Pequot chief

Mononotto. Yet when Magawisca intercedes to save Everell just as he faces execution, she loses her arm. Following her dismemberment, the narrator and characters no longer treat her as a possible love interest for the young white man. Instead, the titular Hope Leslie enters the text and dominates the action, usurping Everell as well as every other character in the text. In the story's final pages, Hope and Everell have their union blessed by Magawisca, a move that inaugurates their actual betrothal to each other. The characters feel fascinated, repelled, and reverential toward the native woman who rejects any bond with the settlers. The author allows her to hover on the margins in contrast to texts that depersonalize indigenous characters or treat them as haunting specters, suggesting that Magawisca's refusal to disappear completely prevents the Puritans from forgetting what has been lost.[26]

But replacing Magawisca with Hope as the center of the text, Sedgwick also promotes racial segregation to protect against interracial marriage that would realign power hierarchies. Instead of having a "natural" right to the land through their heritage or through the toil of settlement, the English orphan Hope Leslie establishes power by reimagining American womanhood. Hope's strong foothold in Boston, despite her lack of roots in the New World, distracts from other kinds of prohibitions against interlopers. If indigenous people and Europeans marry, the text suggests, then settlements may unravel. Sedgwick has Magawisca feel wretched when Sir Philip describes Everell as unfeeling toward her. While Magawisca sits in jail, Sir Philip visits her cell and taunts her, "Methinks if [Everell] had a spark of thy noble nature, maiden, he would burn the town, or batter down this prison wall, for you" (255). Yet the kind of love Philip describes has a destructive bent. Just as Magawisca's sacrifice of her arm for Everell's life does not bridge the divide between the factions but instead incurs more losses, the self-immolating love Philip describes would harden grudges from the past. Colonial enterprise, the narrator suggests, needs individuals who will sustain each other and thus stabilize Winthrop's "city set on a hill" through major economic and social changes (Sedgwick 158).[27] Hope may embody a new attitude toward indigenous people, but by the time she arrives in the colony it is too late to act on her generosity or sense of fairness. She remains a safe vehicle for imagining an alternative relation between settler and indigenous person. Hope epitomizes the agential self whose desires will propel the colony to independence through her willingness to enter the field directly and through her discerning attentiveness. She has the resourcefulness to survive on the frontier while promoting the sanctity of life; she helps Nelema and Magawisca to escape from unjust imprisonment, even though she fails to tolerate her sister's marriage to the Pequot Oneco. At the same time, Sedgwick makes clear that remnants of the old order, like rakish white men, continue to threaten Hope's safety when she tries to strike out alone.

The narrator frequently welcomes the young people's ascendancy over the old guard. By the early nineteenth century, Sedgwick claims American culture has become youth driven: "This was, certainly, an almost unparalleled presumption, in those times, when youth was accounted inferiority; but the very circumstance that, in one light, aggravated her fault, in another, mitigated it" (119). Hope represents American transgressive innocence born of daring and kindness. Rather than a subservient or cloying wife, American women will have to act, not just socialize men to act as virtuous citizens to perpetuate "republican motherhood." If Hope sometimes offends Mrs. Winthrop by overstepping the boundaries of Puritan propriety, then she also offends her Aunt Grafton, whose commitment to consumption and fashion fails to interest her niece. Hope instead models a new mode of American womanhood. She tells Everell, "Aunt Grafton remonstrated, and expressed her natural and kind apprehensions, by alleging that it was 'very unladylike, and a thing quite unheard of in England,' for a young person, like me, to go out exploring a new country. I urged, that our new country develops faculties that young ladies, in England, were unconscious of possessing" (98). According to the narrator, Hope must discard Old World models of womanhood for one of action and exploration. The key word in the paragraph is "natural" to describe Mrs. Grafton's apprehensions. The narrator invokes the word "natural" frequently in descriptions of women, especially when highlighting socially constructed or habituated behaviors to render its meaning closer to "accustomed."

Sedgwick's text prompts women to embrace censure without changing their behavior. The text begins with the younger William Fletcher disappointing his uncle because he prefers liberty to property, as does Hope, who invites the ire and condemnation of her elders. The Puritans bristle at Hope's independence. Sedgwick has the characters condemn Hope for attributes that seem necessary for forging new world settlements. The governor admits that he is "impatient to put jesses on this wild bird [Hope], while she is on our perch" by marrying her to someone like Sir Philip; in Hope's case, one sees the shift from using women to socialize men to using the institution of marriage to socialize women (155). Irony undergirds the older characters' remonstrance; for the narrator lauds her behavior that elicits condemnation by Hope's elders. Hope is characterized as straightforward or as lacking the "art of diplomacy" (175); she is athletic, with a "quick hastened foot," and mouthy: Esther reprimands her for her "blameable freedom of speech" (175) and later that "you do allow yourself too much liberty of thought" (180). Sedgwick provides a model and a precedent for American womanhood if women were to take advantage of the freedoms available to them in the new republic. Sedgwick uses the disjunction between Hope and her community to dramatize the ironies of the process of transvaluation. Yet Hope, in her rebelliousness, seems like an alien figure compared to the heroines created by American writers in the 1850s or even other novels by Sedgwick, such as the too-good-to-be-true Jane Elton in *New-England Tale* (1822) or Ellen Bruce in *Redwood* (1824).[28] Hope then stands as the virtual figure—one that almost was or could have been.

Sedgwick's attempts at transvaluation lead her to draw a character who flails against her community's moral compass. Hope's feeble moments of self-recrimination recall Mark Twain's "All right, then, I'll go to hell" speech in *Huckleberry Finn* in which Huck allows the runaway Jim to remain free even though it breaks his culture's strictures. Likewise, Hope breaks the law to liberate indigenous women who have been unjustly incarcerated. Sedgwick mocks Hope when she chastises herself for feeling bad about losing Everell. Hope aims to "to expel every selfish feeling from her heart, and to live for the happiness of others," rather than indulge in love sickness (213). Yet living for the public good leads to inefficiencies and mismatched couples. When she sacrifices for others, she creates disharmony, as when she proposes marriage to Esther for Everell in an act of self-abasement. The novel suggests she cannot act completely on her own counsel; she needs a coconspirator.

The text's progressive vision of American womanhood is undercut by the text's insistence on heteronormativity at its center by propelling by the plot with Hope and Everell's eventual, if at times unlikely, attachment in marriage and the substitution of Esther as a rival for Hope instead of Magawisca. Throughout the text, Hope fails to confide in Everell in ways that work to her detriment. Yet her self-reliance, if at times misguided, serves to shape the self prior to marriage, most prominently when Hope escapes Mononotto's attempt to kill her and flees into the woods. Like other frontier heroes, she must confront darkness, dense forests, vegetation, storms, but, unlike her male counterparts in the American literary canon, she also confronts a possible gang rape. Hope runs into a group of drunken Englishmen in the dark forest. When she asks for their aid and even promises them money if they can convey her back to Boston, they scoff: "'There's no reward could pay for you, honey,' replied the fellow, advancing towards her" (240). Despite Hope's representation as the new, brave, independent version of American womanhood, in an instant she can be objectified and turned into a new form of currency "no reward could pay for." Yet her journey into the wilderness leaves her poised to confront the challenges of forging a New Canaan, if not a New Israel, not necessarily as a mother but as a joint partner to Everell. Instead of spawning similar characters like Hope, it seems that the types of women available in fiction became more constricted by mid-nineteenth century. As historian Laurel Shire notes with westward expansion, "American politicians thus cast white women in two roles: the innocent victim and the civilizing agent" (Shire 139). These categories dominate the literature as well. In contrast, Hope assumes neither the role of victim nor civilizing agent but that of advocate. Nonetheless, despite her agency, she must tie herself to Everell through marriage to participate in the public sphere.

Hope's connection to Everell forecloses one between him and Magawisca; the nascent love story between the American-born Puritan boy and the Pequot girl appears in the early chapters of the book. But Sedgwick portrays Magawisca's commitment to her people as overriding her desire for Everell. The transition of the book's focus from Magawisca to Hope creates a sense of loss in the reader. Aesthetically, the text does not cohere. It forces the reader to question race prejudice and Hope's ascendency on the frontier. If the women characters compete with each other for Everell (as some characterize the plot), then Hope's marriage to him confirms a strain of the text: one cannot compete with people, like Hope, who have already abandoned their people by emigrating. On the one hand, Magawisca remains loyal to her father and thus cannot admit Everell into her life. On the other, Hope is an orphan who has also lost her sister; she is free to make new attachments without betraying others. Settling the new world incurs loss upon loss, *Hope Leslie* implies. When the domestic space is a militarized place of conflict acted upon by outside forces, then one has to prepare for loss. Hope loses her father, mother, country, the

Fletcher family (except for Everell and his father), and then her sister to her husband, Oneco (Magawisca's brother). If one gets caught up on vengeance or in trying to salvage the past, then one loses an opportunity to rebuild. The second half of the book traces Hope's failure to recapture her sister. The sister is not lost or killed, nor is she a spectral presence who haunts. Instead, she wants nothing to do with Hope's world and, in a stinging reversal, she does not seek to be rescued.[29] Rather than indulging in her affliction in her sister's rejection, Hope moves forward to transform the community and marry Everell.

In *Hope Leslie*, despite its overtures to reach some future audience, Sedgwick repeatedly denies Hope public recognition for her boldness in suturing white settler-indigenous relations. Hope ignores her community's norms and laws but without incurring any personal costs; her mindset is decidedly forward facing. When other characters try to teach her about the past or admonish her, her mind is elsewhere. Defiance, it seems, with a nostalgic bent is self-annihilating. Magawisca interposes herself in Everell life by altering his point of view through her version of history and then saves his life from execution by literally "interposing" her arm to save his neck.[30] Hope, though, never demands the same kind of political recognition. Instead, she employs subterfuges and disguises to transgress colonial law. To escape notice, she plays upon gender stereotypes, as when she weeps to manipulate a jailer into letting her pass into the prison to see Magawisca without the proper permit. Even during her journey into the wilderness, she takes on the guise of the Virgin Mary to adapt to the worldview of the boatman who saves her. Barnaby, the jailer, lets Hope break rules because "the sight of you always brings to mind your kindness to the dead and the living" (323). Barnaby remembers her at his daughter's wedding and his wife's sick bed when she died. Hope is not a cipher for repressing the memories of the dead. Rather she brings forth virtual memories of the dead: Barnaby's wife, Mrs. Fletcher, and her mother. Hope Leslie animates life's high and low points. Hope is an ideal person to recompense colonial violence and preserve virtual history because her transgressions remain unimpeachable. Sedgwick undercuts the portrayal of her rebelliousness because she does not seek political recognition. Her self-directedness is subsumed by her self-effacement.

Hope seamlessly weaves together the family and the state despite the glaring tension between the two in colonial settlements that require individual prostration to the law to maintain the colony's hold on the land. Hope's triumphs turn her into an anti-Antigone. Indeed, she lets her sister go without killing her or burying her. She violates the state as though the state wishes to defy the laws it cannot abide, and thus the magistrates use her as a scapegoat for allowing transgressions that it cannot openly reconcile with its strict adherence to the letter of the law. The adaptability of Hope rests on her self-effacement. Antigone has become the figure for philosophical inquiry into the thwarted possibilities of citizenship. Hegel famously uses Antigone to tease out a dialectic of political reconciliation; Judith Butler, though, interprets Antigone's story as a figuration for modes of loving (in particular, of and for sisters) and mourning that cannot be acknowledged. She describes it as "an allegory for the crisis of kinship: which social arrangements can be recognized as legitimate love, and which human losses can be explicitly grieved as real and consequential loss?" (24). And Lee Edelman interprets Antigone as the embodiment of those who abandon hope in the future, who "insist on the unintelligible's unintelligibility" (106).[31] In a text seeped in recalling the past, Hope, unlike Antigone, moves forward without calling the political order to account for her familial sufferings. For all the text's representations of the need for women in the political and military realms, it suggests that they do so while disavowing political recognition.

In contrast to Hope, Magawisca asks for recognition and remains loyal to her father even in the face of colonial justice. The need for recognition marginalizes her. Sedgwick describes Magawisca and Mononotto's father-daughter relationship as more extreme in its chauvinism than the one between the Puritan husband and his subservient wife. Magawisca "soon imbibed his melancholy, and became as obedient to the impulse of his spirit, as the most faithful are to the fancied intimations of the Divinity" (194). Magawisca does not just bend to her father's will but empathically becomes one with him, now described by the narrator as "an insane person" (194). She, too, cannot thrive in this new world order just like Esther or Rosa or those women who become vacant, because Magawisca sacrifices Everell "on the altar of national duty" (194). Magawisca's choice to turn back to her father rather than toward Everell again reiterates that loyalty or fixed prejudices prove a liability in the American spheres. Instead of evoking Pocahontas, as she does in other respects, Magawisca evokes an enabling daughter who cannot challenge her father. In contrast, historians often interpret Pocahontas anachronistically as a republican hero for the way she seemingly defied her father to save John Smith. According to Robert Tilton, Pocahontas represents, along with George Washington, "defiance of patriarchal power, a fearlessness of the consequences of such defiance, and an appeal to a form of honesty, whether in response to a direct question or to the emotions engendered by an impending event, as the key to unlock an expression of paternal love" (Tilton 53). Rather than separate from her insane father, she commits her life to his project.

In Sedgwick's formulation, the failure of Mononotto and Magawisca's attempt to thwart the English settlers lies in their severing of the domestic and the political rather than merging them as the Puritans had. As he becomes radicalized against the settlers for their rampage at Mystic, he stops interacting with his family: totally intent on violence, "he neither spoke nor looked at his wife, or children" (50). The inability to capitalize on the political power of the heterosexual couple costs the Pequots. Magawisca's mother pleads, "Go forth and avenge us" (52). When Mononotto concurs, he explains, "When women put down their womanish thoughts and counsel like men, they should be obeyed" (52). But "going forth" to fight, away from his family, costs him his sanity, and when his wife counsels him to fight she unsexes herself: she "counsels like men." It is the English who embody the easy vacillation between war and peace in the guise of domesticity. Sedgwick hints that Oneco, Mononotto's son, was perhaps better suited to fighting the English on these terms. His father "felt Oneco's volatile unimpressive character was unfit for his purpose, and he permitted him to pursue without intermission, his pleasure—to hunt and fish for his 'white bird,'" that is, his white wife (194). This perspective on Oneco is filtered through Mononotto and therefore based on his "feelings" of disappointment that his son will not act as insane as him. When Oneco wants to effect something, he does it with purpose as when he recaptures his wife from the Puritans.[32] The emphasis on their happy interracial marriage allows him to "pursue . . . his own pleasure." Oneco fights when necessary, but it does not consume him. He can forge a life with his wife without making himself subservient to the past or his father. Oneco is the best representation of someone living an entirely "domestic" life.

. . .

Of late, American literature scholars have used *Hope Leslie* to trace the workings and misdirections of cultural amnesia during a time when authors

wrote within the genre of sentimental literature. Some authors, like Sedgwick, sought to tap into sentimentality to foster a sense of belonging, despite
the racial and socioeconomic diversity of the US. Yet by ending the text with
Hope and Everell's marriage without ever portraying them as an intimate
pair, the text's central portrait of intimacy remains Everell and Magawisca's
relationship developed at the beginning of the novel. Not only does Everell
and Magawisca's nascent love cross racial boundaries but it also highlights
the construction of history, the processes that lead to cultural amnesia, and
the intimacies of intersubjectivity. Magawisca evokes Pocahontas for saving
Everell's life and her marriage to John Rolfe because the Pocahontas-Rolfe
connection allows Americans to indulge in regret about how intermarriage
failed to become widespread between English settlers and indigenous people.
Robert Tilton observes how "[c]ommentators could muse that had other Europeans followed Rolfe's example and intermarriage become commonplace
from the outset of the colonial enterprise, the ongoing, apparently irreconcil-
able, conflict between the Anglo-American colonists and the native cultures
might have been avoided" (3). The subjunctive "could" remains the key word
because Pocahontas scenarios provide a template for fantasizing about different ways settlement might have unfolded without requiring any action to
rectify what did happen.

As noted, the text itself offers a metacommentary on history making.
Susanne Opfermann maintains that *Hope Leslie* "is remarkable because it
questions cultural norms and the processes by which they are generated"
(42). Weierman echoes this sentiment: "Challenging the collective, enforced
amnesia concerning the Indian presence in Stockbridge and elsewhere, Sedgwick reminds readers that the lives of those 'tribes of human beings' held
meaning and value, even if their values did differ from Anglo-Americans"
(429). The work of bridging this historical impasse undergirds Everell and
Magawisca's nascent love. Their relations prove intellectual, not sexual or national. At one point, the narrator describes Magawisca's fondness for Everell:
"He had opened the book of knowledge to her—had given subjects to her
contemplative mind, beyond the mere perceptions of her senses; had in some
measure dissipated the clouds of ignorance that hung over the forest-child,
and given her glimpses of the past and the distant; but above all, he had grat-
ified her strong national pride" (263). Not only does Everell's transmission
expand Magawisca's worldview but his teachings also do not force her to

reject or forget the story of her people's terror and displacement. Magawisca, too, teaches Everell through stories by telling him her version of the first attacks of the Pequot wars. Everell finds himself "unconsciously lending all his interest to the party of the narrator" (48). From her, Everell learns about the power of point of view to shade events. In her account, she explicitly draws upon the destruction: "the bodies of our people were strewn about the smouldering ruin; and all around the palisade lay the strong and valiant warriors—cold—silent—powerless as the unformed clay" (48). For Everell, "from Magawisca's lips [the Pequot war] took a new form and hue," not because of the poignancy of her loss but because of their growing intimacy (53).

These stories lead to a paradigm shift in Everell's thinking: "This new version of an old story reminded him of the man and the lion in the fable. But here it was not merely changing sculptors to give the advantage to one or the other of the artist's subjects; but it was putting the chisel into the hands of truth, and giving it to whom it belonged" (53). Everell must hold incommensurable ideas about the Pequot war as he tries to reconcile Magawisca's first-person account and the ways "[h]e had heard this destruction of the original possessors of the soil described" by whites. As the narrator forthrightly describes how Everell learned that the Pequots were burned alive: "'it was a fearful sight to see them thus frying in the fire, and the streams of blood quenching the same, and the horrible scent thereof; but the victory seems a sweet sacrifice, and they [the Puritans] gave the praise thereof to God'" (54). The narrator, like Everell, identifies with Magawisca as she re-members the virtual history of the confrontation engaging the sight and sounds and smells of the massacre.

The dead letters of history are charged with meaning and clarity through Everell's growing intimacy with Magawisca; Sedgwick uses the syntax to collapse past and present versions of this story. Everell has heard these stories orally, whereas nineteenth-century people find it in books ("we find in the history of the times"). Her reference to history books, though, breaks the narrative thrust to remind her readers that Magawisca's version of the war has not been shared or preserved. Sedgwick, referring to her people as "the original possessors of the soil" concretizes their presence in the territory. Yet following the exchange of histories with Magawisca, the narrative gives way to instability, enacting how the dominant culture's point of view can skew one's perception of marginalized others. Gould outlines the "epistemological traps" Sedgwick lays in her framing of scenes and in the omission of others in the second half of the novel (Gould 110). He maintains, "The text's narrative gaps and chronological ruptures consistently frustrate readerly cognition of both character and plot. . . . [They] all destabilize the reading process by exposing our own limitations as readers" (Gould 110). Her telling therefore emphasizes the epistemic confusion which settlers faced before their experiences were fully understood or put into totalizing narratives.

Sedgwick, like Magawisca, tries to draw readers in while acknowledging the atrocities of the Puritans. She looks plainly at them and acknowledges they killed Quakers, or women "as witches, innocent, unoffending old women!" (16). She does not turn a blind eye to slavery either, as she concedes she might want to erase that mark of the past: "I blush to say it . . . [some Indians] were sent into slavery in the West Indies" (20). There remains a dark undercurrent to the book. When the elderly woman looks on the Fletcher baby, she remarks that it would be better if he were dead: "[T]his world is all a rough place—all sharp stones, and deep waters, and black clouds" (36). Her book does not perpetuate American exceptionalism but highlights the mistakes, catastrophes, and transgressions upon which the colonies were forged.

Hope Leslie recasts the story of settlement by offering alternatives to the overemphasis on women's role in perpetuating the ideals of replication motherhood. Against the tide of the press, historians, or literati who shape cultural conceptions, Sedgwick places intersubjective exchange among diverse peoples as fostering new insights into the past. She aids in opening up the different points of view that circulated in the lead up to Andrew Jackson's removal acts. Nina Baym's reminder in 2006 about the contingencies involved in narratives about Manifest Destiny helps articulate the contribution of Sedgwick's text. Baym writes, "In some sense, the nation may have 'congealed' under Manifest Destiny in the 1850s, but at the same time, tremendous debates and conflicts—expressed through competing narratives—marked every step of the way west throughout the century and, indeed, on into our own time" ("Old West" 825). In *Hope Leslie,* we retrace some of those contentious "steps of the way west" through the virtual history it puts forth.

4

The

LIMITS OF
THE IMAGINARY

in the

RECONSTRUCTED US

in

LYDIA MARIA CHILD'S
Romance of the Republic

AS THE UNITED STATES EXPANDED WESTWARD, GATHERING MORE people under its jurisdiction, writers tried out different stories to incorporate new peoples and geographies into the cultural imaginary. Among them, Lydia Maria Child relied on the form of the novel to accommodate the changing criteria for citizenship. Child's writings fit well with the authors discussed as she, like Sansay and Sedgwick, told stories that sought to define a distinct American peoplehood. In particular, her novel *Hobomok* (1824) with its frank depiction of the fraught relations and outright violence between English settlers and indigenous peoples draws upon a similar premise as Sedgwick's *Hope Leslie*. As explained in the introduction, *Hobomok* portrays an indigenous man who marries and fathers a child with a Puritan woman. Still, the novel concludes with Hobomok's withdrawal and his wife Mary marrying her original Anglo suitor, Charles Brown. *Hobomok* participates in mourning indigenous culture as part of the nation's past. Its currency lies in the hauntings of settlement so richly examined by literary scholars for several decades. Other critics, like Gretchen Murphy, though, interpret the text as operating at cross-purposes, as though the text promotes nascent American imperialism. Murphy reads *Hobomok* as enabling a transition between a British and an American identity in the first decades of the republic. She "suggests that the [*Hobomok*]'s valorization of domestic authority and its identification of 'the Indian' with privileged feminine positions contribute to, rather than counter, the novel's fantasy of New World empire" (*Hemispheric* 52). Instead of *Hobomok*, I examine a less widely taught novel by Child whose very title testifies to the ambition she had for the story to refract the United States, *A Romance of the Republic* (1867), to understand how it contributes to formations within a "New World empire." Without the element of hauntings, *Romance* might seem less complex or subtle than *Hobomok*, less likely to spark critical debate, but it puts forth other assemblages of people elided elsewhere.

Published forty-three years after *Hobomok*, *Romance* serves as a vehicle for Child to advocate for marriages between people of different ethnicities and races. *Romance* concerns the joint descendants of white men and Black women and how recognizing the parentage of people who lived under the "peculiar institution" will alter the future course of US policies. The final chapter of the text portrays two American girls flaunting their fluency in German, the first language of their immigrant father, while the girls' mother and aunt talk about their tendency to use Spanish and French terms of endearments. Their cultural amalgamation seems to define familial relations as they exclaim, "What a polyglot family we are!" (432). Moreover, the family expresses relief that they need not fear genetic diseases: "[N]ations and races have been pretty thoroughly mixed up in this ancestry of our children. What with African and French, Spanish, American, and German, I think the dangers of too close relationship are safely diminished" (432). Her text celebrates mixed ancestry because it advances the vibrancy and strength of the nation: there is no threat of biological problems that "too close relationship" might entail. Embracing racial heterogeneity clearly differentiates Child's work from contemporary nineteenth-century discourses that imply a single, homogenous identity for Americans. Like Child, Frank Webb advocated to incorporate African American families into the body politic in his novel *The Garies and Their Friends* (1857). His novel follows a white southern planter in antebellum Georgia who moves his Black wife and children to Philadelphia, where they can live under the protection of the law. Yet, in contrast to Child,

Webb's novel seemingly advocates against amalgamation by having the family torn apart by the prejudice they confront in the North.

A brief sketch of the *Romance* will make the stakes involved clearer. Child's novel weaves together characters from the North and South in a sordid family romance. The villain is a white man named Gerald Fitzgerald who under slavery takes two wives—one of whom under the law is considered a slave and the other one free—and who fathers a son by each. Gerald marries the octoroon (legally his "slave") Rosa Royal after her father's death leaves her vulnerable to public auction. Gerald buys Rosa and her sister to forestall their sale, but his marriage to Rosa has no legality in Georgia where he takes her. After some time, Gerald legally marries another woman, Lily Bell, a rich, Northern, white woman. Lily never learns about her husband's other wife until after his death, in part because he had no legal obligation to inform her. Meanwhile, Rosa discovers her husband's other wife after sneaking away from the small cottage where he keeps her hidden. Rosa succumbs to a nervous breakdown after discovering Gerald's bigamy. Friends plot to help her run away, but, before she escapes, she switches her infant son with Lily's. Child does not reveal the secret of swapped babies until late in the text. Rosa confesses that she suffered from temporary insanity, and, because she believed Lily's son died soon after, she failed to alert anyone to her act. The plot of switched half-brothers allows Child to highlight how physical attributes fail to signal racial classification, since Rosa's biological son (under the law, property of Gerald Fitzgerald) grows up in Boston society as the spoiled white grandson of the racist merchant Mr. Bell, Lily's father. At the end of the text, Rosa and her new husband offer recompense to Lily's biological son since he would have inherited his grandfather's wealth if Rosa had not pretended to be his mother. Meanwhile, Rosa's and her sister Flora's children, despite their various ethnic and racial heritages, conclude the novel reflecting on how they form a microcosm of a diverse United States.

The "polyglot" American family, for Child, sets the terms for the ways in which the United States imagines its cohesive, if diverse, people. *Romance* appears in print after the ratification of the Thirteenth Amendment but before the passage of the Fourteenth Amendment and the start of a new phase of Congressional Reconstruction. Political scientist Catherine Holland argues that the passage of the Reconstruction amendments led the nation to reconceive of its body politic.[1] Prior to the passage of the Thirteenth, Fourteenth, and Fifteenth amendments, the Constitution's language implies a vague aggregate of peoples. These mid-nineteenth-century amendments, however, mention gender ("men"), race, and color.[2] Holland maintains that they ushered in a "shift in American languages of citizenship" (97). She points out that the passage of the amendments changed how the US perceived the body politic, because "[t]he Amendments made the body visible, and they recast its meaning: once a figure of the suppressed past of political life, the raced and gendered body became a symbol of its future" (99); nonetheless, these amendments continued to suppress the "past." Holland bases her thesis on court cases because "gauging shifts in the political imagination of a nation is a tricky business, and especially so when there are few definitive texts that can serve as conceptual or intellectual compasses of the era" (102–3). Child's novel is one such "compass," as are the other texts discussed in the previous chapters, because it makes the body visible, not relegating it to the US past but portraying it as part of the ongoing American project shaping the political imagination.

RACE, THE NATION, AND GEOPOLITICS

The racialization that subtends liberalism in the United States can seem an aberration rather than rooted in its basic premises. Child's text, though, reveals how marriage serves as a cover for denying individual rights, because accepting interracial marriage will be tied to accepting the expansion of rights. As political philosopher Charles Mills, writing in the *PMLA*, explains, "the centrality of racial subordination to the creation of the modern world . . . has to be retroactively edited out of national (and Western) memory because of its contradiction of the overarching contract myth that the impartial state was consensually created by reciprocally respecting rights-bearing persons" (1388). Yet, more importantly for Child's purposes, these amendments, despite a new emphasis on bodily markers of identity, do not mention marriage. By omitting marriage and relegating it to the private realm, and to the states and courts, the Constitution left women unprotected. The family served as a highly regulated site for rights before and after the passage of the Reconstruction amendments, though one that remained seemingly relegated to the private realm. As Michael Warner explains, "As long as people marry, the state will continue to regulate the sexual lives of those who do not marry" (*Trouble* 96).

Indeed, Supreme Court jurisprudence on marriage focuses on the language of the amendments and the Congressional debate that led to their passage; it has concluded that these amendments cannot be used as a guide to determine the legality of interracial marriage. In *Brown v. Board of Education*, the Warren Court stated that regarding segregation the Reconstruction amendments "are inconclusive. The most avid proponents of the post-[Civil] War Amendments undoubtedly intended them to remove all legal distinctions among 'all persons born or naturalized in the United States.' Their opponents, just as certainly, were antagonistic to both the letter and the spirit of the Amendments, and wished them to have the most limited effect." Both proponents and antagonists purposefully kept vague the amendments that gave equal protection to African Americans. The Warren Court in *Loving v. Virginia*, a ruling that overturned Virginia's ban against interracial marriage in 1967, cited this passage from *Brown v. Board of Education* to reiterate how the framers of the Reconstruction amendments seemingly evaded their responsibility to settle questions of segregation, and ultimately interracial marriage, while allowing individual states to create laws that infringed on rights to marry.[3]

If Catharine Maria Sedgwick hints toward but then withdraws the imagined, recuperative union between indigenous peoples and the English in marriage in *Hope Leslie*, then Lydia Maria Child, her contemporary, proves much less recalcitrant in engaging with the long history of sexual desire, intimacy, and transgression between African Americans and whites prior to the Civil War in *Romance*.[4] Child latches onto the possibility of the consensual crossing of ethnosexual boundaries in *Romance* to reconstruct the Union in the aftermath of the war. This novel, in contrast to the other texts examined in the previous chapters, overtly aligns its characters' fates with the nation's. Despite the characters forays to Europe and the text's brief nods toward marginal sites (New Orleans, rural Georgia, and Florida) the main action is set in Boston. It establishes the United States as a bounded nation after the Civil War by simultaneously forging a coherent conception of an American peoplehood and using that concept to advocate for the acceptance of interracial marriage. Europe is portrayed as a liminal space. Sites outside the United States are usually described as destinations for people trying to escape national problems disguised as personal ones. When one upper-class character travels abroad to shake off his attraction to a mixed-race American woman, his friends lament that he lacks a musical hobby to sooth his disappointment in love: "'Yes,' responded Mrs. Delano, 'it might have saved him the trouble of going to Arabia Petraea or Damascus, in search of something new'" (Child 294). The United States, however, comes across as firmly entrenched in the "real," and oppressed others, Rosa and Flora whose father "owned" their mother, rather than haunting the margins of the text, take to the center. Perhaps with so much else in flux—desire, race, social class, and family ties—the nation-state, as imagined in Child's text, must take on an essentialized insularity. As Laura Bieger, Ramón Saldívar, and Johannes Voelz maintain, "the imaginary" can serve "as a spatiotemporal agent of fixity and institutionalization" (Bieger et al. xix), for Child forthrightly positions her text as contributing to a national literature in the hopes of shaping the "public mind."[5] *Romance* hardens conceptions of the borders of the nation-state and thus, unlike other nineteenth-century texts, it does not obscure the ways in which racialized politics in the United States were an outgrowth of its imperial ambitions. Instead, Child advances heterogeneity as a strength for the United States to advance itself geopolitically.

Over the course of her narrative, Child exposes the secret familial history that prevailed under institutionalized slavery in the United States; if revealed, she believed this hidden side to the American family would challenge legal barriers to racial equality. Although the novel failed to galvanize readers into supporting interracial marriage, as Child sought to do, the text gives current-day readers a glimpse into the transitional period between the end of the Civil War and the start of Congressional Reconstruction. Her text allows readers to witness the process by which competing ideologies framed an understanding of racial difference in the mid-nineteenth-century United States, even if an anti-miscegenation stance eventually prevailed, despite the passage of the Thirteenth and Fourteenth Amendments, amendments that ended slavery and gave African Americans equal protection under the Constitution.[6] Moreover, the text traces how the transnational is eclipsed in literature by a portrayal of the nation-state as the foundation for identity.

As such, it serves as a counterpoint to arguments about imperialism and American literature. Gretchen Murphy identifies the problem with linking identity to national belonging in texts by late nineteenth-century US writers: "The tension comes from thinking globally about race on multiple levels. Telling the story of world politics often gives recourse to the clumsy, homogenizing logic that reifies nation states" (*Shadowing* 9). However, Child avoids this stance by emphasizing US heterogeneity as a sign of geopolitical power. Jonathan Elmer has argued against mistaking individual versus state sovereignty by drawing upon the intersection of race and imperial power in British and American literature. He maintains that authors as different as Aphra Behn and Herman Melville, among others, create exceptional characters, like Oroonoko or Babo in "Benito Cereno," who "are attempts to imagine the mystery of autonomy; they are figures who bear the meaning of social collectivity in their very isolation, somehow both mortal like the rest of us and yet able to enter a zone of quasi-immortality" (10). However, Child, in contrast to the examples that Elmer cites, creates a network of characters through whom autonomy is a force that requires mutual recognition. She also undercuts the trope of the "quasi-immortal" status of racialized figures by making a frank case for the restitution and reparations for slavery in post-Civil War United States.

Rather than consigning the racialized other to death, Child considers how to recoup moral *and* financial obligations for the exploited or marginalized Other. Mark Rifkin suggests, "The insistence, then and now, on inherent coherence and contiguity of national geography suggests the political pressure coalesced around the image of unbroken unity within American borders" (*Manifesting* 5). For Child, this mutual recognition among characters hinges on understanding the United States in a global framework as the characters transverse the different worlds of New Orleans, a Georgia plantation, Europe, and Boston. In contrast to Elmer and Rifkin, Amy Kaplan considers imperialism "a network of power relations that changes over space and time and is riddled with instability, ambiguity, and disorder, rather than as a monolithic system of domination," to "emphasize the collapse of boundaries between here and there, between inside and outside, and the incoherence as much as coherence that the anarchy of empire brings to the makings of the U.S. culture" (Kaplan, *Anarchy* 14–15). Using Child's *Romance of the Republic* to enter this debate bears out Kaplan's take because the law and the boundaries it stretches creates an incoherence that counters the homogeneity of European states.

The novel, then, paints a homogenous sense of US national identity despite the heterogeneity of its inhabitants. The text raises a number of ghosts and hauntings only to deconstruct that figuration for moving forward after the Civil War. Instead, Child associates Europe with art and hauntings, like Bellini's opera *Norma* that Rosa performs under the name La Señiorita Rosita Campeneo, whose very story represents ghosts. "Ghosting" the past, rather than confronting injustice or recentering marginalized others, proves unsustainable once back in the United States. In Europe, Rosa's performance of *Norma*, does not lead to revelation; instead, it gives rise to a number of defense mechanisms, such as when Gerald Fitzgerald, the white man who married and then abandoned her to slavery, responds to her performance by shrinking back, and the audience insists on interpreting her expression of anguish as "inimitable acting" and "a remarkable inspiration of theatrical genius" (231). Child unveils the secrets of the slaveholders to move past the haunting of the United States and displace them onto the Old World. Instead of ghosts, she offers a new conception of US peoplehood as constituted by its multiethnic heterogeneity. She suggests that this heterogeneity, as the nation gathers together people from the West Indies, Africa, and Europe, will propel the US geopolitically. Race, as she illustrates in her scenes in Europe, remains "suspended" outside the border of the United States. Within its borders, Child's text promulgates the US people's diversity as way to propel it to international dominance. Murphy, examining late nineteenth-century imperial rhetoric in US culture, notes some nonwhite writers "alte[r] the racial scripts of empire by revealing the U.S. national mission for global power and leadership to be, instead of white, potentially multiracial" (*Shadowing* 2). Child both anticipates this gesture while laying out challenges to its fulfillment. *Romance* reveals the lived experience of persons that other texts render ghosts. Nonetheless, she portrays how unfettered, unscrupulous capitalism works against establishing a multiethnic plurality. Instead, it leads to the theft and hoarding of wealth. The power whiteness confers proves all-consuming when paired with capitalism. What Child gets right are the ways in which capital and the nation-state exist in tension rather than reinforce each other. To evade a self-consuming capitalistic logic, the text touches upon the republic's heterogeneity and its cosmopolitan elements. However, modes of belonging rooted in heterogeneity form no organizing principle within capitalism.

THE POLITICS OF READING
IN THE POST-CIVIL WAR US

A Romance of the Republic cuts across racial and ethnic lines to topple the dominance of race to structure social hierarchies. However, the text represents how difficult that work will be through the character of Lily Bell, the privileged white Northern woman whose "averted gaze" maintains power hierarchies based on race and class even after the Civil War. As Laura Wexler describes, "the 'averted gaze' of domestic sentiment functioned to normalize and inscribe raced and classed relations of dominance during slavery and to reinscribe them after its legal end" (6). Lily Bell's intractability represents how the flows of capital will not stop to mourn or provide recompense for past injustice. She proves a terrifying figure as she makes explicit how even imperial ambitions that drive capital into markets abroad have no investment in national belonging. Capital will rely upon the nation-state to encroach into new markets but is not beholden to it.

Critical attention on the novel has focused on tracing Child's racialized thinking to demarcate the extent of her progressivism and its limitations, especially as it reveals what critics deem her privileging of white, middle-class American values. Even though scholars celebrate Child for her work as an abolitionist and defender of women's and children's rights, some, like Carolyn Karcher, argue that the book "merely provides a means of gradually absorbing people of color into the white middle-class mainstream" ("Abolitionist's Vision" 83). Karcher's view dominates the scholarship on *Romance* because, it seems as though, "[t]hrough intermarriage, [Child] imagined, race itself could be erased, and with it racial prejudice" (*First Woman* 512).[7] The metaphor of "erasing," though, fits uneasily the text's treatment of race. On the contrary, the text calls for an acknowledgement of slavery's most private practices to expose the ignorance of prejudice and to seek financial restitutions for slavery's victims. For Child, the elusiveness of racial identity and at times its stark overdetermination will require a frank appraisal of American life during Reconstruction, one that she puts at the forefront of the US imaginary with her novel. Yet the text then seems literally "haunted by empire," to twist Ann Laura Stoler's phrasing ("Intimidations" xiii) even as it presents itself as unghosting the American past. The "white middle-class mainstream" that Karcher identifies is vaunted in the text not because of its racial purity but because it offers a solid basis from which the US can compete better against other nations. For Child, that "white middle-class" is more formidable because, despite appearances, it is not white but more heterogeneous or, as she puts it, "thoroughly mixed up" (432)

Child attempts to dispel the anxiety that racial and ethnic difference inspires in the US body politic by using the form of the novel to foster a reader's identification with sympathetic characters. While the genres of secret histories and sentimental novels forge an affective unidirectional bond between text and reader, *Romance* exposes this bond as tenuous and temporary and, ultimately, incapable of suturing a democratic republic. In an imagined community, one cannot know everyone. Therefore, rights must precede intimacy. Despite Child's efforts to use literature to change people's attitudes to encompass a more progressive ideal of inclusion, her text challenges the mode of the novel as a viable form for social progressivism following the Civil War. My reading of Child's novel draws from the ideas of political philosopher Charles Mills. Mills advocates an understanding of liberalism as fundamentally racialized: "Liberalism, I suggest, has historically been predominantly a racial liberalism . . . in which conceptions of personhood and resulting schedules of rights, duties, and government responsibilities have all been racialized" (1381). While political philosophy often ignores the racialized thinking that underscores liberalism, Child's 1867 novel reveals these fault lines. By adopting Child's point of view, readers would alter how the United States conceptualizes the expansion of legal rights in the nineteenth century. As Mills attests, "making racial sociopolitical oppression methodologically central would put us on very different theoretical terrain from the start" (1387). Child's text reasserts how marriage as a public means of regulating private choice (or what is perceived as private choice) allows the US legislatures to institute racism without necessarily calling attention to its discriminatory practices.

The lore surrounding the creation of *Romance*, Child's second and last novel, comes from a letter she wrote to a friend a few months prior to starting her interracial love story. Child, a well-known abolitionist and reformer who had already published a long list of nonfiction works, explains why she chose the form of a novel for combating race prejudice following the Civil War: "I wanted to do something that would undermine *prejudice*, and there is such a universal passion for novels, that more can be done in that way, than by the ablest arguments and the most serious exhortations."[8] In the statement, Child confesses to exploiting the "passion for novels" among readers because she guesses that readers' novelistic investment will override their racial prejudices. At this point in her career, Child had already published several works of short fiction that considered interracial love affairs. In *Romance*, she hopes that this "universal" predilection for novel reading will diminish race prejudice in the US. According to the logic of her statement, novel reading already binds the country; therefore, if the novel portrays the newly freed population, then white readers will identify with Black characters and come to accept them as part of the nation. Argumentation or rationalizations, she maintains, will not produce the same solution.

Contrary to Child's aims and despite positive reviews, *Romance* did not capture the national imagination.[9] Throughout the late 1860s, legislatures instituted strong "anti-miscegenation" language into state constitutions to circumvent interracial marriages. *Romance* failed to move public opinion like *Uncle Tom's Cabin* (1851) did (a book to which it was favorably compared in contemporary book reviews). While *Uncle Tom's Cabin* reinforced white hegemony, *Romance* unsettled the foundations of the US as a white nation. Yet Stowe's book, published in 1851, advocates against the Fugitive Slave Law and seeks to end slavery. By the time Child publishes her novel in 1867, a whole new calculus of race emerges as the nation acclimates a new population of freed people while still reeling economically and politically from a drawn-out war. Nonetheless, *Romance* occupies a unique vantage point of a failed national narrative and highlights the competing ideologies for understanding difference in the mid-nineteenth-century US.

Around the same time, Rebecca Harding Davis published *Waiting for the Verdict* (1868), a tale about the possibility of accepting interracial marriage after the Civil War. Yet her novel repeatedly draws upon fixed notions of race even if her text does question the motivations behind proscribing intermarriage. Her character Dr. Broderip, who hides his status as a formerly enslaved person, feels an immediate sense of "kinship and brotherhood" with other African Americans (295). Race, in Davis's work, continues to hold essentializing power over one's "instincts" and responsiveness to others. The novel reveals unease with the idea of amalgamation, whereas Child advocates for intermarriage by firmly situating it as an ongoing practice in the United States long before the Civil War and by undercutting the fixity of race. As William Andrews explains, "In response to America's fear of the mulatto as a racial subversive, much post-Civil War race fiction placed mulattoes in situations in which assimilation into white society is possible but is high-mindedly refused" (308.) In contrast, Child thrusts her characters into genteel Boston society.

Narrative constructs surrounding the integration of the newly freed citizens would have enduring consequences. Historians note how Black sexuality was encoded after the Civil War in ways that have dominated the American imagination since. Just as slavery reinforced white power, sexual taboos allowed whites to maintain systems of power. Hodes explains, "The idea of manhood, which had long implied the rights and responsibilities of citizenship in American political thought, now took on connotations, in white minds, of black male sexual agency, and specifically of sexual transgressions with white women" (404). Anxiety about sexual transgressions obscured larger economic and political concerns: "[F]or the first time, black men possessed political power, as well as opportunities for greater economic and social power. White Southerners thus conflated those powers with a newly alarmist ideology about black male sexuality. Armed with such an ideology, they hoped to halt the disintegration of their racial caste system" (Hodes 415). By launching a full attack against the idea of interracial marriage, white stakeholders restricted African American political power under the guise of regulating familial ties rather than property rights. This indirect regulation of property through the regulation of marriage obscures the way racialized thinking forms the very basis of rights, as Charles Mills argues.[10] As Eva Saks notes, "Miscegenation law responded in varied ways to the assault on white property represented by the abolition movement and, later, the Civil War Amendments. On the political level, states passed stricter miscegenation statutes during Reconstruction" (67). While civil rights entrenched itself in calls for voting rights, full citizenship, and desegregation, historian Peggy Pascoe observes that "this very inattention to interracial marriage is an indication of how thoroughly and effectively the concept of 'miscegenation' was woven into the fabric of American law and society" (1). Rather than a site where individuals express an individual preference, marriage serves various functions for the state. Pascoe explains how "[t]he many functions of marriage—the gendered molding of husbands and wives, the containment of sexuality, the raising of children, the linking of the private family to the political and economic figure of the male householder, the orderly handing down of property from generation to generation—made it an institution of singular importance to the state" (Pascoe 23). Marriage proved useful for attenuating rights of Black Americans. This was made manifest in state antiamalgamation laws and then in prohibitions in the South against couples held in slavery from marrying. As Hendrik Hartog explains, "By marriage, a host of property rights, obligations, losses, gains, immunities, exemptions, remedies, and duties came into one's life. . . . And the sharp boundary between marriage and nonmarriage was everywhere in the law" (93). By simply placing marriage off-limits, enslaved people and later emancipated ones were silently stripped of access to other legal rights and protections.

Twenty-first-century debates for and against marriage equality articulate some of the stakes involved in the state's regulation of marriage rights in the nineteenth century. Warner explains how "[m]arriage sanctifies some couples at the expense of others. It is selective legitimacy" (*Trouble* 82). Because marriage also serves to regulate sexuality, those outside its sphere of legitimation, such as mixed-race couples in the nineteenth century, internalize a sense of shame. Warner also highlights how privileged white people depend upon others' exclusion from marriage to legitimate their own. Although Warner, writing in 1999, refers to heterosexual married couples, I am applying his logic to white, upper-class women in the nineteenth century, like the character Lily Bell in *Romance:* "They need some token, however magical, of superiority" in their access to marriage that excludes others like Rosa (*Trouble* 82).

The relation between civil rights and sexuality seems most pointed when advocates for equality were accused of secretly desiring more sexual partners. Elise Lemire writes at length about stories ridiculing the motives of abolitionists such as a scheme to force intermarriage between unwilling participants.[11] As Lemire succinctly writes, "[I]nter-racial sex is here again the dangerous outcome of liberal democracy" (18). Sexuality in Child, however, serves as the site where liberation is possible. Heteronormative desire fosters not only social and economic viability but also political participation. While slaveowners' argument that racial equality is really a Trojan horse for intermarriage remains baseless, it points to an underlying premise that links marriage rights to economic and social equality.

IMAGINARIES
OF BELONGING

Since the reemergence of *Romance* in the late 1990s, scholars have interrogated Child's vaunted egalitarianism. Critics such as Debra Rosenthal, Karsten Piep, and Kimberly Snyder Manganelli lament that in her portrayal of her two main characters, Rosa and Flora, whose father was a white man from New England and whose mother was descended from a love match between a Spanish gentleman and a woman held in slavery from the French West Indies, Child fails to evoke, either through phenotype or culture practices, an African American heritage for the characters. Moreover, critics reject the standard *topos* of the "tragic mulatto" that Child participates in and perpetuates. In contrast, Eve Raimon defends Child's use of the "tragic mulatto" figure—a literary device frequently criticized for narrowly portraying Black American experience.[12] She states, for Child, "her subject matter, plot, and characters were devised to appeal to a large readership and to effect in them a moral and spiritual conversion" (41). Julie Cary Nerad, likewise, offers a probing analysis of the critical response to Black characters "passing" as white in American literature, particularly in Child's novel, by delineating how critics reessentialize racial categories by expecting fictional characters who are of mixed-race heritage to exhibit an essential blackness. She asks readers to reexamine the ways in which "[s]cholars who criticize Child for making Rosa and Flora too white, reveal more about our current expectations of racial identity and behavior than about Child's weakness as a defender of racial equality" (Nerad 836). On the whole, though, critics lament Child's tendency to "erase" markers of racial difference. Yet that failing provides insight into her conception of race. Rather than depict race as an essential category of identity, Child depicts perceived race as a matter of political standing; therefore, proclaiming or hiding one's ancestry becomes a way of avoiding or embracing the ways in which socioeconomic ideology codifies one's rights. Child seizes on an opportunity to reimagine race once chattel slavery no longer serves to govern relationships among races, and once freed peoples have the opportunity to assess their complex racial heritage.

Indeed, Child seems to argue that people of mixed racial heritage are already part of mainstream culture and that any "white" mainstream is a fiction that the country seeks to maintain to its detriment; it requires an expenditure of energy not equal to the financial costs. While Child frames race as an unstable political category—the characters do not seem to struggle with race as an identity but rather as a modality of political standing that confers or defers certain rights—she also seems to foreshadow the danger of treating racial intermarriage as a matter for toleration or circumspection rather than a legal right. In fact, the text portrays race-based discrimination and prejudice as thoroughly immersed in the social and state order and marriage as the vehicle through which to maintain power hierarchies.[13]

In Child's novel, reasons for marrying oscillate between pursuing familial (and by extension race) interests and reinforcing often-inexplicable attraction. Whether attraction involves relationships between characters or between readers and characters, these relationships prove tenuous. One must find firmer ground principally through the rule of law. If bigots are able to marshal the rule of law, then proponents of equality need to challenge them in the courtroom or show their invalidity. Even if race, for Child's main characters, functions as a matter of choice rather than an immutable category of identity, the country cannot function as though one's tolerance for race is, likewise, a matter of personal preference. Toleration, as Wendy Brown states in *Regulating Aversion,* marks the powerful (those who tolerate) and the subordinate (those tolerated). "Passing" is never an individual choice but often is conferred as an option through a number of factors largely outside an individual's control: physical characteristics, social class, and the material conditions of the individuals involved. Therefore, for Child, interracial marriage becomes the site, par excellence, for working through these national problems, because it shows how the choice of a marriage partner is filtered through family, the local community, and above all, the state. Scholars continue to fetishize the racialized thinking that the novel works to problematize. Child, however, rather than reinforcing white, middle-class values, exposes them as insidiously supporting a segregated social system for marriage. Marriage functions under the guise of personal preference, while serving to determine property rights and social standing. *Race* may be an unstable marker of identity; *marital status* when contracted through the state is not. While Child, at times, deploys the novel to prompt readers to identify with her fictional characters in order to overturn widespread and institutionalized racism following a long, bloody, and bitter Civil War, the text serves as a warning against using affective solutions to resolve national problems. Child seemingly commits what Brown terms "depoliticization" or the tendency to "substitute[e] emotional and personal vocabularies for political ones in formulating *solutions* to political problems" (16). Although Child deploys the form of the novel and attempts to manipulate the reader's empathetic identification with the main characters Rosa and her sister Flora, the text complicates any such reading by outlining the limitations to that vision.

The first part of the text compounds secrets as Gerald Fitzgerald accumulates wives and his first wife switches her baby with his white wife's baby, but as the narrative moves into the Civil War, the secrets emerge among the family, if not the larger public. After the two boys who have grown up under mistaken identities and Gerald Fitzgerald dies, Lily Bell, Gerald's widow, must learn the truth regarding the boys' identities. While secret, the relationship that binds Lily and Rosa, leaves everyone at risk of social infractions: the boy, Gerald, lusts for his biological mother Rosa; Lily idolizes her husband's secret wife while trying to attach her son to his biological sister; Rosa's new husband is ready to take his family away to Europe to halt the fascination between biological mother and son, thinking it is the start of an extramarital affair. Yet their true relations leave the characters equally on unsure footing. Furthermore, the revelation that Gerald is Rosa's son and therefore part Black (one-sixteenth) means that Gerald is not the legal heir of his maternal grandfather, and it means that Lily's white son has been consigned to a life of slavery. Lily may have been the legitimate wife of Gerald Fitzgerald, but she was in fact his second and concurrent wife.

Lily Bell operates as the model reader that Child's text invites into its world and then admonishes. Lily finds herself fascinated by the seemingly white Rosa. This plot device adds credibility to critics who suspect the sentimental tragic mulatto draws in white women readers to her plight, especially since the mulatto's status, as victim, does not threaten the power white readers hold. Child's depiction of Lily's response to Rosa troubles this standard *topos* because the mulatto Rosa overcomes her victimization and leaves Lily reeling when she confesses to stealing Lily's child and informing her that Lily has raised Rosa's son. Once affective identification leads to direct infringement on Lily's life and family history, Lily's fascination with Rosa dissipates. Even though Child wants to entice readers through *Romance* in order to inculcate a more tolerant attitude toward intermarriage, she provides insecure ground on which to effect social change. Repeatedly, attraction gives way to indifference and contempt. Moreover, one cannot alter the body politic of the United States by relying on sympathy. Rather, one needs a more stable standard for conferring rights. As Lauren Berlant puts forth, "The displacement of politics to the realm of feeling both opens a scene for the analysis of the operations of injustice in lived democracy and shows the obstacles to social change that emerge when politics becomes privatized" (*Cruel* xii). Indeed, Child lures in the sentimental reader, but that reader must move beyond affective identification to the realm of politics; likewise, loving an African American does not lead to granting them political efficacy.

White women will be called upon to recompense people formerly held as slaves. Lily learns the truth from the white Northerner Alfred King, who married Rosa. After she hears the complicated history that unites their families, Lily Bell declares, "But we had better not talk any more about it now. I am bewildered and don't know what to think. Only one thing is fixed in my mind: Gerald is *my* son" (363). "Fixed in my mind" is exactly the mindset that Child seeks to undo; for racial prejudice proves fluid, and the characters must work to keep their racialized notions fixed or immovable. The novel highlights the emotional costs to the unveiling of slavery's secrets. It does not gloss over the hard work Reconstruction will require. While Gerald assures his mother that they remain mother and son, when he goes to see Rosa, he addresses her as "'My mother!'" and "she flew into his arms and wept upon his neck" (363). The revelation radically alters the character of the boy, but it hardens the prejudice of the white Lily Bell, who willfully ignores the truth. While many abolitionist texts written in a sentimental vein seek to draw in white Northern women readers, Child instead reveals white women's culpability and cowardice in the face of slavery's true costs.

Child's Story, "The Quadroons"

Child's novel also portrays the unstable foundation of attraction, and the risks it poses to women, without the institutional support or contract of marriage. Attraction can wax and wane, and without marriage the relationships have no legal ground for dissolving. Gerald Fitzgerald tires of Rosa and eventually tires of his legitimate wife Lily Bell, but his contractual obligations to Lily's family force him to bear out his responsibilities to her and their child. While many readers have noted similarities between *Romance* and Child's short story "The Quadroons" (1842) (in fact many consider the story a first draft of the novel), the short story published twenty-five years earlier highlights the dangers of relying on love and desire as a basis for maintaining equity. It encapsulates how the family depends on recognition from the state to maintain some semblance of stability.[14]

Legal marriage, which recognizes the history and ubiquity of interracial coupling, would expand to other rights such as claims of inheritance and property. Limited marriage rights harden the arbitrariness of racial distinctions. At the center of Child's short story "The Quadroons" (1842) is a tragic mulatto woman who cannot marry the white man she loves because of the interdiction against interracial marriages in the state of Georgia. Instead, the heroine Rosalie tells her lover, "Let the church that my mother loved sanction our union, and my own soul will be satisfied, without the protection of the state. If your affections fall from me, I would not, if I could, hold you by a legal fetter" ("Quadroons" 62). The narrator goes further to declare, "It was a marriage sanctioned by Heaven" (62). Yet, as with Gerald Fitzgerald in *Romance*, the husband's influence in the public sphere in the story "The Quadroons" needs to be cemented through marriage to a white woman with a powerful and politically connected father. Without the protection of the state, the husband need not ask Rosalie for a divorce or explain to his new bride that he already has a wife. Meanwhile, Rosalie remains at risk for exploitation because she believes that her love supersedes social conventions. She, for example, does not make any demands of the white man; in fact, she states, "I would not, if I could," reiterating her lack of control. Her capitulation is tied to her sense of self-worth ("I would not . . . hold you by a legal fetter"). While the white man regrets abandoning Rosalie, he realizes that he cannot sever his engagement to the white woman without considerable trouble: "At that moment he would have given worlds to have disengaged himself from [the white] Charlotte; but he had gone so far, that blame, disgrace, and duels with angry relatives, would now attend any effort to obtain his freedom" ("Quadroons" 67–68). The state and social conventions both reinforce his marriage to the white woman and limit his personal choice.

More humiliations follow when Rosalie's daughter, Angelique, finds her legal status as a slave invoked once her "owners" find themselves in financial trouble. In "The Quadroons," as in *Romance*, there is no guarantee of safety in a slave-owner's promises, especially when one faces the threat of a slave-owner's need for financial expediency: "His heirs had lately failed, under circumstances which greatly exasperated their creditors; and in an unlucky hour, they discovered their claim on Angelique's grandchild" ("Quadroons" 73). Subjectivity can never emerge, as slavery always circumscribes autonomy and interpersonal relations. Even though Southerners deemed their economic system a hybrid of feudalism and capitalism, a capitalistic society that demands liquidity reinforces the inhumanity of slaveholding because people held in slavery were viewed as fluid capital. At any moment, a person legally considered a slave, like Angelique, can have her life overturned because of a slave-owner's need for cash, despite whatever love or affection she inspires in white people.

Marriage serves as a rich problematic for Child's purpose, because it, paradoxically, obscures and highlights how familial relations intersect with individual choice and group dynamism. One may choose an individual to marry or even in some cases to adopt into the family, yet that choice reverberates throughout the extended family and community. Marriage functions as an interpersonal *and* social contract. Gerald Fitzgerald violates these contracts when he abandons his "slave" wife Rosa in part because she has no family to protect her or advocate for her. Alfred King who later becomes the adoring husband of Rosa initially rejects his feelings for her because he imagines his mother would object to them. He knows that "My good mother shares the [race] prejudice. How could I introduce them to *her?* Then, as if impatient with himself, he murmured in a vexed tone, 'Why should I think of introducing them to my mother'" (14). Child italicizes "her" to reiterate how attraction is not merely dyadic but involves many other stakeholders. Sexual attraction, thus, remains an unstable basis for rights. Alfred's initial attraction to his wife is undercut and repressed by fears that it would offend his mother if he were to marry a woman with a Black ancestor. Child's depictions warn readers that an individual's control over her children is tenuous: once his mother dies, Alfred feels no impediment to marrying Rosa, despite her racial background and her illegitimate marriage to Gerald Fitzgerald. Instead of appealing to her readers—in this case, white Northerners—she repeatedly demonstrates the illusions that undergird their world.

Capitalism and the Law

When a New England woman, Mrs. Delano, adopts Rosa's sister Flora, she tries to keep her from society because of her racial ancestry. Still, the young girl's beauty inevitably attracts suitors. A Boston gentleman eventually comes to propose marriage to Flora. But when Mrs. Delano tells him that she is an octoroon, he withdraws his proposal and lashes out, "Do you deem it right, Mrs. Delano, to pass such a counterfeit on society" (277). When Mrs. Delano demurs, the suitor responds, "You certainly have a right to choose a daughter for yourself though I could hardly have imagined that any amount of attraction would have overcome such obstacles in the mind of a lady of your

education and refined views of life. Excuse my using the word 'counterfeit'"
(278). These lines bring the many threads of the text together. While the gentleman concedes Mrs. Delano has a "right" to adopt whomever she pleases,
her "choice" and "right" are ironized by the social price he thinks she forces
everyone else to pay. His astonishment does not stem from Flora's secret
identity; instead, he implies that Mrs. Delano's should have been immune to
"attraction" by the institutional prejudices inculcated by her "education."
Mrs. Delano admits that Flora's "beauty and vivacity captivated me before I
knew anything of her origin; and in the same way they have captivated you"
(278). Indeed, the man offers no apologies for rejecting the daughter on the
grounds of race, ancestry, or legal standing; instead, his apology focuses on
his diction. He apologizes for calling Flora a "counterfeit" because it has the
potential to tarnish Mrs. Delano, not because it serves as an inapt description
of Flora as someone who poses as the real currency—a white woman. Still,
Mrs. Delano's "choice" has wide-ranging effects, and eventually she stops
entering society, resigning herself to a small circle of Flora's acquaintance. As
Wendy Brown cautions, "choice can become a critical instrument of domination in liberal capitalist societies; insofar as the fiction of the sovereign subject
blinds us to powers producing that subject, choice both cloaks and potentially
eroticizes the powers it engages" (197). Mrs. Delano's "choice" must not
affect others with whom she associates. Social norms and personal choice
nullify each other to cause negative consequences within the community and
to the individual. In fact, the pejorative term "counterfeit," when white society characterizes the individual with Black ancestry as illegal tender, limits
American ontologies.

Likewise, Child warns that empathy, like attraction, cannot substitute for
legal status. Although Harriet Beecher Stowe's *Uncle Tom's Cabin* repeatedly
stages scenes that imply that equality depends on an immediate, intimate
relation between others—Senator Byrd must meet the runaway Eliza, who
is young, beautiful and white; St. Clair must interact with Uncle Tom to
ameliorate his (and the reader's) racial prejudice,—Child's text reveals the
limits of affective identification. Although family ties may lead to empathy
for a minority or disenfranchised group, it cannot supersede legal status. A
democracy with robust due process rights cannot depend upon the individual
epiphanies of bigots who must experience sympathetic identifications with
others before granting them full rights. In *Romance*, an antislavery sympa-

thizer cautions the capitalistic Mr. Bell for his blasé attitude about the rights of people who ran away from slavery: "If your grandson should be claimed a slave, I rather think you would consider the writ of *habeas corpus* a wise and just provision" (315). The subjunctive case ("if") implies that one accepts federal authority and laws based on how they affect one's family.

Yet Child's text repeatedly warns against such an attitude. Characters sometimes choose to disown family members. By the time Alfred tracks down Mr. Bell's legitimate grandson living in slavery, the old man has died, and the boy's mother refuses to see him. Political equality must withstand the prejudices of ruthless capitalists, even those who are relatives. For these reasons, Child's text illuminates the specters that polite society wishes to conceal. As the capitalist, Mr. Bell complains, "You fanatics, with your useless abstractions about human rights are injuring trade, and endangering the peace of the country" (317). Under liberalism, capitalist enterprise limits the extension of rights to disenfranchised groups.[15] The key word in Bell's rant is "useless," for trade and use-value trump rights. When Lily Bell and her father, a ruthless businessman, fix upon a marriage between her son Gerald and Rosa's daughter, Mr. Bell, the grandfather, announces "Capital match" (347). Later the reader learns that the young people are brother and sister. Child's pun on "capital" suggests that "capital" blindly corrupts when it seeks to forge connections. When Alfred tells Mr. Bell that he himself bear responsibility for returning his own grandson to slavery when he tried to run away in Boston, Mr. Bell declares, "that story might sell for something to a writer of sensational novels" (391). Mr. Bell's association with ruthless capitalistic markets may seem over-the-top, but again Child portrays him as conceptualizing everything in capitalistic terms; for him, the truth "might sell for something" as a sensational novel.

When the state accedes to tendentious interests, it enacts laws that undermine the country. In Child's estimation, the state needs to recognize the lived experience of its citizens. To propound this vision, Child repeatedly undercuts the authority of the Constitution and valorizes the abolitionist principles undergirding Massachusetts's response to slavery. Mr. Bell, who imports goods from the South, declares, "It's a great disgrace to Massachusetts, sir, that she puts so many obstacles in the way of enforcing the laws of the United States" (315). The Constitution becomes an impediment to equality because it preempts thinking about ongoing questions of fairness and equality. Mr. Bell laments that he cannot assert a political will against slavery, because "I stand by the Constitution, . . . I don't presume to be wiser than the framers of that venerable document" (316). Child demonstrates how a written text from the beginning of the republic stultifies thinking. He "stands" by the Constitution, even as he does not read or interpret it. This passage insists that the only way forward after the Civil War is a direct confrontation with the nation's past and a renewed understanding of its founding documents, rather than inert allegiance.[16]

Child's text not only exposes the secret history of the nation in ways that Sansay merely skirts in her *Secret History* of Haiti's Revolution but also rewrites the foundation for its exceptionalism. Rather than situating the American story as one emerging from a city on a hill, she interprets the nation's greatness as linked to its heterogeneity. Alluding to Mme. de Stael, she declares, "It is a seething cauldron, this great nation. There is a great simmering together of Jew and Gentile, Catholic and Protestant, extreme Asiatics, and extreme Westerners, Red, and White, Yellow and Black. What will be the product, God alone knows, but I have faith that it will be good, and that we shall fulfill our mission as 'vanguard of the human race.'"[17] Child may draw upon the rhetoric of a "mission" that America fulfills, but she offers an alternative basis for the roots of its vigor. While she implies that most nation-states are built on networks of blood or trade or wealth, she imagines the US as adapting to the shifting demographics of the state. The simmering of different peoples undercuts the centrality of one's family or blood relations. This tension between loyalty to family members and the advantages of race and ethnic mixing surfaces in Child's early plans for her novel. She believed a literary work could change readers' attitudes about racial prejudice by manipulating their emotional response to fictional characters, and yet her novel calls for further political action, in the form of reparations, based on that emotional response, not just temporary affective identification.

WHITE WOMEN
AS THE VEHICLE FOR REPARATIONS

Reparations, like the ones made to the real Gerald, further erode the tissues that connect the domestic and the imperial, because Alfred can make his overtures without involving anyone to recompense George, such as the state or even Boston society. In using his money to make amends for Rosa's crime against George, Alfred employs a mercantilist policy of ethics. Their family stole his identity and thus his rightful inheritance. To balance their transactions, they make financial amends. Alfred comes across as misguided in part because his way forward still allows Lily Bell to ignore the past. Her refusal to confront the truth, by attuning her eyes forward, employs a capitalist mindset rooted in self-interest, thus she rushes right past questions of equitable exchange. Her mercenary methods outstrip Alfred's feeble attempts to right the ledger books. Despite Child's efforts to seep her characters into the national consciousness when it seemed malleable, Child seems to make the same mistake as Alfred: she ignores how slavery is rooted in capitalism and any model of recompense (either literary or monetary) will be subsumed in by capitalism's other diversionary tactics.

According to Child in "The Quadroons" and *Romance,* miscegenation laws do not prevent interracial relations but instead foster a disavowal of familial responsibility. *Romance* never fully expiates Rosa and Flora's father, who neglects to manumit them during his lifetime. Under slavery's twisted power dynamics, one cannot depend on indolent or well-intentioned individuals. If a husband or father does not feel compelled to protect a loved one, then his relatives have even less motivation. Alfred King is at pains to explain to Mr. Bell how Bell's biological grandson was switched with a "Black" child when he was a baby. The implications mean that Mr. Bell's legitimate heir has been living as a Black man and that the grandson whom he helped raise is the son of a woman who is legally considered a slave. Repeatedly, he tries to stop Alfred from telling him the truth; he interrupts Alfred: "What interest do you suppose I can take in all this? . . . It's nothing to me, sir. The South is competent to make her own laws" (390). Individuals, like wealthy Northerner Mr. Bell, want to avoid the consequences of slaveholding practices and treat them as a matter relegated to geography.

Mr. Bell's main concern centers on the legitimacy of his white daughter's marriage. Alfred explains that the marriage between Gerald and Rosa was illegitimate because in the South one cannot marry a person deemed a slave under the law. Mr. King replies, "I consider such a law a wise provision. . . . It is necessary to prevent the inferior race from being put on an equality with their superiors. . . . You may be an advocate for amalgamation, but I am not" (390). In Mr. Bell's mind, the basis of marriage as an institution that cements equality is unqualified: marriage would put whites and Blacks on equal footing. To keep Mr. Bell's attention, Alfred says, "I would simply ask you to observe that the law you so much approve is not a preventative of amalgamation. . . . The only effect of the law was to deprive her of a legal right to his support and protection, and to prevent her son from receiving any share of his father's property" (390). Again, Child's text highlights the repercussions of antimarriage laws. Yet Alfred asks Mr. Bell to do more than "observe" but confront the true relations among Americans of different races; it is an interest that must go beyond familial connections to strike at the heart of the liberal project of equality undergirded by the US at its founding and repledged after the abolition of slavery through the Thirteenth Amendment. Indeed, when Mr. Bell learns that he bears direct responsibility for the return of a runaway to the South who happens to be his biological grandson, he appears greatly agitated. Mr. Bell, however, reveals the cause of the emotion: "Do you suppose, sir, that a merchant of my standing is going to leave his property to negroes?" (393). While his grandson is legally white, Mr. Bell dismisses this fact because his grandson has married a "mulatto." Slavery has long been understood as consigning the condition of the child to follow that of the mother, but Child's text reveals a more insidious process whereby the condition (slave-status) of one spouse can affect the legal status of the other; the danger in this proposition is *not* that a white person might be unlawfully enslaved but that a nonwhite person might have access to property. Many readers scoff at notions of fetishizing "pure" blood lines, but the anxiety of racial "mixing" usually veils unspoken threats to ownership and inheritance.

The public avowal of interracial relatives under slavery would reveal how individuals of mixed-race parentage have always been a part of American culture. Late in the text, when the characters assemble in a ballroom, the narrator observes that, unbeknownst to them, blood ties crisscross the room, but they remain secret because of slavery's lingering shame. The author notes, "Ah, if all the secret histories and sad memories assembled in a ball-room should be at once revealed, what a judgment night it would be!" (299). The text serves as that judgment and draws attention to the myriad bonds between its fictional characters. These bonds, Child argues, are a living testament to the nation-state that supersedes "dead" documents. But to the characters it makes manifest unappealing financial obligations.

The text flirts with gothic elements in its early chapters, like using the living Rosa to appear on the margins of a white character's perceptual field to produce a ghost-like effect. But Child's language of "sperits" and "spectral" presences dissipates once the past of sham marriages and switched identities are exposed. The secret at the heart of the text is not an unremarked racial ancestry but Rosa's act of switching her baby (born the child of a woman considered a property) with his half-brother (born the child of a rich, white, free mother). It is not her race but Rosa's crime that sets her apart from others and leaves her with a hidden shame. Even as the act of switching the children haunts the text, the act does not completely define Rosa. Rather the characters interpret it as a temporary state of insanity ("savage paroxysm of revenge" [198]) brought about by the mistreatment and cruelty of her first husband. Following this act, Rosa goes to Europe, where she takes on a new identity, as a reclusive opera singer. Child portrays Europe as awash in ghosts that Americans perpetuate by participating in Carnival and by viewing art at night with "torchlight" to increase the spectral effect (213–14). Despite the shadowy atmosphere of Europe, Rosa remains clear-eyed on her purpose: "I wish to earn money fast," she tells Alfred in order to put her crime to right (250). Instead of relying on ghosting in the text, Child makes the phantoms of slavery present, and, to dissipate their power, she has the characters offer them the truth about their parentage and cash. Without that revelation, sexual jealousy seeks to undermine the fabric of an orderly society. It threatens incest and loss of fidelity whereby a sister feels attracted to her (unknown) brother, son is attracted to his (unknown) mother.

The book concentrates on overlapping networks of wealth, family, sexual jealousy, and nationality. These networks place the white, legitimate wife of Gerald Fitzgerald, Lily Bell, a minor character, at its center. The revelations the text unfolds all but crumple the world of Fitzgerald's legitimate wife, intimating the untidy implications of the secret histories that could end up upending the nation. Lily Bell is the white establishment figure who must confront the new political order. Under slavery, she fell captive to the allure of slave figures (Rosa's singing has a mesmeric effect upon her), but eventually she became inured to slavery's abuses. Nothing in her life prepares her for the truth of her husband's conduct or for perceiving the broad institutional structure that enabled it. This white woman has to live through and answer for the injustices that emerge as the nation transitions from slave to free, for her husband, father, and son all die before the end of the Civil War. Child, however, represents and indicts her for cowardice in the face of the secret history that is revealed to her.

Three key conversations mark her invitation into this brave new world of the postbellum social order. The paradigm Lily models for readers demarcates the overlap between private and public realms; Lily negotiates her relationships to absolve herself of any responsibility—socially or financially—for her biological son and his wife. Lily can take this stance because intermarriage becomes a site for tolerance rather than legal recognition. She prefers her child did not have a Black wife; her intolerance of his choice lets her disavow any obligation to them. Wendy Brown in *Regulating Aversion* maintains that toleration involves "the negotiation . . . between what is deemed private or individual choice appropriately beyond the reach of law (hence tolerable) and [what] is deemed a matter of the public interest (hence not a matter of tolerance)" (12). Consigning amalgamation to a matter of tolerance gives Lily unlimited power to thwart the hereditary transfer of property.

With each conversation that the Kings initiate with Lily Bell to atone for Rosa's act of switching the two boys, Lily recedes further away from them. Rosa confesses to Lily Bell as a way to atone, but Lily Bell treats the story as a dispute over property. When Rosa says she does not mean to claim her son Gerald, Lily wonders, "If you don't intend to take him from me, what was the use of telling me this dreadful story?" (361). Lily's fears have some basis, for Gerald does start to confide in Rosa and her husband more than in Lily. Yet her phrasing draws attention to the ways in which she will distance herself from the truth. First, she sees no "use" for the information; a similar mental tic for registering truth in terms of use-value was exhibited by her father. Second, she understands Rosa as imparting "a story" rather than revealing their true relations. Lily sees no reason to provide financially for her husband's biological son even if it turns out, in this case, that it is her biological son as well. Yet Child's text hints that reparations must be paid, even by "innocents" like Lily Bell who disavow any involvement in amalgamation.[18] Lily's refusal to confront the full costs of slavery will mark the next hundred years of US narrative-making about slavery's legacy until the mid-twentieth-century civil rights movements.

The second conversation involves Lily and Alfred, when he informs her that her biological son (now named George) is alive. Raised in slavery, he has married a racially mixed woman. Lily's new family ties point to a US peoplehood that does not correspond to the national imaginary as rooted in a shared white ancestry. As one character explains, "Mr. Bell and Mrs. [Lily] Fitzgerald would prefer to have it all sink into oblivion; but that does not change our duty with regard to the poor fellow" that is the real Gerald (384). Child's text models the kinds of reparation obligated by emancipation. While Alfred tries to include Lily Bell in the decision making about what to do with the real Gerald, she responds with annoyance: "please leave Gerald and me in peace; and do what you choose about the other one. We have had sufficient annoyance already; and I never wish to hear the subject mentioned again" (386). Many texts of the abolitionist era sought to appease the white, female, middle-class reader. Harriet Jacobs is especially sensitive to the prejudices of "ye women of the North," as she calls them in her autobiographical *Incidents in the Life of a Slave Girl* (1861), a text edited by Child. Jacobs is explicit, though, in reminding her anticipated readers that, unlike her, their homes are protected by "law" (54); a woman legally deemed a slave, like Jacobs, has no recourse to law to protect her "home" from the intrusions of her master or to keep her white lover accountable for the promises he makes her.

Child's text, in contrast, grates against white women's sensibility to avoid unpleasant subjects to force them to make a full reckoning with slavery. Child repeatedly portrays Lily Bell as attempting to insulate herself from the difficult truths that the "real" Gerald raises. Although Lily's denial leads her to frame Alfred's actions as a "choice" ("do what you choose about the other one"), she then ignores what is right by law and duty and, to a certain extent, what is just based on her husband's paternal obligation to both sons. Alfred's good graces leave him culpable for enabling Lily's forced repression of the truth. He decides to bear the cost of reparation for Lily's son not only because he feels responsible for his wife's conduct in switching the children but also because he wants to keep the scandal private. Furthermore, Lily continues to use language to distance herself from what she knows. Instead of registering this child as lost, she refers to him as "the other one," as though he will cease to distress her if she refuses to acknowledge his existence.

Child's text depicts the uncomfortable truths that the country must acknowledge. Even though Lily Bell had idolized Alfred and Rosa King, her new intimate connections to them (she and Rosa share a husband and sons) cause her liking to wane: "They had disturbed her relations with Gerald, by suggesting the idea of another claim upon his affections; and they had offended her pride by introducing the vulgar phantom of a slave son to haunt her imagination" (396). Toni Morrison has written eloquently on the way an Africanist presence "haunts" early American literature by providing "the vehicle by which the American self knows itself as not enslaved, but free; not repulsive, but desirable; not helpless, but licensed and powerful; not history-less, but historical; not damned, but innocent; not a blind accident of evolution, but a progressive fulfillment of destiny" (52). As quoted earlier, Ann Laura Stoler echoes this language of haunting to discuss the imbrications of intimacy with imperialism. Child "disturbs" our relations to each other as Americans, revealing how this haunting process sediments little by little for Lily until she employs full repression of the truth by casting another human being (Rosa) as "the idea of another claim," using a commercial term as though a business context frames encounters with people formerly held in slavery. Moreover, she is not so much haunted by the idea that her child was stolen from her; instead, she depicts her anxiety as provoked by the "vulgar." Child, though, unrelentingly advances her claim that slavery is not merely an annoyance, a disagreeable aspect of life, or a "peculiar" Southern institution. For instance, all these characters reside in Boston. Yet Alfred and Rosa's strategy of appeasing Lily at every turn undermines their larger aim of atoning for the larger institutional effects of Rosa's act of identity theft.

Alfred King still seeks to protect his family's secrets and refuses to reveal pertinent information about the past to his children, the next generation. While Lily's pride may be hurt by these phantoms, Child underscores how the people, such as the real Gerald, are left "phantoms" who "haunt" because Alfred and Rosa refuse to acknowledge publicly their relationships to them. In this way, Lily functions as a proxy for the specter of the reader who wants to avert her eyes from the country's past. Child's fantasy of public atonement undercuts her indictment of Lily Bell. Alfred and Rosa are likewise captive to the same feelings of gentility. They prefer their daughter to feel jilted by Gerald rather than tell her that her suitor is her biological half-brother. Likewise, Mrs. Delano's adoption of Rosa's mulatto sister Flora involves hiding Flora's legal status and ushers in Delano's withdrawal from society, even if she offers one mode for white Northern women to take responsibility for economic reparations to people formerly held in bondage. As Jeffory Clymer argues, Mrs. Delano's adoption of Flora hinges on creating a new familial tie to her that will transfer wealth (*Family Money* 110–11). Yet the entire text undercuts the family as a viable unit for transferring wealth.

By the end of Child's novel, the context has altered for all the characters and with this new context they must find new reasons to support their prejudices. The Emancipation Proclamation has ended legalized slavery, and Rosa's biological son Gerald Fitzgerald has died in action in the Civil War. In her third and final discussion with Alfred King, Lily refuses all knowledge and responsibility for her biological son, who is now a free man. It is not his former slave status that makes her renounce him or even that he is Black (for both his parents are white), but his marriage to a mulatto. Lily Bell ends the book refusing to recognize the "real" Gerald: "I shall never recognize any person as a relation who has a colored wife. Much as I love Gerald, I would never have seen him again if he had formed such an alliance; not even if his wife were the most beautiful and accomplished creature that ever walked the earth" (420). Lily's point is absurd since her own husband knowingly took an enslaved woman as a wife. Child calls on readers to reject Lily's attitude. Alfred replies to her, "I think you would soon forget her origin, also, if you were in a country where others did not think of it. I believe our American prejudice against color is one of what Carlyle call the 'phantom dynasties'" (421). Alfred concedes that institutional forces in American culture have affected her and inculcated this prejudice. Nonetheless, he buffers those institutions because he demurs to Lily Bell's fastidiousness regarding the color line. He demurs, "I would gladly adopt [George], and have him live with us; but . . . his having a colored wife would put obstructions in his way entirely beyond our power to remove. But the strongest objection to it is, that such an arrangement would greatly annoy Mrs. Fitzgerald, whose happiness we are bound to consult in every possible way" (416). He fails to see that she objects to marriage more than "color"; furthermore, it is not skin color but marriage rights that lead Alfred's family to take in and educate the real Gerald's (George) mulatto wife, Henriet.

Marriage continues to determine rights even within the individual household where members are keenly aware of equitable treatment. The Black servants in Alfred's house are befuddled by a system wherein they labor but the Black woman Henriet is educated: "When black Chloe saw [Henriet] learning to play on the piano, she was somewhat jealous because the same privilege had not been offered to her children. 'I didn't know Missy Rosy tought thar war sech a mighty difference 'tween black an' brown,' said she. 'I don't see nothin' so drefful pooty in dat ar molasses color'" (419). The key difference between Chloe and Henriet lies in the rights conferred by marriage. Critics focus so much on skin color, especially Henriet's, and appearance that they neglect to account for how much marriage creates its own claims to rights or in some cases creates "obstructions," as Alfred puts it. After the Civil War ends, marriage will be the site where prejudices are maintained or dispelled. While Child embraces the material need for redress, supporting George financially does not seem to require sacrifice, nor does Alfred openly acknowledge his connection to his benefactors.

Child's *Romance* makes visible the ties between marriage rights and full citizenship; it remains a singular example of a text by a major American author in the nineteenth century that attempts to challenge a concerted campaign to stigmatize interracial marriage. For marriage rights dovetail with social and economic issues rather than simply political ones. Beneath this prejudice lie fears about property.[19] Peggy Pascoe notes how laws that forbid marriage between white men and Black women "prevented masters from turning slaves they slept with into respectable wives who might claim freedom, demand citizenship rights, or inherit family property, and so undermined the foundations of racialized slavery" (27). Ultimately, Child's attempt to recast interracial marriage in the American imagination must acknowledge the consequences in the form of the transfer of property if these former relationships are recognized and legitimated in the faith that it will strengthen the US even if it involves short-term loss.

However, Child tries to remedy a social ill using the form of the novel, as though it will forge a new basis for understanding US identify as rooted in robust human rights, regardless of the economic costs. She sought a radical paradigm shift in attitudes toward wealth, race, property, and restitution. After the book was published, Child echoes the same language she used prior to publication in explaining to Robert Purvis, an African American activist, her reason for choosing a romance: "In these days of novel-reading, I thought a Romance would take more hold of the public mind."[20] Yet no matter how much a novel engages an individual's attention, it cannot overcome deeply engrained attitudes about race. The power of her novel seems to derive less from its portrayal of what Jane Tompkins, characterizing nineteenth-century sentimental fiction by women, called "a blueprint for survival under a specific set of political, economic, social, or religious conditionals" (xvii); rather, *Romance* seeks to "take hold" of the mind by seducing the reader into the emotional world of its characters. In other words, it indulges in the cult of sensibility rather than sentimentality.[21] Through the novel, Child sought to, in Karcher's terms, "create the consciousness appropriate for a multi-racial, egalitarian society" (*First Woman* 491). After the book's failure to capture the public's imagination, she stopped writing novels, because she felt "weary of imparting my mind to others, since it is a commodity that nobody wants."[22] Again Child emphasizes the power of the mind, even if it is reified through the act of writing and book selling. From a twenty-first-century perspective, Child comes across as an idealist whose project was doomed to fail. Stowe's *Uncle Tom's Cabin*, in contrast, displaced real solutions into an emotional register. Child, though, sought change through the economic and legal institutions but calls for change stoke rather than dispel racial prejudice; perhaps, the unspoken propagation of a mixed-race nation to advance US imperial ambitions proves too subtle. Still, the text reveals how affective ties are not commensurate with economic ones.

Although her book, which casts new light on past conduct, did not shape a new national narrative, Child exposes social networks that, in her mind, should have eradicated slavery and should have eased the transition into Reconstruction. More important, she traces the ways in which institutions maintain economic power by perpetuating racial prejudice. Travis Foster mentions the gothic sensibility that "Child participates in as a genre that critics and writers have long linked to African American presence" (Foster 16). Foster goes on to mention Richard Wright and Toni Morrison, linking the gothic genre to an "African American presence" in fiction by nineteenth-century American writers, like Poe and Melville. Yet *Romance* puts forth gothic aspects only to debunk this aesthetic as useless for forging a national imaginary that seeks to recognize people as citizens and compensate them with money. But for Child, in contrast to these other writers, the process of unveiling produces aesthetic asymmetries. Moreover, her text showcases how a white character like Lily Bell might prefer a shadowy sensibility, like the one offered by a gothic text, and how she has the power and money to veil her unsavory actions.

Child exposes the currency with which Americans assert their belonging—white skin—as illusory tender.[23] In the end, one risks becoming "an imposter" to oneself, as the character Gerald exclaims when he learns about his true ancestry as the son of a woman who is legally a slave. Slavery has made all citizens counterfeiters, to borrow a term from the text.[24] Through these secret histories, Child forces readers to reckon with a legacy of obscured paternity that has been swept aside rather than properly interrogated, one she tries to position as an asset in a global marketplace. *Romance* drags forth a paradigm of social progressivism at home as a means to shore up the US's global competitiveness, a move that seems familiar within neoliberal politics of the early twenty-first century. Nonetheless, she de-eroticizes these secret histories by pointing readers to consider their implications: financial reparation and uncovered familial connections. No matter how much these revelations disturb genteel society, she suggests that economic, not just political, restoration is in order to reconstitute the United States following the Civil War.

5

MASSACHUSETTS

in the

AMERICAN

IMAGINATION

in

HARRIET JACOBS'S

Incidents in the Life of a Slave Girl

AS A YOUNG WRITER, LYDIA MARIA CHILD CAME TO THE DEFENSE of Catharine Maria Sedgwick to challenge a misimpression about the supposed rivalries among women writers.[1] Later, as an elder among reformist writers, Child came forward to aid new writers, perhaps most famously, Harriet Jacobs, who had written a narrative of her life in slavery and needed the imprimatur of a white writer to authenticate her anonymously published text. Unfortunately, Child's editing of the manuscript and preface for Jacob's work led to confusion about the authorship of *Incidents in the Life of a Slave Girl* (1861). It was not until the 1980s that Jean Fagan Yellin put to rest doubts about Jacobs's authorship and Child's limited role as editor. The circuitous route to publication, though, seems fitting for a text that seems to reach out to readers who do not yet exist. Despite Jacobs's overt addresses to her audience as "ye women of the North," her supposed audience, the text also signals toward other readers, "future generations" (200). In examining Jacobs's text in the final chapter, I break the chronology of my study in part because *Incidents* provides a point of contrast to the other texts as she speaks out on her own behalf and on behalf of other women who are held in bondage. The study concludes with *Incidents* because Jacobs's life writing should be considered not only in terms of its 1861 publication but in terms of its republication in 1987 with her name affixed to it. As Martha Schoolman suggests, because abolitionist writers struggled to be heard within the literary print marketplace of the mid-nineteenth century, they all, she argues, exhibit an "untimeliness" (11).[2] Still, when Saidiya Hartman put forth claims about Jacobs and her future readers, Caleb Smith accuses Hartman of making "unhistoricized" claims about *Incidents*. Smith writes, "But the sense that Jacobs's narrative was an irresistible force, compelling the assent of every reader, seems to be projected onto 1861 from the perspective of a late twentieth-century interpretive community, where Jacobs's critique of the slave system has become a norm" (751). Although Smith proves correct in nudging scholars to discover "transnational, multiracial, and militant movements of [Jacobs's] time" in *Incidents* (763), his criticism of Hartman is not convincing. Hartman is correct to imply that Jacobs's supposed readership proves broader than the white, middle-class women of the North she directly addresses. Instead, her text seems oriented toward future readers who might understand her better than those with whom she lived.

Unlike the other authors studied here, Jacobs writes directly about her personal experience. However, she constructs an imaginary history for herself to antagonize her enslaver, a man named Dr. Flint in the text, with whom she engages in "war." The terms of the war, her book implies, is neither personal nor singular: Dr. Flint might act as her antagonist, but the terms of his and her behavior seem set by the institution of slavery and therefore affect not just her but women within slave territory. Catherine Gallagher, in her study of alternative histories, identifies as a primary feature of counterfactual narratives a tendency to "scale up" or move away from the novel's identification with individual characters to "scale up into larger collectivities, stretching our normal view of what can count as a character" (14). Jacobs, who refers to herself as a mere "Slave Girl" in her title, tells her individual story to refract wide-ranging national stories about women just like her. She understands that Dr. Flint's treatment connects her to countless other women over whom he had power and to other women she will never meet across plantations and households in slaveholding states. Her life writing seeps itself into that "third horizon" of a text, the one oriented toward subsequent generations of readers. To requote Paul Armstrong, "To reduce meaning to 'meaning then' by privileging the contexts governing the moment of production is to rob the situation of writing of its historicity by suppressing its futurity" ("In Defense" 94). Although readers would be hard-pressed to identify Jacobs's life writing as a counterfactual text, the story within the story she weaves for Dr. Flint about her running away creates its own counterfactual trajectories. That story enables her to manipulate him into action that will expend his time, energy, and money and keep her hiding space secure. It also refracts the decisions Jacobs makes in directing the attention of her readers.

Scholarship in book history has raised important questions about the overdetermination of a text's date of first publication. Meredith McGill, writing in *American Literature* in 2016, observes that "[d]espite our disciplinary practice of referring to a text by its year of initial publication—the year in which it first passed from author's manuscript into printed form—the production, distribution, and consumption of a literary work is not simultaneous or immediate, but staggered and mediated" (2). Few texts have such a fraught relationship to their initial publication date as Jacobs's *Incidents*. Jacobs, despite living and working in the household of publishing bigwig and scion N. P. Willis, faced an uphill battle getting her life writing into print. Yellin has reported how Jacobs first sought unsuccessfully to publish her manuscript in England, and then how US publishers required her to have a famous white woman write the preface. And even once she secured publication in the United States, the publishing house went bankrupt before printing it. In the face of setbacks, Jacobs relied on her own ingenuity to make her story public. After the publisher started to fail, she had the American Anti-Slavery Society help fund the typesetting. When production stalled, she bought the plates from the publisher and printed the book herself. She then traveled city to city to sell and promote it (Yellin, *Harriet Jacobs* 144–46). Despite her efforts, her text seems to fade into obscurity and, worse, the authorship of *Incidents* was misattributed to Child, who wrote the preface, even though her preface sought to corroborate that the anonymous author's story was authentic.[3]

While her text fits nicely with late-twentieth-century disciplinary practices to widen the literary canon to include more women and African American voices, I seek to place Jacob's autobiography in current conversations in American studies about empire. Schoolman argues that scholars need to have a more expansive conception of how geography intersected with abolitionist literature to move beyond the usual coordinates of North versus South or westward expansion (1). She maintains "the possibility that abolitionists' explicit investment in American geography was precisely arrayed against the expansionist machinations of the U.S. state in its increasingly desperate efforts at self-preservation" (Schoolman 5). Gretchen Murphy's scholarship on American nationalism observes how imperialism and the tension inherent in the dialectic of US insularity and expansion "submerges any one national history as it calls attention to interconnected historical processes of colonization, revolution, nation formation, and the displacement and destruction of natives" (Murphy, *Hemispheric* 2). Jacobs weaves her life together as part of these processes of imperialism, revolution (her own declaration of independence), and other historical forces her text cannot control or foresee. However, unlike Schoolman and Murphy, I am interested in not just real geographic spaces but also imagined ones.

Although Jacobs might seem like she would break the stranglehold that Massachusetts has on the American literary canon up to the late nineteenth century, in the following pages, I make the case that Massachusetts becomes a site onto which Jacobs and others project some future perfection. Catharine Maria Sedgwick tries to imagine a new past for the Massachusetts Bay Colony in *Hope Leslie,* and Child tries to imagine a new future for Massachusetts forged through ethnic and racial heterogeneity in *A Romance of the Republic.* Jacob, though, strikes right at the heart of how Massachusetts looms in the American imagination and the gap between its idealization and its lived reality. I concur with Jennifer Rae Greeson that we should "relocate Jacobs—as a brilliantly perceptive reader and analyst of U.S. culture in New York City, her home for two decades before the publication of her North Carolina narrative" (280).[4] In this chapter, though, I am more interested in the imaginative *topos* of northern cities that Jacobs creates and relies upon in the first part of her narrative. As Greeson points out, an irony emerges in the text when Jacobs finds herself emancipated but still "victimized by the middle-class Northern society inhabited by the very reformers and readers who have taken up her cause" (300). Jacobs's conception of the Commonwealth of Massachusetts breaks down the monolithic conception of America. In the first part of her narrative, Jacobs employs *the scandal of Massachusetts* to protect herself while hiding in the South—a scandal that establishes Massachusetts as a place besotted with slave-loving abolitionists. But in the second half of her story in the North, she finds herself subjected to the scandal of Massachusetts—the scandal that reveals the gap between Massachusetts's claims to equality while it perpetuates racial injustice and inequality. Treating Massachusetts as a scandal plays into reabsorbing it into the US imaginary as an errant aspect rather than one that dismantles the federation of states. As Greeson succinctly comments, "At the end of Jacobs's narrative, the interpenetration of these generic conventions disrupts the moral-spatial bifurcation of abolitionist narrative, so that slavery is no longer unequivocally aligned with the South, freedom no longer surely attributed to the North" (302). The critical overemphasis on the garret where Jacobs hides in the South allows critics to avoid discussion about the disillusionment Jacobs undergoes once she starts living in northern cities.

BEYOND

THE GARRET

The geographies of *Incidents* are often submerged as critics interrogate the same middle chapters in which Jacobs records her confinement in a small garret in her grandmother's house in Edenton. Jacobs's four-chapter rumination on the seven years she spent hiding in that tiny space monopolizes scholarship on the text, although a handful of critics, like Mark Rivkin, Lauren Berlant, and Jennifer Greeson, establish the national and even transnational reach of *Incidents*. Nonetheless, most criticism of the text repeatedly locks Jacobs back into the confines of the garret, especially as the garret serves as a grim figuration of cloistered domesticity.[5] The dark, confined, poorly insulated rooftop, measuring seven feet by nine and only three feet high, above her grandmother's shed, leaves Jacobs isolated from other humans and exposed to wind, rain, snow, heat, and vermin. Long after she leaves the South for refuge in the North, her body bears lasting pain from her prostrate stay in cramped quarters. The space, referred to as the "loophole of retreat," offers a small aperture from which she witnesses the horrors of slavery and the daily affairs of her family without participating in them. As Sally Gomaa observes, "Rather than becoming the object of voyeurism, Jacobs turns the voyeuristic gaze against itself" (376). Confined physical spaces often permeate slave narratives. Zoe Trodd writes, "The abolitionist hole story imagined historical space as physical space. . . . The closets, garrets, boxes, crevices, and dark holes of abolitionist literature are the forgotten spaces in history's house" (Trodd 69). Laura Doyle emphasizes Jacobs's gothic allusions while living in hiding and ignores other allusions, like her reference to herself as Robinson Crusoe. Moreover, she renders Jacobs a sort of ventriloquist of an "Anglo-Atlantic narrative" that undercuts Jacobs's own creative power. Instead, in Doyle's version, Jacobs is reduced to ghost metaphors: "Her voice in this sense is a ghostly one, speaking doubly and from nowhere, expressing an illicit freedom" (259). Doyle makes these claims even though Jacobs's voice as the writer of her story comes years after she has left the garret, the South, and as a free woman in the eye of the law. Jacobs's text memorializes her confinement and the scenes she witnessed from the loophole. Though crucial to understand the horrors Jacobs endured to escape slavery, the focus on the garret seems to stow Jacobs safely away from other conversations about political power and expansion. It encapsulates, as Lisa Lowe explains, how "the autobiographical genre illustrates how liberal emancipation required a literary narrative of the self-authoring individual to be distilled out of the heteronomous collective subjectivity of colonial slavery" (50). The story of Jacobs's stay in the garret moves her testimony about the general lives of women in slavery to her specific, unique movement, or, rather, lack of movement, from slavery to freedom.

Jacobs's text challenges a monolithic conception of US nationhood, and the attempts to rein her in not only undercut her individual volition but also tether her to a domestic narrative that would advance a more coherent national identity from which the United States can better participate geopolitically. However, Jacobs's text depends on figuring the United States as a fractured federation of states even if the other characters in her text and even literary critics undercut this dimension of the text. Thus, Jacobs often serves as a point of contrast by providing a domestic account of life in slavery to counter slave narratives penned by emancipated men. Wresting Jacobs away from this critical paradigm demonstrates how her text engages with empire. Indeed, her autobiography is constructed around Jacobs's ability to identify the structuring principles that undergird her private turmoil. It also leads her to rely on cultural paradigms, especially as they involve political geographies, to challenge the system of sexual exploitation she identifies within slavery. Jacobs responds to her exploitation by using the imaginary to shape a direct relation to the state rather than one mediated through marriage. Jacobs "authors" her own life by relying on what we now term "new historicist" interpretation in her dealings with others, especially Dr. Flint, as she negotiates the limits of her agency. Or as Christopher Freeburg maintains, "Therefore, defeating Flint means defeating the matrix of physical and ideological forces against her" (108). Furthermore, she presents her life story to the reader as representative of life in slavery without employing the narrative techniques that hook a reader—the very narrative techniques that she deploys to control her adversaries in real life.

Rather than portray the usual predicament of a woman who undergoes temporary exile before marrying (like Unca Eliza or Hope Leslie) or a obtaining a man's protection (like Mary in *Secret History*), Jacobs presents herself as uncannily prescient about others' conceptual worlds and uses that knowledge to carve out a life independent of marriage. Try though she does, Jacobs finds that marriage and its illusory sources of protection are even forbidden her by her owner (who refuses to let her marry a free Black man) and by the law (she cannot marry her white lover). As Hendrik Hartog explains, "Slave marriage, if recognized, would have threatened the central need of slave owners in a capitalist economy: to keep capital mobile" (194). Yet her position as a slave grants her the perspective that reintegrates the mutually constitutive realms of private and public. Lauren Berlant and Michael Warner have offered a cogent analysis of how heteronormativity depoliticizes intimacy: "Intimate life is the endlessly cited *elsewhere* of political public discourse, a promised haven that distracts citizens from the unequal conditions of their political and economic lives, consoles them for the damaged humanity of mass society, and shames them for any divergence between their lives and the intimate sphere that is alleged to be simple personhood" (Berlant and Warner 553). Living in such a society, Jacobs seems keenly aware of how this disjunction between "intimate life" and one's lived experiences entrenches political power while alienating individuals. Thus, she finds a solution in garnering "mass society" around her, even in an imagined sense, to ward off threats to her personhood. Thus, she overturns autobiography's tendency to reify the liberal subject. Instead of finding consolation in the possibilities of the intimate, she identifies the dominant narratives that shape "fantasies of the good life," to borrow Lauren Berlant's phrase in *Cruel Optimism* that describes the ineluctability of individual solutions to mass problems.

Jacobs's discursive uses of Massachusetts enable her to assert mastery over others. She has no recourse to the imaginary "elsewhere" or "promised haven" to which Warner and Berlant refer; at the same time, as a unit of "mobile capital," to revive Hartog's language, she subverts the system of slavery by entering the imagined "elsewhere" of others, such as Flint's. Yet her ability to project a worldview for others refracts the aesthetic dimensions of her text. As the "slave girl," she lays traps for others through discursive means; but as the narrator Jacobs simultaneously speaks to future readers and creates a sensibility for them to interpret her text by refusing to employ manipulative narrative ploys that would hold readers' attention captive. In the text, Jacobs creates a *nom de guerre* for herself as Linda Brent. Throughout this chapter, though, I refer to Jacobs as Jacobs instead of Linda Brent because my focus is on Jacobs as an author. Otherwise, I refer to the people by the fictional names she gives them in the text.

Jacobs's *Incidents* has long invited critical inquiries into the spaces of the text, both physical spaces and figurative blank spaces. Jacobs leaves a textual blank regarding the setting where most of the action takes place, refusing to name Edenton or North Carolina, where she was born and raised, for fear of exposing herself and others to recrimination for her escape from slavery. In contrast, her brother, John, who also writes an autobiographical slave narrative, begins his text with "I was born in Edenton, North Carolina" (J. Jacobs 207).[6] Instead, *Incidents* remains vague about the actual geographic setting until Jacobs arrives in the North. Present-day readers can reconstruct her early life because of Yellin's thorough biographical work tracking the people and places that Jacobs masks in the text. Still, Jacobs's refusal to name the setting of her early life allows her to erase engrained spatial ideologies of the South and her hometown. She refuses its status as the metropole from which her life emanates.

In Jacobs's *Incidents,* the Commonwealth of Massachusetts serves as an imagined space that promises refuge to African Americans deemed slaves, not merely as a free state in the North but also because of its reputation as a place populated with fervent abolitionists who not only fight to end slavery but who also harbor animus toward slave owners. The tight spaces in which she hides from her enslaver threaten to overwhelm critical examination of Jacobs's life writing, making her contribution to American letters narrower than it is. Rather than relegated to confined spaces, she manipulates the social construction of space, specifically geopolitical space, to shift the power dynamics between enslavers and those held in bondage in a way that challenges US imperial ambitions. Her narrative fills the discursive gaps that people refuse to utter about slavery, because of her attunement to how time and language disarm each other. At one point, she makes an observant point about white people's empty promises: "I was too familiar with slavery not to know that promises made to slaves, though with kind intentions, and sincere at the time, depend upon many contingencies for their fulfillment" (H. Jacobs 134). She can project herself into a future, unlike those white people who make promises they never keep; it seems as though even the powerful cannot apprehend how contingencies are exacerbated by the asymmetry of master/slave relations. Because Jacobs remains aware of the wide-ranging effects of slavery as an institutional practice—in which the lived experience of labor, family, and the law converge—she realizes that "[s]lavery is a curse to the whites as well as to the blacks. It makes the fathers cruel and sensual; the sons violent and licentious; it contaminates the daughters, and makes the wives wretched" (52). Jacobs observes how the master class cannot grasp how slavery as an institution confines them and uses her knowledge to thwart their control.

Sociologist George Lipsitz maintains that an imagined spatial ontology precedes the formation of the United States, one that reveals how spaces shape power differentials in what he terms a "black spatial imaginary." Lipsitz argues, "The relationship of race to the Enlightenment—as its always disavowed yet universally produced product—makes it necessary to struggle in separate sites to unearth and identify the occluded and disavowed historical genealogies and ideologies of racialized space particular to specific locations" (12). Jacobs draws forth the overdetermined meanings Massachusetts bears in the American imagination. Her text serves to "identify the occluded and disavowed" by working through these two separate sites—"the South" and "Massachusetts"—as each produces a separate history of constructing race. Indeed, the signification of Massachusetts permeates conceptions of the founding of the nation as it connotes Puritanism, the Salem Witch Trials, or Revolutionary fervor. In the twenty-first century, Massachusetts continues to focus the nation on innovative political conceptions to promote egalitarianism and a shared sense of belonging: universal healthcare, marriage equality, and even state-mandated open-source software. Yet its innovation and progressivism have led in the past as well as in the present to a focus on its contradictory sexual mores in which it is portrayed as cold, sexually repressive, Puritanical. and at other times as boldly nonnormative in its sexual expressions. The latter is portrayed in both *A Romance of the Republic* and *Hope Leslie* and transcended through the promise of interracial relationships.

This two-pronged conception of the commonwealth's sexual mores was repeatedly staged during debates about slavery's legality. By projecting desire for interracial sex onto abolitionists, pro-slavery factions attempted to distance themselves, in fact, to deny, the long-standing practice of master-slave relations that marked plantation life.[7] When famed abolitionist and Bostonian William Lloyd Garrison was asked if he would let his daughter marry a Black man, he responded, "I am not married—I have no daughter. Sir, I am not familiar with your practices; but allow me to say, that slaveholders generally should be the last persons to affect fastidiousness on that point; for they seem to be enamored of amalgamation" (qtd. in Lemire 82). To rebut accusations that he promotes interracial marriage, Garrison denies his own sexuality: he has no wife and therefore no daughter. Moreover, because he claims he is "not familiar with your practices," he provides a framework that resists enslavers' efforts to sexualize abolitionism and therefore cast it to the margins of society as an advocacy movement organized to legitimate a personal desire. Nonetheless, Massachusetts's ideological purity regarding slavery—its state Constitution outlawed slavery in 1780—prevents slave owners, like Flint, from daring to penetrate past it.[8] If Jacobs has no recourse sexual propriety, she then appropriates Massachusetts's inviolateness, linking it to her own "black spatial imaginary."

Jacobs proves adept at rooting out the racial dimensions in the construction of different settings, as Lipsitz suggests is necessary because race is "always disavowed yet universally produced." As such, she can navigate and create new spaces, literal and figurative, to evade her master's sexual possession. As Foucault has written, "Endeavoring . . . to decipher discourse through the use of spatial, strategic metaphors enables one to grasp precisely the points at which discourses are transformed in, through, and on the basis of relations of power" (*Power* 70). While Jacobs's text elucidates how the identity categories of race, gender, and sexuality intersect in a narrative of American life, it should also serve more broadly as the preeminent text for nineteenth-century studies of how political geography and power subtend identity categories. By attending to spatial metaphors, as Foucault suggests, we can observe the negotiations and reversals of power between Jacobs and Flint.

Jacobs details more specific northern geographies even before she arrives there. Just when she seems unmoored from space—suspended in the small, dark garret—she claims for herself a physical presence rooted in the large northern cities, whether New York or Boston. *Incidents* creates a tension between imagining and eliding space through textual representation. Wayne Franklin and Michael Steiner, in the introduction to their edited collection *Mapping American Culture,* make a distinction between "space" and "place," with the openness of space giving way to the specificity of place (4). Jacobs's narrative, however, swaps these terms: *home*—whether Edenton or the hiding spots where she dwells—denotes "spaces" in the text, and those unknown spots representing freedom in her imagination denote "place." Indeed, it is through her manipulation of spaces that she can best assert power in social relationships. As Lipsitz suggests the erasure of race entails these kinds of reversals to make present a black spatial imaginary. Jacobs further plays upon, relies upon, and subverts the site of Massachusetts in her text, because her conception of space is discursive. Having never traveled North, Jacobs knows Massachusetts only through printed texts and oral testimony. She occupies Massachusetts discursively as well through the counterfeit letters she writes and that she has posted for her from the North to correspondents in North Carolina. The only way to shift the power in communicating with Flint is through the vicarious protection offered by her supposed stay in Boston.

Jacobs's text shows how space obscures the cultural work it produces.[9] As Mary Pat Brady argues, "spatial processes attempt to keep that shaping power largely hidden, so that space is seen as a background, a setting, rich and interesting, but not in any sense interactive or formative" (8). Sara Blair also explains how space studies seek the "articulation of space as a social product, one that masks the conditions of its own formation" ("Cultural Geography" 544). Likewise, Patricia Yaeger comments on how social spaces "repress" their history: "And this repression is exacerbated by the quiddity and seeming impenetrability of created social space" (25). In contrast to these theories that hinge on invisibility: "the hidden" (Brady), "masks" (Blair), and "impenetrability" (Yaeger), I posit that Jacobs draws attention to the potential of spaces to operate discursively independent of one's actual location in space and time. In the ante-bellum United States, at a time when space is overdetermined by politics, where borders denote the differences between slave state and free, Jacobs exploits the fears geography inspires in her owners. Her freedom, she imagines while still in the South, interdepends on geography. Therefore, she can write herself into the North and achieve limited freedom from Dr. Flint. When she finally arrives in the North seven years after running away from him, Jacobs's lived experiences cause some disillusion about her imagined freedom, but while trapped in the garret, geographic space takes on greater importance because of her seeming fixity in one location. In other words, she can assert a firm grounding in imaginary space through her letters because she perceives and manipulates the social construction of spaces.

Hsuan Hsu provides a vocabulary, borrowed from cultural geography, to think about how nineteenth-century American writers conceived of space through spatial scales, either to gain a footing or to express anxieties about space. The sense of scale runs through Jacobs's text, especially as she occupies coffin-like spaces, under floorboards and in between ceilings and roofs, while trying to navigate politically diverse geographies along the Eastern Seaboard of the United States.[10] As Hsu argues, "By attending to the literary rhetoric and form, we can perceive not only attempts at 'cognitive mapping' but also a process of affective mapping that produced and unraveled subjective identifications with different kinds of place" (17). Nowhere does space become more vexing than in the constant push and pull in the early United States between free and slave soil.

The concept of scales of space proves particularly useful for Jacobs as she and Flint rely on gradations of spatial areas to control one another, whether in the doctor's private office in the middle of Edenton or in Northern states when Flint's presence in New York leaves her racing to Boston. The critical focus on the garret diminishes the sophisticated spatial figurations. For Jacobs's use of Massachusetts continues even after she finally arrives in the North. Although she lives in New York to be near her daughter, she repeatedly returns to Boston to evade potential slave catchers. Her attitude toward Massachusetts continues to evolve. Once in the North she becomes attuned to institutionalized racism, not just slavery, and thus her valorization with Massachusetts diminishes, especially after the passage of the Fugitive Slave Law: "I knew my old master was rather skittish of Massachusetts. I relied on her love of freedom, and felt safe on her soil. I am now aware that I honored the old Commonwealth beyond her deserts" (H. Jacobs 187). Furthermore, she feels deep disappointment that her bill of sale is made out in New York (200). Even though antislavery attitudes pervade there, Jacobs learns that the people in the North continue to recognize slavery as a legal institution and share the South's attitudes of racism. Yet, despite her observations of racism in the North, she still can manipulate southerners who have absorbed discursive formations about "the North" as offering a haven to people who have run away from slavery.

ABANDONING
THE MARRIAGE PLOT

Because Jacobs, under slavery, has no access to the "marriage plot," her narrative confounds the standard templates for narrativizing one's life within the sentimental or seduction genre. Marriage was not legally recognized for African Americans in North Carolina prior to 1865. This vulnerability, though, leads Jacobs to improvise by placing herself imaginatively in the North and to implement a more enduring relationship to the state, which is less dependent on the changing attitudes and attention of a man. Her tale does not conform to other texts or even to other slave narratives of her time. In fact, this might explain why her text left few traces within the canon of abolitionist texts until the 1980s, when Yellin found evidence that corroborated Jacobs's authorship. Yet her defiance of genre, like her defiance of her owner, opens new possibilities for Jacobs to imagine life as a Black woman in the antebellum United States. Those possibilities rely on her adept manipulation of space. She intuits how Flint's obsession with her hinges on spatial dynamics shaped by the social forces of her town, social forces that are repeatedly naturalized.

The form of *Incidents* draws upon multiple genres while also offering a fresh perspective on them. Leigh Gilmore and Elizabeth Marshall succinctly describe how, "[t]hrough her uses of Garrisonian abolitionism, the seduction novel, spiritual autobiography, and the sentimental novel, Jacobs develops an account of the gendered violence of slavery that distinguishes her text within the archive of primarily male slave narrative" (670). I want to add to this exhaustive list that Jacobs also uses metanarrative, because she often situates herself as a text that Dr. Flint must read and respond to; their relation, with Jacobs as author and Flint as reader, then reverberates back onto the one between Jacobs and the reader of *Incidents*. The key scene informing her narrative is an anecdote about her brother, who as a young child was posed with an intractable dilemma: he is called simultaneously by his father (who is "owned" by a different person) and by his mistress. The boy at first halts but then decides to answer his mistress. The father "reproved him for it" (9). Jacobs writes, "'You are my child,' replied our father, 'and when I call you, you should come immediately, if you have to pass through fire and water'" (9). The paragraph ends without Jacobs's commentary on her father's words. Instead, she sympathizes, "Poor Willie!" (9), but the entire book outlines how she navigates these two lines of authority and how she shifts between the roles of "slave girl" and (grand)daughter. The scene is key because Jacobs sees it happening to someone else. She identifies how the system of slavery leads to self-recrimination even as individuals confront institutional problems over which they have no control or means of resisting.

Jacobs realizes people are terrible at reading their own lives because they read "ahistorically." She forces them again and again to "historicize" and thus flummoxes their attempts to control her. Shortly thereafter she re-counts another incident with her brother. Just as she laments her life, wishing she were dead, her brother meets her and admits, "I wish I had died when father died" (18). Although she might have commiserated with him, she instead buoys his spirits by comparing their relative comfort compared to others. As an aside, she confesses, "While I advised him to be good and forgiving I was not unconscious of the beam in my own eye" (19). As her life's story unfolds, Jacobs learns to distance herself from a situation and review it as both a participant and as an observer; she, indeed, avoids acting "not unconscious."

Jacobs as a narrator can describe her mistreatment in impersonal and self-effacing terms, revealing a radical empathy and at times a Benjamin Franklin-type equipoise in the face of adversity. Her cognizance of slavery's corruption leads her to feel empathy for Flint's wife, because she perceives how the system of slavery disempowers each of them as women, even as this same woman blames Jacobs for her husband's misdeeds. She grasps how life as a whole and her moment-to-moment reality interrelate; she then starts to shape events around how she expects someone to behave by attuning herself to the political constructions of space. This tactic does not seem like speculation, which involves chance, but more like an author who weaves a hermeneutic circle for readers through a text. She becomes attuned to how the power dynamics in her community operate, and, as an author of her life, literally and figuratively, she has the greatest impact on using context—setting—to control others. Jacobs's *Incidents* not only reveals how race intersects with space in slave narratives but also how politics inflects spatial constructions and how those politics mobilize opposition politics elsewhere. In examining nonwhite writers in the late nineteenth century, Gretchen Murphy notices how "[b]y revealing interior frontiers, heterogeneous histories, fictive national ethnicities, and transnational comparisons, these writers' works do more than change the color of U.S. national power on the global stage; they also represent that power as fragmented, internally divided, and historically embedded in ongoing, multipolar, colonial processes" (*Shadowing* 224). In *Incidents,* Jacobs's iterations of internal divisions with US polity fracture a cohesive sense of "U.S. national power." Yet she seizes on those fractures for the cover they provide in key moments in the text.

Jacobs carries no illusion of personal volition, but she manipulates the lives of others by mastering the narratives that structure the South. She highlights the illusion others entertain about their own agency. Berlant defines how an "intimate public sphere" is "shaped by an expectation that the consumers of its particular stuff *already* share a worldview and emotional knowledge that they have derived from a broadly common historical experience" (*Female Complaint* viii). Jacobs, though, has no access to an "intimate public sphere," but through her text she seeks to create one by drawing upon northern women's disapprobation for the Fugitive Slave Law. For women, slavery is not only a laboring practice but also a psychosexual identity that alienates them from the dominant culture's social-moral codes, family, and their own children. Her text cannot rely on the usual *topos* because her very life depends on undermining the narratives to which others cling, to their detriment.

In her text, she conjures Massachusetts to provide her with legal and social status outside the confines of civil marriage. Throughout Jacobs's famous account of her time in slavery, she deplores how her slave status impedes her access to marriage and therefore recourse to state-sanctioned rights and protections. But she finds that cultivating relationships offers no sustainable protection. Although, years later, her lived experience in the North disabuses her of its claims to equality and civil rights, Jacobs, despite her disenfranchised state, draws on the public conception of geopolitical sites as opportunities to test out modes of agency. Her text enables readers to understand how political positions extend beyond sanctioned borders; the nineteenth-century patchwork of legal rights in the United States is fraught with danger for

Black people, but it also undermines marriage as an institution that regulates rights and thus leads one to experiment with new opportunities to establish one's self-direction. For Jacobs, Massachusetts secures her not only from life in slavery but also from the sexual violation constantly threatened by her enslaver, Dr. Flint. It remains an imagined sanctuary, because Jacobs's initial venture as a runaway leaves her trapped, hiding in the South, while her owner believes that she has escaped North. Jacobs's use of Massachusetts tantalizes Dr. Flint by telling him exactly where he can find her. Paradoxically, she excites his power of possession by her seeming presence in a geographic spot that obstructs, and in many ways deconstructs, the practice of slavery.

Jacobs's life writing raises three interrelated points about the United States. First, rights sanctioned in one geopolitical space cannot be contained even if they do not transfer to others; indeed, they erode or strengthen (as a countermove) legal distinctions elsewhere. That is, in Jacobs's mind, other communities extend the possibilities for liberation and at times supersede her immediate sphere. Second, conservative and patriarchal interests attempt to contain political advocacy within specific geographic spaces by ascribing nonnormative erotic impulses to people who live there. Third, Jacobs's ultimate decision to disavow her predilection for marriage or a man's protection leads to a new social and legal imaginary in which state-sanctioned individual rights would diminish the need to patrol marriage rights, specifically interracial marriage; marriage would no longer serve as the contractual relationship among men, women, and the state, and thus marriage need not serve as the institution through which the state extends liberal rights related to property, ownership, suffrage, or citizenship.

The second point requires elaboration about the sexualization of political advocacy. At times, opposition groups derogate activists as compelled by an individual compulsion, refusing to countenance that they pursue a social mandate to redress wrongs. In particular, in the nineteenth-century United States, abolitionists faced repeated accusations that their true motives were to advance amalgamation, as though the campaign to end slavery is rooted not in the political ideals of the Declaration of Independence but in an effort to fulfill an individual's private, erotic desire.[11] This maneuver to characterize abolitionists as harboring secret aims to encourage amalgamation distracts from how the United States fostered a widespread system of sexual exploitation of Black women in the South. In some cases, it diverts energy from activists advocating for a cause to defending their sexual practices. Advocates find themselves constantly pledging their impartial desire for the end to slavery. When Stephen Douglas tried to impute sexual desire for Black women as the reason for Abraham Lincoln's disavowal of slavery during the famous Lincoln-Douglas debates held in 1858, Lincoln responded, "I protest, now and forever, against that counterfeit logic which presumes that because I did not want a negro woman for a slave, I do necessarily want her for a wife." Lincoln accuses Douglas of faulty logic, but he adds the transitive phrase "now and forever" in order to foreclose charges of sexual freedom that might reappear when people are emancipated. The paratactic syntax, which creates a rhetorical symmetry between "for a slave . . . for a wife," though, further juxtaposes the two positions as alternatives—perhaps mutually exclusive alternatives. The opposite of a slave woman is a wife; that formulation highlights how the position of slave excludes one from the multitudinous protections (and limitations) of legal marriage.

Abolitionists therefore had to defend themselves against self-interest in advancing the end of slavery. A letter to the editor printed in 1840 in the *Boston Courier* encapsulates the pressures abolitionist sympathizers faced as the opposition did not simply refute their stand but instead attacked their unspoken motives of promoting sexual freedom. The sleight of hand of the proslavery factions not only diverts the question of slavery as a violation of human rights but also leaves the abolitionist endorsing racist practices, such as laws against amalgamation. The 1840 letter admonishes a Mr. Baxter for impugning those who signed a petition for abolition as also calling for interracial marriage. The letter writer points to the hypocrisy of such an accusation because the impropriety actually lies in the sexual exploitation of individuals by the enslaver class. The letter writer explains that slaveholding's "tendency is to encourage, not to prevent, amalgamation. It is so, because it allows any unprincipled man to take to himself a wife differing from him in complexion, whenever he chooses—provided he can find some one to solemnize the marriage, which it is not difficult to do—with the privilege of living with her so long, and only so long as he pleases. In the same manner, he may take another and another. . . . It is directly encouraged by the law" ("Letter to the Editor"). At times, fighting against a misimpression about the sexualization of abolitionism takes center stage. In Boston's *The Liberator* in 1853, one writer outlines how "[r]ather than fighting for the abolition, advocates had to battle with misconceptions about their aims." The proslavery factions pollute the message of the opposition by sensationalizing its agenda. *The Liberator* denies the portrait that proslavery factions paint of abolitionists, listing the opposition's hyperbolic visions of emancipation that bring forth "[m]assacres of the masters, slaves contented and happy, amalgamation of races, colonization, and similar fallacies—these are the refuges of lies which the abolitionists have swept away, and the issue between them and their opponents is narrowed to the simple question of material success and self-interest" (131). In this way, the "massacres of the masters" and the end of marriage prohibition are equated. Each is part of the "refuge of lies."

For abolitionists who do promote intermarriage, their beliefs are cast as "open," as though other abolitionists are simply hiding their real agenda. One outraged citizen writes in the *New-York Spectator* in 1835 about an English activist who "is not only an immediate abolitionist, but an open and avowed maintainer of the justice and propriety of amalgamation, nothing short of this will content him. He does not hesitate to express his firm belief that, at no distant day, all distinction of color will be lost from the human race, a shade of brown becoming the universal complexion, by means of a general amalgamation" ("Amalgamation Avowed"). Notice the writer's focus on how the activist "does not hesitate" and "open and avowed," yet still the writer relies on hyperbole by claiming "nothing short of this will content him." In the minds of proslavery advocates, "amalgamation" becomes the abolitionists' overriding passion even though the practices of "amalgamation" may fittingly describe the institution of slavery as a lived reality. In this context it puts Jacobs's sexual history into relief when we realize that discursive formations for emancipation are riddled with questions about sexual freedom. When Jacobs seeks freedom, her sexual motives are questioned. Likewise, she uses her sexuality to create temporary reprieves from Flint's domination over her. Nonetheless, the opposition's focus on sexuality keeps politics insular, domestic, and private rather than collective. No matter Jacobs's insistence on creating a clear context for her decisions or lack thereof, she knows readers may interpret her life in narrow, moralistic terms that reinscribe separate private and political spheres. By attending to the ways in which abolitionists were sexualized, one sees the interlocked modalities of oppositional politics, sexual aspersions, and social constructions of space in the mid-nineteenth-century United States in her text.

CALCULATED

RECKLESSNESS

The borrowed agential power that Jacobs appropriates from Massachusetts is central to her story of the ongoing antagonism between her and the man who owns her. She conceives of their antagonism as a "war" (19), while also realizing that, for her, any victory would be pyrrhic. Growing up in the South, Jacobs finds herself unwittingly caught in a series of love triangles with Flint, who over several years tries to coerce Jacobs into consenting to a sexual relationship. Jacobs cannot extract herself from these scenarios of love and jealously that Flint manifests. His power over her leads Jacobs to mount a series of tactical maneuvers against him. In the first part of the narrative, these maneuvers offer only short-lived respite until Jacobs realizes she must alter the settings of their encounters to shift the power differentials between her and Flint. In the South, the arbitrary differences in power are always disavowed; if she invokes Boston, Flint's subjectivity is threatened. She must rely on other spaces, not just people, to position herself as a subject. First, she receives the marriage proposal of an African American free man, but Flint refuses to give his consent for her to marry because he wants her for himself. Next, Jacobs tries to gain protection from Flint's wife, whose possessive jealousy of her husband seems to offer her some degree of safety, but Flint manipulates each woman to maintain his advantage. When confronted, Flint lies to his wife by admitting to an affair with Jacobs. Jacobs explains, "It was to show me that I gained nothing by seeking protection of my mistress; that the power was still all in his own hands" (34). His wife's repeated attempts to wrest information from Jacobs regarding her husband's fidelity reveals how little power or influence she has over his conduct. Hovering over Jacobs while she sleeps, the mistress eventually inspires Jacobs to fear for her life. Next, Jacobs accepts the attention of a white gentleman, named Mr. Sands in the text, whom she takes as a lover. Even after she has two children with him, he fails to offer any lasting relief from Flint. In taking a lover, Jacobs incurs Flint's wrath, the condemnation of her grandmother, and new worries about the fate of her children in a slave system.

Finally, though, the imagined space of Massachusetts confers power that allows Jacobs to imagine and enact a reversal of the master and slave relationship with Dr. Flint even though she remains in North Carolina. From the beginning, their relationship relies on mediated contact. Once Flint knows Jacobs can read and write, he begins writing her letters that he sends to her via her brother. This pattern of indirection leads to further mediation through the use of spaces, whether specific rooms in a building or broad geographic territories. Meanwhile, Jacobs repeatedly uses her grandmother's house as a haven from Dr. Flint's abuses, and at his house she secures her safety by sharing a bed with her aunt. She realizes that her family's respectability and the doctor's necessary capitulation to the social mores of the town, at least in name, give her leeway to protest her treatment: "How often did I rejoice that I lived in a town where all the inhabitants knew each other! If I had been on a remote plantation, or lost among the multitude of a crowded city, I should not be a living woman at this day" (35). Unlike other works of nineteenth-century literature that expose the narrowness of small-town America, *Incidents* celebrates the intruding gaze of neighbors and the lack of privacy, which save Jacobs from Flint's sexual aggression.

All of Dr. Flint's schemes to take Jacobs as a lover rely on spaces; yet his conception of space seems unidirectional and ahistorical. He can only perceive how those spaces further his desires, and thus he is blind to the methods others employ to thwart his construction of space. First, he plans to take his daughter, Jacobs's charge, into his bedroom; Jacobs avoids incurring his close proximity because Flint's jealous wife obstructs the move. Flint then threatens Jacobs with jail if she does not acquiesce to his wishes, to which she replies to him, "As for the jail, there would be more peace for me there than there is here" (40). Flint takes umbrage, for within their struggle the discourse of "here" means in his presence and "jail" means safe from his advances. Next, he considers taking Jacobs to New Orleans, leaving his wife in Edenton; this plan that never materializes: he sends his son to do reconnaissance, but his son, lacking his father's obsessive purpose, nixes the plan. Finally, Flint takes considerable expense to build a cottage for Jacobs four miles out of town, where he intends to keep her as a mistress, promising that there she shall be a "lady," not a slave (35). Frequently, the cottage serves metonymically for Flint's plans to make Jacobs his mistress. Much of her war with Dr. Flint occurs against the background of his building her the house where he plans to keep her isolated from the town. The cottage proves just as illusory as his other schemes to find an extranational space that permits sexual license for a relationship with Jacobs involving mutual consent.

Jacob's ability to conjecture correctly about Flint's plans reveals her ability to take his point of view. As Freeburg describes, "Jacobs depicts Flint as mono-maniacal and obsessed, and in the end, while she does not destroy him, she does expose the falsity of absolute power in which Flint devotedly believes" (Freeburg 107). Jacobs's life writing bears witness to her family's aspirations toward respectability and the stratagems enslaved people employed to outwit their enslavers and limit attempts to compound their exploitation. These two strains in Jacobs's text move her in contradictory directions because her ability to outmaneuver Flint undercuts her ability to live according to her manumitted grandmother's aspirational ideals of middle-class sexual propriety. The impossibility of living according to social mandates of decorum does not diminish her self-recrimination. Instead, Jacobs seemingly moves between these two modes. Like her brother facing the dilemma of whom to answer, his father or his mistress, she must repeatedly choose between her commitment to her grandmother and her commitment to her war with Flint. Much like the fictional women characters who must negotiate militarized private spheres, surveyed in the previous chapters in *The Female American, Secret History, Hope Leslie,* and *A Romance,* Jacobs tries and fails to compartmentalize her life as daughter. Her "war" with Dr. Flint spills into every aspect of her lived experience.

Indeed, in taking another white man as a lover to defy Flint, she loses the respect of her grandmother, and, in fleeing Edenton to escape his control, she must separate from her family. She reifies her life and her ability to design it when thwarting Flint but then shifts out of this mode when she considers her love for her grandmother. When it comes to her grandmother, Jacobs's perspective narrows, and she proves much more susceptible to imbibing her grandmother's point of view. Nonetheless, she insists on thwarting Flint not merely by escaping his control but by controlling his obsession with her. Her ability to split the self is most pointed in her mercenary affair with Mr. Sands. Although she never allows Flint to seduce her, she enters a consensual relationship with Sands to evade Flint's advances.

Jacobs refuses to narrate a love story involving this shadowy figure; she provides almost no details about how they carried on their affair. Her summation of their relationship bears no resemblance to popular seduction stories. In contrast, Lydia Maria Child, in her short story "The Quadroons" (1842), sets up a romantic tale of true love between a mulatto girl and a white man who eventually abandons her. Jacobs, however, treats her children's father as an inconsequential figure, barely mentioning his name; even the fake name she uses, Mr. Sands for the real Samuel Tredwell Sawyer, conveys his lack of form or presence. She represents no direct dialogue from him until late in the text, years after their affair has ended, when he is about to leave for Washington, DC, to serve in Congress. Thus, rather than focusing on him, she spotlights her act of consent in agreeing to be his lover. As she explains, "There is something akin to freedom in having a lover who has no control over you, except that which he gains by kindness and attachment" (55). As Casey Pratt argues, "freely choosing one's lover is *not* freedom, it is only akin to freedom. Even when Linda Brent's narrative is ostensibly about interpersonal sympathy, the theme of freedom holds the foundational position" (69). Moreover, until this late scene in her grandmother's kitchen, as he is about to leave town, Mr. Sands does not exist in any space. She reveals nothing about where they conducted their affair away from the watchful eyes of the town, her grandmother, or her owner. Just as Jacobs directs and misdirects her owner's attention, she deftly structures her narrative to keep the reader focused on her war rather than indulging in details about her love affair.

In reifying her life, Jacobs recounts how she made decisions in order to control others' impressions, as though she were the "author" of her life. Her choice of Sands, as a lover, offers her many possibilities for humiliating Flint based on her sense of contrast and the power hierarchies of Edenton. Jacobs always historicizes. However, her flouting of Flint reproduces her quagmire: she gives birth to a girl, who under the law belongs to Flint as "property." Jenny Sharpe struggles to articulate Jacobs's claims to autonomy even as she has to serve as Sands's "concubine" (Sharpe xxi). Even that characterization jars, because Jacobs uses the diction of "lover." Yet her choice is less about having a lover than about how to evade Flint. Sharpe's characterization therefore contorts Jacobs's story to put in a more familiar paradigm of a love triangle. As Saidiya Hartman explains, "Jacobs requires that we consider not only the restricted scope of black humanity but also the effort to act as a desiring subject in a context in which consent inadequately designates the enactment of possibility and the constraints of agency" (102). On the whole, though, Jacobs creates the impression that her interest in Mr. Sands is mercenary. She does not hesitate to admit that his position as an upper-class white gentleman gives her pride in attracting his attention. She recognizes his relative power over Flint based on her canny sense of power hierarchies of race, class, and sex in Edenton. According to Yellin, because her lover, Mr. Sands, occupied a higher social class station than Flint, Jacobs remained safe: as a physician, Flint's "rank was high, but it fell well below that of a man like [Sands], a descendent of colonial aristocracy" (*Harriet Jacobs* 31).

Besides her excited vanity and her sense of agency in choosing a lover, she admits to other feelings as well, though not her feelings for Sands or even sexual desire. Instead, she specifically catalogs her vitriol for Dr. Flint: "Revenge, and calculations of interest, were added to flattered vanity and sincere gratitude for kindness [from Mr. Sands]. I knew nothing would enrage Dr. Flint so much as to know that I favored another" (H. Jacobs 55). This passage is representative of her discussion about the man who fathers her children. While she only refers to him in pronouns "him" and as "another," Dr. Flint's proper name reverberates throughout the chapter. Indeed, the central scenes of the chapter are not between Jacobs and Sands but are rather the two major confrontations with Flint about her pregnancy. Furthermore, she admits that she held no illusions about Sands's promises to her, though she never elaborates on those promises (54). She doubts he will remain a constant in her life even as she plunges ahead with her plan. She understands the triangulation she enters has less to do with her desire for Sands than with her desire to rebuke Flint. As Sharpe observes, Jacobs "manipulated a system in which slave women were sexual victims because she was not in a position to challenge it" (xx). Hartman adds more nuance, "This exploration implicitly renders a more complex vision of power and the possible and circumscribed terms of agency by refusing to pose the question of desire in terms of compulsion versus unhindered choice" (104). Hartman's use of the word "system" is interesting because Jacobs sees her situation as part of a system when others do not. Jacobs perceives how the system holds everyone hostage and how they delude themselves otherwise.

Jacobs's confession unfolds amid a number of tensions, not least the tension that she expects from her anticipated readership who will judge her lack of sexual propriety. Nonetheless, Jacobs asserts that she willingly enters a relationship Sands. She explains, "The influences of slavery had had the same effect on me that they had on other young girls; they had made me prematurely knowing, concerning the evil ways of the world. I know what I did, and I did it with deliberate calculation" (54). Her assessment of her decision marks a clear line between cultural influences from which she cannot escape ("other young girls") and her individuality ("I know what I did"). The admission of "deliberate calculation" marks her newfound control over her sexuality and identifies her as a tactician cognizant of how she can battle Flint even if it involves sexual abasement. Yet in the very next paragraph as she seeks exoneration from the reader—imagined by Jacobs to be white northern women—for her lack of virtue, she declares, "I felt as if I was forsaken by God and man; as if all my efforts must be frustrated; and I became reckless in my despair" (54).[12] On the same page, she diminishes the cunning of her stratagems, describing them as emotional responses ("reckless in my despair"); then, in other moments, she plots a series of deliberate small victories over Master Flint, culminating in her eventual departure North.

Her wavering confidence, as when she reimagines "calculation" as "recklessness," measures how much her victories cost her personally, because her stratagems never offer lasting security. Peter Coviello comments on Jacobs's shifting characterization as evidence for language's inability to tell Jacobs's story adequately: "Conspicuously, there seems for Jacobs to be no secure ground in which to stake such claims of, in essence, agency and constraint in simultaneity" (139). However, as an alternative to interpreting this passage to further isolate Jacobs—her shame, or in Coviello's terms, her "dispossession" of her own life—I argue that her rhetorical shifts reveal her ability to exist in several planes at once. Her passages are rhetorically controlled despite the ambiguities they engender when juxtaposed. They register her actual "possession" of language and storytelling and her dexterity in controlling her narrative focus: Jacobs obscures the white gentleman who fathered her children while keeping Flint central to the story she tells the reader; likewise, she is not just Flint's "slave" but her grandmother's granddaughter. Too little attention is paid to Jacobs as an artist and how she infuses artifice in her dealings with others while projecting an authentic narrative of the "unsayable" to her readers. In her work all facets of American life are exposed and "break open." To create a hermeneutic circle for the reader, she invokes the grandmother to put him/her on familiar ground.

Jacobs claims that, despite his desperate attempts to seduce her, she and Flint were never lovers. Her refusal to consent to his sexual advances persists in the face of an outright obsession with her that lasts until the end of his life. Some literary critics treat her claims with great skepticism. P. Gabrielle Foreman suggests, along with other critics, that Jacobs denies any sexual contact with Flint to soothe the sexually conservative sensibilities of her white readership: "Although Jacobs would have at least a segment of her reception community believe that her owner never 'succeeded' in his ultimate assault, *Incidents*'s simultextuality suggests that [Dr. Flint] did rape his much-desired slave girl" (29). Foreman defines her neologism "simultextuality" as an author's method of expressing multiple subjectivities through writing; in this case, she posits that Jacobs can write to two audiences simultaneously: affirming to white women readers that Flint never assaulted her while subtly gesturing to Black readers that he did. As Laura Laffrado contends, "Furthermore, Jacobs's naming of black female/white male sexual intercourse disrupted multiple taboos regarding sexual desire, interracial sex, and rape. However, in other salient parts of the text, Jacobs repeatedly foregrounded the nineteenth-century construction of devoted motherhood, aligning herself with white female readers" (Laffrado 13). Whether or not he assaulted her, simultextuality encapsulates Jacobs's rhetorical modes because she has to appease different audiences simultaneously in her text just as she sought to please her master and mistress on one side and her grandmother and family on the other while living in Edenton.

Jacobs perceives how her sexual exploitation is not individuated: she bears witness to the lives of other women under slavery and the treatment of white wives and their daughters on plantations. Flint's obsession with Jacobs endures long after she finally escapes the South. Flint's easy dismissal of Black women with whom he had children contrasts with his strong desire to control Jacobs. After she runs away from his son's plantation where he had sent her to be reined in, Flint makes three trips to New York, often paid for by borrowing money on interest, to find her. No matter how much money friends offer him to buy Jacobs to remove her from his house, Flint refuses despite his often difficult pecuniary state. When Jacobs finally leaves the garret to escape North and writes an authentic letter to him, he immediately sets after her again even though he has not seen her in seven years. From the beginning, he not only threatens Jacobs that he can possess her sexually with or without her consent, but he also tries to seduce her with promises of his devotion: "I would cherish you. I would make a lady of you. Now go, and think of all I have promised you" (35). Yet Flint continues to conjure schemes to isolate Jacobs from others to possess her body away from the community and even from the institution of slavery: "I would make a lady of you." Jacobs has witnessed enough of his behavior toward other women not to trust him. At one point, Dr. Flint promises to get her uncle out of prison if Jacobs accepts him as a lover (25). Jacobs reports, though, "I had seen several women sold, with his babies at the breast. He never allowed his offspring by slaves to remain long in sight of himself and his wife" (55). One woman whom he sells parts from Flint by saying, "You *promised* to treat me well" (13). Master Flint, according to whispered accounts, fathered at least eleven children with other women; he also hints to Jacobs that, as a physician, he can help women abort an unwanted pregnancy, implying that he may have fathered even more (35). Lauren Berlant argues that Jacobs exposes how the private realms of experience are shaped by restrictive public, political domains. She claims that narratives like Jacobs's "refuse to affirm the private horizon of personal entitlement as the cause of their suffering. America becomes explicitly, in this context, accountable for the sexual exploitation it authorizes in the guise of the white male citizen's domestic and erotic privilege" (Berlant, "Queen" 554). Jacobs illuminates how national problems are often naturalized or treated as individual impediments.

Flint always interprets Jacobs's desire for freedom as a cover for her sexual desire for other men, just as abolitionists are impugned by the insinuation that they seek to end slavery as part of an individual sexual fetish. Just as abolitionists face recrimination for advancing a cause because of their supposed sexual desire for African Americans, Jacobs is repeatedly accused of desiring a man rather than her manumission. His lack of imagination makes it easier for Jacobs to access how he will interpret her behavior. When a slave trader seeks to buy Jacobs, Flint becomes paranoid that they are secret lovers even though Jacobs had never met the man: "No jealous lover ever watched a rival more closely than he watched me and the unknown slaveholder, with whom he accused me of wishing to get up an intrigue" (H. Jacobs 81). Even after Jacobs fulfills her convoluted schemes to thwart Flint by having Mr. Sands's children, she still must rebuff Flint's advances. He continues to pursue and punish her for her "unfaithfulness" to him. If she forswears the father of her children: "I will procure a cottage, where you and the children can live together. Your labor shall be light—a home and freedom!" (83). He promises her "freedom" in the abstract, not to manumit her. Jacobs can contrive against him successfully because his obsession creates predictable lines of behavior that she has observed in his dealings with other women. However, she never deludes herself into feeling flattered by his attention. She knows that his true obsession lies not with her but by manipulating space to tighten his power over others.

Much like the women characters surveyed in previous chapters, Jacobs conceives of her war with Flint as discursive. Directly after Dr. Flint announces that her cottage is complete, Jacobs informs him that she is pregnant with Sands's child. She had anticipated and plotted the revelation:

> As for Dr. Flint, I had a feeling of satisfaction and triumph in the thought of telling him [about the pregnancy]. From time to time he told me of his intended arrangements [to move her away from town], and I was silent. At last, he came and told me the cottage was completed, and ordered me to go to it. I told him I would never enter it. He said, "I have heard enough of such talk as that. You shall go, if you are carried by force; and you shall remain there."
>
> I replied, "I will never go there. In a few months I shall be a mother."
>
> He stood and looked at me in dumb amazement, and left the house without a word. I thought I should be happy in my triumph over him. But now that the truth was out, and my relatives would hear of it, I felt wretched. (56)

As usual, she codes her refusal to be Flint's lover as a refusal to enter certain spaces. Jacobs frames the passage with her "feelings" prior to and following her admission as she vacillates between "triumph" and "wretchedness." Yet her feelings before and after telling Flint about her baby locate the two spheres that Jacobs never reconciles: the one sphere involves her war with the master that places her and him in their own plane engaging in their antagonistic struggle over her body, and the other sphere involves her extended family and community and their unremitting commitment to moral paradigms that the practice of slavery renders impossible. She relishes telling Flint about her pregnancy—she considers her dealings with him in terms of "triumph" and "satisfaction"—but once she has told him, her "triumph" dissipates because she remains unmarried, pregnant, and legally under his control. As Berlant has argued, Jacobs "mimed the privileges of citizenship" (*Queen* 227) in wresting control of her life away from her enslaver. Still, no matter how much she tries to claim a victory over Flint, she finds her powers undercut by her position as a woman under slavery. To her family, her pregnancy is a source of shame, despite how common Jacobs's predicament was for other Black women in the South.

Flint also operates within an imaginary sphere but a more limited one; therefore, Jacobs can anticipate and outmaneuver him. Mastery gives an illusion of control. He thinks a cottage four miles out of Edenton will isolate Jacobs from her family. She testifies that amid his plans, she was "silent." When she finally protests, Flint demurs, "I have heard enough of such talk as that," which implies that he has imagined her continued protestations. Ultimately, though, Jacobs leaves Flint speechless with her bombshell: "he stood and looked at me in dumb amazement." A number of contradictory feelings emerges. On the one hand, Jacobs has successfully bested the master, leaving him abject. On the other, she must live with the consequences of an unplanned pregnancy with a child who will be born into lifelong servitude.

WRITING
FOR FUTURITY

Jacobs as the author of *Incidents* seems astutely aware that the same techniques that she employed to manipulate Dr. Flint may be used to structure her narrative and control the reader's affective response; however, she avoids employing them in her life writing. She offers no surprise plot twists or strange elisions or even distracting moments of suspense. She structures scenes to avoid some of the games authors play with readers. For instance, she does not dramatize her love story with Mr. Sands and thus does not inspire mimetic desire in the reader. Moreover, her refusal to build suspense is most striking in the complicated scheme to have her lover secretly buy their children from Dr. Flint. The story has several built-in suspense points. First, Jacobs is in hiding, so she lived the actual suspense of not knowing how the scheme unfolded. Second, Jacobs has a nightmare in which the children appear dead before she learns they are safe. Third, she places her trust in white people. She and her coconspirators have to place their trust in a slaver who has promised not to tell Dr. Flint the identity of the buyer. She also has to trust her lover to spend money to buy not only their children but also her brother. Fourth, the plan hinges on Dr. Flint's impulsiveness. The scheme works because she can anticipate his sensibilities and blind spots. After selling them impulsively, he later adds a caveat to the sale, demanding that the children must be sold out of state, but he only thinks of this after the sale has transpired. Jacobs narrates the successful coup but then recounts, "I had no share in the rejoicing of that evening. The events of the day had not come to my knowledge. And now I will tell you something that happened to me" (107). She spares the reader anxiety even at the cost of building suspense into her story. Philip Gura explains that the *National Anti-Slavery Standard* praised Jacobs's work for "its avoidance of sensationalism" (159). Her narrative strategy avoids capturing or controlling the reader's attention, her way of emphasizing the text's importance to future readers for whom the central questions of the text (the Fugitive Slave Law and abolition) are presumably already settled.

The lack of figurative language in her text also avoids the mediation and distancing of metaphor that would impede the reader's focus on the story. Her use of analogy is usually simple: the phrase "the war of my life" describes her antagonism with Flint and "slowly murdered" describes Aunt Nancy's death after a lifetime of servitude (145). Her use of hyperbole in these examples amplifies the degradations of slavery. The paratactic syntax gives the text a journalistic style and allows Jacobs to avoid excessive subordinate clauses; thus, she gives all facets of her life writing equal significance. She also at times provides an ironic narration to proffer multiple points of view but without immersing the reader in them. Instead, she allows the reader to examine them even as she openly worries about the reader's reception of her tale. In her chapter on the death of her Aunt Nancy, who also served the Flints for decades, Jacobs includes a long description of how a visitor from the North would interpret the scene, if she were to pass the funeral with no context of the situation, except for the southern propaganda that seeps into the northern presses: "Northern travelers, passing through the place, might have described this tribute of respect to the humble dead as a beautiful feature in the 'patriarchal institution'; a touching proof of the attachment between slaveholders and their servants; and tenderhearted Mrs. Flint would have confirmed this impression, with handkerchief at her eyes" (146). Jacobs teaches her reader to be skeptical of "proof" or evidence that seems to "confirm" southern lies about master-slave relations. She broadens the reader's "horizons of intelligibility" by giving the scene greater scope and historical relevance.

Not only does she catalog decades of abuse directed at Aunt Nancy, but she then heightens her take as an "author" by referring to herself in the third person: "We could also have told them of a poor, blighted young creature, shut up in a living grave for years, to avoid the tortures that would be inflicted on her, if she ventured to come out and look on the face of her departed friend" (147). Jacobs's use of the subjunctive reiterates the text's engagement with metanarrative, for her entire text fulfills her wish that she "could have told them." By distancing herself through third person, she can expand on the contradictions and symmetry of the scene: the young woman caught in the oxymoron of a "living grave," who, even in her quasi-death, cannot commune with those who are literally dead. The "poor, blighted young creature," Jacobs herself, is alienated from the living and the dead. Paul Armstrong suggests literary critics who rely on cultural studies methodology often "neglect futurity" in favor of emphasizing the specific context of the moment of writing or publishing a text ("In Defense" 94). Another horizon emerges in which the author flexes certain rhetorical moves to adapt to her conjectures about future readers. Jacobs anticipates Flint's behavior while also anticipating the reader's. In using an ironic tone to convey the hypocrisy of slave owners, this third horizon that attends to futurity emerges. She trusts to future readers to see more than the "Northern visitor" and bear witness to her family's abjection to the Flint family.

To compare her treatment of the reader to her treatment of Flint, one must consider the master-slave power dynamic as transposed when Jacobs assumes the role of writer and Flint the role of reader. The vacillation between "calculation" and "recklessness" encapsulates Jacobs's work as the author of her life and her life writing. She calculates her rhetorical moves but then must wait to see their effect on others. Jacobs relies on discursive means to defy time and space. Her reification of her life, as she imagines herself free and inhabiting the North, depends on her use of print culture. Jacobs stays in Edenton, hiding for seven years, not only because she finds it difficult to escape but also because she hesitates to leave her children and she capitulates to the anxious pleading of her grandmother to stay with her. As proof that she fled North, Jacobs decides to send letters to Flint posted by intermediaries in the North back to North Carolina without telling her grandmother, even though, if these letters were found before they were mailed, she would have endangered all their lives. Again, she does not toy with the reader about the risks that she and others incur to build suspense. Dr. Flint had already made three separate trips to New York to find her at considerable expense before she decides to solidify his suspicions that she resides in the North by writing and sending false letters to him. Her relationship with Dr. Flint remains mediated through the written word. Her game depends on several misdirections that Jacobs can foresee, and these misdirections depend on the politics that northern spaces metonymically convey. Slight shifts in setting and thus context realign the power matrix. In these letters, she lays several traps. First, she encloses a letter written to her grandmother along with the one to the Flints; yet she knows the Flint family will intercept it and never deliver it to her grandmother. Indeed, Flint substitutes his own fake letter for Jacobs's fake to control the information he gives to the grandmother. Second, her letter states that, although she lives in Boston (which Flint fears entering), she happens to be staying in New York because if she lives in New York, Flint will not abandon his plans to retrieve her. Her canny use of the metonymic political significance of these two sites both frustrates Flint (as she claims to live in Boston) and keeps the chase alive (though she sometimes goes to New York).

Jacobs's "abductive reasoning," *à la* Poe's Detective Dupin, her grasp of others and how they will respond, gives shape to her stratagems and reveals her pleasure in dramatic irony. Jacobs directs action from above despite her passive, prostrate position in the garret. This kind of play animates not just Jacobs's interactions with Flint but also slave narratives in general, in which Black men and women are forced to feign ignorance—whether about their literacy or where to find runaways when confronted by white people. Zoe Trodd points to the game playing in the upstairs garret in Stowe's *Uncle Tom's Cabin,* in which the slave Cassie plots to make Legree think that a ghost lives in the attic (72). Derrick Spires has written that these "trickster" moves in African American literature, especially "[i]n contrast to the stability of Harriet Beecher Stowe's Uncle Tom," include "Harriet Jacobs, who creatively uses space and language to gain freedom" (Spires 199). Yet the games between Jacobs and Dr. Flint defy even the genre of the slave narrative. Trodd notices how Jacobs's "letters to Flint lead him in circles, transforming the garret from a no-man's-land into a site of power" (83).

Jacobs explains how she devised her scheme through secondhand knowledge of geographies she gleaned from printed texts, to give her setting authenticity. Notice, though, that that kind of geographic specificity is lacking in terms of its Edenton, North Carolina, setting: "Early the next morning, I seated myself near the little aperture to examine the newspaper. It was a piece of the *New York Herald;* and, for once, the paper that systematically abuses the colored people, was made to render them a service. Having obtained what information I wanted concerning streets and numbers, I wrote two letters, one to my grandmother, the other to Dr. Flint" (128). Jacobs juxtaposes the large metropolitan site of New York with her cramped living corners to illustrate how her power to control Flint defies boundaries. She nestles into a corner of the garret where a little light intrudes to study the newspaper to ascertain geographic spots in New York to give her letter authenticity. In the letter to her grandmother, she "asked her to direct her answer to a certain street in Boston, as I did not live in New York, though I went there some-times" (H. Jacobs 129). Jacobs's tactical skills result from her willingness to see past her lifetime servitude. While she recognizes the *New York Herald* as a racist paper, she makes use of it to further toy with Dr. Flint. In this instance, the newspaper does her "a service." She is a canny reader who can interpret the paper's racist content. She then dismisses the paper, as though the paper were a disagreeable servant, once she "obtained what information I wanted concerning streets and numbers." She uses the information they report to create an alternative reality in which she transverses distant cities. For Flint, however, the geographies are tangible to him, so they take on an outsized im-portance because he equates getting to these locations with possessing Linda.

Within the games she constructs, Jacobs has to account not only for imag-ined space but for imagined time. She "dated these letters ahead, to allow for the time it would take to carry them and sent a memorandum of the date to the messenger" (129). "Allowing for time" might be the best way to describe Jacob's narrative techniques as she trusts to a future, when readers will be able to understand the stakes of her situation as a woman, not as an enslaved person. Yet Jacobs's letter does not conclude the matter, because she wants to hear the result of her game: "I told my grandmother Dr. Flint would be sure to come, and asked her to have him sit near a certain door, and leave it open, that I might hear what he said. The next morning I took my station within sound of that door, and remained motionless as a statue" (129). While the imagined runaway in the North transverses New York and Boston, the real Jacobs lies entombed ("motionless") in her small-closeted space where any slight movement could mean detection. Jacobs's plot works. She anticipates Flint's every move ("Dr. Flint would be sure to come") and then listens to him, while hidden from sight, as her conjectures are proven correct.

Despite Jacobs's absence from the town, Dr. Flint continues to obsess over her. Nonetheless, he refuses to seek her out himself if she is in Boston; Jacobs's reliance on the commonwealth's reputation proves prescient. Dr. Flint, in an effort to control the exchange, reads the letter from "Linda" aloud to the grandmother. It quickly becomes apparent that he has written a false letter in which Jacobs laments running away and begs to return to the South. He claims that she wants her children sent to her either in New York or Philadelphia, and thus the geographic games continue as Flint offers to entice Jacobs away from Boston without directly stating why. Dr. Flint reports to her grandmother: "I know exactly where to find her; but I don't choose to go to Boston for her. I had rather she would come back of her own accord, in a respectable manner" (129). Flint's control remains firmly rooted in geography: "I know exactly where to find her," he reiterates. His admission that "I don't choose to go to Boston" highlights how he must conceptualize his weak position in their power games as a personal choice even as he plans to spend money for this fool's errand.

The lynchpin for Jacobs, though, is the metonymic registers of claiming to reside in Boston. Jacobs's presumed presence in Boston creates several complications for Flint, complications that he repeatedly denies. Flint renders his lack of choice—he cannot risk seeking her in Boston—as magnanimity in allowing Jacobs the power of choosing to "come back of her own accord, in a respectable manner." He refuses to order her Uncle Phillip to bring her home directly. Instead, he is willing to pay to send and return the uncle to Massachusetts. But Uncle Phillip balks at Flint's scheme: "from what [Uncle Phillip] had heard of Massachusetts, he judged he should be mobbed if he went there after a runaway slave" (130). The doctor dismisses his concerns:

> "All stuff and nonsense, Phillip!" replied the doctor. "Do you suppose I want you to kick up a row in Boston? The business can all be done quietly. Linda writes that she wants to come back. You are her relative, and she would trust *you*. The case would be different if I went. She might object to coming with *me;* and the damned abolitionists, if they knew I was her master, would not believe me, if I told them she had begged to go back. They would get up a row; and I should not like to see Linda dragged through the streets like a common negro." (130)

Phillip states the matter directly. He fears an abolitionist mob will prevent him if he goes to Boston. Dr. Flint brushes aside his fear; at the same time, he suggests that Phillip retrieve his niece "quietly," a suggestion that contradicts his assurances. He concedes that "damned abolitionists" would make it oner-ous for him, as her owner, to take her. Moreover, he cannot give a consistent account of Jacobs. He concedes she might object to coming with him, but by the end of his utterance he imagines the possibility of her "beg[ging] to go back" with him. He then reverses his role as slave owner with Jacobs's, as though the abolitionists would "drag" her through the streets rather than him. In addition, Dr. Flint writes to the mayor of Boston to ascertain if Linda lives there. Her grandmother laments, "What will you do if the mayor of Boston sends him word that you haven't been there? . . . . O Linda, I wish you had never sent the letters" (131). Jacobs replies, "The mayor of Boston won't trouble himself . . . for Dr. Flint. The letters will do good in the end. I shall get out of this dark hole some time or other" (131). Jacobs's letters achieve her ends, because the idea of Massachusetts keeps Dr. Flint at bay. Unlike her grandmother and Dr. Flint, who make moment-to-moment decisions, her future-oriented stance as an author focuses on "the end" result, such as her poignant reference to "some time or other."

But Jacobs's letters prove more powerful than the mayor, because of her assured ability to anticipate how these men will behave. As Lipsitz argues, the white spatial imaginary hinges on exchange value that Jacobs perceives: the mayor "won't trouble himself." The mayor of Boston would reap noth-ing from seeking out Flint's property. Just as she uses letters to manipulate Flint, she sees the results of her victories in more letters: "The fact that Dr. Flint had written to the mayor of Boston convinced me that he believed my letter to be genuine, and of course that he had no suspicion of my being any-where in the vicinity. . . . I resolved, therefore, to continue to write letters from the north from time to time" (131–32). Even though he seeks Jacobs's whereabouts to make her vulnerable to detection, the letter he sends to the mayor actually provide Jacobs with proof that Flint has been fooled by her stratagems. Meanwhile, Jacobs's confederates, who gain nothing by helping and risk a great deal, navigate between Edenton and Boston. In fact, these confederates help contrast the black spatial imaginary with its emphasis on "use value" from the white spatial imaginary that organizes itself based on "exchange value," to borrow terms from Lipsitz (13). Her friends who travel from port to port facilitate Jacobs's stratagems because they can be "useful" to her and therefore will help her even if it means putting their lives at risk.

While hiding in town, Jacobs's fake letters give her time to make a real escape. The imaginary recourse she has to the North enables her real venture there, collapsing the real and the imaginary in the text. Just as Jacobs once imagined herself alternating between New York and Boston to evade Flint, she finds herself facing this predicament when she actually does start working in New York. Yet once Jacobs physically goes North, her control over Flint's movements diminishes. Every time she knows he is coming North for her in New York, where she works, she goes to Boston to evade him. She has lost discursive control. Space shapes the mindset of its inhabitants. While Flint's licentiousness extends even into New York, where he personally goes in search of Jacobs, it cannot aid him in entering Massachusetts. Instead, he treats the Bay State as an inviolate, chaste woman. Jacobs appropriates its guardedness against slave owners since she cannot do so on her own. Indeed, in fleeing to Boston, the general disapprobation toward slavery secures her from Flint even as he exercises his rights granted by the Fugitive Slave Law.

Because of Harriet Jacobs's precarious position under slavery, these safe zones, whether the garret or Massachusetts, do not provide lasting safety either. As Patricia Yaeger contends, any discussion of space must include an analysis of language that "addresses the ways in which the physical world first elicits desires, then disappoints or reapportions these desires, and finally masks the ache of this disappointment or asymmetry" (25). The process Yaeger describes sounds similar to Berlant's concept of "cruel optimism." As Berlant explains, "[A] relation of cruel optimism exists when something you desire is actually an obstacle to your flourishing. . . . [These desires] become cruel only when the object that draws your attachment actively impedes the aim that brought you to it initially" (*Cruel* 1). Or as Freeburg explains, "*Incidents* places Dr. Flint in his own state of impasse, with his slave object out of reach—his beliefs disputed, he has a glimpse of the larger threat to his way of life through Jacobs" (108).

Once Jacobs experiences racism in the North, Massachusetts loses some of the ideological registers it had acquired, such as freedom and justice. Furthermore, she finds herself overwhelmed in actual northern cities by the sights, sounds, and people, a sensory overload that is exacerbated by her long imprisonment hiding in the garret. Yet Jacobs never becomes totally susceptible to the signification of sites, in part because her early life in slavery braced her for the slippage between space and sociocultural practices. Jacobs's ability to perceive the power dynamics that undergird sites is not the same as the vision that W. E. B. Du Bois famously termed "double consciousness." Rather Jacobs seems to understand and manipulate the paradigms that give shape to a consciousness, whether doubled or not. As Sally Gomaa maintains, "To be known fully, slavery has to be experienced. But to enter this experience, one has to be narrator and narrative as well as spectacle and spectator. Jacobs, therefore, consciously draws attention to how she occupies this double position" (377). This "double position" is facilitated by geography.

Jacobs's successful manipulation of her position as a slave and her escape to the North depends on access to competing narratives of ethical practice. Yellin explains that, since Edenton was a port town, "Edenton's black seamen, both slave and free, could not be prevented from communicating, as they always had, with their free brothers and sisters in New England, Haiti, Central America, Mexico, and Bolivia—where slavery had ended. . . . Still, the white South could try to control the channels of information" (*Harriet Jacobs* 38–39). In particular, those in Edenton vilify the abolitionist stronghold of Boston; this hostility provides Jacobs and others with a counter paradigm to their lives in the South.

Likewise, Boston's progressivism unsettles life in North Carolina. After Nat Turner's rebellion in 1831, North Carolina made it a crime to possess or circulate abolitionist literature, literature that originates in Massachusetts. Yellin reports how in Raleigh in 1831, the publishers of William Lloyd Garrison's Boston-based *Liberator* were indicted for breaking North Carolina sedition laws (*Harriet Jacobs* 39). The North Carolina authorities feared the importation of political beliefs. Jacobs hears a story about a girl who ran away from slavery in Edenton to New York only to find herself begging in the street and pleading with a slaveholder to take her back to the South (43). Jacobs testifies, "Many of the slaves believe such stories, and think it is not worthwhile to exchange slavery for such a hard kind of freedom" (43). Despite the slaveholders' attempts to keep their enslaved people ignorant of politics and slaveholding laws in the Northern United States, Jacobs reports, "even the most ignorant have some confused notions about it" (45). Because she can read, others seek her out for information: "I was often asked if I had seen any thing in the newspapers about white folks over in the big north, who were trying to get their freedom for them. Some believe that the abolition-ists have already made them free, and that it is established by law, but that their masters prevent the law from going into effect" (H. Jacobs 45). While northern states may opt for different laws regarding slavery, the implications of those laws cannot be contained, despite anti-literacy laws and censorship; likewise, the newspapers circulate information and opinions that readers or listeners then improvise upon or reimagine.

Because New York and Boston recur so frequently in the texts that circu-late through North Carolina, it is not surprising that, when Jacobs imagines herself free, she places herself in these Northern cities. Matthew Wilkens has sorted through the number of times different geographic locations are men-tioned throughout nineteenth-century American literature. His calculations affirm that between 1851 and 1874 New York State dominates, with references to it totaling 14,899. Massachusetts in the same period comes in fourth with 6,733, behind "None/multiple" at 14,155 and Virginia at 8,213 (Wilkens 3). Wilkens asserts, "[G]eographic information is tremendously important if we are to understand the issues that shaped not only literary and cultural production in the nineteenth century, but also the ways in which Americans construed their social, political, and economic projects in the following years" (10). Indeed, the ties between cultural production and geography remain central to Jacobs's life, especially since she eventually forges a life in the North, crisscrossing between New York and Massachusetts and even across the Atlantic to England.

The cultural imaginary of Massachusetts as a space where people firmly advocated for universal emancipation was propagated by its citizens, who took pride in their progressivism and celebrated it as a hallmark of their ties to the true spirit of the United States as a nation founded on the principles of equality and freedom. Historian Margot Minardi writes that the people of Massachusetts "argued that their Commonwealth was the historical model and ideal for the nation. In the second quarter of the nineteenth century, the cultural element of this 'sectional nationalism' was eminently effective, giving Massachusetts claim to historical preeminence in texts and images circulated throughout the United States" (Minardi 7). The newspapers in North Carolina, however, portray Boston, in its opposition to slavery, as hostile to the Constitution. Nonetheless, Jacobs learns to associate the place with the cognitive dissonance she feels under slavery. Discussing her reasons for choosing to post her letters from Boston, she writes, "But even in that dark region [of the South], where knowledge is so carefully excluded from the slave, I had heard enough about Massachusetts to come to the conclusion that slaveholders did not consider it a comfortable place to go in search of a runaway" (131).

Indeed, this proves temporarily true for Jacobs and her brother, who also escapes from slavery. Once she makes her way North after living for seven years in the garret, she finds employment in New York, but she makes several trips to Boston to evade Dr. Flint, southern tourists, or relatives of her owners who visit the North. When John Jacobs, her brother, flees from his enslaver in New York, he quickly goes to Boston and then New Bedford, Massachusetts. Yellin conjectures as to why the brother goes to Boston: "[P]erhaps he saw copies of William Lloyd Garrison's newspaper *The Liberator,* which for a dozen years had made 'abolition' synonymous with 'Boston'" (*Harriet Jacobs* 75). Jacobs reiterates slave owners' fears of going into Massachusetts territory. Mr. Sands frets that the abolitionists will "decoy" Jacobs's brother away from him. When her brother runs away in New York, Mr. Sands continues to ascribe responsibility to activists but not John. Jacobs narrates: "He had not been urged away by abolitionists. He needed no information they could give him about slavery to stimulate his desire for freedom" (125). Despite its notorious reliance on exploited immigrant labor during the same period and despite depictions of a coldness of manner in its people in nineteenth-century popular literature, Massachusetts represents a fervid animosity to slavery.

This sentiment about the Bay State animates abolitionist slave narratives and speeches in the antebellum United States. In an 1848 letter from the abolitionist Wendell Phillips to Frederick Douglass, Phillips juxtaposes Massachusetts to the Carolinas to predict that Massachusetts will metonymically suggest freedom to those living in remote US spots. He describes how, despite slavery's hold on the Union, "New England, cutting loose from a blood-stained Union, shall glory in being the house of refuge for the oppressed,— till we no longer merely 'hide the outcast,' or make a merit of standing idly by while he is hunted in our midst; but, consecrating anew the soil of the Pilgrims as an asylum for the oppressed, proclaim our *welcome* to the slave so loudly, that the tones shall reach every hut in the Carolinas, and make the broken-hearted bondman leap up at the thought of old Massachusetts" (Phillips 279). The passage encapsulates how Massachusetts breaks from the

Union only to return the nation to its authentic position as a safe ground for the oppressed, a position formed by its early settlers, the Pilgrims. Massachusetts's post-Revolutionary history of declaring slavery illegal, its refusal to return fugitives, the volubility of its abolitionist leaders had given it a reputation as a safe haven for individuals seeking asylum. Minardi reports that the *Massachusetts Abolitionist* paper began its inaugural issue with this editorial in 1839: "MASSACHUSETTS! Her very name is the synonym of freedom!" (36). And, in 1850, the *Liberator* waxed, "[E]very fugitive slave shall instantly be transformed into a freeman as soon as he touches the soil of Massachusetts" (qtd. in Minardi 37). This overblown rhetoric not only perpetuated a cohesive ideological stance for the people of Massachusetts but also, because the commonwealth figures itself as the forefront of national trends, it likewise nods toward a federal imaginary of liberality. What is distinct about Massachusetts later transforms into what is distinct about the United States. Paradoxically, its exceptionalism permeates the rest of the nation, transforming the exception to the rule. Jacobs uses Massachusetts to anticipate general turns in the consciousness of readers. However, Massachusetts relies on its attitude toward slavery to create an enduring legacy about its commitment to social justice, even though it continues to perpetuate and institutionalize racialized social formations; ultimately, its hypocrisy toward African Americas reveals how it uses bodies not as chattel but as evidence for its commitment to liberty.

. . .

Yellin reports how Jacobs's autobiography was forgotten while other narratives entered the abolitionist canon, including stories about women like Harriet Tubman and Sojourner Truth, even though neither was literate. Yellin conjectures that "[m]ale turn-of-the-century readers . . . found [*Incidents*] a 'women's book.' White female readers were perhaps put off by Linda's account of her scandalous sexual history" (*Harriet Jacobs* 262). The true plight of women in slavery remained shrouded. Jacobs's story reveals how people's entry into shame, secrets, and silence is rigged from the start. As Berlant argues, "The work of 'women's culture' enacts a fantasy that my life is not just mine, but an experience understood by other women, even when it is not shared by many or any" (*Female* x). Jacobs's story troubles this fantasy only because of the silence that pervades US culture about the sexual abuse of women under slavery. One can observe how this silencing operates by examining Jacobs's brother John's narrative. In his life writing published the same year as *Incidents,* John includes his sister's tale but swaps her story of sexual harassment with a story about his sister (Jacobs) facing the constant threat of a lashing (J. Jacobs 210). Masking sexual violation with physical violation reveals the unease sexual relations inspire and how that unease covers over the truth about life in slavery. Therefore, Jacobs's story is both everybody's and no one's because, despite the number of women who also endured sexual exploitation and aggression, no one will confirm how pervasive it was. Yellin writes, "By creating a narrator who presents her private sexual history as a subject of public political concern, Jacobs moves her book out of the world of conventional nineteenth-century polite discourse" (Yellin, Introduction xvi). Yet the phrase "out of the world" is revealing. For Jacobs, there is no world outside of "polite discourse." It has been my argument that Jacobs writes for a futurity rather than her contemporaries. Again, it is useful to cite Armstrong's telling point about the three horizons to which we need to attend: "Contextual historical studies that take into account only two of those three horizons—the text's relation to its contemporaneous situation and the traces of the past in its originating circumstances—but those that neglect futurity, the third horizon, are fatally incomplete. They take the historicity out of history because the indeterminacy of what is to come signals our particularity and contingency" ("In Defense" 94). The stakes as the author of her life could not be higher. Her need to shape experiences by anticipating Flint's future behavior while anticipating the reader's as well appears astute. If the book is not a conventional nineteenth-century text, then perhaps it fits in better in some distant time. The text depends on future readers, readers whom Jacobs cultivates through the act of sharing her life writing and to whom she outlines the dimensions of a black spatial imaginary. She addresses her audience as "ye, [white] women of the North," but she cannot rely on them. On her first night in northern territory, she listens to a well-intentioned, if hurtful, warning that people will not sympathize with her story if she reveals her status as an unwed mother. Therefore, she pleads with her readers: they cannot understand her situation unless they have lived it; as such, these readers cannot pass recriminating judgment on her: On reuniting with her son, she asks, "Oh reader, can you imagine my joy? No, you cannot, unless you have been a slave mother" (173). But she needs the political capital of these women to advocate for overturning the Fugitive Slave Law. She realizes that politics is structured by the people's will and that will must be courted through identificatory practices to which she has no access; therefore, she cannot pledge herself to sentimentality. Instead, by coming forward with her tale of sexual exploitation not just of her but of women under slavery, she raises the stakes for her readers. As Gilmore and Marshall note, "Jacobs places cross-racial female solidarity and institutional change at the center of her project, fraught as that potential alliance must be" (674). She offers these women readers no vicarious pleasure through her story. As Yellin explains, "Jacobs's Linda Brent does not seek to inspire her audience to overcome individual character defects or to engage in reformist activity within the private sphere, but urges them to enter the public sphere and work to end chattel slavery and white racism" (Introduction xxxiv). Lydia Maria Child echoes this sentiment when, as Jacobs's editor, she writes that she helped publish Jacobs's text despite its "delicate" subject matter in the "hope of arousing conscientious and reflecting women at the North to a sense of their duty in the exertion of moral influence on the question of Slavery" (Child, Preface 4). Sexual mores obscure the actual power nexus in US cultural geography. These Northern women seem as mythic as the Boston of Jacobs's imagination. Jacobs, in her narrative, paradoxically, relies upon those myths while overturning them for her purposes.

EPILOGUE

NATHANIEL HAWTHORNE'S *The Scarlet Letter* (1850) OFFERS TWO
visions of women's futurity. Early in the text, the character Hester's delib-
erations on her plight as an outcast in seventeenth-century Puritan Boston
lead her to conclude that women's liberation will entail a radical overthrow
of society: "As a first step, the whole system of society is to be torn down and
built up anew. Then the very nature of the opposite sex, or its long hereditary habit, which has become like nature, is to be essentially modified before
woman can be allowed to assume what seems a fair and suitable position"
(165). Hester's vision of emancipation will affect everyone, not just women,
especially as she suggests gender is a social construct and identifies the process of its naturalization. Hers is not a tepid call for change; instead, she
embraces a destructive vision that desacralizes the current order. In the text's
conclusion, though, the reader learns that Hester's views have altered entirely. She now offers a hopeful version of women's future happiness, despite
no changes to the status quo. Living alone in her cottage, she tells the women
who seek her counsel that it is "[h]er firm belief, that, at some brighter period,
when the world should have grown ripe for it, in Heaven's own time, a new
truth would be revealed, in order to establish the whole relation between man
and woman on a surer ground of mutual happiness" (263). Instead of a fixed
plan to tear down society ("as a first step"), Hester now encourages a passive
acceptance of some unknown truth that will appear at some indeterminate
time. As a futurist, Hester mollifies the unhappy by substituting her "firm
belief" for action. By claiming this "new truth" will emerge "when the world
should have grown ripe for it," she places responsibility for inequities on
individual people who are not ready rather than the society that fosters them.

As an unhappy outcast, Hester seeks to overturn society, but later as a
contented community elder, she urges individual resignation. Hester's con-

ception of futurity is undercut at other points in the text by her belief in immortality. Several times her mind ponders how she and the Reverend Mr. Dimmesdale, with whom she committed adultery, will forge a life together in hell. The narrator details how she represses the joy she feels at the idea of her and Dimmesdale "connected in union, that, unrecognized on earth, would bring them together before the bar of final judgment, and make that their marriage-alter, for a joint futurity of endless retribution" (72). Even as Dimmesdale lies dying on the scaffold at the end of the text, she whispers to him, "Shall we not meet again . . . Shall we not spend our immortal life together" (234). She urges him to reassure her that their fates are intertwined: "Thou lookest far into eternity, with those bright dying eyes! Then tell me what thou seest?" (234). Meanwhile, Dimmesdale expresses horror at the thought of compounding their sin just as he is about to die. Hester's late resignation seems undergirded by a belief in immortality, even immortal punishment in hell. Through Hester, Hawthorne acknowledges the foundations of sexist double standards in the social and political order even as he seems to ignore racial injustice. But then Hawthorne diminishes even his acknowledgment of sexism in two ways. First, he establishes that Hester's longing for romantic union in "a joint futurity of endless retribution" voids the need to reorganize society; second, he suggests that women should not bother to imagine, let alone try to implement, solutions to overturn the double standard toward them, because problems will resolve themselves if one relies on the passage of time. Many critics have seized on these final lines of the text and Hester's decision to resume wearing the scarlet letter, after she returns to Boston from England, as evidence of Hawthorne's ideology of incrementalism toward political questions like women's rights and abolition.[1]

The Scarlet Letter remains a quintessential text that cements American literature as distinct from British or Anglophone literatures and repurposes the Puritan past through individual characters, as though the story acts as an antidote to the transgressions of colonial settlers, despite few references to indigenous peoples in the text. According to novelist Bharati Mukherjee, the text stands as "a psychologically complex portrait of the seventeenth-century dissident: a free-thinking woman making what peace she can with the demands of submission to a doctrinaire religion and gender inequality" (272). Although Mukherjee makes the text sound subversive, that interpretation places too much emphasis on an individual as she faces problems that require system-wide change. In *The Scarlet Letter,* individual complexity dominates, in contrast to the texts analyzed in the previous chapters, which outline the possibilities for widespread change within the operations of empire. The passivity of Hester to effect change contrasts with the bold imaginings and deeds of the women characters analyzed here: Unca Eliza, Mary, Magawisca, Hope Leslie, Linda Brent, and Rosa. Instead, the women authors examined in the previous chapters all seem attuned to the ways in which conceptions of time—"the promise of one day"—further desubstantiate their political visions of egalitarianism or women's empowerment. They do not go so far as Lee Edelman's bold call, in *No Future,* to reject discourse about some distant time when justice will emerge, but their texts challenge the normalization of time or "chrononormativity," a term coined by Elizabeth Freeman to explain how "[m]anipulations of time convert historically specific regimes of asymmetrical power into seemingly ordinary bodily tempos and routines, which in turn organize the value and meaning of time" (*Time Binds* 3). In these early American texts, the anonymous author of *The Female American,* Sansay, Sedgwick, Jacobs, and Child provide alternative modes for engaging with imperial sites that invite reader participation to sort through, unpack, and perhaps ameliorate the racial and gender injustices they represent.

The future horizon that the authors shape negates familiar constructions of the past. They establish power through indirect means that seem to characterize empire building in the twenty-first century, as described by Michael Hardt and Antonio Negri, as "filled by intellectual, immaterial, and communicative labor power" (29). In their argument, Hardt and Negri refer to the widespread networks of capital and communication technologies of the late twentieth century. The characters under discussion in the previous chapters use more rudimentary communication tools—whether counterfeit letters (Jacobs), operatic performances (Child), ancient oracles (Winkfield), oral storytelling (Sedgwick), even the mediating figure of a disgraced former vice president (Sansay)—to challenge hegemonic power and seize it for themselves while making explicit how social and economic power in the domestic sphere is propped up by Christianity, militarization, fractured political geographies, or property laws. These books imagine how women might use discursive means to claim power over others, even as these representations reveal an undercurrent of anxiety about powerful women and how these women assuage that anxiety.

Imaginary Empires demonstrates how literature that provides an alternative rendering vis-à-vis historical development offers a new vantage point from which to evaluate the relationship between literature and culture. In the texts studied here, we find women authors who imagine what it would be like to wield power over others, whether over whole populations of people or suitors or even enslavers. Because of the wide circuit of geographies covered in these literary works, they further inscribe the transnational as a disciplinary category in cultural studies. As Laura Stevens maintains, "Even our interpretations of texts and issues apparently rooted in the domestic realm are enriched now by understanding how they were inflected by the implications of Europe's interactions with the peoples of Africa, Asia, and the Americas" (199). Thus, these works fall neatly into new disciplinary figurations of the transnational while troubling the notion of the nation as a stable social formation. The easy transversal of spaces is central to each of the works. Travel develops these women's sense of sociopolitical mechanisms, allowing them to establish their autonomy separate from the family. Or as the character *Hope Leslie* suggests, "[O]ur new country develops faculties that young ladies, in England, were unconscious of possessing" (Sedgwick 98). The worldviews and attitudes these characters highlight are not always emancipatory or egalitarian. Instead, they use, at times, the power of empire for their own self-serving purposes.

For the past few decades, literary scholars have identified how the operations of empire emerge in transatlantic literary culture, broadening their scope to include the contributions of otherwise neglected figures. These studies often rely heavily on new historicism and archival research in the service of contextual readings that, at times, have identified convincing convergences between text and context, but the connections scholars identify between world happenings and literary representations, at times, seem predetermined.[2] As historian Sara Maza observes, historical methodologies "can show you what happened to majorities in 'society,' but not what individual social actors did or what those actions meant to them" (21). With characteristic directness, Rita Felski states, "*History is not a* box—that is to say, standard ways of thinking about historical context are unable to explain how works of art move across time. We need models of textual mobility and transhistorical attachment that refuse to be browbeaten by the sacrosanct of period boundaries" (*Limits* 154).[3]

A paradigm shift is in order in which literary scholars attend to texts that offer an *imaginary* that defies the contained and sterile constructions of historical narratives but nevertheless gestures at and includes the multiple actors within empires rather than treating them as occluded and, therefore, undemanding presences. The imaginary, like the word "fiction," evades definition because it has no ontology except as it is combined with other concepts. As Wolfgang Iser claims, it is "a featureless and inactive potential" (*Fiction* xvii). For Iser, the imaginary relies on fiction to activate its potentialities. Scholars attempting to define the imaginary usually cite psychoanalysts, like Jacques Lacan, or social scientists, like Benedict Anderson. For my purposes, Paul Armstrong provides the clearest articulation of the imaginary when summarizing Iser: "The imaginary is the featureless, otherwise inaccessible capacity for making meaning to which fictions give form. . . . The imaginary mediates between the fictive and the real and animates their interaction, but it is knowable only through its effects. Not a faculty or an essence, it is the power of human plasticity to create forms, play with the given, and overstep limits" ("Politics of Play" 212). Emphasizing acts of imagination rather than the historical connections involved in literary texts widens the ways in which we perceive the past; it enables different stimuli and modalities to foster alternative modes of being and in some cases to formulate the terms for a more equitable future.

Historical context, though, hangs about a text and cannot be shaken off, even if it does not provide the historical trajectory that literary scholars are interested in tracing. Catharine Maria Sedgwick's invocation of John Milton in her highly allusive *Hope Leslie* offers a figuration for thinking about a text's relation to its context. During a scene when the jailed indigenous woman Magawisca is visited by the villain (a secret Royalist) Sir Philip who tries to align with her against the Puritans, Sedgwick alludes to a scene in *Paradise Lost* in which Milton describes Satan's surprise as he enters Eden to tempt Eve in Book IV of *Paradise Lost* (1667) and discovers that, despite moving through space, he still remains in hell because:

The hell within him; for within him Hell
He brings, and round about him, nor from Hell
One step, no more than from Himself, can fly
By change of place (IV.20–23)

I suggest that we can use Sedgwick's allusion to Milton to describe the ways in which critics have internalized the historical imperative. Just as Satan carries hell "round about him," a literary work—if narrowly defined and propagated within certain historical resonances—carries its historical context no matter when or where the text is read or by whom. The example of Milton's Satan may seem overwrought as it implies infernalization, but it can seem as though a literary work's historical context not only merges with the text but also blights it.

Sedgwick's allusion to Milton also includes the image of the "meridian" that I would like to tease out for the way it encapsulates her attempt to represent racialized and gendered others, like the Pequot Magawisca, as agential characters, and her attempt to represent the white settlers' anxiety, fears, desire, and anger as they operate in the "contact zone." The metaphor of "meridian" in *Paradise Lost* (and alluded to by Sedgwick) may rejuvenate how readers conceptualize their engagement with the past, which is not only fraught, biased, and partial (like a horizon) but also multiple and shifting with illusions of total perceptual power (like that offered by a meridian). Let's look at the passage Sedgwick quotes from Milton's poem. As Satan reflects on what sufferings he will bring about by his temptation of Eve, Satan looks:

Sometimes towards Heaven and the full-blazing Sun,
Which now sat high in his *Meridian Towre* (IV.29–30, emphasis mine)

In *Hope Leslie*, Sedgwick alludes to Milton's lines when describing how her villain Sir Philip looks upon the indigenous woman, Magawisca, with the same "askance" look as Satan when he eyed "the sun in his 'high meridian tower'" (Sedgwick 257). At noon or when the sun is at its "Meridian Towre," Satan is reminded of his past and former glory. Sedgwick's allusion to Milton then establishes Magawisca, in Sir Philip's eyes, as the figure who governs over and illuminates her land. Indeed, Satan apostrophizes the sun as forcing him to grapple with his motivations even if they highlight his heresy:

O thou that, with surpassing glory crowned,
Look'st from thy sole dominion like the god
Of this new World—at whose sight all the stars
Hide their diminished heads (Milton IV.32–35)

His grand encomium to the sun ("like the god / Of this new World") bespeaks Satan's enmity. In particular, Satan's heresy is on full display as he idolizes the sun, and he imagines himself as a "diminished" star. And, likewise, Sir Philip's feelings toward Magawisca, whom he likens to the sun, radiate from awe to impatience to "wrath": at first, "Sir Philip's eye fell, and his heart quailed before the lofty glance, and unsullied spirit of the Indian maiden" (257), but then just as abruptly he experiences a "feeling of almost insupportable meanness" (257). Sedgwick's allusion to the sun in its "meridian tower" encapsulates the contrary feelings that the New World colonies and its subjugated people, like Magawisca, inspire in white settlers: reverence, meanness, and misdirected anger.

In identifying and recognizing the contrarieties within expressions of imperial power, one finds characters neglected by other early American and transatlantic texts. The authors studied here present the multitudinous psychological responses (besides silence or a metaphoric "amnesia") that the racialized and gendered other evokes and how those "othered" by white settlers respond to the violence that attends encroachments on them. As Felski explains, literary texts "do not just represent, but make newly present, significant shades of social meaning" (*Uses* 104). These texts position the reader, especially some future reader, to notice, and in some cases experience the awe and frustration that asymmetrical power arouses when reading literature about the settlement of colonial sites and about emerging nation-states with imperial ambitions.

Notes

INTRODUCTION

1. In 1991, Michael Kammen wrote about the idea of cultural amnesia or what he termed "apparent social amnesia" (533). His language offers more precise accounting for historical omissions: "Historians on the left are surely correct in referring to 'the social production of memory,' and in positing the existence of dominant memories (or a mainstream collective consciousness) along with alternative (usually subordinate) memories. Such historians are equally sensible to differentiate between official and spontaneous or populistic memories" (Kammen 9). Yet many critics working in American literature and culture make no such distinction between official and populist memories and follow the lead of Michael Warner's claim that "National culture began with a moment of sweeping amnesia about colonialism. Americans learned to think of themselves as living in an immemorial nation, rather than in a colonial interaction of cultures" (Warner, "What's Colonial" 63). Lindsay DiCuirci, moreover, argues that "efforts toward historical preservation in America always carried with them the collective amnesia that absolute claims to territory require," as she traces the reemergence of records from colonial settlers into print in the nineteenth century (27). Yet the very terms "efforts" and "amnesia" seem contradictory. More explicit language like Jillian Sayre's might be more precise when she states that, in early US texts, certain "discourse aggressively excludes" marginalized others (76).

2. Likewise, this study understands the United States' formation in terms set out by Edward Watts, who, summing up empire studies from the last quarter century of American studies, notes, "Reframed then as invasion and occupation, the white inhabitation of North America and the founding of the United States become closer to ordinary events in human history, not markers of epochal transformations" (*Colonizing* 14). For more on the United States and its emergence as an empire distinct from British politics and culture, see my cowritten introduction with Denys Van Renen in *Beyond 1776: Globalizing the Cultures of the American Revolution* (U of Virginia P, 2018).

3. For an expansive tracing of the intersection among freedom, racialism, and the "English-language novel" marked by a kind of death ("swooning") and rebirth in particular texts, see Doyle's *Freedom's Empire*.

4. Marianne Noble has made a convincing case for the way representations of women's "masochism" has been ignored in studies of nineteenth-century sentimental fiction: "Female

sentimental authors were not simply victims who were silenced or forced to function as mouthpieces for patriarchal ideology, nor simply virtuous crusaders for truth and justice. They were authors eager to empower themselves and ambitious to explore and put into words their thoughts on a range of subjects not confined to tender love, regional portraiture, and womanly desires for kindness and compassion" (Noble 5).

5. I am not equating North American settlements with later iterations of European colonialism. Throughout this book, I refer to colonial or pre-Revolutionary times using the term "colonial," and I use the term "imperialism" to refer to the emergent United States' domestic and foreign policies. Still, books like *The Female American* are difficult to call part of British America because the author remains unknown. Perhaps it fits best as part of what Jace Weaver terms the "Red Atlantic." Nonetheless, I am aware of limitations of this term as it defines European colonialism in the nineteenth and twentieth centuries. As Michael Warner explains, "The benign idea of settlement continues to be the main obstacle against recognizing the history of British American colonies as a story of colonialism rather than of mere colonization" ("What's Colonial" 56).

6. Insko offers a sustained critique of the dominance of new historicist practices in nineteenth-century American literature to explicate what he terms "Romantic presentism." Insko makes a compelling case that "historicism tends to produce what we might call a kind of 'complacent' presentism. . . . [that] assumes the present, the critic's present, as more advanced than, not just different from, the past" (*History* 10).

7. Since the 2006 publication of Mary Carruth's edited collection *Feminist Interventions in Early American Studies,* several special journal issues on women, imperialism, and early America have appeared in *Legacy* and *Early American Literature.* As Tamara Harvey observes, "Work on women throughout the Americas, including European, African, and Native women, both free and enslaved, has profited from decades of groundbreaking scholarly attention not only to those whose names appeared on the title pages of books but also to women whose texts were hidden in the works of others, stagnating in untapped manuscript archives, or awaiting interpretive methodologies that could address oral and material texts" (159).

8. Carrie Hyde has likewise theorized how literature shapes the "political subjunctive," in particular citizenship before the passage of the Fourteenth Amendment, or an "aspirational mode of politicking [that] concretizes different ways of envisioning political membership" (*Civic* 16) She also argues that "the subjunctive offers a uniquely instructive paradigm for understanding the political power of rhetoric writ large, because . . . its modal . . . framework isolates the speculative mode that fiction exemplifies" (*Civic* 16).

9. Many of these monographs rely on Michael Hardt and Antonio Negri's *Empire* and Amy Kaplan's *The Anarchy of Empire.*

10. Ed Larkin makes explicit the ties literary critics see between the novel and empire: "Regardless of which explanation for the emergence of the novel in English we subscribe to, its implication in the history of eighteenth-century empire is clear. From early British examples such as *Robinson Crusoe* and *Moll Flanders* to American counterparts such as *The Algerine Captive* and *The Pioneers,* the themes and narrative forms of the novel were shaped by the experience of a rapidly expanding world and its impact on the social, economic, and political life of the time" (Larkin 3).

11. Indeed, Jacobs seems in line with Denys Van Renen's characterization of Olaudah Equiano's life writing about his own emancipation: "Equiano's narrative rejects reductive identities offered by aesthetic forms or national and individual identities. . . . The emancipated slave does not validate the so-called American individual; instead Equiano exhibits and imagines himself in a rotating cast of roles to adapt to various nations or cultures" (229).

12. My argument is informed by Rita Felski's *The Limits of Critique*, in which she points out an overreliance on the hermeneutics of suspicion in literary studies. Felski suggests that "rather than scanning texts for signs of transgression or resistance, . . . —for its hidden causes, determining conditions, and noxious motives—we might place ourselves in front of the text, reflecting on what it unfurls, calls forth, makes possible" (*Limits* 12).

13. The idea that a single critic or author can erase whole peoples seems a bold assertion and one that overemphasizes the role of an individual in a culture or even a field of study. For instance, I find Bow's assertion that Toni Morrison somehow erases the work of Edward Said unconvincing; Bow claims that "it is Edward Said's *Orientalism* (1978) that I would highlight as one 'ghost in the machine' of Morrison's influential work, a ghost whose presence is echoed philosophically, methodologically, and at times linguistically" (558).

14. In the study, I use "indigenous people" to refer to peoples who lived in the Western Hemisphere before European conquest, rather than "Native American," because the phrase is more inclusive for a transnational study like this one that examines settings outside the present-day United States.

15. The full title of Mary Rowlandson's text is often rendered as *The Sovereignty & Goodness of God, Together, With the Faithfulness of His Promises Displayed; Being a Narrative Of the Captivity and Restauration of Mrs. Mary Rowlandson.*

16. A search on MLA International Bibliography shows forty-two results for *Hobomok* and nineteen for *A Romance of the Republic*, though the database would not be inclusive for all published essays and books on those texts.

17. Many of the books in empire studies reference ghosts or haunting in their titles, such as *Ghosts of Slavery* by Jenny Sharpe; *Haunted by Empire* by Laura Ann Stoler; *Specters of the Atlantic* by Ian Baucom; *Cities of the Dead* by Joseph Roach; *The National Uncanny: Indian Ghosts and American Subjects* by Renée Bergland; and *Haunting Realities: Naturalist Gothic and American Realism* edited by Monika Elbert and Wendy Ryden.

18. My identification of two strains is not an exhaustive survey of the field. I acknowledge the concomitant rise of criticism that sought to temper or at least question new historicism's dominance.

19. These two articles appear first on their respective journal's web pages as "sample articles" and, as such, I presume to call them "representative articles" as well.

20. The literary and cultural scholarship devoted to what one may term "hauntology" comes across not merely as scholarly inquiry but social justice activism. As Jacques Derrida maintains, "If I am getting ready to speak at length about ghosts, inheritances, and generations, generations of ghosts, which is to say about certain *others* who are not present, nor presently living, either to us, in us, or outside of us, it is in the name of *justice*" (*Specters of Marx* xix).

21. Hauntology within American studies has a whole subdiscipline often referred to as the "vanishing narrative" of indigenous people. Repeatedly, scholars collapse literary texts

and federal policy. For an extensive overview of the trope of Vanishing Americans, see Sayre (73–78), who explains how "The trope of the Vanishing American thus served not only to elide the violence of conquest and naturalize claims for removal, but it also functioned as a historical foundation for narrating the historical romance" (74).

22. Even Michel Foucault, whose writing informs the presuppositions of contemporary humanities scholarship, cautions against the conflation of "lack" with ghosts: "The statement is not haunted by the secret presence of the unsaid of hidden meanings" (*Archaeology* 124) even as he parsed the distinction between "the lack that is characteristic of an enunciative regularity" and "the meanings concealed in what is formulated in it" (*Archaeology* 124).

23. Anna Brickhouse calls for more scholarship that invokes "an alternative history—one that . . . draws on Native American studies' multilayered concept of sovereignty to reconsider a canonical episode of colonial history"—in her case the episode refers to the first encounters between Christopher Columbus and indigenous translators ("Mistranslation" 938). Brickhouse, like many who take issue with available archives, points out the gothic elements that punctuate the historical record. Indeed, she writes about Spanish ships in the sixteenth century that crossed the Atlantic only to find colonial settlements destroyed, the people missing: "first discovery becomes a southern gothic as the ship arrives" ("Mistranslation" 941). An appealing anachronism undergirds Brickhouse's metaphor to describe a Spanish colonial ship in the early sixteenth century as part and parcel of an aesthetic form associated with the nineteenth-century US South. Elizabeth Freeman is more explicit when she revises the genre of the gothic based on new historicist practices: "the gothic was a kind of historical novel *in extremis*, a register for encountering the past felt precisely at the boundaries of what could be encompassed by secular, disciplinary, and even 'scientific' notions of history" (*Time Binds* 98).

24. In pursuing a study that looks at individual texts, I purposely reject the practices of distant reading that use books like these as "props" to aggregate texts from a certain set time period in order to cull "data." Distant reading commits itself to the date of a text's first printing as a way to set a comparison or control group even as critics have begun to question an overreliance on first publication date. *See* McGill, "Echocriticism."

25. Laura Doyle, in contrast, argues that Jacobs's remarks on the bill of sale implodes narratives that tie literacy and freedom; instead that false tie "re-imprisons her in the very moment that it frees her" (Doyle 360).

26. Jacobs in some respects enacts Lee Edelman's calls to repudiate the future as figuring the possibility of political emancipation; she both invokes the future and then renders it irrelevant, see Edelman, *No Future*.

27. Lisa Lowe articulates how thinking of alternative histories develops a "two-fold attention": "The past conditional temporality of the 'what could have been' symbolizes aptly the space of a different kind of thinking, a space of productive attention to the scene of loss, a thinking with twofold attention that seeks to encompass at once the positive objects and methods of history and social science and also the matters absent, entangled, and unavailable by its method" (Lowe 40–41). The texts under discussion activate reader's twofold attention by engaging with possible futures.

28. The realms imagined in fiction are often termed "alternative worlds" or even "better worlds" (Bieger et al., vii, x). At times, this language can seem inexact, especially for texts that

rely on mimetic realism. Rather, some texts remain firmly grounded in the reality of this world (even if that term is epistemologically and ontologically incoherent); instead, they imagine "alternative" attitudes toward the world they inhabit.

29. Catherine Gallagher notices how the counterfactual narratives she studies share a "predilection for catastrophic histories" (7). For instance, she analyzes texts that offer worlds in which Nazi Germany successfully took over Europe. Jillian Sayre further complicates the whole genre of counterfactual. Drawing upon Robert Pogue Harrison, Sayre comments on the entanglement of the dead (past) and unborn (future) in acts of commemoration. She explains how a "story, arriving from and for future's past, is narrated in the future anterior, the will-have-been. This structure does not describe a conditional or possible future, but rather a backward glancing prognostication" (27).

30. One reason that the word "fantasy" bristles is because it is, as defined by Freud and Jacob Arlow, "primarily the imagined gratification of libidinal drives and is engendered by emphasizing what he calls hierarchies of fantasies . . . [that] have at their core early drive-related wishes and instinctual fixations" (Levin 137–38). Fantasy seems regressive and imagination progressive.

31. A substantial number of studies has extended Linda Kerber's original claim about the central role of republican motherhood in the formation of the United States. See "The Republican Mother."

32. My reading differs from Doyle, who argues that in characterizing the Pequots as a "race," Sedgwick "assures Magawisca's assimilation into an Anglo-Atlantic narrative" (279). Moreover, Doyle claims that "in casting the war as the Indians' race drama, this rhetoric elides English colonization as cause of the war" (281).

I.

THE "FANTASY" OF A WOMAN IN CHARGE
IN *The Female American*

1. Among these, Matthew Reilly makes a strong case for the way Arabic and Quaker texts may have influenced the text's treatment of subjectivity in "'No eye has seen, or ear heard.'"

2. The word "fantasy" modifies not so much the plot of the text but rather the gender of the central character. Betty Joseph describes the plot as one "where the founding father has been displaced by the not-quite-white mother, and where Christianity becomes *a female fantasy of total being* that rescues the native population from the history of Anglo founding and Anglo (male) missionary projects" (317, emphasis mine). Michelle Burnham also uses the word "fantasy" when describing the text as a "fantasy of female power" (Introduction 19). The exception is Anna Brickhouse, who, writing on *The Female American*, refers specifically to Defoe's *Robinson Crusoe*'s engagement with the "English fantasy of access to Spanish and Portuguese wealth derived from the Americas" ("Indian Slave Trade" 116–17).

3. In Weaver-Hightower's analysis, the presence of a hermit who already inhabited the island and later the presence of Unca Eliza's male cousin marginalizes her role as a Crusoe figure. Even in texts like *The Female American*, Weaver-Hightower maintains, "By consigning

women firmly to the margins of island and empire, island narratives show women as largely incidental to the island colonization, reflecting their political invisibility in real-world imperial society" (55). Yet Weaver-Hightower's analysis, in which these texts both "show" women and render them invisible women, captures the anomalous effects of having a woman protagonist.

4. See McGrath, "Rousseau's Crusoe."

5. Hans Turley adds nuance to interpretations of *The Female American* as a Robinsonade by claiming that Unca Eliza's story compares to volumes 2 and 3 of the *Robinson Crusoe* trilogy rather than the first and more famous story from volume 1 of Crusoe marooned on a deserted island. See "Protestant Evangelism, British Imperialism, and Crusonian Identity."

6. The anonymous author relies on the name Winkfield (or Wingfield), which is the actual name of a Virginia settler. Still, according to scholars, her characters are fictional. Winkfield, for instance, had no children. See Burnham, Introduction 27–28.

7. Mary Helen McMurran, though, makes the case that the text enlarges the definition of the novel because of the way it evades realist modes of telling. Building upon McMurran's claims, one can argue that the text not just alters the form of the novel but also alters the paradigms for representing New World exploration by cataloging the losses incurred by settlement and by tracing how Europeans coalesce power by capitalizing on asymmetrical knowledge.

8. The text perhaps fits best located within the "Red Atlantic." Jace Weaver extends Paul Gilroy's figuration of the Black Atlantic to revise the notions of disciplinary boundaries drawn by nation-state and literary period. In this case, Weaver's purpose is "to restore Indians and Inuit to the Atlantic World and demonstrate their centrality to that world" (x). Weaver considers *The Female American* "*the* quintessential novel of the Red Atlantic" (233).

9. Denise Mary MacNeil observes in *The Female American* how the "handling of European American prisoners is markedly benign in tone, even when violence is involved" (*Emergence* 93).

10. Roxann Wheeler examines how the book evades questions about intermarriage in late eighteenth-century Virginia by setting the story in the distant past before the influx of people from Africa into the colony. Indeed, Virginia outlawed all interracial marriages by 1691. At the same time, Wheeler notes how *The Female American* "promotes the notion that however unsettling dark color may be, it is ultimately insignificant" (168).

11. Elizabeth Barnes has written convincingly about the dynamics of coercion and consent in the seduction novels that proliferated in the years of the early republic: "Though depicted as antithetical models of heterosexual relations, both marriage and seduction symbolize the complicated relationship between coercion and consent characteristic of democratic disciplinary agendas" (Barnes 11). However, a work like *The Female American* would not fit her thesis not only because it precedes the American Revolution but also because it does not participate in the sentimental genre. Nor does it relate the shifts in social classes as in texts by English authors, like Samuel Richardson. Moreover, in the first part of the text, it is the father, not the mother, of Unca Eliza who is seduced and abused by the desiring indigene women.

12. Unca Eliza, in contrast to the Hermit, asserts power not through writing but an ephemeral performance through which she co-opts the ruins and burial sites she finds on the remote island. Diana Taylor argues against focusing exclusively on archives of "enduring materials" and opens up the possibilities of studying "so-called ephemeral *repertoire* of embodied practice/knowledge" (19). In *The Female American*, Unca Eliza destroys access to the ruins as a

way to ensure her performance as a prophet remains "ephemeral." April London comments, "Masculine writing here gives way to female orality" (London 99). Yet in my reading of the text, it makes Unca Eliza usurpation of power more insidious as opposed to emancipatory.

13. Unca Eliza expressed surprise when she confesses, "I soon found that they were confounded in their ideas about me, and conceived of me, as one more than mortal" (116), as though she had not carefully cultivated that very impression.

14. *The Female American* also seems to "unsettle" Europeans' encroachments. I use this term as Anna Brickhouse does: "But *unsettlement* also argues for the kinds of counterfactual historicist practices that work against the assumed inevitability of European settlement in the Americas and of the institutions and legacies of conquest" ("Mistranslation" 942). Unca Eliza shores up her own power even if the text as a whole contradicts Unca Eliza's fantasy of taking the parts of colonialism that she likes and discarding the rest.

15. London cogently describes how "Her reluctance to accept John's proposals stands in contrast with the well-known textual and visual images that figured the New World as a welcoming and fertile woman eager for union with an Anglo-European male colonizer" (193).

2.

TALKING SEX AND REVOLUTION IN SAINT-DOMINGUE
IN SANSAY'S *Secret History*

1. The full title is *Secret History; or, The Horrors of St. Domingo, in a Series of Letters Written by a Lady at Cape Francois to Col. Burr, late Vice-President of the United States, Principally During the Command of General Rochambeau.* Sansay was known by a number of names, as has been detailed in scholarship by Michael Drexler and Angela Vietto. The title page of the book refers to the author simply as "A Lady at Cape Francois."

2. Sansay's emphasis on verbal power places her firmly within the context of early US writers and their attentiveness and sensitivity to the links between eloquence and power. The importance of oratory or verbal eloquence in effecting the American Revolution and the centrality of "declaring" independence from Great Britain have long shaped an understanding of early American public life. See, especially, Jay Fliegelman, *Declaring Independence;* Sandra Gustafson, *Imagining Deliberative Democracy;* and Christopher Looby, *Voicing America.*

3. Michelle Burnham argues for a transoceanic reading of the text that takes into account Europeans' growing interests in Pacific and Caribbean economies during the early 1800s. See *Transoceanic America.*

4. Discussing the social imaginary that forms in the United States in the early nineteenth century, Anna Brickhouse writes, "Fraught with cultural anxieties and desires that attested to a larger crisis of national identity, this imaginary was from the beginning riddled with the contradictions and rhetorical impulses attending a nation whose geographic borders were expanding even as its imagined racial borders were narrowing and calcifying" (*Transamerican* 6–7).

5. Tessie Liu sees an immediate shift in racial discourse following the outbreak of revolution in Haiti at the end of the eighteenth century and the first years of the nineteenth century: "Rebellion and insurrectionary struggles in the intervening years transformed the racial dis-

course of slavery and slaveholding. Specifically, what could be said and what could be believed about black power and agency necessarily changed with the latter's military success and legal emancipation" (Liu 415).

6. Carol Smith-Rosenberg offers a telling comment on Sansay's writing: "Despite such rhetorical evocation of the American Revolution however, the United States plays but a shadowy role in" the revised version of the novel (261). Smith-Rosenberg's language poses a powerful juxtaposition of the rhetoric usually reserved for people held in slavery. In her formulation, the United States acts as a shadow to the events playing out in Haiti. Later, though, Smith-Rosenberg reverts to the formulation that people who lived in bondage operate as a shadow haunting the United States: "savage black tyranny casts its dark shadow over the island" (261). This oscillation between placing Haiti at the center to moving the United States to the center shapes Sansay's text as well.

7. Indeed, Burnham offers an engaging analysis of several overlooked passages and contexts for reading Sansay. She notes how the "blurring of acts of extreme corporeal violence with acts of routine consumption (whether commercial, sexual, or culinary) perfectly describes the tone and content of Sansay's *Secret History,* which is littered with vignettes that amount to a kind of capitalist pornography" ("Female Bodies" 188).

8. As Michael Drexler argues, "We might provisionally speculate that publication substituted for the absence of an established salon culture or for Sansay's class estrangement from the forms of the salon that did exist in the United States" (Introduction 35).

9. Sarah Maza has written on the extensive market for printed trial briefs among the French reading public prior to the French Revolution. According to Maza, dominant theories about the impetus for the French Revolution neglect to consider how public fascination with the private lives of people made public through legal briefs printed and published among booksellers created a framework for individual political interest and later individual political participation. She goes further to argue for "the interrelation of public and private issues in the genesis of political ideologies; with the relationship between narrative and ideology; and, more broadly, with the status of fiction in historical analysis" (Maza 10).

10. According to David Geggus, "When the French Revolution broke out, Saint-Domingue was home to almost half a million slaves, about 30,000 white colonists, and a roughly equal number of free people of color" (3). He continues, "During the five years before the uprising, the colony absorbed nearly two-fifths of all the Africans being brought to the Americas, breaking all records for the Atlantic slave trade" (7). Geggus, though, remains skeptical of claims that frame the Revolution as inevitable based on its demographics.

11. Jenson provides a succinct encapsulation of the far-reaching effects of Toussaint's rhetorical powers: "Toussaint expertly deployed an Enlightenment and sentimental rhetoric that veiled his challenge to the workings of hemispheric notions of race in transatlantic print culture even as he brought questions of universal human rights back to his own subjectivity, his own lived history, and implicitly, his own body" (10).

12. But as Ashli White reports, "Americans followed avidly the early moments of Haitian nationhood, especially the deeds and proclamations of its first leader, Jean-Jacques Dessalines. . . . Throughout 1804 newspapers listed the names and numbers of those slain at the hands of Dessalines's army and recounted episodes of violence in grisly detail" (177).

13. Discussions about Haiti's "sovereignty" is complicated by how global interdependencies have impeded its development. Robert Maguire and Scott Freeman, writing about contemporary Haiti, get to the heart of the matter: "In assessing Haiti's ownership, we are compelled to consider the overwhelming evidence that the root of the country's contemporary sovereignty dilemma is ultimately related not just to its internal rumblings but also to roles foreign actors played" (4).

14. Elizabeth Maddock Dillon observes, "By design, however, the madras headscarf became something of a symbol of sexuality rather than a cloaking of it. Thus eighteenth-century writers habitually remark upon the allure of the colorful scarves—an allure clearly associated with the 'excessive' sexuality of creole culture" (Dillon, "Secret History" 89).

15. As Sean Goudie remarks, Sansay's text exposes the ways in which, "amid the chaos of revolution, U.S. American urban economies and merchants operate paracolonially to benefit themselves" (210).

16. Likewise, Brickhouse notes, "Haiti constituted a kind of rhetorical impasse in the U.S. public sphere specifically because of its revolutionary past, which had long been identified with that of the United States in the writings of intellectuals from Emerson and John Greenleaf Whittier and Wendell Phillips" (*Transamerican* 226).

17. See Michelle Burnham, "Early America and the Revolutionary Pacific." *PMLA*, vol. 128, no. 4, 2012, pp. 953–60.

18. Liu raises a key question: "If Clara, who suffered the brutality of her husband and the 'conquest' of Rochambeau, could fight for her freedom, why did Sansay imagine that white women similarly threatened by black men could only choose death? In other words, why did a novel that so forthrightly condemned male prerogatives and presented marriage as a commercial institution create another category of unendurable racialized horror?" (411).

19. Drexler and White report that an ad for Sansay's book appeared on the same page as an ad for Burr trail transcripts in the Democratic Press of Philadelphia in February 1808 (*Traumatic Colonel* 173).

20. In Isenberg's research, Burr "emerged as a feminist—every bit a feminist in a modern sense of the word" (55). Isenberg highlights especially his strong regard for smart women.

21. Elizabeth Maddock Dillon claims, "The violence of patriarchy in the novel is thus clearly related to that of colonialism and race politics, a pairing underscored by the formulation of a quasi-utopic community of unhusbanded Creole women at the close of the novel" ("Secret History" 80). Other critics draw the same conclusion that the text represents freedom from men (Woertendyke 265). Michael Drexler concludes, "Sansay envisions a world in which women's happiness seems all but circumscribed by violent masculinity" (Introduction 33).

22. At this point in the text Sean Goudie identifies Clara as having undergone a transformation that distinguishes her from her sister Mary. Clara "forges a creolizing sensibility marked by her intricate relations with oppressed people across the islands of the West Indies, a development inversely related to Mary's inability to let go of her conservative bourgeois value system" (211).

23. As the United States distanced itself from the Haitian Revolution, the rebelling factions' treatment of the French was characterized by stronger, more violent language. In the revised version of *Secret History*, titled *Zelica* published in 1820, the anonymous author refers to the Revolutionaries' desire for the "extermination" of the French (*Zelica* 12).

3.

THE MILITARIZATION OF HOME
IN CATHARINE MARIA SEDGWICK'S *Hope Leslie*

1. Lucy Maddox's study, *Removals: Nineteenth-Century American Literature and the Politics of Indian Affairs*, presents evidence that counters the idea of widespread forgetting or erasure of indigenous peoples in the nineteenth century. She reminds scholars of how contentious the debates were about the removal of Cherokees from their lands. Moreover, subsequent debates about expansion westward reignited questions about the legitimacy of the Indian Removal Acts. Maddock writes, "The public debate over the political expediency of removal were by no means silenced by the eventual forced resettlement of the Cherokees and other southeastern Indians in the West; the very presence of the Indians within the territory of the United States not only kept alive the sensitive issues associated with Indian removal but extended their implications beyond immediate practical and party questions and into other areas of American public life. . . . the debates became intensified and localized: by the opening of the Oregon Trail, the Mexican War, the gold rush and the annexation of California, the Homestead Act, and so on" (21).

2. Dana Luciano also counters the prevailing argument on the limits of Sedgwick's progressivism: "*Hope Leslie* rechannels the voice that it represents as denied to the Pequots in the 'voiceless' western forests, amplifying the resonance of the un(der)told aspects of the 'vanishing' story. Sedgwick's redeployment of melancholy thus works to restore the sense of *critical* contemplation of the past that is erased by the pathological manifestation of melancholia as a blind spot, since her rearticulation of a melancholy fate as a melancholy state policy can be understood to reflect forward on her own time as well" (Luciano 115).

3. This policy became explicit during the settlement of Florida during the Seminole Wars in part because the federal government faced more resistance from indigenous people ordered to remove. In an aptly named "Armed Occupation Act" (1842), the US government institutionalized a process of moving indigenous peoples out of territories by calling upon households to serve as an extension of the military. See Laurel Shire, *The Threshold of Manifest Destiny*.

4. The scholarship in American Studies on gender and empire emerged from and alongside work by British literature scholars, like Laura Brown, Felicity Nussbaum, Margaret Ferguson, and Catherine Gallagher.

5. Karen Woods Weierman offers a carefully researched overview of Sedgwick's interest in "Stockbridge Indians" from around Stockbridge, Massachusetts, where the family originally settled, and the increasing encroachment of white settlers onto that land in the eighteenth century. Upheavals in Stockbridge continued throughout the nineteenth century with the advent of a railroad (Ellis 181). The home in early America was hardly as stable or safe as some scholarly accounts of domesticity would imply.

6. Jean O'Brien also demonstrates how "New England Indians continued to resist their effacement as tribal nations in the nineteenth century and beyond" (xxiii).

7. Insko provides a sensible reading of the ending of *Hope Leslie:* "But as unsatisfactory as this dénouement may appear to the modern reader, its reliance on the myth of the vanishing

American may have less to do with the 'constraints of Sedgwick's culture than with the formal constraints of the novel itself . . . it has to end" (*History* 74).

8. Judith Fetterly offers an intriguing analysis of Everell's attraction: "Everell's 'universal' desirability—all the girls adore him—leads one to suspect that he functions less as an object of love than as the sign of a desired state of being, a desired subjectivity. He is what the girls want to be rather than have" (84).

9. See James Machor, *Reading Fiction in Antebellum America*. Laurence Buell, in his book on the "great American novel," mentions *Hope Leslie* in passing while referencing Nathaniel Hawthorne's Hester Prynne: "The refractory Puritan daughter had been a familiar motif in New England historical romance well before *The Scarlet Letter*, pioneered a generation before by the feminist writers who inaugurated the genre, Lydia Maria Child (*Hobomok*, 1824) and Catharine Maria Sedgwick (*Hope Leslie*, 1827); but Hawthorne took the theme to a further degree of aesthetic finesse and ethical complexity" (Buell 79). Buell's remarks encapsulate attitudes toward *Hope Leslie*, which interpret it in association with other novels by women rather than on its own terms.

10. Irony underscores those who placed Sedgwick's novel in the category of juvenilia since she pointedly rejects the figure of the child as the root of regeneration or "the Child, as disciplinary image of the Imaginary past or as site of a projective identification with an always impossible future" (Edelman 31).

11. My argument provides an alternative to ones like Dana Nelson's in which she argues that Sedgwick's novel does not provide space to imagine an alternative futurity: "*Hope Leslie* is finally equivocal. While Sedgwick clearly sees the necessity of reenvisioning racial constructs, she is so clearly invested in Anglo-America's historical inheritance that she cannot resolve the 'Indian problem' in any meaningful way for her contemporary readers" ("Sympathy" 202).

12. Hyde has made a compelling argument "to illuminate the formative political power of aesthetics—a power that has been difficult to address in literary criticism, which has for several decades, turned to historicism in search of something more solid and 'real' than the complexities of 'literary ambiguity'" (Hyde, *Civic* 15).

13. Magawisca, early in the text, describes to Everell how the English attacked her tribe (48–55).

14. My interpretation of Magawisca contrasts with Gustavas Stadler, who identifies a different dynamic: "Throughout the novel, Magawisca's 'form' helps the English characters—especially female characters—to regulate their psychological states" (Stadler 43). In my interpretation, Magawisca unsettles, rather than "regulates," their psychological defense mechanisms.

15. Sedgwick mentions Mungo Park to point out how acts of humanity did emerge amid the terrible bloodshed of the Pequot wars. These humane acts "will be gathered and treasured in the memory, with that fond feeling with which Mungo Park describes himself to have culled and cherished in his bosom, the single flower that bloomed in his melancholy track over the African desert" (57).

16. Christopher Castiglia argues that Hope, as a woman, represents a different kind of frontier hero: "While masculine extra-vagrance seeks to leave behind a stifling community in favor of a romanticized solitude, female extra-vagrance offers escape from a stifling isola-

tion into an empowering community" (Castiglia 5). See also Denise Mary MacNeil on Mary Rowlandson as the first American frontier hero: *The Emergence of the American Frontier Hero*.

17. Milette Shamir has discussed how private homes in the early decades of the nineteenth century were much more open to public view. The architecture of homes became increasing more hidden with more walls and private nooks in the middle of the century. See, Milette Shamir, *Inexpressible Privacy: The Interior Life of Antebellum American Literature*. U of Pennsylvania P, 2006.

18. Many critics, like Dana Nelson, Dana Luciano, Gustavas Stadler, Michelle Burnham, and Deborah Gussman, have noted that this ending, which focuses on Esther and not the couple (Everell and Hope), is "atypical" for its genre and unanticipated in terms of the narrative's trajectory (Gussman 252).

19. Despite Sedgwick's encomium to single life and her own decision not to marry, her last work of fiction, *Married or Single?* (1857), seems to argue that women's best chance for thriving is in heteronormative marriage.

20. Nathaniel Hawthorne's debt to *Hope Leslie* is often alluded to but, for the most part, overlooked. Not only does Hawthorne choose to set his story of Hester Prynne in the same period as *Hope Leslie*, but he also echoes Sedgwick's hypotactic syntactical style. *Hope Leslie* also mentions an alcohol imbiber sentenced to wear a placard with the word "toper" on it much like the emblem of the letter A in *The Scarlet Letter*. Critics, though, frequently cite his praise when he referred to her as America's "most truthful novelist" (*Wonder Book* 7:169). Still, it is curious that his own text excludes any principal indigenous characters.

21. Indeed, the entire passage not only reminds one of Hawthorne but also seems to recall the writings of the Jameses (William and Henry) because of its emphasis on transitive words and on the notion of "attention," respectively. I am thinking especially of Richard Poirier's and Jonathan Levin's analyses of the Jameses.

22. Sedgwick looks plainly at them and acknowledges Puritans killed Quakers, or women "as witches, innocent, unoffending old women!" (15). At times, however, Sedgwick seems sober but unequivocal about what she calls the "extermination" of indigenous people by the English (54). In detailing aggression by white Europeans, she labels them "heathen Christians" (40) and repeatedly has characters describe Pequot aggression as "provoked" by white violence.

23. As James Machor succinctly reports, "antebellum readers came to the novel already steeped in cultural ambivalence about the Puritan colonists" (223).

24. See Linda Kerber, "The Republican Mother." Many studies have drawn upon Kerber's central premise that "The republican ideology that Americans developed included—hesitantly—a political role for women. It made use of the classic formulation of the Spartan Mother who raised sons prepared to sacrifice themselves to the good of the polis" (188). See Fetterly for a different take on how *Hope Leslie* approaches republican motherhood, "'My Sister! My Sister!'"

25. As Gustavas Stadler states, "rather than trying to politicize privacy by sanctifying it, Sedgwick's novel attempts to undermine the status of privacy by revealing, in what will prove an ambivalent political gesture, its construction on the grounds of history and the forced removal of native peoples" (44).

26. As Michael Warner explains, "And in the variety of colonialism that distinguishes the English mainland colonies—settlement plantation—the relation of settlers and indigenes does not take the visible form of super- and subordinate so much as of center and margin" ("What's Colonial" 54).

27. When Everell considers helping Magawisca flee her cell, Digby warns him that if he is caught, "nothing can ever be done for her" (258).

28. Joel Pfister reports that standards for women's behavior narrowed decades after the publication of Sedgwick's text. He argues that "Sections of mid-nineteenth-century medical texts, even those that stereotype women, criticize the narrowing of women's sphere and comment upon the appearance of feminine palefaces. Some physicians suggested that women were undergoing a radical transmutation at the hands of culture" (320).

29. As Sedgwick portrays it, even after Hope rescues Faith, "There was nothing in the intercourse of the sisters to excite Hope's affections. Faith had been spiritless, woe-begone—a soulless body—and had repelled, with sullen indifference, all Hope's efforts to win her love" (359). Indeed, Faith is all corporal body and thus has no spirit with which to haunt.

30. Erica Burleigh argues that "interposes" is the central figuration of *Hope Leslie*; see *Intimacy and Family in Early American Writing*.

31. Edelman discusses queer and nonnormative sexualities, but his thinking might also apply to the dénouement of *Hope Leslie* when the three friends must part and Hope gives up hope of reclaiming her sister from her Pequot husband. Rather than Hope abandoning her sister, Faith abandons Hope in favor of her husband. Cathy Davidson observes, "one character, Faith Leslie, might be better off in her Indian life than she was in her restrictive, misogynistic Puritan community" (viii).

32. Critics are correct in noticing how Sedgwick overdetermines race by making Faith Leslie's assimilation into Pequot culture so total and complete. See Weierman 429.

4.

THE LIMITS OF THE IMAGINARY IN THE RECONSTRUCTED US IN LYDIA MARIA CHILD'S *Romance of the Republic*

1. Karen Sánchez-Eppler argues the same in *Touching Liberty* when she observes a shift in how social protest highlighted identity as tied to the body; she points to "the abolitionist concern with claiming personhood for the racially distinct and physically owned slave body, and the feminist concern with claiming personhood for the sexually distinct and domestically circumscribed female body" (1).

2. Indeed, the infamous "three-fifths persons" clause of Article 1, Section 2 of the Constitution, which explains that representatives from slave-owning states would determine state population by counting each slave as three-fifths of a person, does not mention race or slavery but instead notes that free persons will be counted and "excluding Indians not taxed, three fifths of all other Persons," leaving the idea of "persons" vague and not tied to a physical body, an omission that exposes a reluctance on the part of the framers to make a direct statement about race.

3. Supreme Court jurisprudence depends upon an undefined standard regarding "fundamental rights." In a 1997 case involving assisted suicide, the Court reasoned with regard to Fourteenth Amendment in most cases, "the Court has regularly observed that the Clause specially protects those fundamental rights and liberties which are, objectively, deeply rooted in this Nation's history and tradition. *E.g., Moore v. East Cleveland,* 431 U.S. 494." Indeed, the case cited as precedent defined a family as a grandmother and two grandsons rather than through the relationships within a nuclear family. At issue here, though, is what "history" and "tradition" will justices call upon? In his 1997 dissent to *Lawrence v. Texas,* a case involving Texas anti-sodomy laws, Antonin Scalia argues that engaging in private sex acts is not a right "deeply rooted in this Nation's history and tradition" and therefore needs no protection. What "history and tradition" Scalia refers to are left vague.

4. Karen Sánchez-Eppler argues, "Antislavery fiction's focus on miscegenation evades the difficulties of representing blackness by casting the racial problematics of slavery into the terms of sexual oppression. In defining the question of ownership of one's body as a sexual question, the ideal of liberty and the commercial concept of ownership attain not only an intimately corporeal but also explicit marital or domestic dimension" (Sánchez-Eppler 41).

5. Child used the phrase "public mind" to describe her purpose publishing the text (qtd. in Dana Nelson, Introduction vii.)

6. Indeed, the word "miscegenation" was constructed during this period, specifically the presidential election of 1864, as a way to shape negative public perception of interracial couples. See especially, Peggy Pascoe, *What Comes Naturally.*

7. According to Karsten Piep, "*A Romance* insists that amalgamation and the complete absorption of blacks into the white mainstream are the only practical means of ensuring the continued existence of an American society whose core principles are threatened by the immoral and potentially destructive institution of slavery" (172).

8. Qtd. in Karcher, *First Woman* 505.

9. See Karcher, *First Woman* 529–30.

10. As Eva Saks notes, "Miscegenation laws responded in varied ways to the assault on white property represented by the abolition movement and later, the Civil War Amendments. On the political level, states passed stricter miscegenation statutes during Reconstruction" (67).

11. See further discussion of this point in chapter 5.

12. As Werner Sollors reminds readers, "if one correlated the various 'typical' plot lines that have been offered as constituting *the* Tragic Mulatto, one would be surprised by the differences between one and the next version of the stereotype" (238).

13. As Lisa Lowe outlines, "The abstract promises of abolition, emancipation, and the end of monopoly often obscure their embeddedness within colonial conditions of settlement, slavery, coerced labor, and imperial trades" (16).

14. When a man tried to unburden himself from his wife by claiming that she had a Black ancestor, rather than declaring the marriage null, the Courts usually sided with the wife. In rendering their judgment in an 1870 case, the Georgia Supreme Court declared, "If [the husband] may cast [his family out], they will in many instances, fall a weighty burden on the

public. To allow a husband to indulge in scruples about the pedigree of his old wife, when her youth, beauty and strength have all waned, and thus escape responding to her claim for reasonable alimony, would be unwise in policy, unsound in principle" (qtd. in Saks 158).

15. Contemporary critiques of neoliberalism have made the imbrications of social and economic injustice clearer. Writing about turn-of-the-twenty-first-century neoliberalism, Lisa Duggan articulates how "In the real world, class and racial hierarchies, gender and sexual institutions, religious and ethnic boundaries are the channels through which money, political power, cultural resources, and social organization flow" (Duggan xiv).

16. Child here participates in a long-standing debate among abolitionists about the efficacy of the Constitution because of the way it strengthens slaveholding interests.

17. Qtd. in Karcher, *First Woman* 507.

18. Jeffory Clymer also argues that *A Romance of the Republic* advocates for economic reparations for slavery. He claims the book "represents a major effort to present alternative routes, justifications, strategies for, and the potential results of economic redistribution from whites to blacks" (*Family Money* 97). Clymer's metaphor of "alternative routes" is particularly compelling because Child's novel presents a road not taken regarding reparations following the US Civil War. Moreover, Clymer correctly refers to it as "redistribution"; my argument differs in that I maintain that Lily Bell, and thus white women, in particular, are called upon by Child to initiate this step toward economic sanctions and redress.

19. Clymer examines the economic structures subtended by bans against interracial marriage in antebellum literature. By the time Child writes, a new set of legal restrictions arose to prevent the distribution of wealth from white property owners to their mixed-race wives or children. See "Family Money."

20. Qtd. in Nelson, Introduction, vii.

21. Jerome McGann as defined the difference between the two: "the discourse of sensibility is the ground on which the discourse of sentiment gets built. . . . sensibility emphasizes the mind in the body, sentimentality the body in the mind" (7).

22. Qtd. in Karcher, *First Woman* 575.

23. See Germana, "Counterfeiters."

24. See Child, *Romance* 278. The lines about passing and counterfeiting are discussed in section two.

5.

MASSACHUSETTS IN THE AMERICAN IMAGINATION IN HARRIET JACOBS'S *Incidents in the Life of a Slave Girl*

1. For further discussion of Child and Sedgwick, see chapter 3.

2. Schoolman, writing about Martin Delany's *Blake*, notes, "At one level, *Blake* will always be untimely, doomed by the chaotic publishing conditions that particularly afflicted African American writers' attempts to make political arguments through books" (11).

3. The scholarly edition of Jacobs's text with her name attached was not published until 1987. Yellin admits she approached Harvard University Press to publish *Incidents:* "Because

the academic community judged *Incidents* an inauthentic slave narrative, it was important to find a prestigious academic publisher" (*Harriet Jacobs* xx).

4. Most critics seem to follow the lead of Anne Bradford Warner and interpret Jacobs as a Southern writer. See "Harriet Jacobs at Home."

5. For scholarship on the garret chapters as central to the text, see Burnham, "Loopholes of Resistance"; Kawash, *Dislocating the Color Line*; O'Neill, "'Shape of Mystery'"; Wardrop, "'I Stuck the Gimlet in.'" Wardrop focuses on a tool Jacobs finds in the crawl space. Most critical inquiry into the text follows Caitlin O'Neil's claims that "Jacobs's most significant theoretical contribution to [black feminist theory] is her discussion of the garret—a nine-feet long, seven-feet wide, and three-feet high hide-away where she would subsist for seven years before fleeing north. Although her writing on the garret is brief, Jacobs's time spent in it is crucial to her activist beginnings and is the site of her self-actualization" (56). O'Neil even goes so far as to claim that Jacobs's time in the enclosed spaces transforms her into "a watchful monster lurking in the attic of their home whose 'bird-eye-view' of the plantation landscape makes her preternaturally knowledgeable of the inner workings of slavery" (56). I, however, argue that she possesses a bird's-eye-view much earlier in her childhood, as evidenced by her ability to view her circumstances impersonally, as though at a distance, during her face-to-face war with Dr. Flint.

6. John Jacobs (known as William in the text) published his life story in four installments in 1861, the same year as *Incidents*, in the periodical *The Leisure Hour: A Family Journal of Instruction and Recreation*.

7. As Diane Somerville notes, "Privileged men and women of the plantation South of course knew that despite these proscriptions, interracial sex abounded, especially between slaveholding men and slave women. Yet it was in their interest to deny its existence or at least ignore it. Two worlds were separated by little to no geographical space, but segregated completely and wholly by social space" (7).

8. The Massachusetts Constitution's prohibition of slavery was determined in a court case in 1783.

9. Henri Lefebvre's foundational theory about how social relationships and power converge out of the social production of space also elucidates Jacobs's manipulation of Flint.

10. See especially, Georgia Kreiger's article "Playing Dead: Harriet Jacobs's Survival Strategy in *Incidents in the Life of a Slave Girl*" as it demonstrates how Jacobs's removal from slavery pantomimes a kind of death.

11. The term "amalgamation" here refers to interracial coupling. The term "miscegenation" was not coined until the end of the Civil War.

12. Indeed, Jacobs at times seems to imagine a much larger audience. Her participation in the American Anti-Slavery Society and her reading of *The Liberator* and *The National Anti-Slavery Standard* acquainted her not just with a wide network of African American writers but also with African American readers. Andrea Powell Wolfe, in "Double-Voicedness," offers an intriguing argument that one can find traces in Jacobs's texts that she anticipates a black female readership. While the book offers evidence for it, more pointedly, it is a future audience that Jacobs seems to imagine reading her text and one that took over a century for her to reach.

EPILOGUE

1. See, especially, Sacvan Bercovitch's *The Office of the Scarlet Letter.* Johns Hopkins UP, 1991.

2. Indeed, Nicholas Paige observes how finding connections between text and context "is not evidence of a link; it is evidence of the human propensity to see patterns" (32).

3. Elizabeth Freeman articulates another limitation of a narrowly historicist perspective: "whether imaginative texts are perceived as mere effects of larger cultural forces, as equal to them, or as indistinguishable from them, the result is a certain homogenizing of matters aesthetic" (*Time Binds* xix).

Works Cited

"Amalgamation Avowed." *New-York Spectator*, 27 July 1835, www.loc.gov/item/sn83045488/

Andrews, William. "Miscegenation in the Late Nineteenth-Century American Novel." *Interracialism: Black-White Intermarriage in American History, Literature, and Law*, edited by Werner Sollors, Oxford UP, 2000, pp. 305–13.

Armstrong, Nancy. *Desire and Domestic Fiction: A Political History of the Novel*. Oxford UP, 1987.

Armstrong, Paul. "In Defense of Reading." *New Literary History*, vol. 42, no. 1, 2011, pp. 87–113.

———. "The Politics of Play: The Social Implications of Iser's Aesthetics Theory." *New Literary History*, vol. 31, no. 1, 2000, pp. 211–23.

Bannet, Eve Tavor. *Transatlantic Stories and the History of Reading, 1720–1810: Migrant Fictions*. Cambridge UP, 2011.

Barnes, Elizabeth. *States of Sympathy: Seduction and Democracy in the American Novel*. Columbia, 1997.

Bauer, Dale. *Sex Expression and American Women Writers, 1860–1940*. U of North Carolina P, 2009.

Bauer, Ralph. "Early American Literature and American Literary History at the 'Hemispheric Turn.'" *American Literary History*, vol. 22, no. 2, 2010, pp. 25–265.

Baym, Nina. *Feminism and American Literary History: Essays*. Rutgers UP, 1992.

———. "Old West, New West, Postwest, Real West." *American Literary History*, vol. 18, no. 4, 2006, pp. 814–28.

Benot, Yves. "The Insurgents of 1791, Their Leaders, and the Concept of Independence." *The World of the Haitian Revolution*, edited by David Patrick Geggus and Norman Fiering, Indiana UP, 2009, pp. 99–110.

Bergland, Renée L. *The National Uncanny: Indian Ghosts and American Subjects*. UP of New England, 2000.

Berlant, Lauren. *Cruel Optimism*. Duke UP, 2011.

———. *The Female Complaint: The Unfinished Business of Sentimentality in American Culture*. Duke UP, 2008.

———. "The Queen of America Goes to Washington City." *American Literature*, vol. 65, no. 3, 1993, pp. 549–74.

———. *The Queen of America Goes to Washington City: Essays on Sex and Citizenship*. Duke UP, 1997.

Berlant, Lauren, and Michael Warner. "Sex in Public." *Critical Inquiry,* vol. 24, no. 2, 1998, pp. 547–66.

Best, Stephen, and Sharon Marcus. "Surface Reading: An Introduction." *Representations,* vol. 108, no. 1, 2009, pp. 1–21.

Bieger, Laura, et al. Introduction. *The Imaginary and Its Worlds: American Studies after the Transnational Turn,* edited by Bieger et al., Dartmouth College Press, 2013, pp. vii–xxviii.

Blackwell, Jeannine. "An Island of Her Own: Heroines of the German Robinsonades from 1720 to 1800." *The German Quarterly, vol.* 58, no. 1, 1985, pp. 5–26.

Blair, Sara. "Cultural Geography and the Place of the Literary." *American Literary History,* vol. 10, no. 3, 1998, pp. 544–67.

———. "Home Truths: Gertrude Stein, 27 Rue de Fleurus, and the Place of the Avant-Garde." *American Literary History,* vol. 12, no. 3, 2000, pp. 417–37.

Boe, Ana de Freitas, and Abby Coykendall. Introduction. *Heteronormativity in Eighteenth-Century Literature and Culture,* edited by Boe and Coykendall, Ashgate, 2014, pp. 1–22.

Bow, Leslie. "*Playing in the Dark* and the Ghosts in the Machine." *American Literary History,* vol. 20, no. 3, 2008, pp. 556–65.

Bowen, Scarlet. "Via Media: Transatlantic Anglicanism in *The Female American.*" *Eighteenth Century: Theory and Interpretation,* vol. 53, no. 2, 2012, pp. 189–207.

Brady, Mary Pat. *Extinct Lands, Temporal Geographies: Chicana Literature and the Urgency of Space.* Duke UP, 2002.

Brickhouse, Anna. "The Indian Slave Trade in Unca Eliza Winkfield's *The Female American.*" *Yearbook of English Studies,* vol. 46, 2016, pp. 115–26.

———. "Mistranslation, Unsettlement, La Navidad." *PMLA,* vol. 128, no. 4, 2013, pp. 938–46.

———. *Transamerican Literary Relations and the Nineteenth-Century Public Sphere.* Cambridge UP, 2004.

Brody, Jennifer DeVere. "Memory's Movements: Minstrelsy, Miscegenation, and American Race Studies." *American Literary History,* vol. 11, no. 4, Winter, 1999, pp. 736–45.

Brooks, Lisa. *Our Beloved Kin: A New History of King Philip's War.* Yale UP, 2018.

Brown, Kathleen M. *Good Wives, Nasty Wenches, and Anxious Patriarchs: Gender, Race, and Power in Colonial Virginia.* U of North Carolina P, 1996.

Brown, Laura. *Ends of Empire: Women and Ideology in Early Eighteenth-Century English Literature.* Cornell UP, 1993.

Brown, Wendy. *Regulating Aversion: Tolerance in the Age of Identity and Empire.* Princeton UP, 2006.

Bruyneel, Kevin. *Third Space of Sovereignty: The Postcolonial Politics of U.S.-Indigenous Relations.* U of Minnesota P, 2007.

Buell, Lawrence. *The Dream of the Great American Novel.* Harvard UP, 2014.

Burleigh, Erica. *Intimacy and Family in Early American Writing.* Palgrave, 2014.

Burnham, Michelle. "Female Bodies and Capitalist Drive: Leonora Sansay's *Secret History* in Transoceanic Context." *Legacy: A Journal of American Women Writers,* vol. 28, no. 2, 2011, pp. 177–204.

———. Introduction. *The Female American,* by Unca Eliza Winkfield, edited by Burnham and James Freitas, Broadview Press, 2001, pp. 9–32.

———. "Loopholes of Resistance: Harriet Jacobs' Slave Narrative and the Critique of Agency in Foucault." *Arizona Quarterly,* vol. 49, no. 2, 1993, pp. 53–73.

———. *Transoceanic America: Risk, Writing, and Revolution the Global Pacific.* Oxford UP, 2019.

Burr, Aaron. *Political Correspondence and Public Papers of Aaron Burr.* Edited by Mary Jo Kline et al., Princeton UP, 1983.

Butler, Judith. *Antigone Claim's: Kinship between Life and Death.* Columbia UP, 2000.

Cameron, Sharon. *Choosing Not Choosing: Dickinson's Fascicles.* U of Chicago P, 1992.

Carruth, Mary. *Feminist Interventions in Early American Studies.* U of Alabama P, 2006.

Casimir, Jean. "From Saint-Domingue to Haiti: To Live Again or to Live at Last!" *The World of the Haitian Revolution.* Edited by David Patrick Geggus and Norman Fiering, Indiana UP, 2009, pp. xi–xviii.

Castiglia, Christopher. "In Praise of Extra-Vagant Women: *Hope Leslie* and the Captivity Romance." *Legacy: A Journal of American Women Writers,* vol. 6, no. 2, 1989, pp. 3–16.

Castiglia, Christopher, and Russ Castronovo. "A 'Hive of Subtlety': Aesthetics and the End(s) of Cultural Studies." *American Literature,* vol. 76, no. 3, 2004, p. 432.

Castronovo, Russ. "'On Imperialism, See . . .': Ghosts of the Present in *Cultures of United States Imperialism.*" *American Literary History,* vol. 20, no. 3, 2008, pp. 427–38.

Cayton, Andrew. *Love in the Time of the Revolution: Transatlantic Literary Radicalism and Historical Change, 1793–1818.* U of North Carolina P, 2013.

Child, Lydia [Francis]. "Miss Sedgwick's Novels." *Ladies' Magazine,* vol. 2, 1829, pp. 234–38.

Child, Lydia Maria. *Hobomok. Hobomok and Other Writings on Indians.* Edited by Carolyn L. Karcher. Rutgers UP, 1986.

———. Preface. *Incidents in the Life of a Slave Girl.* 1861. Edited by Jean Fagan Yellin. Harvard UP, 2000.

———. "The Quadroons." *Fact and Fiction Collection of Stories.* C.S. Francis & Co., 1846.

———. *A Romance of the Republic.* 1867. Edited by Dana D. Nelson. UP of Kentucky, 1997.

Clavin, Matt. "Race, Rebellion, and the Gothic Inventing the Haitian Revolution." *Early American Studies,* vol. 5, no. 1, 2007, pp. 1–29.

Clymer, Jeffory. *Family Money: Property, Race, and Literature in the Nineteenth Century.* Oxford UP, 2013.

———. "Family Money: Race and Economic Rights in Antebellum U.S. Law and Fiction." *American Literary History,* vol. 21, no. 2, 2009, pp. 211–38.

Cott, Nancy. *The Bonds of Womanhood: "Women's Sphere" in New England, 1780–1835.* Yale UP, 1977.

Coviello, Peter. *Tomorrow's Parties: Sex and the Untimely in Nineteenth-Century America.* New York UP, 2013.

Crick, Julia, and Alexandra Walsham. "Introduction: Script, Print, and History." *The Uses of Script and Print 1300–1700, by Crick and Walsham.* Cambridge UP, 2004.

Dash, Michael J. *Haiti and the United States: National Stereotypes and the Literary Imagination.* Second Edition. Macmillan Press, 1997.

Daut, Marlene L. *Tropics of Haiti: Race and the Literary History of the Haitian Revolution in the Atlantic World, 1789–1865.* Liverpool UP, 2015.

Davidson, Cathy N. Preface. *A New-England Tale,* by Catharine Marie Sedgwick, Oxford UP, 1995.

Davis, Rebecca Harding. *Waiting for the Verdict.* Sheldon and Company, 1868.

Defoe, Daniel. *Robinson Crusoe.* 1719. Norton, 1994.

D'Emilio, John, and Estelle Freedman. *Intimate Matters: A History of Sexuality in America.* Harper & Row, 1988.

Derrida, Jacques. *On Cosmopolitanism and Forgiveness.* Translated by Mark Doole and Michael Hughes. Routledge, 2001.

———. *Specters of Marx.* Routledge, 1994.

Dickinson, Emily. *The Poems of Emily Dickinson.* Edited by R.W. Franklin. 3 vols. Belknap Press of Harvard UP, 1998.

DiCuirci, Lindsay. *Colonial Revivals: The Nineteenth-Century Lives of Early American Books.* U of Pennsylvania P, 2018.

Dillon, Elizabeth Maddock. *The Gender of Freedom.* Stanford University Press, 2004.

———. "The Original American Novel, or the American Origin of the Novel." *A Companion to Eighteenth-Century English Novel and Culture,* edited by Paula R. Backscheider and Catherine Ingrassia, Blackwell, 2005, pp. 235–60.

———. "The Secret History of the Early American Novel: Leonora Sansay and the Revolution in Saint Domingue." *Novel,* vol. 40, no. 1–2, 2007, pp. 77–103.

Donegan, Kathleen. *Seasons of Misery: Catastrophe and Colonial Settlement in Early America.* U of Pennsylvania P, 2014.

Douglas, Ann. *The Feminization of American Culture.* Knopf, 1977.

Doyle Laura. *Freedom's Empire: Race and the Rise of the Novel in Atlantic Modernity, 1640–1940.* Duke UP, 2008.

Drexler, Michael. Introduction. *Secret History: or The Horrors of St. Domingo and Laura,* Broadview Editions, 2007, pp. 10–38.

Drexler, Michael, and Ed White. *The Traumatic Colonel: The Founding Fathers, Slavery, and the Phantasmatic Aaron Burr.* New York UP, 2014.

Dubois, Laurent. "Avenging America: The Politics of Violence in the Haitian Revolution." *The World of the Haitian Revolution,* edited by David Patrick Geggus and Norman Fiering, Indiana UP, 2009, pp. 111–24.

Duggan, Lisa. *The Twilight of Equality?: Neoliberalism, Cultural Politics, and the Attack on Democracy.* Beacon Press, 2003.

Edelman, Lee. *No Future: Queer Theory and the Death Drive.* Duke UP, 2004.

Edwards, Bryan. *The History, Civil and Commercial, of the British West Indies,* Vol. 3. G. and W. B. Whittaker, 1819.

Ellis, David Maldwyn. *Landlords and Farmers in the Hudson-Mohawk Region, 1790–1850.* Cornell UP, 1946.

Elmer, Jonathan. *On Lingering and Being Last.* Fordham UP, 2008.

Felski, Rita. *The Limits of Critique.* U of Chicago P, 2015.

———. *Use of Literature.* Wiley-Blackwell, 2008.

Female American, The. See under Winkfield, Unca Eliza.

Fetterley, Judith. "'My Sister! My Sister!': The Rhetoric of Catharine Sedgwick's *Hope Leslie.*"

Catharine Maria Sedgwick: Critical Perspectives, edited by Lucinda L. Damon-Bach and Victoria Clements, Northeastern UP, 2003.

Fick, Carolyn. "The Saint-Domingue Slave Revolution and the Unfolding of Independence, 1791–1804." *The World of the Haitian Revolution,* edited by David Patrick Geggus and Norman Fiering, Indiana UP, 2009, pp. 177–98.

Fleissner, Jennifer L. "Is Feminism a Historicism?" *Tulsa Studies in Women's Literature,* vol. 21, no. 1, 2002, pp. 45–66.

———. "When the Symptom Becomes a Resource." *American Literary History,* vol. 20, no. 3, 2008, pp. 640–55.

Fliegelman, Jay. *Declaring Independence: Jefferson, Natural Language, and the Culture of Performance.* Stanford UP, 1993.

Foreman, P. Gabrielle. *Activist Sentiments: Reading Black Women in the Nineteenth Century.* U of Illinois P, 2009.

Foster, Travis M. "Grotesque Sympathy: Lydia Maria Child, White Reform, and the Embodiment of Urban Space." *ESQ: A Journal of the American Renaissance,* vol. 56, no. 6, 2010, pp. 1–32.

Foucault, Michel. *The Archaeology of Knowledge.* 1969. Translated by A. M. Sheridan Smith, Routledge, 2008.

———. *The History of Sexuality.* 1978. Translated by Robert Hurley, Random House, 1990.

———. *Power/Knowledge: Selected Interviews and Other Writings, 1972–1977.* Edited by Colin Gordon, Pantheon Books, 1980.

Franklin, Wayne, and Michael Steiner. *Mapping American Culture.* U of Iowa P, 1992.

Freccero, Carla. "Figural Historiography: Dogs, Humans, and Cynanthropic Becomings." *Comparatively Queer: Interrogating Identities across Time and Cultures,* edited by Jarrod Hayes, Margaret R. Higonnet, and William J. Spurlin, Palgrave, 2010, pp. 45–68.

Freeburg, Christopher. *Melville and the Idea of Blackness : Race and Imperialism in Nineteenth Century America.* Cambridge UP, 2012.

Freeman, Elizabeth. *Time Binds: Queer Temporalities, Queer Histories.* Duke UP, 2010.

———. *The Wedding Complex: Forms of Belonging in Modern American Culture.* Duke UP, 2002.

Freud, Sigmund. "Mourning and Melancholia." 1917. *The Standard Edition of the Complete Psychological Works of Sigmund Freud,* edited and translated by J. Strachey, vol. 14, Hogarth Press, 1955, pp. 243–58.

Gallagher, Catherine. *Telling Like It Wasn't.* U of Chicago P, 2018.

Geggus, David. "Saint-Domingue on the Eve of the Haitian Revolution." *The World of the Haitian Revolution,* edited by David Patrick Geggus and Norman Fiering, Indiana UP, 2009, pp. 3–20.

Germana, Michael. "Counterfeiters and Con Artists: Money, Literature, and Subjectivity." *American Literary History,* vol. 21, no. 2, 2009, pp. 296–305.

Ghachem, Malick. *The Old Regime and the Haitian Revolution.* Cambridge UP, 2012.

Gillman, Susan, and Forrest G. Robinson. "Introduction." *Mark Twain's* Puddn'head Wilson. Duke UP, 1990.

Gilmore, Leigh, and Elizabeth Marshall. "Girls in Crisis: Rescue and Transnational Feminist Autobiographical Resistance." *Feminist Studies,* vol. 36, no. 3, 2010, pp. 667–90.

Girard, René. *Deceit, Desire, and the Novel: Self and Other in Literary Structure*. Johns Hopkins UP, 1966.

Gomaa, Sally. "Writing to 'Virtuous' and 'Gentle' Readers: The Problem of Pain in Harriet Jacobs's *Incidents* and Harriet Wilson's *Sketches*." *African American Review*, vol. 43, no. 2–3, 2009, pp. 371–81.

Gonzalez, John M. *The Troubled Union: Expansionist Imperatives in Post-Reconstruction American Novels*. Ohio State UP, 2010.

Goudie, Sean. *Creole America: The West Indies and the Formation of Literature and Culture in the New Republic*. U of Pennsylvania P, 2006.

Gould, Philip. *Covenant and Republic: Historical Romance and the Politics of Puritanism*. Cambridge UP, 1996.

Greeson, Jennifer Rae. "The 'Mysteries and Miseries' of North Carolina: New York City, Urban Gothic Fiction, and *Incidents in the Life of a Slave Girl*." *American Literature*, vol. 73, no. 2, 2001, pp. 277–309.

Gura, Philip. *Truth's Ragged Edge: The Rise of the American Novel*. Farrar, Straus and Giroux, 2013.

Gussman, Deborah. "'Equal to Either Fortune': Sedgwick's *Married or Single?* and Feminism." *Catharine Maria Sedgwick: Critical Perspectives*, edited by Lucinda L. Damon-Bach and Victoria Clements. Northeastern UP, 2003, pp. 252–67.

Gustafson, Sandra M. *Imagining Deliberative Democracy in the Early American Republic*. U of Chicago P, 2011.

Habermas, Jürgen. *The Structural Transformation of the Public Sphere*. Translated by Thomas Burger, MIT Press, 1991.

Hardt, Michael, and Antonio Negri. *Empire*. Harvard UP, 2000.

Hartman, Saidiya. *Scenes of Subjection: Terror, Slavery, and Self-Making in Nineteenth-Century America*. Oxford UP, 1997.

Hartog, Hendrik. *Man and Wife in America: A History*. Harvard UP, 2000.

Harvey, Tamara. "Women in Early America: Recharting Hemispheric and Atlantic Desire." *Legacy: A Journal of American Women Writers*, vol. 28, no. 2, 2011, pp. 159–76.

Hawthorne, Nathaniel. *The Scarlet Letter* (1850). *The Centenary Edition of the Works of Nathaniel Hawthorne*, vol. 1, The Ohio State UP, 1962.

———. *A Wonder Book*. *The Centenary Edition of the Works of Nathaniel Hawthorne*, vol. 7, The Ohio State UP, 1982.

Hodes, Martha. "The Sexualization of Reconstruction Politics." *Journal of the History of Sexuality*, vol. 3, no. 3, 1993, 402–17.

Holland, Catherine. *The Body Politic: Foundings, Citizenship, and Difference in the American Political Imagination*. Routledge, 2001.

Hsu, Hsuan. *Geography and the Production of Space in Nineteenth-Century American Literature*. Cambridge UP, 2010.

Hyde, Carrie. *Civic Longing: The Speculative Origins of U.S. Citizenship*. Harvard UP, 2018.

———. "Novelistic Evidence." *American Literary History*, vol. 27, no. 1, 2014, pp. 26–55.

Imada, Adria. *Aloha America: Hula Circuits through the U.S. Empire*. Duke UP, 2012.

Insko, Jeffrey. "Anachronistic Imaginings: Hope Leslie's Challenge to Historicism." *American Literary History*, vol. 16, no. 2, 2004, pp. 179–207.

————. *History, Abolition, and the Ever-Present Now in Antebellum American Writing*. Oxford UP, 2018.

Isenberg, Nancy. *Fallen Founder: The Life of Aaron Burr*. Viking, 2007.

Iser, Wolfgang. *Fiction and the Imaginary: Charting Literary Anthropology*. Johns Hopkins UP, 1993.

————. *The Implied Reader*. Johns Hopkins UP, 1974.

Jacobs, Harriet. *Incidents in the Life of a Slave Girl*. 1861. Edited by Jean Fagan Yellin, Harvard UP, 2000.

Jacobs, John. "A True Tale of Slavery." *Incidents in the Life of a Slave Girl*. 1861. By Harriet Jacobs, edited by Jean Fagan Yellin, Harvard UP, 2000, pp. 207–28.

Jenson, Deborah. *Beyond the Slave Narrative: Politics, Sex, and Manuscripts in the Haitian Revolution*. Liverpool UP, 2011.

Joseph, Betty. "Re(Playing) Crusoe/Pocahontas: Circum-Atlantic Stagings in *The Female American*." *Criticism: A Quarterly for Literature and the Arts*, vol. 42, no. 3, 2000, pp. 317–35.

Kammen, Michael. *Mystic Chords of Memory: The Transformation of Tradition in American Culture*. Knopf, 1991.

Kaplan, Amy. *The Anarchy of Empire in the Making of U.S. Culture*. Harvard UP, 2002.

————. "Manifest Domesticity." *American Literature*, vol. 70, no. 3, 1998, pp. 581–606.

Kaplan, Amy, and Donald E. Pease, eds. *Cultures of United States Imperialism*. Duke UP, 1992.

Kaplan, Carla. *The Erotics of Talk: Women's Writing and Feminist Paradigms*. Oxford UP, 1996.

Karcher, Carolyn. *The First Woman in the Republic: A Cultural Biography of Lydia Maria Child*. Duke UP, 1994.

————. "Lydia Maria Child's A Romance of the Republic: An Abolitionist Vision of American's Racial Destiny." *Slavery and the Literary Imagination*, edited by Deborah E. McDowell and Arnold Rampersad, Johns Hopkins UP, 1989, pp. 81–103.

Kauanui, J. Kēhaulani. "'A structure, not an event': Settler Colonialism and Enduring Indigeneity." *Lateral*, vol. 5, no. 1, 2016, https://doi.org/10.25158/L5.1.7.

Kawash, Samira, *Dislocating the Color Line: Identity, Hybridity, and Singularity in African American Narrative*. Stanford UP, 1997.

Kerber, Linda. "The Republican Mother: Women and the Enlightenment: An American Perspective." *American Quarterly*, vol. 28, no. 2, 1976, pp, 187–205.

Kreiger, Georgia. "Playing Dead: Harriet Jacobs's Survival Strategy in *Incidents in the Life of a Slave Girl*." *African American Review*, vol. 42, no. 3–4, 2008, pp. 607–21.

Laffrado, Laura. *Uncommon Women Gender and Representation in Nineteenth-Century U.S. Women's Writing*. The Ohio State UP, 2009.

Larkin, Ed. *The American School of Empire*. Cambridge UP, 2016.

Lefebvre, Henri. *The Production of Space*. 1974. Translated by Donald Nicholson-Smith, Blackwell Publishing, 1991.

Lemire, Elise. *"Miscegenation": Making Race in America*. U of Pennsylvania P, 2002.

"Letter to the Editor." *Boston Courier*, 3 February 1840, vol. 1647.

Levin, Kenneth. "Unconscious Fantasy in Psychotherapy." *American Journal of Psychotherapy*, vol. 50, no. 2, 1996, pp. 137–53.

Liberator, The. 19 August 1853, p. 131.

Lincoln, Abraham. *Complete Works: Comprising His Speeches, Letters, State Papers.* Vol. 1, edited by John George Nicolay, Cornell UP, 2009.

Lipsitz, George. "The Racialization of Space and the Spatialization of Race." *Landscape Journal,* vol. 26, no. 1–07, 2007, pp. 11–23.

Liu, Tessie P. "The Secret beyond White Patriarchal Power: Race, Gender, and Freedom in the Last Days of Colonial Saint-Domingue." *French Historical Studies,* vol. 33, no. 3, 2010, pp. 387–416.

London, April. *Women and Property in the Eighteenth-Century English Novel.* Cambridge UP, 1999.

Looby, Christopher. *Voicing America: Language, Literary Form, and the Origins of the United States.* U of Chicago P, 1996.

Love, Heather. "Critique Is Ordinary." *PMLA,* vol. 132, no. 2, 2017, pp. 364–70.

———. *Feeling Backward: Loss and the Politics of Queer History.* Harvard UP, 2007.

Lowe, Lisa. *The Intimacies of Four Continents.* Duke UP, 2015.

Luciano, Dana. *Arranging Grief: Sacred Time and the Body in Nineteenth-Century America.* New York UP, 2007.

Machor, James. *Reading Fiction in Antebellum America: Informed Response and Reception Histories, 1820–1865.* Johns Hopkins UP, 2011.

MacNeil, Denise Mary. *The Emergence of the American Frontier Hero: 1682–1826.* Palgrave Macmillan, 2009.

———. "Empire and the Pan-Atlantic Self in *The Female American; or, The Adventures of Unca Eliza Winkfield. Women's Narratives of the Early Americas and the Formation of Empire,* edited by Mary McAleer Balkun and Susan C. Imbarrato, Palgrave, 2016.

Maddox, Lucy. *Removals: Nineteenth-Century American Literature and the Politics of Indian Affairs.* Oxford UP, 1991.

Madsen, Deborah L. "'A for Abolition': Hawthorne's Bond-Servant and the Shadow of Slavery." *Journal of American Studies,* vol. 25, no. 2, 1991, pp. 255–59.

Maguire, Robert, and Scott Freeman. *Who Owns Haiti?: People, Power, and Sovereign.* UP of Florida, 2017.

Manganelli, Kimberly Snyder. "The Tragic Mulatta Plays the Tragic Muse." *Victorian Literature and Culture,* vol. 37, no. 2, 2009, 501–22.

Marsh, Clayton. "Hawthorne's Distillery: Time and Temperance in 'The Birth-Mark' and Other Tales." *American Literature,* vol. 88, no. 4, 2016, pp. 723–53.

Matthiessen, F. O. *American Renaissance.* Oxford UP, 1941.

Maza, Sarah. *Private Lives and Public Affairs: The Causes Célèbres of Prerevolutionary France.* U of California P, 1993.

McGann, Jerome. *The Poetics of Sensibility: A Revolution in Literary Style.* Claredon Press, 1996.

McGill, Meredith. "Echocriticism: Repetition and the Order of Texts." *American Literature,* vol. 88, no. 1, 2016, pp. 1–29.

McGrath, Brian. "Rousseau's Crusoe: Or, On Learning to Read as Not Myself." *Eighteenth-Century Fiction,* vol. 23, no. 1, 2010, pp. 119–39.

McKeon, Michael. *The Secret History of Domesticity.* Johns Hopkins UP, 2005.

McMurran, Mary Helen. "Realism and the Unreal in *The Female American.*" *The Eighteenth Century,* vol. 52, no. 3–4, 2011, pp. 323–42.

Melville, Herman. *Billy Budd, An Inside Narrative.* U of Chicago P, 1962.

Merish, Lori. *Sentimental Materialism: Gender, Commodity Culture, and Nineteenth-Century American Literature.* Duke UP, 2000.

Mills, Charles. "Racial Liberalism." *PMLA,* vol. 123, no. 5, 2008, pp. 1380–97.

Minardi, Margot. *Making Slavery History: Abolitionism and the Politics of Memory in Massachusetts.* Oxford UP, 2010.

Morrison, Toni. *Playing in the Dark: Whiteness and the Literary Imagination.* Vintage Books, 1992.

Mukherjee, Bharati. "*The Scarlet Letter,* 1850." *The New Literary History of America,* edited by Greil Marcus and Werner Sollors, Harvard UP, 2009.

Murphy, Gretchen. *Hemispheric Imaginings: The Monroe Doctrine and Narratives of U.S. Empire.* Duke UP, 2005.

———: *Shadowing the White Man's Burden: U.S. Imperialism and the Problem of the Color Line.* New York UP, 2010.

Nagel, Joane. *Race, Ethnicity, and Sexuality: Intimate Intersections, Forbidden Frontiers.* Oxford UP, 2003.

Nash, Gary. *Red, White, and Black: The Peoples of Early North America.* Prentice Hall, 2010.

Nelson, Dana. "Sympathy as Strategy in Sedgwick's *Hope Leslie.*" *The Culture of Sentiment: Race, Gender, and Sentimentality in Nineteenth-Century America,* edited by Shirley Samuels, Oxford UP, 1992, pp. 191–202.

Nelson, Dana D. Introduction. *A Romance of the Republic,* by Lydia Marie Child, edited by Nelson, UP of Kentucky, 1997, pp. v–xxii.

Nerad, Julie Cary. "Slippery Language and False Dilemmas: The Passing Novels of Child, Howells, and Harper." *American Literature,* vol. 25, no. 4, 2003, pp. 813–41.

Noble, Marianne. *The Masochistic Pleasures of Sentimental Literature.* Princeton UP, 2000.

North American Review, The. Vol. 26, no. 59, 1828, pp. 403–20.

O'Brien, Jean. *Firsting and Lasting: Writing Indians Out of Existence in New England.* U of Minnesota P, 2010.

Ogle, Gene E. "The Trans-Atlantic King and Imperial Public Spheres: Everyday Politics in Pre-Revolutionary Saint-Domingue." *The World of the Haitian Revolution,* edited by David Patrick Geggus and Norman Fiering, Indiana UP, 2009, pp. 19–96.

O'Neill, Caitlin. "'The Shape of Mystery': The Visionary Resonance of Harriet Jacobs's *Incidents in the Life of a Slave Girl.*" *Journal of American Culture,* vol. 41, no. 1, 2018, pp. 56–67.

Opfermann, Susanne. "Lydia Maria Child, James Fennimore Cooper, and Catharine Maria Sedgwick: A Dialogue on Race, Culture, and Gender." *Soft Canons: American Women Writers and Masculine Tradition,* edited by Karen L. Kilcup, U of Iowa P, 1999, pp. 27–47.

Paige, Nicholas. *Before Fiction: The Ancien Régime of the Novel.* U of Pennsylvania P, 2011.

Pascoe, Peggy. *What Comes Naturally: Miscegenation Law and the Making of Race in America.* Oxford UP, 2009.

Pfister, Joel. *The Production of Personal Life: Class, Gender, and the Psychological in Hawthorne's Fiction.* Stanford UP, 1991.

Phillips, Wendell. "Letter from Wendell Phillips, Esq." *The Narrative of the Life of Frederick Douglass, Slave Narratives,* Library of America, 2000.

Piep, Karsten H. "Liberal Visions of Reconstruction: Lydia Maria Child's *Romance of the Republic* and George Washington Cable's *The Grandissimes.*" *Studies in American Fiction,* vol. 31, no. 2, 2003, pp. 165–90.

Pratt, Casey. "'These Things Took the Shape of Mystery': *Incidents in the Life of a Slave Girl* as American Romance." *African American Review,* vol. 47, no. 1, 2014, pp. 69–81.

Pratt, Mary Louise. *Imperial Eyes: Travel Writing and Transculturation.* Routledge, 2008.

Raimon, Eve. *The Tragic Mulatta Revisited: Race and Nationalism in Nineteenth-Century Antislavery Fiction.* Rutgers UP, 2004.

Reed, Ashley. *"Hope Leslie* and the Grounds of Secularism." *ESQ: A Journal of Nineteenth-Century American Literature and Culture,* vol. 66, no. 1, 2020, pp. 89–132.

Reilly, Matthew. "'No eye has seen, or ear heard': Arabic Sources for Quaker Subjectivity in Unca Eliza Winkfield's *The Female American.*" *Eighteenth-Century Studies,* vol. 44, no. 2, 2011, pp. 261–83.

Retallack, Joan. *The Poethical Wager.* U of California P, 2003.

Rifkin, Mark. "'A Home Made Sacred by Protecting Laws': Black Activist Homemaking and Geographies of Citizenship in *Incidents in the Life of a Slave Girl.*" *d i f f e r e n c e s: A Journal of Feminist Cultural Studies,* vol. 18, no. 2, 2007, pp. 72–102.

———. *Manifesting America.* Cambridge UP, 2009.

Rosenthal, Debra. "Floral Counterdiscourse: Miscegenation, Ecofeminism, and Hybridity in Lydia Maria Child's *A Romance of the Republic.*" *Women Studies,* vol. 31, no. 2, 2002, pp. 221–45.

Rowlandson, Mary. *The Sovereignty and Goodness of God: with Related Documents.* Edited by Neil Salsbury, Bedford/St. Martin's, 1997.

Rust, Marion. *Introduction. Women's Narratives of the Early Americas and the Formation of Empire,* edited by Mary McAleer Balkun and Susan C. Imbarrato, Palgrave, 2016.

Ryan, Delmot. *Technologies of Empire: Writing, Imagination, and the Making of Imperial Networks, 1750–1820.* U of Delaware P, 2013.

Saks, Eva. "Representing Miscegenation Law." *Interracialism: Black-White Intermarriage in American History, Literature, and Law,* edited by Werner Sollors, Oxford UP, 2000, pp. 61–80.

Sánchez-Eppler, Karen. *Touching Liberty: Abolition, Feminism, and the Politics of the Body.* U of California P, 1993.

Sansay, Leonora. *Secret History: or The Horrors of St. Domingo.* 1808. Edited by Michael Drexler, Broadview Editions, 2007.

Sayre, Jillian J. *Mourning the Nation to Come: Creole Nativism in Nineteenth-Century American Literatures.* Louisiana State UP, 2019.

Schoolman, Martha. *Abolitionist Geographies.* U of Minnesota P, 2014.

Secret History: or The Horrors of St. Domingo. See under Sansay, Leonora.

Sedgwick, Catharine Maria. *Hope Leslie; or the Early Times in the Massachusetts.* Rutgers UP, 1987.

Sharpe, Jenny. *Ghosts of Slavery: A Literary Archaeology of Black Women's Lives.* U of Minnesota P, 2003.

Shire, Laurel. *The Threshold of Manifest Destiny: Gender and National Expansion in Florida.* U of Pennsylvania P, 2016.

Smith, Caleb. "Harriet Jacobs among the Militants: Transformations in Abolition's Public Sphere, 1859–61." *American Literature,* vol. 84, no. 4, 2012, pp. 743–68.

Smith, John. *The Generall Historie of Virginia. Capt. John Smith: Writing,* edited by James Horn, Library of America, 2007.

Smith, Rogers M. *Stories of Peoplehood: The Politics and Morals of Political Membership.* Cambridge UP, 2003.

Smith-Rosenberg, Carol. "Black Gothic: The Shadowy Origins of the American Bourgeoisie." *Possible Pasts: Becoming Colonial in Early America,* edited by Robert Blair St. George, Cornell UP, 2000.

Sollors, Werner. "Introduction: Black—White—Both—Neither—In-Between." *Neither Black Nor White Yet Both: Thematic Explorations of Interracial Literature.* Oxford UP, 1997.

Somerville, Diane. *Rape and Race in the Nineteenth-Century South.* The U of North Carolina P, 2004.

Spires, Derrick R. *The Practice of Citizenship: Black Politics and Print Culture in the Early United States.* U of Pennsylvania P, 2019.

Stadler, Gustavus. "Magawisca's Body of Knowledge: Nation-Building in *Hope Leslie.*" *Yale Journal of Criticism,* vol. 12, no. 1, 1999, pp. 41–56.

Stevens, Laura. *The Poor Indians: British Missionaries, Native Americans, and Colonial Sensibility.* U of Pennsylvania P, 2004.

Stoler, Ann Laura. *Carnal Knowledge and Imperial Power: Race and the Intimate in Colonial Rule.* U of California P, 2002.

———. "Epistemic Politics: Ontologies of Colonial Common Sense." *The Philosophical Forum,* vol. 39, no. 3, 2008, pp, 349–69.

———. "Intimations of Empire: Predicaments of the Tactile and Unseen." *Haunted by Empire: Geographies of Intimacy in North American History,* edited by Ann Laura Stoler, Duke UP, 2006.

Stowe, Harriet Beecher. *Uncle Tom's Cabin.* Norton, 2010.

Sweet, Nancy F., "Dissent and the Daughter in *A New England Tale* and *Hobomok,*" *Legacy: A Journal of American Women Writers,* vol. 22, no. 2, 2005, pp. 107–25.

Taylor, Diana. *The Archive and the Repertoire: Performing Cultural Memory in the Americas.* Duke UP, 2003.

Tilton, Robert. *Pocahontas: The Evolution of an American Narrative.* Cambridge UP, 1994.

Tompkins, Jane. *Sensational Designs: The Cultural Work of American Fiction 1790–1860.* Oxford UP, 1985.

Traister, Bryce. "Mary Rowlandson and the Invention of the Secular." *Early American Literature,* vol. 42, no. 2, 2007, pp. 323–54.

Trodd, Zoe. "A Hole Story: The Space of Historical Memory in the Abolitionist Imagination." *Agency in the Margins: Stories of Outsider Rhetoric,* edited by Anne Meade Stockdell-Giesler, Fairleigh Dickinson UP, 2010, pp. 68–90.

Turley, Hans. "Protestant Evangelism, British Imperialism, and Crusonian Identity. *A New Imperial History: Culture, Identity, and Modernity in Britain and the Empire, 1660–1840,* edited by Kathleen Wilson, Cambridge UP, 2004.

United States, Supreme Court. *Brown v. Board of Education. United States Reports*, vol. 347, 17
May 1954, /www.loc.gov/item/usrep347483/.

———. *Lawrence v. Texas. United States Reports*, vol. 539, 26 June 2003, www.loc.gov/item/
usrep539558/.

———. *Loving v Virginia. United States Reports*, vol. 388, 12 June 1967, www.loc.gov/item/
usrep388001/.

Van Renen, Denys. "'Walk upon water': Equiano and the Globalizing Subject." *Beyond 1776:
Globalizing the Literatures, Cultures and Community of the American Revolution*, edited by
Maria O'Malley and Denys Van Renen, U of Virginia P, 2018, pp. 230–52.

Vietto, Angela. "Leonora Sansay." American Women *Prose Writers to 1820*, vol. 200, edited
by Carla Mulford and Amy E. Winans.,Gale Research, 1999, pp. 330–36.

Wardrop, Daneen. "'I Stuck the Gimlet in and Waited for Evening': Writing and *Incidents
in the Life of a Slave Girl*." *Texas Studies in Literature and Language*, vol. 49, no. 3, 2007,
pp. 209–29.

Warner, Anne Bradford. "Harriet Jacobs at Home: *Incidents in the Life of a Slave Girl*." *Southern Quarterly*, vol. 45, no. 3, 2008, pp. 30–49.

Warner, Michael. *Publics and Counterpublics*. Verso, 2005.

———. *The Trouble with Normal: Sex, Politics, and the Ethics of Queer Life*. Harvard UP, 1999.

———. "What's Colonial about Colonial America." *Possible Pasts: Becoming Colonial in
Early America*, edited by Robert Blair St. George, Cornell UP, 2000, pp. 49–71.

Watts, Edward. *Colonizing the Past: Mythmaking and Pre-Columbian Whites in Nineteenth-
Century American Writing*. U of Virginia P, 2020.

———. "Settler Postcolonialism as a Reading Strategy." *American Literary History*, vol. 22,
no. 2, 2010, pp. 459–70.

———. *Writing and Postcolonialism in the Early Republic*. U of Virginia P, 1992.

Weaver, Jace. *The Red Atlantic: American Indigenes and the Making of the Modern World,
1000–1927*. U of North Carolina P, 2014.

Weierman, Karen Woods. "Reading and Writing *Hope Leslie:* Catharine Maria Sedgwick's
Indian 'Connections.'" *The New England Quarterly*, vol. 75, no. 3, 2002, pp. 415–43.

Wexler, Laura. *Tender Violence: Domestic Visions in an Age of U.S Imperialism*. U of North
Carolina P, 2000.

Wheeler, Roxann. *The Complexion of Race: Categories of Difference in Eighteenth-Century British
Culture*. U of Pennsylvania P, 2000.

White, Ashli. *Encountering Revolution: Haiti and the Making of the Early Republic*. Johns Hopkins UP, 2010.

Wilkens, Matthew. "Geolocation Extraction and Mapping of Nineteenth-Century US Fiction." *Chicago Colloquium on Digital Humanities and Computer Science, Loyola University
Chicago*, vol. 20, 2011, pp. 1–11.

Winkfield, Unca Eliza (anon). *The Female American*. 1767. Second Edition. Edited by Michelle
Burnham and James Freitas, Broadview Press, 2014.

Winnicott, D.W. *The Collected Works of D. W. Winnicott*. Oxford University Press, 1960.

———. "The Location of Cultural Experience." *Playing and Reality*. Routledge, 2005, pp.
95–103.

Woertendyke, Gretchen. "Romance to Novel: *A Secret History*." *Narrative*, vol. 17, no. 3, 2009, pp. 255–73.

Wolfe, Andrea Powell. "Double-Voicedness in *Incidents in the Life of a Slave Girl:* 'Loud Talking' to a Northern Black Readership." *American Transcendental Quarterly*, vol. 22, no. 3, 2008, pp. 517–25.

Wolfe, Patrick. *Settler Colonialism and the Transformation of Anthropology.* Continuum, 1999.

Yaeger, Patricia. *The Geography of Identity.* U of Michigan P, 1996.

Yellin, Jean Fagan. *Harriet Jacobs, A Life.* Basic Civitas Books, 2004.

———. Introduction. *Incidents in the Life of a Slave Girl: Written by Herself,* by Harriet A. Jacobs, edited by L. Maria Child, Harvard University Press, 2000, pp. xiii–xxxiv.

Zelica, The Creole. Vols. 1–3. William Clowes, 1820.

Index

abolitionism, 5, 126–27, 138, 148, 162–64, 179–85, 207n1, 208n10, 208n13, 209n16; Lydia Maria Child and, 123, 135; Harriet Jacobs and, 151, 154–56, 159, 180

alternative history. *See* counterfactual narrative

amalgamation, 89, 116–17, 137–38, 140, 210n7, 210n11; abolitionist movement and, 156, 162–64; antiamalgamation laws, 125–26, 163–64; antimiscegenation laws, 120, 125–66, 137, 208n4, 208n6, 208n10, 209n19, 210n11

American Revolution, 1, 201n2; in relation to Haitian Revolution, 53, 202n6

amnesia, 7; cultural amnesia, 1–2, 5–8, 80, 90, 111–12, 194, 195n1, 204n1; Haitian Revolution and, 53

Antigone, 109–10

Antislavery. *See* abolitionism

Armstrong, Paul, 2, 49, 148–49, 192

Bauer, Ralph, 55

Baym, Nina, 81, 114

Berlant, Lauren, 82, 130, 151, 153, 161, 172–73, 181, 185

Brent, Linda. *See* Jacobs, Harriet

Brickhouse, Anna, 23, 198n23, 199n2, 201n14, 201n4

Burnham, Michelle, 43, 199n2, 201n3, 202n7

Burr, Aaron, 54, 58, 75; in *Secret History* (Sansay), 17, 52, 54, 58, 74–77

Child, Lydia Maria, 85–86, 115–46, 150, 190; *Hobomok*, 8–9, 116; on Sedgwick, 85–86; preface to *Incidents* (Jacobs), 147, 149, 187; "The Quadroons," 131–33, 137, 167; *Romance of Republic*, 8, 18–19, 115–46

Christianity, 104, 190; in *Female American* (anon), 26, 34–35, 44–46, 199n2; in *Hope Leslie* (Sedgwick), 104

colonialism, 28–29; difference from imperialism, 196n5; in *Female American* (anon), 46–47, 195n1; settler colonialism, 84. *See also* imperialism

Constitution, US, 128; slavery and, 135–36, 183, 207n2, 208n3, 209n16

contextual readings, 9–10, 13, 191–93, 196n6, 211n2, 211n3; of *Female American* (anon) 30; of *Incidents* (Jacobs), 149, 186; presentism, 196n6

counterfactual narrative, 8, 14–15, 22, 54, 81, 87, 114, 148–49, 191, 198n23, 198n27, 199n29, 201n4

Daut, Marlene, 53, 69

Davis, Rebecca Harding, 125

Defoe, Daniel, 21, 22; *Robinson Crusoe*, 21, 24–26, 37–38, 152, 196n10, 199n2

Derrida, Jacques, 1, 10, 197n20

Dillon, Elizabeth Maddock, 36, 82, 95, 203n14, 203n21

double consciousness, 182

THE GHOST LOCKET

THE GHOST LOCKET

ALLISON RUSHBY

WALKER
BOOKS

First published in Great Britain 2022 by Walker Books Ltd
87 Vauxhall Walk, London SE11 5HJ

2 4 6 8 10 9 7 5 3 1

Text © 2022 Allison Rushby
Illustrations © 2022 Rovina Cai

This book has been typeset in Centaur, Antigua and Atmosphere

Printed and bound by CPI Group (UK) Ltd, Croydon CR0 4YY

British Library Cataloguing in Publication Data:
a catalogue record for this book is available from the British Library

ISBN 978-1-5295-0599-3

www.walker.co.uk

Prologue

SPITALFIELDS, LONDON

I am eight. I'm standing outside a tall terrace house that has fancy green shutters and a solid black front door. I don't want to go inside the house. Something about it doesn't feel right. I have that feeling. That funny feeling that I get in my stomach sometimes.

"Freya?" I look up.

"Mmm-hmm?" She turns on the pavement, busy digging for her phone in her bag.

"Have I been to this house before?"

She stops digging. "Why do you ask that?"

"Um, I don't know." I do know. I already know not to talk to Freya about the feeling I'm having. "It just . . . it feels like I've been here before. Like I remember it."

"Well, yes. You have been here before. A long time ago. Several times, in fact."

"Okay." If I've been here before, it should be all right. It's just that I think there might be something that lives inside the house … I used to call them shadows, but now I'm older I know they're not. They're people. People who used to be alive. People who are stuck between this world and what comes next. I call them spirits now. When I notice one, I just do this thing where I pretend I haven't seen it at all. The spirit will usually go away then.

"Coming?" Freya is at the door, framed by the ivy that climbs up either side. A glass-and-iron pendant light hangs heavy overhead.

I nod. I want to see Elsie and I know she's inside. Elsie is Freya's great aunt and she's one of my favourite people in the world. Elsie comes to visit us every year in Singapore, but this year we've come to her instead.

Freya grabs the iron knocker and knocks twice. It takes a few moments before the door creaks open.

"There you are!" Elsie beams as she opens the door wide. She is all silvery hair and rosy cheeks.

I hesitate in the doorway. Something feels … wrong. Like I'm not welcome inside.

"Come on, Lolli, where's my hug?" Elsie says.

Of course I'm welcome inside. I dash past Freya into the hallway and am enveloped by Elsie's soft folds.

"Come here, you," she says over the top of me, pulling in Freya as well.

Still a bit unsure, I peek around Elsie's skirt.

What a strange place. It's almost like I've stepped into the past. The entrance hall is gloomy, the walls layered thick with years of creamy paint. The only light comes from some old glass lamps on the wall with candles in them. The flames flicker and dance. All the things I can see — a heavy bench seat, a little hall table, the bumpy, uneven floor — look ancient and worn. A set of dark wooden stairs looms. The good news is, I can't see any spirits. As Elsie draws back, I relax.

"Now, I've prepared some fun for this afternoon. I've found an old waffle iron and I've whipped up some batter. I thought we could make some waffles over the open fire, Lolli. Would you like that?"

I nod, barely hearing her question. The thing is, the moment I relaxed, a different feeling had come creeping in. Before it had been a bad feeling that I'd had. But this ... if it's a spirit, it's a friendly one. I'm surprised. Sometimes they seem confused, or worried, or look lonely, but I don't think I've met a friendly one before.

While the grown-ups talk, I continue to look around. A clock I can't see *tick-tocks* and the house *creaks* and *groans*, as if it's talking to me.

Maybe it is?

Freya has told me Elsie's house is famous. I know not to call it a museum, because it isn't. It's an art installation. I don't really understand what that means, but when Freya explains it, she says the house isn't about artefacts, red ropes and reading labels. Apparently it's about emotions and drama. That still doesn't make complete sense to me, so I try to think of it like a ride where you experience the past. It's not expensive for the public to get in here, but it can take ages to get a ticket. Especially at Christmastime, because Christmas at the House in Spitalfields is special. Every Christmas the house is crammed full of festive decorations, holly and ivy. It's made all cosy and inviting and visitors are plied with mulled wine and mince pies by the hearth.

"Come on, Lolli. Let's go down to the kitchen and make some waffles the old-fashioned way," Freya says.

There's a mirror behind her reflecting a room and in it I see a flash of something. "Who's in there?" I ask Elsie, turning to point at the room itself.

"In the dining room? No one. It's just us. The house is closed today."

"There is. I think I saw someone. In the mirror." I regret the words the moment they come out of my mouth, because I know what I just saw.

"You saw someone in the mirror?" Elsie says quickly. "Who? A girl?"

"I . . ." I start, but then stop as a feeling overtakes my body. Whatever I saw, whatever I felt that was kind and good just moments ago has gone. It has been chased away by something else. The something I felt a tingle of before when I was standing outside. Something angry. Something dark and hateful that is pressing down heavily from above, building and growing and doubling like an incoming deep, dark storm cloud. Now I've let it in, it grabs me with two hands. It sucks all the air from my lungs. Presses tight around my head. I know I'm not going to have the strength to push it away. It's too late. I'm too late. It warned me and I didn't listen. Now I can't move my feet. I'm stuck here.

I'm at its mercy.

And it's coming.

Coming.

Barrelling down the stairs like a wave.

Coming to take me.

To drown me.

Tick-tock, tick-tock, tick-tock, the clock says, not caring.

Creak-crack, the stairs groan as the thing hurtles downwards.

I put my hand out, scrambling for something to hold on to. I grab at the wall, but it's no good; my fingernails only slide down the layers of paint.

"Freya!" I panic. "Freya!"

I try the wall again, scratching, grasping. I have to hold on. It's pulling me under.

Just as I think there's no hope, the wall seems to shift. My fingers catch on something, taking hold as a shape forms, thrusting outwards. Something warm. Something ... doughy. And then I see what that shape is.

A nose. Two eyes. A gaping hole of a mouth.

"Leave," the face says, the lips shifting. "Leave this place, girl."

I do the only thing my frozen body can do.

I scream.

I scream and I scream and I scream.

It's Elsie who saves me. She grabs me. Grabs me tight. So tight.

"Get away from her," I hear her hiss. "Get away from her, you nasty old bat."

She picks me up, presses me to her and runs, my body jolting as we go. I keep screaming. Because it is everywhere. All around me. The house is full of it. This being that has swallowed me alive. Elsie keeps running. Along the hall. Down some stairs. And I keep screaming. I'm not sure I'll ever be able to stop.

"Lolli!" I hear Freya's voice in the distance. "What's wrong? What is it? Are you sick? Where does it hurt?"

Elsie keeps running.

Until we stop.

It feels like a hundred years before the pressure starts to release.

"It's all right," a voice soothes. "It's all right. It's all right …"

I dare to open an eyelid.

We're sitting. I'm on Elsie's lap. There is light. Warmth. Nice smells — toast, tea, cinnamon, spicy ginger, sweet marzipan. A fire crackles. Now the tight feeling around my head is not the work of a spirit, but of Elsie's soft hand, cradling me to her.

The person, the face, the spirit is gone.

Elsie bends her head down to me. Her eyes meet mine and she whispers. "Listen to me now. Listen carefully. You are always safe by the hearth, Lolli. Always. Remember that."

LONDON

Three years later...

1

Each footstep brings me closer to the place of my nightmares.

I long to turn around and retrace the path we've taken. I want to scurry back to our hotel. Back to that ripple of a building, all modern, shiny glass that reflects the Thames. I want the doorman to give me that nod – the one that says, "I have no idea who you are, young lady, but lovely to see you again". I want to slot the key in the door, feel the plush carpet underfoot, dive deep down under the smooth white sheets on my bed. There I'll stay, forever and ever, no one knowing, the world passing by outside.

I love hotels.

"Olivia!" Freya calls out as I begin to lag that bit too far behind. "Come on!"

I'm only ever Olivia when I'm in trouble. I'm Lolli the rest of the time, because I couldn't say my name properly when I was little. Sometimes I wonder what I'd be called if my mum was still here and Freya was just her best friend, like things should have been.

Freya doesn't wait for my excuses but continues to stride ahead. She's upset with me for several reasons. These reasons include:

1. we're staying in a hotel (I've always refused to stay at her great aunt Elsie's, which is next door to the place of my nightmares);

2. I've dawdled all morning, taking too long having breakfast, spending ages in the shower and changing outfits three times because I couldn't decide what to wear; and

3. we said we'd be at the place of my nightmares at 9 am and we're definitely not going to be there at 9 am, because it's already 9.32 am.

The place of my nightmares is a house called the House in Spitalfields. I'd looked it up on the internet last night. Stared at photos and read people's reviews, even though I already knew everything about it. I'd even checked maps and made a note of the side streets that we'd walk past on our approach.

And now we're almost there.

I take a deep breath. Time to focus.

I've practised for this moment over and over for weeks now. I have to be prepared for the feelings. When they come, I must catch them with both hands. I'll then drive them back behind a door I created in my mind a long time ago. I will slam that door shut and lock it tight.

The house isn't haunted, like some people say it is. That's just their imagination.

My imagination.

I notice a woman up ahead, standing by herself. She peers this way and that, looking a little confused. I am instantly on alert. They often look like that. But then another woman approaches her and the pair smile and hug and go on their way. It's okay. Reminding myself to be careful, I fix my gaze on the bright, newly hung Christmas wreaths that decorate the traditional-looking lampposts above. The wreaths are made of brand new plastic. New things tend to be good. Safe. Wiped clean of history. I'm particularly nervous because we're in Spitalfields now, which is an old place with a long history. Freya's even told me how it got its name – from an old priory and hospital called St Mary Spital. It had the largest infirmary in medieval London. It can't have been a very good one, because apparently there are burial pits close by with over 4,000 bodies in them.

We turn the corner, leaving the world of business behind us and are presented with a row of fine red-brick Georgian terraces. Elsie owns two of them – they've been in her family for over one hundred years, mostly rented out to other people. I know the story, because Freya has told me so many times. Elsie had just graduated from art school and decided she wanted to turn one of the terraces into something that was a cross between a museum and a piece of art. She had flipped a coin and the terrace on the left ended up becoming that piece of art. Elsie wanted to try and make people believe they'd wandered into the past. As if they'd walked into an old, still-life painting. Nothing would be labelled. Everything would be for looking. For *feeling*.

Well, I'd certainly felt something when I'd gone inside. That was for sure.

And that's when it comes into view. Just as I remember from the nightmare I have almost every single night – green shutters, solid black front door.

I come to a complete stop.

"Lolli!"

"*Coming.*" I run the few steps over.

Freya huffs. "Honestly, if I ever find out who told you about that ridiculous ghost, I'll . . ."

"No one told me. I know what I saw. I think I've always known what's inside. You said yourself I've always hated it here. That I'd scream even when I was a tiny baby."

"That's what tiny babies do everywhere they go. I haven't asked you to come here for years because of your aversion to the place. But you're eleven years old now and big enough not to believe in silly stories."

I open my mouth to argue, then close it again. There's no point. We've discussed this a hundred times. I feel a bit bad because I know I'm ruining this trip for her. Freya's always been entranced by the House in Spitalfields. When she was younger, she'd spend her school holidays staying with Elsie and helping out her great aunt, especially during the Christmas season. She's told me about those days lots of times.

Freya turns away and I remind myself that I need to concentrate. As I take those final few steps over and stand in front of the terrace house, I brace myself. I hadn't known to do that when I was younger. Over the years I've worked out how to block spirits — how to make them think I haven't noticed them at all. Not that I see them every day. I don't. The thing is, I think it's rare for a spirit to remain in this world. Or maybe it's common and I can only see some of them. I don't know. It isn't something I talk about, because the few times I have, Freya has absolutely lost it and dragged me to see psychiatrists and psychologists. They never believe me, of course. And why should they? I wouldn't, if I was them.

Push it down. Close it off. Block. Breathe. Don't engage.

Freya stands on the doorstep, waiting. Her gaze softens when she looks at me — I must seem worried. This is not a good sign. I shouldn't look scared. I shouldn't look ... well, like anything. What is inside the house can sense fear. It likes it. Feeds on it. Of that much I'm certain.

Freya's hand rests on the door. "We have to, Lolli."

"I know."

"We promised Elsie we'd help. We both agreed."

"I *know*." Freya is right — I had agreed. But that was months ago and a world away, when Elsie had visited us in Singapore. I hadn't really thought the time would actually come.

Unfortunately, it has.

"There's so much to do for the opening of the house this weekend. Tanice needs us to pitch in."

Tanice is the house curator. We've only met a couple times and never here, at the house itself, but she's really nice and I know she needs our help.

"In two weeks we'll be gone. We'll be back home in Singapore." Freya keeps at me, wearing me down.

"I know. I'm not arguing! Let's just get inside already!" All this chattering is only making things worse. How am I supposed to concentrate?

Freya turns her key in the door of the House in Spitalfields and pushes it open. "In you go, then."

I duck past her and run for my life.

2

I bolt down the hallway, swing around the newel
post with one hand and run down the stairs to
the kitchen and the hearth.

Push it down. Close it off. Block. Breathe. Don't engage.

I smell the kitchen before I see it. The sweet,
smoky smell of the wood fire. Cloves and orange,
gingerbread, icing sugar.

Safety.

I burst inside the small room, its warmth
embracing me. But then I draw back. I'm not alone.

"Lolli! Welcome!" Tanice, the house curator,
stands before the huge dresser, stacked with its rows
of mismatched blue-and-white porcelain. Cups hang,

a white maid's cap dangles from a peg, an apron lies abandoned on a chair. Everything used. Worn. Loved. Nothing here is perfect. Nothing is meant to be. Tanice herself is a bright pop of colour with her green-rimmed glasses and fitted fuchsia jacket.

"Hi, Doctor Cole," I say. Freya has reminded me I should use Tanice's proper title.

"Oh, Tanice is just fine. Now, you haven't met my daughter Jada before. She's been looking forward to you coming."

I look over to see a girl my age – a mini Tanice, just with cool cornrows and no glasses – sitting at the wide wooden table.

"Hi," she says, with a smile and a wave.

The fire crackles and pops and I jump. "Hi," I say. I have to calm down. I am safe here. Safe by the hearth. Safe with Tanice and Jada who are very much alive.

"Lolli!" Freya enters. "Not so fast down those steep stairs, please. Ah, Tanice, Jada! We're finally here. Sorry to have kept you waiting."

"It's fine." Tanice comes over to give Freya a hug. "Just fine. We definitely need your help. There's still quite a bit to do before the weekend."

"I almost hate to ask you," Freya continues. "I need to pop next door. I just wanted to say hello first."

"Of course. I'll make us a quick pot of tea before we start."

"Perfect. I won't be long. You'll be all right, Lolli?" Freya gives me a look.

"Mmpf."

Freya takes this as a yes and leaves with a wave. Tanice turns back to the dresser where she'd been sorting through some small metal tins.

"Well, I would make tea, but it seems we're almost out. Jada, sweetie, would you mind running to the storeroom? Actually, no, wait. You get the biscuits from my bag, which I've left in the parlour and I'll get the tea, because I haven't unlocked the storeroom yet."

"Okay," Jada says, getting up from the table.

"Won't be a moment, Lolli," Tanice says.

Before I can protest about being left on my own, they are both gone.

You are always safe by the hearth, Lolli.

I inch closer towards the fire and inspect the string of gingerbread men that are strung from one side to the other. Their little currant eyes stare back at me.

"Like them?" Elsie says. "Tanice put them up just this morning."

I almost jump out of my skin. I hadn't spotted her there, in her favourite spot by the fire.

"Elsie!"

"And who else would be in my chair?"

I can't help it. I begin to cry. The last time I'd seen Elsie had been in Singapore. She'd come to visit us and we'd had a bit of a fight before she left. Then she'd got sick again. Really sick. "I thought … I thought I'd never see you again."

"I thought you'd never get here!"

I laugh. And sniff.

"Now, come sit here by me. Quickly, before the others come back."

I go over and sit in the other wooden chair.

Elsie gives me a look. "I wasn't joking – I was beginning to think you weren't coming."

"Hello! We promised we'd come. You made us promise over and over!"

"Yes."

"And here we are."

"Yes. And now I need you to do something else for me."

Typical Elsie — straight to the point. "Seriously, I told you in Singapore. I don't want to talk about it. I don't like thinking about it."

This was what we'd fought about. Elsie was always trying to talk to me about what had happened all those years ago, when the face came out of the wall. She was always trying to explain. And I was always trying to explain to *her* that I didn't want to know.

Another pop from the fire breaks the spell. I turn in my seat, inspecting the room. Wary, as I remember where I am and what once happened upstairs. I'd stopped concentrating some time ago. That door in my mind might be shut tight, but I'd let something seep out through the gap underneath.

Big mistake.

I stand. "I can't be here."

"You can, Lolli. You have to. It's important. There's something I need you to do."

"No. I have to go. I thought I could keep it away, but I can't." I'm already moving towards the door.

"Lolli, wait. Wait!"

I shake my head. No. It's coming again. Just like last time. And it's stronger than me. So much stronger.

"You tricked me." I point my finger at Elsie. "You tricked me into coming here."

I don't wait for her reply. There's no time. There's only time to run.

3

I make it out just in time. The spirit is still upstairs; the hallway wall remains smooth.

I pass Jada as I go. "I'm going to see Freya next door," I yell back at her.

"But ..." She holds up the packet of biscuits.

I bang the front door closed behind me and sink down onto the front step, unsure if my shaky legs can carry me any further.

She tricked me.

She really did.

When Elsie had visited us in Singapore, I thought she was being melodramatic about how much help she'd need at the house at Christmastime. I knew she'd had cancer in her leg a while ago, but she'd had treatment and she looked good. Almost back to normal, even if she did have a cane and super-short hair. Unfortunately, at her last check-up they'd found the cancer had come back again. She'd brought her visit to Singapore forward so that she could come and see us before she started another round of treatment. Freya had taken some time off from the art gallery and, during her stay with us, Elsie had constantly been trying to corner me whenever Freya was out of earshot. It was always the same. She wanted to talk about the spirit I'd seen in the house when I was eight.

I didn't.

On her last day with us, Elsie had wanted to visit the Botanic Gardens. Freya hadn't been sure.

"There'll be a lot of walking," Freya had said.

"So, I'll sit down when I have to."

"I don't think . . ."

Elsie had given her a very Elsie look.

"Fine. If that's what you want to do."

So that's what we'd done. We'd gone to the gardens and sat about and just looked. We'd been in the lush ginger garden, admiring a little waterfall when Freya had suggested ice-cream, leaving the two of us on a bench while she went to find some.

"I don't want to talk about it," I'd said as soon as Freya was more than a few steps away.

"You're never going to want to talk about it, but this may be your last chance."

"I seriously doubt that. You're going to bug me about this forever."

"Lolli, you know I'm sick again. You know I have to go for more treatment when I get home. I can see that you don't want to visit the house again, but Tanice can't handle the special Christmas installation and viewings all on her own and Freya has just the right touch."

"I'm not saying I won't come and help. I'm just saying I don't want to talk about it. About the house, I mean. And what's in it."

"You need to talk about it, Lolli. We need to talk about it. It's vital that you understand. I'm not going to live forever."

"Don't say that." I'd shifted in my seat. "I don't like it."

"Nobody lives forever, Lolli."

"Some people do," I'd replied. "I've seen them.

And so have you. There was one in the market yesterday. When we were getting lunch. Sitting right across from us. Did you see her?" There'd been one near the entrance to the gardens today too, but Elsie obviously didn't see him.

"No, I didn't. You're stronger than me. I don't think I can see ... all the spirits you see. Anyway, I don't think that's what you want for me, is it? To live forever as some poor, wandering spirit."

We both knew the answer to this.

"You're a smart girl, Lolli. Haven't you wondered about the spirits? Wanted to know more?"

Yes. "No."

"I'm sure that's not true. Do you know something? I think after eighty years I've finally found out why we see them."

I'd stared at the little rock waterfall in front of us and tried to act like I didn't care. The truth was, I wanted to hear what she had to say about this. Of course I'd always wondered why. Why did I see spirits? Why did Elsie? And if I could see spirits, why had I never seen my mother? It didn't make any sense.

"I was at a lecture a few weeks ago. It was given by a theologian and she was talking about religions and differing beliefs about the afterlife and whether or not the living can have contact with it. I was most interested to hear what she had to say, of course. Anyway, she said something that made me think a great deal. It all centred on one belief about newborns. She said that some people believe that when you're a newborn baby, you have a thousand portals open in your mind that link directly to all the energy and information in the cosmos. Those pathways shut down quickly and by the time you're one year of age, they're all closed off. But if you have a traumatic event when you're small, those pathways can be damaged. They can remain open and information can continue to flow through. I was six months old when my family's London home was bombed to smithereens during the Blitz, remember? We were lucky to survive. And you were only weeks old when your mother died. Maybe that's why your gift is stronger than mine?"

"I wouldn't call it a gift."

"I would. It makes us different. Special." Elsie sighed. "Lolli, I'd hoped by now you'd have stopped fighting it. That you'd be open to knowing more. Especially about what happened to you at the house."

I'd shrugged. What Elsie didn't get is that I wanted to know more, but at the same time, I couldn't. Because to know more, I would have had to think back to that day. And everything inside fought me on returning to that place. That horrible moment.

"It's important that you understand what happened to you," Elsie continued, almost as if she could hear my thoughts. "Do you remember how you said you saw someone in the mirror?"

I shook my head. Hard. "I told you I don't want to talk about that day. Ever."

"Lolli, you can't go through your life denying this."

I was pretty sure I could. That was my plan, anyway.

"Look at me. Right now, please."

I'd looked at her through narrowed eyes.

"Lolli, it's not good for you to be this way. You can't go through your life being so ... disconnected."

"I'm not disconnected."

Silence. In it, I focused on the waterfall and hoped she'd stop talking.

Elsie didn't take the hint.

"We're all connected, Lolli. To each other. To the past. To the present and future. It can't be just you.

On your own. It's not healthy. It's not how things are meant to work."

I'd shrugged. "Like I said, I'm not disconnected. I have Freya. And you."

"That's not enough."

"I ..."

Elsie had held up a hand. "No. I don't want excuses, or arguments. I want you to think about what I've just said. Really *think* about it. And when you come to London at Christmas, we'll discuss it further. The thing is, I need your help with the spirits in the house. But you have to be ready. You have to be open to listening. There's no point in discussing it with you until you are."

4

don't want to go back inside the house, but Tanice will be sure to come looking for me if I stay out here too long. I decide to go next door — to Elsie's house — to see what Freya is doing. With no modern oven, or central heating, or other things like that, the House in Spitalfields isn't really the sort of place you'd want to live in. In Elsie's words, "There's a lot that I love about electricity."

The door to Elsie's house is slightly ajar, so I push it open and enter.

Inside is not like next door at all. It's bright and modern. The floors are a blond wood, the slim hallway table is painted a warm cream. There are light switches.

I'm sure I've been here before as well, but I don't remember it at all.

In other words, I don't need to worry about things coming out of the walls in here.

"Freya?" I call out.

"Oh, Lolli!" Her voice carries down from upstairs. "Come up here!"

I make my way upstairs.

There, the first room I pass is filled with old furniture, boxes and a few larger items on display that are a strange mix of bits and pieces. Treasures, Elsie and Freya call them. I spy a unicorn horn (okay, narwhal tusk), a huge paper wasp nest, an automaton of a devil that pokes its tongue out, decorated nautilus shells and vintage Happy Meal toys. There is also a long glass box, covered by a white sheet. That's the lady. At least, that's what I call her. She was super expensive — Freya and I flew all the way to Florence to see her and buy her — but I think she's worth it, because I could stare at her for hours. I go over and lift the corner of the sheet, peering inside. She is what's called an anatomical Venus. Human-sized and made out of wax, she is extraordinarily beautiful with long, curled, real hair, rosy cheeks and pearls at her neck. She looks like she's asleep. But that's not the best bit. If you look further down her body, you realise her torso is a sort of lid. You can lift it off and take her insides to pieces. That's what she's for — she is an anatomical sculpture from the late 1700s.

Sounds weird?

It is.

And it's meant to be. Because that's what Freya collects. For years she's been acquiring items of curiosity. Not just old things, but new things too. Anything that is curious and amazing and holds your attention. It's Freya's dream to open her own installation — a house-sized cabinet of curiosities. Cabinets of curiosities started to become popular in the 1500s and were rooms rather than pieces of furniture. These rooms were filled with interesting objects belonging to nature, the world of art, archaeology, religion … anything, really. I guess you could say they were what came before museums.

"Lolli?"

"Coming!"

Freya's head appears in the hallway. "Quick! You've got to see this!"

I run down there. "What is it?"

"It's Elsie. She's so funny. I had no idea about this."

I step into the room. And then I start laughing. Because in here are more boxes. But in the corner, there is something else. There, space has been cleared and a scene has been set up. There is a little wooden table with a pristine white tablecloth set for high tea, a gleaming silver cake stand stacked with pink-rose porcelain, fake *petit fours* and ribbon sandwiches. Two friends sit at the table, having a marvellous time together — an arm flung outwards, a head tipped back in mirth. Oddly, one of them is a stuffed tiger in a cricket outfit and one of them is an alligator in a tutu. In front, a tiny mole valiantly pushes a tea trolley, as if it's possible for him to deliver the large pot of tea sitting atop.

Freya and I look at each other and we both burst out laughing.

Finally, she wipes her eyes. "The little mole! So funny! But so naughty of Elsie to spend time on this. It must have taken up so much energy."

"When do you think she did it?"

"It must have been a while ago. Maybe even before she came to visit us in Singapore. But we really must get back to Tanice. I only meant to drop a few things off. We've got to have the parlour finished today if we want to stay on track. Let's go."

I know there's no point in arguing — Freya is going to make me help out at the house. If I'm going to be spending a lot of time in there, I need to be prepared. So, those portals that Elsie had spoken of in the ginger garden — the ones that have been left open for the spirits to enter? In my mind I picture them as one doorway. And then I imagine that I am sealing that doorway tight. Funny how I'd thought the spirits communicated with me through a door even before Elsie had spoken of portals. Because a door is a kind of portal. You're never really sure what's behind a closed door. It could lead anywhere. Open up to reveal anything — a wintry kingdom called Narnia, Wonderland, or an Other Mother with button eyes.

Doorways are not to be trusted.

I take a moment to add some details. I visualise an iron door — I'd seen a movie a while ago where someone had said spirits don't like iron and I'd squirrelled the information away. I make sure the lock is covered. And that there's a good, thick draught stopper. No spirit seepage here. That had been my mistake in the kitchen before.

Back at the house, Tanice and Jada have brought up a tray of tea and biscuits to the parlour. There's a lot to do. The parlour is probably the most decorated part of the house during the Christmas period. It's the room people seem to love the most, because it feels like the way people imagine Christmas should be. It's a Victorian-style room, full of little knick-knacks and fripperies. The mantelpiece is cluttered with vintage Christmas cards. There is a real fir tree, a roaring fire and two large comfortable armchairs. In between the armchairs sits a tiny table and on top of it rests a plate with a mince pie, a bite taken out of it. A hardback book has been placed upside down on one of the chairs and some slippers have been kicked off to warm by the grate, where a snoozing cat (stuffed) rests. It's as if the reader has just paused in his or her reading and ducked out. This is what the house aims to do in every room — give the impression that you have just chanced upon a moment in time. That the maid has just left the kitchen, that the master of the house has just left the parlour, that the mistress of the house has just left the bedchamber. All through the house, speakers play sounds as you enter and exit the rooms to heighten this feeling.

I know everything about this house. I love this house. I just happen to hate being in it.

I've read pretty much all of the reviews that have appeared in newspapers. Some of them have complained that the house is "ridiculous" and nothing more than a "Hollywood set". One journalist wrote a whole piece on how she'd spotted some plastic-wrapped candy canes right in this very room. Elsie never cared what people said. About the candy canes, she'd replied, "Your eye can seek out such discrepancies, or you can stand back and imagine and wonder. The choice is yours to make."

I stand in the doorway for a moment or two and really drink in the scene. "It looks like Christmas vomited in here," I finally say.

Tanice laughs. "I think that's the decorating style the Victorians were going for. They were not a subtle people. Now, do you think you two could manage the tree by yourselves?"

Jada looks over at me.

"I guess so," I say.

Freya steps in. "Here's a photo from last year. All the decorations are in the two boxes over there. Just be extremely careful unwrapping them. Lots of them are glass and quite a number of them are actually Victorian and quite delicate."

"We'll be careful." I give Freya a look. I know better than to just throw everything at the tree. This will have to be meticulously done. The photo studied, each decoration thoughtfully and carefully placed. I know the sort of glass ornaments she's talking about; if you breathe too hard, you feel as if they might shatter. I move over now to inspect the special wooden boxes they're housed in, divided so that each ornament is cocooned safely in its own nest of tissue paper. I run my finger gently over a Saint Nicholas, removing a stray piece of shredded paper from his face.

Jada nods. "I know what to do. I helped Mum last year. We didn't lose one decoration."

"You did amazingly well. Funny, though, that we've already lost quite a few of the chocolates and we haven't even opened to visitors yet," Tanice says, looking over at the half-eaten tin.

"Someone has to make it look like the family who lives here has been nibbling away at them." Jada grins. "It's about authenticity."

Freya laughs. "I can help you with your authenticity, if you like."

"It's okay, I can manage on my own."

"You're all very amusing," Tanice says. "Should we start with the greenery, Freya?"

"Sounds like an idea."

The pair head over to the corner where there is a pile of holly, ivy and mistletoe waiting to be strung. It all has to go up. Today.

We work for hours, stopping only for a short break for some sandwiches that Freya ducks out to buy. By the time Jada and I have finished the tree, I'm exhausted from concentrating on both the tree and keeping myself firmly closed off to any feelings brewing upstairs.

"It looks beautiful, you two," Freya says. "Just beautiful. Which is more than I can say for my fingers." She holds them up. Over the day more and more medical tape has been wound around them as her fingers have been nicked by the foliage.

"The pain and suffering and blood loss is worth

it, though," Tanice says. "Because, behold, Christmas has come to the House in Spitalfields!"

We all look around us. Tanice is right. The room looked Christmassy enough before, but the beautifully decorated tree and the greenery have taken it to the next level. I'd like nothing more than to curl up in one of the armchairs, inhaling the bright pine smell and finishing off that mince pie. If only it wasn't for what's upstairs, I could spend hours in here pretending. Imagining. Dreaming.

"Speaking of Christmas being here, during the Christmas break, Jada tends to spend quite a bit of time with her grandmother, who lives with us. I thought Lolli might like to hang out at our place too."

"Oh, that sounds nice. We can't keep you two cooped up here all the time," Freya says. "What do you think, Lolli?"

I look over at Jada. I'm not sure what to say. I don't want to seem rude, because Tanice is really nice and Jada seems nice too, but the truth is that people really aren't my thing. "Um, thanks."

"No need to let me know right now. The offer is there."

"It's very kind of you." Freya eyeballs me.

All this talk of hanging out with people makes me think about something else — someone else. Elsie. Elsie who is downstairs, all alone. The kitchen is safe, it's the getting there that worries me. But I have to do it. I take a deep breath.

"I'm going to get some water," I say. "Anyone else want some?"

"I'm okay," Jada says.

Both Tanice and Freya shake their heads.

"I think we'll just finish tidying up in here and we'll be done for the day," Tanice tells me. "You run on down to the kitchen and we'll be there in a moment."

5

With Freya not looking, I don't run down the stairs to the kitchen. I sprint.

Push it down. Close it off. Block. Breathe. Don't engage.

It feels like forever before I reach the hearth.

I slip into the chair beside Elsie's. "I'm sorry," I say, panting. "About before. I don't want to argue with you all the time."

Elsie flicks a hand. "Oh, I knew you'd come back. Eventually. I didn't mean to frighten you. I know it's hard for you to be here."

"Let's talk about something else," I say.

Elsie sighs. "Always with the something else. All right, then. How about Tiny Pieces? You're going to help out there as well, aren't you? You did promise."

"Um, when I said let's talk about something else, I meant like the weather. Not another one of your lectures." Tiny Pieces is this mosaic club that Elsie helped to found a number of years ago. It helps people who are having a few problems get their lives back on track through art. I haven't actually been to their workshop before, but I've met Suzie lots of times. Suzie is the social worker who oversees the program. She knew my mum when she was alive, and my mum was Freya's best friend.

Elsie waits for my answer, grinning at me the whole time. Because how can I say no?

I groan. "Yes, we're going to help at Tiny Pieces. Just like we promised."

"Good. Because Suzie's expecting you. Anyway, it's no great hardship. You'll love it there."

I pull a face.

"You will. You'll see. I know you better than you think. Also, I wanted to point out that you were wrong about what you said before. I didn't trick you into coming here. I was quite upfront about it. Don't you remember what I said in the ginger garden? I told you to think about what I'd said and we'd discuss everything when you came at Christmastime."

"How could I forget?"

"So, did you?"

"Did I what?"

Elsie huffs. "You know very well — think about what I said."

I grunt.

"I know you did, Miss Lolli. Of course you did. But I see you're as stubborn as ever, so I suppose I'll just have to continue to wait for you to be ready."

"Ready for what?" That's the second time Elsie's said this. I don't like the sound of it.

"It's as I've said before — there's no point in discussing it until you're ready."

"How am I supposed to know if I'm ready, when I don't even know what it is I'm supposed to be ready for? It's impossible!"

"What rubbish. You'll know. But hurry up about it. I'm not sure how much time we have. And Clara's waiting."

Elsie looks at me expectantly. I can see she wants me to ask who Clara is.

So I don't.

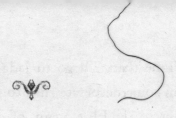

It's early evening by the time Freya and I get back to our apartment. We shower, order some food and flop in front of the TV.

Halfway through some baking show, Freya's phone starts pinging. She grabs it.

"It's Suzie. We'll go to Tiny Pieces in the morning and then over to the house after that." She shifts in her seat, turning to face me. "By the way, that was rude this afternoon. It was very kind of Tanice to offer you some time with her mother and Jada. You completely blanked her."

"No, I didn't. I said thanks. It's just ... I don't know them."

"What? We've known Tanice forever."

"You have. Not me."

Freya gives me a look. I can see what she's thinking — maybe I'd know Tanice better if I'd just go to the house? I give her a look back — do we have to go through this again?

"Well, I think it's very nice of Tanice," Freya finally says.

"Fine then, I'll go to Jada's place." It's not like I'm in some desperate rush to go back to the house. I want to see Elsie again, of course. I'm even a bit curious about whatever it is she's going on about that I need to be "ready" for and who Clara is. But having to navigate the hallway and those stairs again ... I can wait, thanks very much.

The next morning we get out of the apartment a lot faster. I don't drag my heels nearly as much because I know we're not going to the house, but to a row of shops near Old Spitalfields Market. Freya and I walk almost exactly the same way we'd travelled yesterday morning, then a few streets further to make it to the market. Everywhere we look it's Christmas. Coffee shops advertise peppermint lattes, Christmas carols wind their way out of shop doors, charity workers shake donation buckets. Everything is "merry" and "bright" and decorated with tinsel and holly.

"It's just down there." Freya points as we turn a corner. "The yellow one."

In the midst of a row of quite plain shopfronts, the wood painted white, or black, or grey, the daffodil yellow paint is sunshine itself.

Freya checks the time on her phone. "Quick. We have to be there for nine o'clock exactly." She hurries me along.

"Why?"

"You'll see."

As we approach, I can see a pretty mosaic artwork sign above the glass that reads "Tiny Pieces" in all the colours of the rainbow. Freya pushes the door open and ushers me inside. Several people look up from long wooden tables, where they're busy organising plastic boxes and metal tools. Every single person is wearing a red felt Santa hat.

"Freya! Lolli! Oh, it's so good to see you." Suzie rises from one of the tables to come over and greet us. "Merry Christmas!" She gives Freya a kiss on the cheek and places a hand on my shoulder.

"Merry Christmas to you too, Suz," Freya says.

"You're here just in time. Now, Santa hats first, because ... well, just because." She pops one on each of our heads. "And with that we're good to go. Ready, everyone?"

Suzie runs over to pick up what looks like a wedge of clear, green glass and some sort of tool. I look around to see that everyone in the room seems to be holding similar objects — pieces of differently shaped and coloured glass and that same small tool.

"Three, two, one . . ." Suzie continues.

"Snap!"

I jump as everyone in the room clips at the same time, cutting their pieces of glass. So that's why we had to be here at nine o'clock.

Suzie laughs at my expression as she comes back over to join us again. "Cute, huh? It's a little ritual of ours — we find it starts the day off right if we all start together. And now that's done, let me introduce you to everyone. Everyone, this is Freya and Lolli, old friends of mine. Freya and Lolli, this is Dani and Peta, Roberta, Lisa and Britt."

We get lots of waves and nods.

"Don't forget Alfie," Britt says, pointing under the table.

I duck down to see a little black, curly-haired dog asleep on the floor. He has a Santa hat on too.

"I could never forget Alfie," Suzie replies.

"He'll wake up when the biscuits come out,"

Britt says as I stand again. "Never misses a biscuit. You can pat him then if you like. He'll love you forever if you scratch his belly. Alfie's a toy poodle. Kind of a funny-looking one. Probably crossed with something."

"Okay." I'm not sure how to answer, but I know I'll be happy to scratch Alfie's belly.

"Britt's been coming along to sessions for a few weeks now," Suzie said. "Alfie too, of course. Anyway, now that you've met everyone, come and put your things down and maybe we can put you to work for an hour or two? We're a bit behind. We're supposed to be launching a special mural in March and time is flying by. I don't want to reveal too much, but I know you'll both love it." Suzie leads us through to the back of the room. She takes my backpack and Freya's bag, tucking them neatly into a storage cabinet that's been painted the same cheery yellow as the shopfront.

It's quieter in the back of the room and Suzie turns so that her back is to the group. "I heard your birth grandmother died, Lolli. I'm sorry."

I look up at Freya. "I'm not."

"Lolli ..." Freya warns.

Suzie steps in. "It's all right. It's a complicated situation. It's okay to have mixed feelings about it."

I don't have mixed feelings about it, but Suzie is right — it is a complicated situation. This is how it goes. My mother, Clementine, had been Freya's best friend at boarding school. They hadn't seen a lot of each other after they'd finished school, because Clementine had some mental health problems. But Freya had kept in touch and would call Clementine every so often to see if she was okay. Her face always lit up when she talked about Clementine. "I just adored her," Freya would always say. "She was always so much fun. We were always laughing. I think what I loved most about her was how real she was — she never tried to be someone else. It didn't matter what anyone else thought about something, she was never scared to give her own opinion, or to stand up for someone else's. She understood me. Really understood me. She knew what it felt like to be dumped at that school. To not want to go home for the holidays."

Things got steadily worse. Clementine got in trouble with the police. And then she got pregnant. She was determined to have the baby. To be a better mother than her mother had been. Freya tried to get her to move into her apartment. If she wanted to have a baby, she had to be healthy. Look after herself. But Clementine didn't want to move in. Not with Freya's partner, Phillipa, there. Freya said she and Clementine had had a terrible fight about it all. After that, Clementine's phone stopped working. She disappeared. Freya had no idea if Clementine had had the baby or not. Until, one day, a woman Freya didn't know rang her doorbell.

"You Freya?" she'd said.

"Yes."

"Clem gave me your address a while back. Just in case. There's been a bit of a situation."

"What? What do you mean ..."

The woman had thrust a baby so roughly at Freya, that she'd almost had to catch it. And then she'd run off down the street.

That baby was me.

"I didn't even know your name," Freya always said.

Freya had thought Clementine would show up later that day. Definitely by late evening. She didn't. Freya had had to call a friend over who'd had a baby the year before and find out what she needed to do.

What formula to give me. How to change a nappy. She had no idea. Over the next twenty four hours, Freya tried every number she had for Clementine. She contacted every friend who might know where she was, or how to get in touch with her. She came up with nothing. Desperate, she tried Clementine's mother.

"How on earth would I know where she is?" the woman had said. "To be honest, I probably wouldn't want to know."

"I'm not sure what to do. I've got her daughter here. Your granddaughter. I think she must be about a month old."

"What are you saying? That you want me to come and get her?"

Clementine had told Freya all about her childhood when they were at school. About how her mother would drink too much. How she'd say terrible, horrible things that would go around and around in Clementine's head. Freya had stared at the baby in her arms — there was no way she would let Clementine's mother take her. It would never happen. Never.

"Do you know who the father is?" Freya tried.

Clementine's mother had laughed.

And so Freya had hung up.

She'd gone to the police after that.

"It's not that I didn't like you," she'd say, "it's just that I honestly didn't know what to do. And Phillipa had been pushing to go to the police all along."

As it turned out, Phillipa had sort of been right about going to the police. Because when Freya went to the police and told them about me, about Clementine and about where she thought Clementine had been living, everything sort of unravelled. It turned out there had been a situation, like the woman on Freya's doorstep had said. Clementine had been involved in a fight. She'd been pushed and had fallen and hit her head. Badly. And then ... well, she'd died.

Things unravelled further over the following few days.

My grandmother didn't want me. And then she did want me. And then she wasn't allowed to have me and got super angry about that and hired a lawyer.

No one knew who my father was.

I would go into foster care.

Except Freya wasn't going to let that happen. "By then I'd completely fallen in love with you," she'd tell me when we got to this part of the story. "You were so, so tiny and so, so perfect. I couldn't believe it when they told me you were healthy. I knew then that Clem must have listened to what I'd said. That she must have tried very, very hard to look after herself and you. She'd even managed to make it to most of her antenatal check-ups. And then when you smiled at me — a real, proper smile — well, it was a done deal. I knew Clem had sent you to me because I was the only person in the whole world that she trusted with something so precious."

You'd think this is where things might have got better, but they didn't. They sort of got worse.

Freya's partner Phillipa moved out. Freya had to go to court with Clementine's mother. Freya's parents argued with her — she wasn't thinking this through, people would talk, there would be something wrong with me that the doctors had overlooked.

"But Elsie," Freya would say. "Elsie was amazing. We'd always been close — she loved children and I was the only child in the family. She hadn't been able to have any children herself, but she'd spent time with so many that she somehow knew what to do. And if she didn't know, she knew who to ask —

she really does know everyone. She stepped in and helped me in so many ways and—"

"Lolli?"

I wake from my daydream to see Suzie and Freya have moved off. Suzie beckons me over.

"Why don't you come and sit next to Britt and give her a hand?"

6

*B*ritt wears a camouflage shirt and pants and talks a lot. I'm wary. Sometimes I don't get on with people who have a lot to say. They often ask a lot of questions. But Britt doesn't ask too many questions. She just likes to talk. So far she's told me how long she's been coming here (three weeks), where she's from (Essex), how many brothers she has (two) and how she bought a Christmas pudding on sale this morning to have on Christmas Day. Apparently it has little gold leaf flakes that you scatter over the top. She's especially looking forward to that bit.

"Here." She hands me some clippers and a piece of clear yellow glass.

The glass is smooth and heavy in my hand, with a vein of gold running through it. "It's beautiful."

"Yeah. It's going to make up part of a big sun. So, what you have to do is pretty easy. You just snip little pieces off like this, see?" She demonstrates how you snip off a little shard of glass from a larger piece. "You've got to try and make them even and about the same size. You'll probably mess a few up before you get the hang of it. I did. Just have a go. Don't worry, you'll get it in no time."

I try snipping off a few pieces. The first two aren't the best, but the third one is okay.

"See? You're a natural."

"Oh!" Something lands on my right foot under the table. I look down to see Alfie has wriggled over and settled in.

Britt takes a look. "I can move him if you want."

"No, he's okay." It's actually kind of nice. He's warm. *Snip, snip, snip.*

"I guess you're wondering if I was in the army. Because of my clothes. People always ask me that. I wasn't. I wanted to be when I was at school, but they wouldn't have me." She leans in. "Too many problems, you know?"

I don't know, but I nod anyway.

"Everyone here has problems of some kind or another. I like wearing this army gear because it's a reminder that I have to protect Alfie. I got him from this program that matches up people with dogs. He saved me, really. Gave me someone to think about other than myself. Now I have to put him first — what he needs. I have to get up and go out every day. Make sure he has food. Vaccinations. All of that. He likes it here, so we come."

I keep snipping as Britt keeps talking.

Every so often, she stops talking for a bit and we snip in silence.

In one of those breaks, I begin to see that Elsie was right. I kind of like this place. Some people talk. Some people don't. But all the time everyone is busy with their hands, so it doesn't seem to matter either way.

"So how do you know Suzie?" Britt asks. "You guys seem to know her pretty well. I don't like many social workers, but I like her. She's nice."

"Um, well, I know her through Freya and Elsie, I guess. Suzie knew my mum when she was alive. Her name was Clementine. She died when I was three weeks old."

"Oh. Sorry."

Underneath the table I feel Alfie rise. "Alfie's getting up."

Britt ducks her head down to take a look.

"Alfie says it's time for a tea break," she calls out.

"We'll have to go soon, Lolli," Freya says, getting up from the table she's sitting at.

"Quick cup of tea before you go?" Suzie says. "Or a hot chocolate, Lolli?"

I look at Freya, who nods. "If you like."

"Yes, please," I say.

"I think it's my turn to do tea," Suzie says.

"I'll give you a hand," Freya offers.

Britt and I snip in silence for a while. My hot chocolate comes, I drink some and take a biscuit from a packet that is passed around.

"Here. Want to give Alfie his?" Britt passes me a little bone-shaped biscuit as well as the packet I'd taken a biscuit from. "You've got to pretend you've taken it out of the human biscuit packet, or he won't eat it."

"Really?"

"I know it's weird, but that's Alfie for you."

I kneel down on the floor. Alfie eyes the bone-shaped biscuit with disinterest. But then I push it inside the biscuit packet and pretend to take it out again. He jumps up and practically bowls me over trying to get at it. I give it to him and he gobbles it up in seconds.

And then starts licking me.

I laugh and give him a pat.

"I told you so," Britt says as I get up again.

"Time to go, Lolli. We really need to give Tanice a hand. Thanks for having us, Suzie." Freya grabs our things and makes her way over to me. "Come and see the house over the weekend. If anyone's interested, we'd love for you all to come through and take a look."

"That sounds lovely," Suzie says. "And thanks for checking in."

Freya gives me a nudge.

"Thanks, Suzie."

Another nudge.

"Thanks, Britt. And Alfie," I add.

"Come back, eh?" Britt says. "We need all the help we can get if we're going to have this mosaic finished on time."

Freya picks up some s̶a̶n̶d̶w̶i̶c̶h̶e̶s̶ and
we head over to the house.
more I begin to tense up, readying
feelings I know are coming.

When we get there, Tanice is out front. She's set up
a real Christmas tree and is busy chaining its trunk to
the black iron railing at the front of the house.

"I wish I didn't have to use the chain, but I most
definitely do," she says with a sigh.

I stand back and try to look like everything's
fine. Like I can't already feel the dark anger that
swirls inside the house. I look up at the tall, narrow
building's windows – three sets of three. As soon as
my gaze hits the top row, my stomach rolls.

"Madame LeNoir," I say, the words coming out
of nowhere.

"What was that?" Freya says, busy talking to
Tanice.

I shake my head. "Nothing. Just talking to myself."

Madame LeNoir. That's the name of the angry
spirit in the house. Have I always known this?
Maybe. But I'd chosen to block it out. Like Freya
had mentioned, it's common knowledge the house
is haunted. It's famous for it. But I'd always refused

anything about it. Freya wouldn't let people mention it around me anyway. Not after what had happened when I was younger. Anyway, I'm not sure what I've heard, or where I've heard it, but something deep inside me knows that Madame LeNoir is her name and she lives up there, on the top floor. That's why it takes her a while to make it down the stairs.

Clara.

Madame LeNoir and Clara.

I look away from the windows and take a deep breath.

Push it down. Close it off. Block. Breathe. Don't engage.

"Everything all right, Lolli?" Tanice looks over.

I nod. "I just feel a bit sick."

"It's probably the heating. It gets so stuffy. Maybe you could help outside this afternoon? We need to wind the ivy around the iron railings. It takes forever. Trust me, I know. I did it last year."

"Sure," I say quickly. Anything not to have to go inside.

Freya gives me a look.

"What? I'm offering to help."

Another look.

Freya and Tanice discuss the logistics of the afternoon. They end up deciding they'll decorate the dining room, which is right up the front of the house, directly in front of the railings I'll be weaving ivy through.

"So we'll be right here if you need us," Freya says.

"Okay."

The weather has turned cold, so Freya makes me do my jacket up and Tanice wraps her scarf around my neck.

"They're predicting snow," she says. "Can you believe it? Before Christmas!"

"I'll believe it when I see it," Freya says.

"Now are you sure you can manage this on your own, Lolli? I can call Jada's grandmother and get her to bring Jada over to help if you like."

"No, it's okay. I can do it."

Yet another look from Freya.

"But maybe I could go over there tomorrow? Like you said? If that's okay."

"Of course! Jada would love that." Tanice beams.

Freya looks pleased. "It's probably a good idea. It's going to be a long day here tomorrow."

"Most definitely," Tanice agrees.

I look up at the top row of windows again. Something tells me it's going to be a long day here today as well.

Tanice was right about the ivy — it really did take forever. But I didn't care. The angry spirit remained in its hidey-hole upstairs while I hung about on the pavement below. I didn't go inside once. I even ate a picnic on the front step with my sandwich, apple and juice. When I had to go to the bathroom, I offered to go and fetch coffees for Freya and Tanice from the coffee shop down the street and I went there. Sure, I was cold, but I was also safe.

Just after 5 pm, Freya and I begin the walk back to the apartment.

"It's so weird that it's already dark," I say.

Freya turns to look at me. "I always forget. I think you're English. But you're not really, are you? Singapore is all you've ever known. You don't understand seasons."

"Well, I get that they exist. And now I can see that they're overrated. All this putting on coats and taking them off again. Why would you want to do that?"

Freya pokes her tongue out at me. "Maybe to stop from freezing. I miss seasons. They give a sort of shape to the year. A rhythm. Hey," she turns to me. "Why don't we go do something Christmassy?" she says. "We could walk across the bridge to Borough Market. Get something to eat there. Look about."

"No, thanks," I say. I want to go back to the apartment. The nice, new, safe apartment where I can be by myself. Take a shower. Hang out in my spirit-free room.

Freya stops walking. "Don't you want to see any of London? The wonderful place of your birth?"

"Not really."

"What about dinner?"

"We can get something delivered again."

Freya sighs.

Sensing a lecture coming, I attempt to stop it in its tracks. "I said I'd go to Jada's tomorrow."

Another sigh. "Yes. You did say that."

"I'm, like, the perfect child."

Now I really get a look.

"Well, you can't have Jada's and Borough Market. I mean, there's perfect and there's *perfect*."

7

*T*hat night, I have a dream about Elsie. We're sitting on the bench in the ginger garden again. But, this time, we're having a completely different conversation.

"Madame LeNoir," she says. "Madame LeNoir and Clara. Clara and Madame LeNoir and Clara and Madame LeNoir and Clara ..."

She says the names over and over again. Over and over and over until I wake up sweating and kick the sheets off me.

I fall back asleep and have my nightmare.

I stand in front of those dark stairs, the blackness coming to pull me under. And I can't move. Can't breathe.

I wake again and shudder as I suck in some air.

I hate Madame LeNoir.

And Clara, whoever she is.

I hate them both.

When I wake once more, it's because I hear the little coffee machine whirring in the kitchen. Freya's up.

I get up too. I have to look willing to go to Jada's. Because there's no way I'm going to the house after the night I just had. And anyway, my dream has just given me an idea — one that means I need to go to Jada's and not just to avoid the house.

"I think this is it." Freya is staring at the map on her phone. "At least, it should be."

I look up, taking in the old-style grey apartment block that blends into an equally grey sky. Some movement catches my eye. I see a girl in a purple coat wave at me from one of the long walkways.

"There's Jada," I say, waving back.

"Oh, good."

We make our way across a little bitumen basketball court as Jada flies down a set of stairs to meet us.

"Sorry, the lift broke last night. We'll have to walk up."

"That's all right. Good exercise," Freya says.

Jada opens the apartment door. "They're here!" she calls out.

It's a small room that we step into, warm and homey — full of books, a comfy-looking sofa and armchair, rugs and throws and a little dining table. Paper chains and tinsel decorate the bookcase.

An older version of Tanice, complete with salt-and-pepper hair and red-framed glasses, appears from the hallway.

"Beebee!" Freya says. "It's so good to see you again."

"Ah, it's been too long." She comes over to give Freya a hug. "But who is this tall, good-looking thing here? It can't be Lolli, because the last time I saw Lolli, she was just a tiny good-looking thing!"

"Beebee." Jada groans.

"I'm embarrassing all the time now," Beebee says to Freya.

"I know the feeling."

Jada and I look at each other and roll our eyes.

Beebee laughs at us. "I've been looking forward to seeing you again, Lolli," she says.

"Thanks," I say. Remembering I need to keep Freya on side if I want to stay here and not be at the house, I add, "And thanks for letting me hang out here with Jada."

"You are most welcome."

"It's about to get crazy in here," Jada says. "My two aunts are coming over with my little cousins. They're planning the Christmas menu. There's always an argument and then the food is exactly the same every year."

"She's right!" Beebee laughs. "Speaking of which, I was discussing Christmas with Tanice just this morning. What are the two of you doing on Christmas Day?"

"Oh!" Freya says. "I hadn't really thought about it yet." She looks at me.

"Sometimes we go to the movies," I say.

Jada stares at me like I've just said we decapitate puppies or something.

"What? On Christmas Day? No way."

"Sure. It's great. Sometimes we have the whole theatre to ourselves."

"I don't believe you." She looks up at Freya. "Is that true? You go to the movies on Christmas Day?"

"Yes. I don't ... we ... well, I suppose we live overseas and my family ..."

"Not everyone has the same Christmas Day as you, Jada," Beebee says, a warning note in her voice.

"Oh, sorry."

"That's okay," Freya says. "We're unusual people."

"That's the nice way of putting it," I add. Which at least makes everyone laugh.

"Well, if you'd like to come here, we'd love to have you both."

"That's so kind of you to think of us, Beebee. We'll talk it over."

I'm already giving Freya "nooooo ..." looks and she's giving me a "don't you dare, not here" wide-eyed stare.

Freya clears her throat. "Anyway, I'd better go and help Tanice over at the house. We're getting there. It'll be ready on time, but only just."

"Ah, it's the same every year. It always pulls together in the end. Usually with five minutes to spare."

Freya nods. "Fingers crossed this year will be the same."

Not long after this, Freya leaves. The moment the door closes behind her, I'm not so sure about staying here with Jada and Beebee.

"Want to meet my hamster?" Jada says.

What I actually want to do is run after Freya. "Um, okay."

I meet Jada's hamster and help her finish off some Christmas-themed bunting she's making. We're almost done when there's a bang that makes me jump.

"Uh oh. They're here." Jada jumps up and whirls into action. The hamster goes on top of a wardrobe, the paper and stamps get pushed far under the bed. "I have four cousins under five years old." She explains. "They're cute, but they're exhausting."

While the adults bicker about recipes and who will be cooking what, we spend the next few hours running around after Jada's cousins. We chase them. Give them piggyback rides. Play shops. Build a tower with some blocks.

At one point, I slip away into a corner of the lounge room to the bookshelf. When Freya and I had walked into the apartment, a row of books had caught my eye. Five copies of the same book, by the same author.

"How are you going there?" Beebee spots me by myself and comes on over. "Everything okay?"

I nod.

Beebee pushes aside some of the tinsel and pulls out one of the books I'm looking at. "I bet you have this one in your house too."

It's a book about the House in Spitalfields – Elsie's installation. Tanice wrote it. We do have a copy, but it's packed away somewhere because I won't have it anywhere I can see it. I don't say any of that, of course.

"My Tanice. A published author! I couldn't have been prouder the day she brought her book home. I really couldn't."

I stare at the book.

Madame LeNoir. Madame LeNoir and Clara. Clara and Madame LeNoir and Clara and Madame LeNoir and Clara ...

"Do you think I could maybe borrow a copy? It's just ... being here ... I was thinking of re-reading it." I can't tell Beebee I've never read it at all.

"Of course! You can keep it if you like."

"Thanks." I take it from her.

I put the book into the zipped side pocket of my

backpack. I don't want Freya to see that I've got it and start asking questions.

Freya picks me up just after 5 pm.

"I was going to insist we go out tonight," Freya says, as we make our way back to the apartment. "But I think all I'm capable of doing is ordering something to eat and getting an early night. Especially if I've got to do it all over again tomorrow."

"Is there lots more to do?"

"Just little things. But we've got a long list of them to get through."

We walk in silence for a bit, my backpack heavier than before, because of the book.

"Is Beebee her real name?" I ask. I've been wondering all day, but wasn't sure about asking in case it was a rude question.

Freya laughs. "No. Beebee's real name is Joan. I asked her about her name once and she said she was chased by a bee when she was little and her family called her Beebee after that. It's like a family joke. She told me it's quite common in Jamaica to have a pet name. She said she went to an uncle's funeral once and realised she never even knew his real name until she saw it on the order of service."

"I like it. Anyway, Beebee is a really cool name."

"Yes, I like it too."

8

$\mathcal{A}$s soon as I know for sure that Freya is in bed, I start reading. It's not a big book, but it tells the whole tale of the House in Spitalfields. Tanice painstakingly pieced all the information about the house together. She'd had to sift through old newspaper clippings, police reports, letters and diaries.

It had taken years — and a lot of money — to pull the installation together. Elsie had started by standing in each room and asking it what it wanted to be. It took some time before the rooms answered back. The attic was first. It was a strange room with a prickly feeling to it. It didn't like visitors. It didn't like anyone. Used as a storage room for many years, it was full of items — some of them very dusty and very old. It had always been clear that it wanted to be left alone and thus items had accumulated over time and never been discarded. Elsie went through the room, used a few items around the house and then left the room to its own devices. All that was left in there was the original iron-and-brass bed from Victorian times and an old trunk. Then came the parlour. It felt decidedly Victorian, saying late 1830s. A bedchamber wanted to be of the year 1760, but the mistress's dressing-room next door stated it was 1813 and that was that.

While she worked on the house, Elsie moved into the terrace next door and lived there, hoping she wouldn't fall through the floorboards, because that terrace desperately needed renovating too.

I skip over a chapter or two — mostly about how Elsie had furnished each room. It's other information I'm here for.

Information about how and why the house is haunted.

The story of the haunting, when I find it, goes something like this:

Once upon a time there was a husband and wife called Monsieur and Madame LeNoir. They weren't really French. In fact, they had both been born in London itself and their real names were Henry Black and Ellen Walker. Henry came from a poor family, but he was clever and ambitious and wanted to make something of himself. He went to work for an uncle who owned a chemist's shop in Southwark, where poverty and disease were rife. The chemist's shop sold all sorts of medicinal cures that were no better or worse than what would be prescribed by the city's top doctors. Even they could only offer such treatments as blistering, or blood-letting, which tended only to make patients even more ill.

Henry became interested in the craze for mesmerism that was sweeping the city. Some doctors claimed they could put patients into trance-like states and shift the energy field within their body. Painful surgery could then be performed without any pain at all. They even claimed they could cure patients of diseases simply by using mesmerism. Henry decided he had to see this for himself. He began to attend demonstrations of mesmerism in the city and was an instant believer. He watched the doctors very carefully and practised their special hand movements in every minute of his spare time. It didn't take him very long until he knew how to mesmerise people himself.

At one of these mesmeric demonstrations, Henry met Ellen. Ellen came from a family who dabbled in spiritualism. Several members claimed to be in constant contact with the twilight world. They were very happy to take people's money and put them in touch with their loved ones in the twilight world.

Henry and Ellen decided to get married. They formed a plan – they would change their names to Monsieur and Madame LeNoir. And they would set up as Monsieur and Madame LeNoir – Mesmeric Spiritualists. They would combine the best of both their talents – mesmerism and contact with the twilight world.

The pair distributed pamphlets stating that they had discovered putting subjects into a mesmeric trance brought them closer to the twilight world – that it changed their spiritual energy and enabled Madame LeNoir to draw their dear departed loved ones as close to the living world as possible.

Their show was an instant sensation.

The pair travelled the length and the breadth

of the country, filling music halls and giving costly private sittings.

But their show was a sham.

For while Monsieur LeNoir was skilled at putting people into a trance-like state and he had soon taught Madame LeNoir his tricks, neither of them could contact the twilight world. Madame LeNoir had never been able to. What she and her family had always relied upon was their ability to observe people closely, gleaning what information they could from very little. Some blonde hair curled into a mourning brooch? Madame LeNoir would see someone young and fair calling out to her from the twilight. An old lady ready to part with her money? A gentleman associated with the letter "J" had a message for Madame to impart. Did the lady perchance know a John? A Jack? A Joseph? Why, of course it was her brother, Jeremy!

Tired of moving and wanting a base to operate out of, the LeNoirs bought a terrace house in Spitalfields. It wasn't a very nice area, but they needed something large. They wanted to use the bottom floor for their private sittings and to live upstairs. Hopefully they would become even more famous and be able to afford something better shortly.

They hadn't been there long when something remarkable happened.

A mother who lived several streets away heard that the LeNoirs had moved into the terrace house. This mother had a daughter, Clara, who was eight years of age. Clara was always talking about people who weren't there — spirits she called them. The mother called upon the LeNoirs and imparted this information, not knowing who else to turn to. Madame LeNoir, who was an abrupt person, had attempted to slam the door in the mother's face. But Monsieur LeNoir had stopped her. He had looked down at waif-like Clara and seen past her dirty dress and knotted hair. He convinced the mother to leave Clara with them.

The girl would become Madame LeNoir's apprentice.

Within days, Clara's talents became apparent. She chatted easily to anyone and everyone about the spirits surrounding them. Names were correct. Relationships were correct. She would mention the tiniest details — the name of a treasured lapdog, the exact design of a cherished brooch made of Whitby jet, even a favourite hymn.

Monsieur and Madame LeNoir knew they had

discovered a goldmine. They cleaned Clara up. They coiffed her hair, purchased some smart little boots and had some beautiful dresses made. All of the dresses had the same special high neckline that would cover Clara's terrible scars. When she was only hours old, the wrap she had been swaddled in had caught fire and she had been badly burned. She had not been expected to survive. But she had. Some said it was this dance with death that had led to her strong ties to the spirit world.

Clara was paraded. Lauded. Monsieur and Madame LeNoir began to charge more. Much more.

People began to talk about this miraculous child who could speak directly to the deceased. Clara was called upon to visit a Baroness. A Countess. A Duchess, even.

And then the letter came.

Clara would have an audience with the Queen herself.

Queen Victoria had been interested in spiritualism for some time, but especially so after the sudden death of her dear husband, Prince Albert.

But when Clara visited the Queen, Prince Albert's spirit was nowhere to be found.

Monsieur and Madame LeNoir were furious. They knew that this sometimes happened — there had been quite a number of times that Clara had not been able to contact a spirit. But for it to happen on this occasion? It was simply not acceptable. They made their excuses — it might take time for the girl to coax the spirit towards the living world. It would, perhaps, take several sittings.

Clara baulked. She knew that she would never be able to contact the Prince. It didn't matter how many sittings she had with the Queen.

But Monsieur and Madame LeNoir would not take no for an answer and forced Clara to visit the Queen time and time again. They used their contacts to pay for information from the Queen's household. They had Clara mention private details of the Queen and Prince's life together. When Clara divulged the Prince's pet name for his wife, the Queen was in raptures. She sent a present to the house — a beautiful silver locket, engraved with her thanks.

Clara had not wanted to wear the locket, but Madame LeNoir forced her to wear it every single day. She would point out the gift to every client.

Every passer-by in the street. The locket that had been a gift from the Queen herself.

Then, quite unexpectedly, Monsieur LeNoir became sick and died.

Madame LeNoir knew their act would have to change overnight. Mesmerism was viewed as a medical skill — a male skill — while women were seen as being more adept at contacting the twilight world. She would now be completely reliant on Clara for an income. Madame LeNoir began to push harder. She forced Clara to tell more falsehoods and speak to spirits who were not there. Another problem: Clara was growing far too quickly. Four years had passed and Clara was now twelve years of age. Decent food meant that she was filling out. People had preferred her to be that tiny, waif-like creature that had appeared on the LeNoir's doorstep.

Madame LeNoir began to starve Clara. Soon, her eyes became dark hollows. Her dresses began to hang off her.

And then, one night, she ran away.

Clara ran to the place she used to call home. She had seen her family only a few times since being left on the LeNoirs' doorstep. Her family wasn't really sure what to do with her — this strange, grown-up child with curled hair in the beautiful dress and fancy locket. She didn't belong. Not to mention all the money that had been invested in her apprenticeship. Clara's mother dragged her back to Madame LeNoir and handed her daughter into her care.

After that night, no one ever saw Clara again.

I put Tanice's book down in the early hours of the morning, my eyes dry from reading and lack of sleep.

Finally, I properly understand what I've always felt in the house. Two spirits — one dark and one light. Madame LeNoir and Clara. It had been Clara I'd seen that day in the mirror behind Elsie, I was sure of it. That other, fleeting, presence I'd felt — the friendly one — had been her.

I stare at the bedroom ceiling for a while, my thoughts caught up in what I've just learned. I can't figure out why I didn't want to know this information before. Why did I think I was protecting myself in not knowing what it was that lurked within the house?

Why hadn't I asked questions? Hundreds of them? I'd definitely had questions about that house for as long as I could remember. I'd desperately wanted to blurt them all out at Elsie that day in the ginger garden. I'd wanted her to answer them quickly and neatly so that my brain could rest and stop searching. But something had stopped me. Fear? I don't know. But if I thought by not talking about it all that Madame LeNoir was going to go away and leave me alone, I was wrong. That's what Elsie had been trying to explain to me that day, I suppose. I couldn't just deny what I'd experienced and expect Madame LeNoir to magically disappear. I had to deal with her. Maybe even confront her. Something inside me tells me that's what Elsie wants me to do now — this is what I'm supposed to be getting ready for.

I shudder, thinking about it all. Especially about Clara. Had Madame LeNoir really murdered her? That dark, bitter anger I'd felt in the house — it wouldn't surprise me if it was true.

I try to go back to sleep and fail, tossing and turning until Freya pops her head in the door.

"You awake, Loll?"

"Yes. Um, Freya?"

"Mmm?"

"Can I go back to Tiny Pieces today?" I don't think I can go back to the house. Not yet. I'm still trying to take in what I've read. And with little to no sleep, I'm too tired to keep Madame LeNoir's energy at bay, or to deal with Elsie's demands about this thing that I have to be ready for, which I know is to do with the spirits in the house. Right now I don't feel ready for anything.

Freya slips into the room and inspects me for a moment, one eyebrow raised. "Because you want to go to Tiny Pieces, or because you don't want to go to the house?"

Um … "Both?"

She sighs. "It's not an unreasonable request. Let me text Suzie first."

"Okay."

"Go and have some cereal and get ready."

Texts fly. Suzie says she'd be delighted to have me at Tiny Pieces and asks if Jada would like to come along too.

Over a second coffee, Freya leans on the kitchen bench. "So, we have a plan. We'll stop by the house, pick up Jada, and I'll walk you girls over to Tiny Pieces."

"All right." I'm not going to complain about spending a few minutes at the house. As long as I don't have to hang out with Madame LeNoir all day I'm happy.

Freya and I pick up Jada and the three of us make the short walk over to Tiny Pieces, where Suzie opens the door for us. Freya says her hellos and mentions that she has to dash back to the house. "Call me if you need anything or if you want me to come and pick the girls up," she tells Suzie.

"Will do. But we'll be just fine. Truth be told, you're doing me a favour. I could use the help."

"Great! See you soon!" Freya rushes off.

Suzie closes the shop door. "Right. Festive hats first, of course." She bustles about locating my hat, which she's named and a new hat for Jada. These she places on our heads. "It'll just be us for a bit, I'm afraid. The others are at a planning meeting at the site our mosaic will be installed at — just for an hour or so. There's plenty to do here, though, so I hope you're ready to be put to work!" She puts a couple of containers which hold some large wedges of glass down on one of the benches. She passes us some clippers. "Would you mind getting started on these?"

"Sure," I say. "Do you know how to do it?" I ask Jada.

She nods. "I've been here before with Mum and Elsie. It's fun."

"I've just got to send a few emails," Suzie says. "If you need anything, call out."

"Okay," we both say.

Suzie selects a Christmas playlist and Jada and I begin clipping in silence. The more time I spend at this place, the more I like it. It's kind of soothing concentrating on clipping the little pieces of glass and not thinking about too much else.

"Beebee says you took a copy of Mum's book," Jada says.

I stop clipping.

"I mean, she gave it to you. Not that you stole it or something. Haven't you read it before?"

"Do you think the house is haunted?" I blurt the question out.

Jada thinks for a moment before answering. "I know some people come to the door and won't go any further. And lots of them don't even know about Madame LeNoir before they get there. They just say there's a feeling — a bad feeling — and they don't want to go inside."

"Do you think it's true then? That she murdered her apprentice?"

"Clara. Her name was Clara."

I nod. "I know."

Jada shrugs. "There wasn't any real proof that she did. Only talk. The police investigated it, though that was in Victorian times, so I'm guessing it would have been a pretty basic investigation. It all seemed to focus on that locket."

"The one that Queen Victoria gave to Clara."

Jada nods. "Their maid happened to see it lying around after Clara left. That's when all the rumours started about Madame LeNoir murdering her and the police got involved. It was the maid who came out and said what had been going on — that Clara had been starved and that she couldn't contact Prince Albert. But I think everyone was convinced she'd been murdered because the maid had seen the locket. No one could believe that Clara would leave without it. It was valuable and she always wore it."

"What? It makes complete sense that she wouldn't have taken it with her if she'd gone! She'd have hated that locket and everything it stood for. She would only have worn it because Madame LeNoir made her."

"But it was valuable and she had nothing," Jada argues. "Even if Clara did run away, everyone ended up believing that Madame LeNoir had murdered her anyway. It ruined her life and her career. She kind of just hid out in the attic after that and rented the furnished downstairs rooms cheaply, because no one wanted to live there. People weren't interested in her spiritualist sittings anymore. They were scared Clara's vengeful spirit would return and get them." She waggles her fingers at me and laughs.

"It's not funny," I say, shifting in my seat.

"Yeah, I guess not. I don't think Madame LeNoir murdered her, though. It wouldn't have made sense. Clara was how she made her money. I think Clara just ran away again. I mean, the old witch was starving her. I would have kept running away too. I think the second time she just got smarter and didn't go back to her family."

"Is that what your mum thinks as well?"

"Pretty much."

With a shiver, I think about that terrifying face pushing out of the wall. I'm not so sure.

We go back to our clipping.

It isn't long before the Tiny Pieces crew begin to arrive from their meeting.

"Alfie!" Jada jumps up as soon as she sees Britt and Alfie walk past the workshop window. She runs over to open the door for them. Ignoring Britt, she scoops up Alfie, who begins to lick her face excitedly.

"Everyone's always so happy to see me," Britt says with a snort.

Santa hats are located, cups of tea are made and biscuits are shared. Jada gives Alfie his dog biscuits — pretending to take them from the biscuit packet, just like I'd done the other day.

Alfie just wags his little tail and laps up the attention, the pompom on his hat bobbing frantically.

Britt takes a seat beside me and starts clipping.

"You look a bit tired," she says, after a while.

"I stayed up late reading a book about the house."

"Suzie told me it opens up tomorrow. For visitors and stuff."

I nod. "Tanice and Freya have to get everything sorted today."

"They said we could all go and see it for free, but I don't know. It sounds a bit spooky. And no talking? I quite like talking. You might have noticed."

I laugh.

Alfie barks one short bark.

"Right. Off we go." Britt jumps up. "Toilet trip," she explains. She clips Alfie to his lead and the pair make their way outside. I kind of like how she doesn't take off their Santa hats.

As Jada and I continue with our work, I half-watch through the workshop window as Britt and Alfie go on their way. They pause outside on the pavement to talk to a woman and her spaniel. At first the dog tries to jump up, but Britt makes the dog sit obediently and gives it part of a dog biscuit from her cargo pants' pocket. After this, they cross the road. They see someone else with a pug and have a chat. At first the pug is super-excited to see Alfie. But Britt pulls back and makes the dog wait. When it calms, she gives it some dog biscuit, just like she'd done before. After this, she and Alfie disappear into the park for a bit. About ten minutes later, I see them jog back across the road. They're just about to enter the shop again when someone waves to them from down the street. It's another woman and yet another dog — a dachshund this time. I don't think Alfie likes it very much, because he pulls away. But Britt does something different this time — she crushes some dog biscuit and spreads it all over the ground. And while the two dog owners chat, the dogs busily snuffle for biscuit on the ground. Distracted, they get far closer than I think they would have otherwise.

"Did you see that?" I say to Jada, who is busily clipping beside me.

"See what?" She looks up.

"Oh, nothing."

"I did," Suzie says, coming over to stand next to me as Britt enters. "She's brilliant, isn't she?"

Britt takes her place again and Alfie slides back under the table and flops on the floor. "You lazy thing," she says.

"We were just talking about your trip outside," Suzie says.

"Probably about how long Alfie's toilet trips take. By the time he's greeted all his fans, it's practically time to go out for another one."

"I think they're your fans too, not just Alfie's," Suzie says.

I nod. "You were amazing just then! You should be some kind of dog trainer or something. Or one of those people who walks ten dogs at a time."

Suzie leans on the bench. "Funny you should say that, because Britt and I have been talking recently."

"Here we go," Britt says.

"I think dog walking is a brilliant idea, Lolli. How do you think Britt would find people who need their dogs walked?"

I think for a moment. "Well, that first lady you spoke to had a mobility aid. She might not be able to walk far enough to give her dog the exercise it needs. So there might be people you already know who need dog walking. Or they might have friends who do."

"So, word of mouth?"

I nod. "Or you could put a sign up. Outside on the glass here. Or at a supermarket. Sometimes they have noticeboards. And I'm sure there are apps, or local groups on Facebook and things like that."

"Some great ideas there, Britt. I'll leave you to think about them." Suzie grins at her and then leaves.

Britt watches Suzie go. She grunts. "She doesn't stop, that one. Gets you in here with mosaics and the next thing you know you have a dog-walking empire."

10

$\mathcal{B}$ack at the apartment that evening, Freya is lying on the couch, a pot of peppermint tea on the coffee table beside her. "I think we're actually going to do it. A few more tweaks and we'll be ready for the first visitors to come through late tomorrow afternoon."

The apartment telephone rings and we look at each other.

I shrug.

Freya gets up and answers it. "Hello?"

On the other end someone speaks.

And Freya's expression drops.

I go over to her. Something's the matter.

She looks down at me, her brow creased. Pauses for a second. "Well, I don't know. This is all very ... unexpected. How did you even know I was here?"

The voice speaks again.

Freya sighs. "I should have known someone would see me sooner or later and tell you I was in London." She pauses. "Look, I'm going to come downstairs. I don't know if I'll bring Olivia or not. I'll see if she wants to come." She hangs the receiver up.

"Who was that?"

"That," she says, "was my mother."

"Seriously?" Freya hasn't spoken to her parents for years, as far as I know. Not since I was a toddler. Like Clementine, Freya had never really had a great relationship with her parents. They weren't close. She was an only child. When she was little, she had a nanny and then she went to boarding school. She'd come home on the school holidays, but often her parents would be away. Whenever I asked her about it, she would always say things like, "My parents were very busy, Lolli. Too busy and important to spend any time on someone as insignificant as me." When she was older, they disagreed on a lot of things. Like Freya's girlfriends. And then, of course, they had disagreed about me. The thing was, Freya had had to fight for me. She'd had to take Clementine's mother to court. It had taken a lot of time and a lot of money and because Freya's family were wealthy and influential, it had been in all the newspapers. People had gossiped about it. Freya's father hadn't liked that, apparently. He hadn't liked that at all.

"I'm not sure if I told you," Freya says, "but I heard my parents separated a while ago."

"You didn't tell me."

"Sorry. I didn't mean to not tell you. It's just ... to be honest, I don't really think about them all that much. I prefer to focus on the good things in life."

"That's me."

Freya laughs. "It is. And I'm thrilled that I've brought you up to be so modest."

"So are we going down there?"

"You want to go?"

"Sure. I'll go poke the monster."

This really makes Freya laugh. "Sometimes you remind me so much of your mother, it's scary. Come on." She grabs her phone and the room key.

"What do you think's going to happen?" I ask as Freya holds the door open for me.

She sighs. "I think she'll say things that are thoughtless without knowing they're thoughtless. I think she'll believe I'm being unreasonable and not seeing her point of view about everything that's happened between us. I doubt she'll have magically changed into a kind, caring person. I wish she would. That she could. Sadly, I don't really think it's possible."

We continue to stand in the doorway.

"Don't you wish things were different?"

"Of course I do. But they're not. And so I decided a long time ago that I wouldn't dwell on that, but would put my energy into creating what I wanted to have, rather than what I wished I could have. Does that make sense?"

I nod. It makes a lot of sense.

As we walk down the hallway and get into the lift, I realise I'm not scared about meeting Freya's mother again. Freya does tell me about her family if I ask — she's never hidden anything. But I've never had much to ask. They don't sound very nice. She's mostly said they're obsessed with what everyone else thinks and says, instead of doing the right thing, or what will make them happy. "Except for Elsie," she'd always add when she said this. "But Elsie has always marched to the beat of her own drum. And been far, far happier for it, I might add."

As soon as the lift door opens onto the ground floor, I see a woman sitting at a little table and chairs by the large windows that face the river and the spectacular view of Tower Bridge. She stands and I see that she's wearing a crisp, fitted cream skirt and jacket with an emerald green blouse underneath. Everything about her matches — bag, shoes, necklace. Her hair is that sort of hair that doesn't move. Everything is perfect. I glance up at Freya, not entirely believing this could be her mother, even though they sort of look alike.

"I'm already regretting this," Freya says under her breath as we cross the floor.

Suddenly I don't feel quite so brave.

I slip my hand into hers — something I haven't done for a long time.

She gives it three quick squeezes.

I. Love. You.

It's something we used to do when I was little. When I was scared, or worried about something.

I do the same back.

We approach and Freya leads me around so that the table is between us and her mother.

"Hello, darling," she says to Freya, smiling a nervous sort of smile. Even her teeth are perfect.

"Hello," Freya says, her voice giving nothing away. "Lolli, this is my mother, er ... Robyn." There's a pause where she doesn't look entirely sure what to call her. I see the problem. Having barely met, grandmother wouldn't really be appropriate, and Mrs Darlington would seem too formal.

"Hello, Olivia. I mean, Lolli."

"Hi."

"Why don't we sit down?" Robyn says, doing just that. She smooths her already-smooth skirt with her hands.

Freya remains standing for a moment and then sits.

I sit too.

"I'm not entirely sure where to start," Robyn says. "It's good to see you again. You look ... well. You both do."

"Thanks," Freya says. "So do you."

"You're so grown up, Lolli."

I smile. But in my head, I think, *That's because you haven't seen me for so many years.*

"Well. I suppose you heard from someone or other that your father and I separated."

"Yes."

Robyn waits for Freya to say something else about this. But Freya doesn't. Robyn smooths her skirt again, a frown flitting across her brow. "All right, then. I suppose I came today because I wanted to tell you that all those years ago, it was your father's decision to cut ties with you. Not mine. You being an only child and in a relationship with Phillipa ... well, I knew this might be my one chance. To have a grandchild. Not speaking to you wasn't really what I wanted."

Freya's frown deepens as she listens. "And you just decided to go along with what he wanted, despite how you really felt."

"Well, you know what your father's like."

Freya looks away.

"You have to understand that, at the time, it all seemed so impulsive. We were worried you didn't truly understand what you were agreeing to."

"Of course I understood. I was an adult."

"Clementine always managed to twist you into doing what she wanted. She was such a terrible influence."

Freya's head snaps up. "What a thing to say in front of Lolli! Can you even hear yourself?"

"Well, what would you do? If Lolli had a friend who got her into trouble like that at school? Would you be as supportive as you expected me to be? No. Of course you wouldn't."

Freya stands. "This was a mistake."

"Oh, dear. I knew this wouldn't go well." Robyn flusters with her bag. "Here, I brought a present." She brings out a small stuffed toy — an elephant.

Everyone stares at it.

"But now I see it's all wrong. I didn't realise quite how grown up you'd be."

"Um, thank you?" I say. I don't know whether to take the present or not.

"No, I've got it all wrong." Robyn puts the elephant back in her bag. "I'll get something else and give it to you next time."

I almost laugh. She thinks Freya's going to give her a next time? She doesn't know her daughter at all.

"Perhaps at Christmas?" Robyn tries.

"We have plans for Christmas," Freya says.

"After Christmas then."

I go to open my mouth to say we'll be going back to Singapore. But then I think twice and close it again.

"Maybe after Christmas?" Robyn tries again. She looks almost on the verge of tears and I get the feeling crying is not something she does in public.

Ever.

"Maybe." I blurt the word out before I even realise what I'm doing. I think because she's trying so hard and getting it so wrong. I feel sorry for her. I hadn't expected that.

Freya looks down at me, surprised.

"It was lovely. To see you both," Robyn says. "I know I should have called first, but I wasn't sure ..."

We all know how that sentence ends — she wasn't sure if Freya would see her at all.

Freya looks at her mother. She looks down at me again. I nod the tiniest of nods. I want her to keep her options open. Also, now that Clementine's mother is gone, Robyn is the only chance of a grandmother that I've got.

"Look, I'll give you my number." Freya signals to one of the women at the front desk, asking for a paper and pen. Someone brings her one. She writes down her number, rips the piece of paper off and gives it to her mother.

We all stare at it in Robyn's manicured hands.

It's a start. A phone number.

And a maybe. A maybe after Christmas.

"Thank you." Robyn clutches the piece of paper tight.

I realise it's probably the nicest thing she's said during our meeting.

We leave it at that. At "thank you". Freya nods a small nod and I give a small wave and we disappear into the lift.

All the way up to the apartment, we don't speak.

When we finally get inside and Freya closes the door behind us, she sort of . . . deflates. Her shoulders loosen and I can see how hard she'd fought to hold herself together downstairs. She takes a deep breath, sniffs, runs her fingers under her eyes and then pulls me in for a big hug. I hug her back. Tight.

When she pulls back, she holds my shoulders and looks straight into my eyes, unblinking.

"Your mother was a good person, Lolli. And don't ever let anyone tell you otherwise. All she'd want for you in this life is for you to be a good person too. That you are always brave enough to be your best self. That you strive to do the right thing. The good thing. The loving thing. The helpful thing. The kind thing. That's exactly what your mother would have done her whole life long if the world hadn't broken her first."

11

$\mathcal{A}$nother night without much sleep. This time, because I know that in the morning, I'm going to have to do all those brave things that Freya was talking about. I have to talk to Elsie and find out exactly what it is she's so desperate for me to do. But I don't feel brave. I feel scared. I know whatever it is Elsie wants me to do concerns Madame LeNoir. Angry, bitter, mean Madame LeNoir. Who is maybe even a murderer.

I try to tell myself that she can't hurt me. That she's just a spirit.

But, to be honest, I don't know if that's true.

Madame LeNoir is strong. She's far, far stronger than any other spirit I've ever felt before.

Despite my fear, I know I have to be brave and face up to things. Like Freya did with her mother. Elsie needs me to be brave for her right now. And I know one thing for sure: if I ever had to ask Elsie for help with anything, she would help me without question. That's what people who love each other do. Even when they're scared, they show up.

I also feel pretty bad, because I should have said I'd do this thing (whatever it is) long ago. Way back when we were in the ginger garden and she was sitting beside me. I should have tried to find out what she needed. What was wrong. And how I could help.

But I didn't.

And now I hate myself for being like that.

I guess the thing is, I couldn't do it then.

But I can do it now.

I try not to drag my feet too much, but Freya still has to hurry me along for us to get to the house by 9 am.

"Come on, Loll," she pleads as we walk towards Spitalfields, our breath puffing out in the frosty morning air. "The first open is this afternoon. Real visitors will be coming in. Everything needs to be sorted by then. And I told Tanice we'd pick up coffee on the way."

We turn the corner and the house comes into view. My eyes look up, up, up to the attic windows.

A wave of uncertainty hits me.

I'm not sure I can do this. All these years I haven't wanted to know, haven't asked all those questions. I don't know what I'm doing. I'm not prepared for this.

I push my fear aside.

No.

I have to do better than this.

I have to *be* better than this.

But I also know I have to be ready. I have to sort myself out before I go inside. "You go and find Tanice. I'll get two coffees from the shop on the corner."

"Would you? That would be great. Here." Freya gives me some money. "Get a hot chocolate for yourself as well. But don't worry about Jada — Tanice said she won't be here until later."

"Okay." I head off down the street, telling myself I'm not chickening out. I'm just ... taking a moment. (Yeah, right.)

At the coffee shop, I order and then stand to the side to wait for the coffees. I see a little noticeboard and go over to read the flyers and business cards pinned to it while I'm waiting. There's one for a local babysitter, one for French lessons and a little packet of business cards for someone who offers dog training, dog sitting and dog walking. I smile when I see it. That's exactly what Britt should be doing. She would be so good at something like that. I take one and slide it in my pocket.

When I get back to the house, Freya has left the door unlocked. I push it open with my foot and stand in the hallway for a moment, the coffee tray in my hands. I don't rush. I don't run. Instead, I take in the scene around me. The hallway is dark and quiet, lit only by the candles in sconces on the wall. Behind me, care of hidden speakers, is the *clip-clop* of hooves, as carriages drive past. To my right I can hear voices in the dining room. A maid's footsteps on the stairs.

And, overhead, something else entirely.

Something dark and brooding.

I'm not scared of you, I think. *You can't hurt me.*

"Lolli, is that you?" Freya's voice breaks the spell. "We're in the parlour." Her head pokes out of the room down the hallway. "Ah, there you are!"

I bring the coffees in to them. "Here you go."

"Oh, lovely. Thank you so much, Lolli." Tanice takes the cup from me.

"It's freezing in here," I say, looking around at the room I'd spent so much time in the other day, decorating the Christmas tree.

"Yes, it can take a while for the fire to warm the room," Tanice says.

"We've just got to straighten things up and we're done," Freya says. "Why don't you run down to the kitchen for a bit? It's toasty there. I got a text from Suzie while you were out — she's going to bring a few people from Tiny Pieces by later. Do you think that you could do something for us before they get here? We really need someone to have a proper walk-through. Test everything out for us."

Freya gives me this sideways look and I know precisely what she's up to. She thinks I'm all comfortable with the house now. She's testing my boundaries.

"I think you can do it," she adds, confirming my thoughts.

"It would be amazing if you could, Lolli," Tanice says. "We need to see if there's anything we've missed.

I know by this point I tend to have lost all perspective. But only if you're okay with it, of course."

Can we go home already?

"I'll do the walk-through," I say, already regretting it. But I also know it's my decision. I want to do it. Sort of.

"Anyway, go warm yourself downstairs and we'll call you when we're ready."

I grab my hot chocolate and head back out into the hallway.

The festering growth stirs upstairs.

I know you're there, I acknowledge the spirit, wanting to stand up to it. To her. Madame LeNoir.

I walk purposefully towards the stairs and take them at a normal pace.

Around me, the walls remain still and smooth.

I'm in the lovely warm kitchen in no time. It's all set up for the afternoon's visitors, complete with mince pies, sweet little marzipan mice and cups ready for welcoming mulled wine.

The yellow glow of the fire shines bright off the copper pots and pans hanging above.

The fancy jellies on the kitchen table gleam, as if illuminated from within.

The gingerbread men's currant eyes twinkle.

The hearth beckons me towards it.

"So, you're finally ready." Elsie doesn't need to turn around in her chair to know it's me.

I go over and sit down. "Yes. And, um, I'm sorry. For taking so long."

She smiles at me. "That's all right. What made you change your mind?"

"I met Freya's mother last night. Robyn. And ..." I pause, not really knowing how to explain what happened. "It was sort of like everything that came out of her mouth was wrong."

Elsie chuckles. "That sounds like Robyn."

"Anyway, I thought ... I don't want to be that sort of person. The sort of person who's only worried about what *they* want and think and feel. Who can't see what other people need. That's the thing ... I knew you needed my help and I wanted to help you. I was just scared, I guess."

Elsie nods. "I know. And that's nothing to be ashamed of. We all get scared sometimes. What's important is what you do with that fear. I've always found it best to acknowledge it and then to do exactly what it is you know you must do anyway."

"Freya wasn't scared. Of her mother, I mean."

"No. She never has been, really. She was lucky that she made such good friends at boarding school. She made her own family, really. Cobbled it together."

"You're a cobble. I'm a cobble."

Elsie laughs. "And very happy cobbles we are together too."

"Robyn said one thing that made me think. About Clementine. She asked Freya how she'd react if I had a friend who was a bad influence."

"Ooh, that is a tricky one. And I suppose she does have a point. It must be very worrisome to have a child who is getting into trouble at school. But you can't just go around cutting everyone out of your life every time they do or say something that you think isn't right. I suppose the thing about Clementine was that she could sometimes do things and say things to get attention. That was because she'd worked out over the years that her parents wouldn't give her attention any other way. She was a troubled soul. And she could be a difficult person. But being troubled and difficult doesn't make you bad. Far from it. She was someone who felt very deeply and cared very much.

She would have done anything for Freya. And for you. That much I know for certain."

I think about this. "You know that Freya and Clementine fought before Clementine had me? Freya wanted her to move into her apartment, but she wouldn't. But she did listen to her. Freya always says she knows she must have listened, because everyone thought I'd have medical problems when I was born, but I didn't."

"Yes," Elsie says. "That's exactly what I mean. I'm sure Clementine struggled during that time, but she somehow managed to look after herself. For you. And because, deep down, she knew Freya was right, even if she couldn't admit it to her."

I look up at the ceiling, thinking about what's above me.

"I know," I say. "About Madame LeNoir. I mean, I've always known in one way or another. But now I also know some of her story. I read Tanice's book. And ... well, I guess I'm ready. For whatever it is you need me to do."

Elsie stares back at me for what feels like forever before she answers. "You can do this, Lolli. I suspected it would all come down to you right from when you were a baby and you had such strong feelings about being in the house. Your connection to the twilight world is strong. Much stronger than mine. Maybe even as strong as Clara's. And that's who you need to speak to. So you run off upstairs and find her now. Clara will explain everything to you."

I go back upstairs. Tanice and Freya are now in the Regency drawing room. The room is decorated in robin's-egg blue-and-white-striped wallpaper, dotted with gold-framed portraits. It's not like the Victorian parlour, all cosy and snug. It's a very prim and proper room, dotted with little tables and chairs for groups of three or four and one chaise longue that looks really uncomfortable.

I pause for a moment in the doorway, my gaze skimming over all of this. I can't see Clara anywhere.

Slowly, slowly, I open myself up to the energy of the room.

Nothing.

I can't feel Clara's presence at all, though I can feel Madame LeNoir's grinding anger upstairs.

Inside the drawing room, Tanice and Freya are at the side table that runs against one wall, *oohing* and *aahing* over a cake.

"Come and see!" Freya says, beckoning me over. "It arrived this morning."

I walk over to take a closer look. To be honest, it doesn't look all that impressive. It's a big round fruitcake decorated with plain white royal icing, white icing swans circling the top as if they're sitting on a frozen lake. It's the only Christmas decoration in the room.

"I know it doesn't look like much." Tanice seems to guess at what I'm thinking. "But Christmas wasn't really celebrated as we know it until the mid-nineteenth century. This is a Twelfth Night cake, which is what the Georgians would have had. There's a little dried bean and a dried pea hidden inside, the pea on the left side and the bean on the right. Ladies get a slice from the left and gentleman from the right. If they find the pea or the bean, they become Queen or King for the night and rule the household."

"Sounds fun. But I prefer the internet."

Tanice laughs.

"No cake for you," Freya says.

"I came to see if I could do the walk-through now?"

"Sounds like a great idea," Tanice says. "We'll keep working."

"You know the drill," Freya says. "By yourself. In silence. Really take everything in."

"I know." I turn to go.

"Lolli?"

I look back at Freya.

"All good?"

I nod, even though everything feels far from good.

Freya gives me a thumbs up.

"I hope you love it, Lolli," Tanice says. "If you open the front door wide and close it again, the audio will activate and play from the start."

"Okay, thanks." I struggle to keep my voice from shaking.

I leave the room and head back downstairs, all the time dodging and weaving inside—trying to find a way to block Madame LeNoir's energy, while remaining open to Clara's. It takes a lot of concentration and I'm not sure how to do it. Every time I open up to Clara, I find Madame LeNoir's energy seeping in as well.

Standing on the stairs, my hand on the handrail, I imagine that iron door of mine again. I visualise Madame LeNoir's energy behind it. I make another door in front of that. And another. Iron over iron over iron. I shut them all tight. She will be forced to stay behind those doors until I choose to let her out.

When I open my eyes again, I realise it might have worked. The angry spirit seems more distant, the roiling anger still there, but subdued. Held back. Maybe I can do this after all? Maybe I really do have the abilities Elsie thinks I have?

I run the last few steps down and over to the front door, which I open and close quickly. The audio pauses and resets.

I take a deep breath and close my eyes once more. Here we go.

Clip-clop, clip-clop, clip-clop.

My eyelids flicker open.

All is silent and still.

And I am in the past.

The hallway is dim, lit only by the glow of the candles on the wall lamps. Overhead, garlands of holly, ivy and mistletoe hang heavy. I hear the sound of a door slam upstairs. Footsteps. The family who lives here is moving about. Down below, in the kitchen, a voice, the scrape of a chair.

I feel like an intruder. Like I should announce myself.

But, no. There is to be no talking. Only observing. Feeling. Though I still don't feel Clara.

Where is she?

Clara? I call out to her silently as I move down the hall. *Clara!*

A few more steps take me to the first door on my right. I slip inside. It is a Georgian dining room. Painted a deep forest green, the low winter light coming in through the front window gives the walls a glossy sheen. Above, a chandelier is decorated with pine branches and cones and oranges. Dominating the room is a large portrait of a family member. He scowls down from above the fireplace. A dark round wooden table sits in the middle of the room. Four uncomfortable-looking high-backed dining chairs are pushed out at angles around it, as if the sitters have just upped and left the room. Food remains upon their plates. Some shucked oysters, half-drunk wine, clay pipes and spilled tobacco, a bowl of walnuts in their shells, some already cracked, a bowl of Turkish delight. A linen napkin lies scrunched, another rests over the back of a chair. I hear a voice in the hall. Have they gone to greet a family member at the front door? Maybe.

One thing I know for sure – Clara is not here.

I retrace my steps into the hallway and continue on.

I know the next door to my right is a small study. But when I poke my head inside, I am met with nothing but a many-drawered heavy wooden desk and papers everywhere. The important Victorian businessman of the house has been doing his accounts, or Tanice has made it look this way. Before starting, he has made himself comfortable, shedding his silk waistcoat. I can hear his rumbling voice. A laugh. He has taken himself to the dining room for sustenance and will return to work late into the night by candlelight. It's only when I look up that I see Christmas has come to the room – the children of the house have provided paper chains to jolly up Papa's surrounds.

Again, I back from the room. And I'm about to enter the next room on my right – the Victorian parlour – when I pause.

Upstairs.

The feeling is overwhelming.

I need to go upstairs.

Still attempting to keep Madame LeNoir at bay behind those doors in my mind, I place my hand on the rail and start upwards, leaving the crackle of the parlour fire behind me.

Along the landing, the door to the Regency drawing room is still closed. I know the room that lies directly in front of me is the largest bedchamber. Beside it is a lady's dressing-room.

And I know Clara is in that dressing-room, hiding.

Hiding from Madame LeNoir.

I can feel it. Her.

And I can feel that she wants me to come in there.

She wants me to find her.

My heart racing, I enter the room.

It is frothy and frilly. A stuffed canary tweets prettily in a cage upon a small table set for tea. On a wooden dresser, a few small Christmas presents are stacked and others lie waiting to be wrapped.

"*Clara?*" I whisper.

My eye is drawn to the small fireplace and then up to the ornate mirror above it.

I see myself.

And a girl, standing behind me.

I startle and whirl about.

But there is no one there.

I turn back around again to view my reflection and there she is once more. She has beautiful dark loose ringlets and wears a deep plum striped dress with full sleeves and many tucks upon the bodice that lead up to a high frill of lace about the neck. Her mouth has an interesting twist to it and her eyes are bright. She looks clever. As if she knows things. As if she knows me.

"Hello, Lolli," Clara says.

13

"Elsie said you would come to find me."

I try to make sense of what I'm seeing. She is more real than any other spirit I've ever encountered. More present somehow. If I could turn around once more and see her actually standing in the room just as I see her in the mirror, I would believe that she is really, truly here.

But I know I can't do that.

"Don't move," I say into the mirror. "Just . . . stay still. Stay right there." It's not that Clara is scary-looking, but the thought of her moving about if I take my eyes off her for a moment is creepy.

Breathe. Just breathe. In and out. In and out.

"I don't mean to frighten you." Clara looks worried.

"No … it's only …" I've never really spoken to a spirit before. Not properly, like this. Up until now, I've always pretended not to see them. I take a deep breath. "Elsie wanted me to find you. She keeps saying there's something I have to do."

"Elsie's been so good to me. So patient. I only wish we had been successful."

I frown. "What do you mean? Is this about Madame LeNoir?"

"Yes. Elsie told me of your horrible experience with Madame LeNoir. I'm sorry you had to meet her."

"I've just been reading about her. I know that you were her apprentice and that she treated you badly — that you weren't given enough to eat, that she made you lie to the Queen. That you ran away." I stare at Clara in the mirror. For her to appear like this — as a girl of around twelve years or so — the rumours must have been true. Madame LeNoir must have taken her life. How awful. I have to say something. But what do you say about something like that? "I'm, um … I'm sorry that Madame LeNoir … er, you know …"

"Oh! Oh, goodness no." Clara shakes her head, her ringlets swaying. "It's unfortunate that everyone thought as much at the time, but that's not what happened. In fact, I lived a very long and happy life until the grand old age of eighty-nine. I married and had four lovely children. I did feel quite bad about those rumours when I found out. But the truth was I didn't find out that everyone believed this until years afterwards. You see, I ran all the way to Dorset and had no contact with my family after that, or anyone I'd previously known. I was too afraid they would send me back to Madame LeNoir again."

I don't understand. "But if you lived to be an adult, then why do you look like this?"

"Elsie didn't explain?"

I shake my head. "She wants you to explain, I think."

"Ah, I see. Well, the reason I look like this is because Madame LeNoir did something almost as wicked as taking my life — she stole a piece of my very soul. She took it and bound it to something in this house. She thought by doing so that I'd never dare run away again. But I did."

"You mean she bound it to an object?"

Clara's head bobs. "Exactly that. And ever since my passing, I've been stuck here, trying to find out which object it is. Elsie's been helping me."

"I didn't know it was possible to do something like that. And you haven't been able to work out which object it is? Not even together?"

"No. We have no idea."

There's one thing that doesn't make sense to me. "But then why is Madame LeNoir here as well? And why is she so angry? Isn't this what she wanted? For you to be trapped here?"

Clara opens her mouth as if to begin explaining, then pauses. "It's probably easier if I show you. May I?" She takes a tentative step forward.

I pause for a moment as well, then nod. Elsie obviously trusts Clara, which means I should too.

Clara comes to stand close to the mirror and I gasp as she places a palm up to touch it. It's bizarre. Surreal. As if she's on the other side of the mirror itself. Slowly, I bring my own hand up to touch hers.

"Close your eyes," she says.

I'm hungry. So hungry. As if I haven't eaten for days. Weeks.

"Get upstairs. Go! Ungrateful, insolent child."

Someone pushes my back and I lurch forward, stumbling onto a set of stairs. I have to grasp at the handrail beside me to save myself. It takes me a moment to realise where I am. I'm on the stairs in the house. Except everything looks slightly different. A little more worn. Grimier. Another push forces me to start up the stairs, even though I barely have the energy to move. It takes everything I have to drag my feet up one step, then another. I see I'm wearing little leather boots with hard soles. They peek out from beneath my full, striped skirt.

Finally, I understand.

I am Clara. I am seeing the past through Clara's eyes.

Another shove as I round the corner.

"Keep going. All the way. Go!"

I have to drag myself upwards using the handrail, hand over hand. It's as if my stomach is eating itself.

"You think you can leave? After all I've done for you? I gave you a home – a good home – and this is how you repay me?"

This isn't a home, I want to argue. It's a place of lies and fear. Of cruelty and starvation. But there is not enough energy for arguing. I'm not even sure I can make it up the final flight of stairs.

"Get up there! To think you would disappoint the Queen herself. The Queen who only wants to converse with her dear, departed husband. Who do you think you are to deny the Queen?"

I don't know how I do it, but I make it into the attic room. My room. Clara's room. Bare except for a small, hard iron-and-brass bed and a trunk that holds my few items of clothes. I want to fall onto the bed, weak and tired, but I don't dare. There will be no rest until she leaves. Instead, I shuffle over to lean on the wall. I want to run. I want to push past Madame LeNoir like a whirlwind. Bolt downstairs to freedom. But I have used up the little energy I had left running to my family home. The moment my mother opened the door I knew I'd been wrong to do so. The look on her face. And all the things I'd forgotten — the smell. The wracking coughs. The fear in my mother's eyes when she thought Madame LeNoir might believe she had persuaded me to come home. No, there will be no more running. Now I can only lean on the wall. Captured. I am a caged animal in her circus.

"Look at me. Look!"

My eyes lift. She is the same as always. Tall.

Bowed. Hair pulled back into a tight bun. Her round pince-nez glasses make her eyes appear even smaller and meaner. Her black dress — for she is still in deep mourning for her husband — does not suit her. It brings out the grey threads in her dark hair and makes her look even older and more worn.

Her flint-like eyes lock onto mine, narrowing, as she moves in.

"You will never leave this place," she hisses. "Never. I'll make sure of it."

I wait for her hands to wrap around my neck.

But instead something else happens.

Her hands rise. In one of them she holds the locket. The silver locket given to me by the Queen.

It swings rhythmically as her hands pass in front of my face.

Once. Twice. Thrice.

Oh, no. No.

I must look away. Push past her. Run. Fight this.

But I can't. I can't. All I can do is slump against the wall and watch as her hands pass in front of my face. The locket sways to and fro.

"You will never be able to leave this place. You will be bound here forever."

My gaze is locked on her hands. Passing. Passing. Passing in front of my eyes. Soft. Fluid.

She is mesmerising me, Clara, I know it. And I can do nothing. Too weak to move, I can only look on. Helpless.

"A piece of your soul will be bound to an object in this place. Bound forevermore."

Her fingers move back and forth. So smoothly they travel. To and fro. To and fro. But my brow creases. Something is not right. How can she do this? I did not think she had the ability to do this as I can — to bind a soul. It is impossible. She's not strong enough. She never has been. So how did she learn to do so? From me? I told her too much when I first arrived here. I was foolish and boastful. I didn't know then how cruel she could be.

"There is no leaving this house with your soul intact. You know this now. Search as you might, you will never find where this fragment of your spirit resides. It will always elude you. Always."

Smooth as poured cream, as a kitten's fur, as a velvet cape, her hands pass in front of my face, over and over again. I forget the pain in my stomach. The pain in my heart. There is only the truth — that my spirit has been rent in two.

The hands stop.

She pulls back. Inspects me.

"Do you feel it, girl? Do you feel your soul split in two?"

My head dips. I do. I feel it. I feel it deep inside me. I feel like one of those cool, white marble statues that I saw in the long gallery I would walk down to meet the Queen — I am whole but for a missing arm, a leg. It is a strange feeling. A feeling of being incomplete. A gnawing remembrance. A hole.

"Good. That will teach you to go against me." She steps forward and clasps the locket around my neck. It weighs me down like an anvil and I slump to the floor, unable to stand one second longer.

Madame LeNoir laughs bitterly. "For goodness sake, girl. What a performance! You should be on the stage. If you're going to be that dramatic, I'll send some food up. I suppose I must protect my investment. After all, we have another audience with the Queen coming up next week."

The door slams behind her. A key turns in the lock.

And what's left of me is alone.

In the end, it is the meat pie she sends up to my room that is her undoing. It is the food that gives me the energy to take the locket off, to exit via the attic window across the rooftops … to bind a little piece of her soul to mine before I go. For safekeeping.

14

I draw in a huge breath of air as I pull my hand back from the mirror, returning to the present.

Clara also draws back and moves aside a little, giving me some space.

"That was awful," I finally manage to splutter. "You were so hungry. So exhausted. Why did Madame LeNoir treat you like that? Why did she hate you so much?"

"I suppose because I cared about the truth."

"Did you really bind a piece of her soul to yours?"

"I'm not proud of it, but, yes. I knew that I had to leave — that if I stayed I'd be forced to tell more and more lies, but I also knew that I couldn't simply leave part of my soul behind. I couldn't bear to be trapped in this in-between place for all time. I'd seen too many unhappy spirits who lived that way and it looked wretched. I knew I needed to protect myself. The best way to do that was to link my soul to the soul of the one who knew which object I was bound to — Madame LeNoir. That way it didn't matter if she died before me. I would be able to contact her in both the living and twilight worlds."

"So you bound her soul to yours and left."

"Yes. And I never used my gifts for personal gain again. The more I thought about it, the more I realised I was never meant to have them in the first place. I am — we are — an aberration. Me, you, Elsie. We're not meant to be this way. To see the things we see."

"No."

"Elsie told me about your mother," Clara says quietly. "I am sorry."

I nod. I remember how Elsie had tried to talk to me about all of this in the ginger garden. About the portals. About her being bombed. About my mother's accident. Elsie most likely wanted to talk about what had happened to Clara too, to make her this way. Unlike them, I hadn't been hurt, but I'd seen things no child should see and doing so had changed me forever.

In the reflection, Clara tugs at the lace neckline of her dress until I begin to see some terrible red scarring. I remember what I'd read in Tanice's book about how Clara had been badly burned when she was only hours old. "I thought about my accident a lot as I ran from this place. I thought about how strong I must have been to survive. It made me believe I could survive leaving Madame LeNoir's house too. That I could create a new life. A happy life. I had a small amount of money I'd hidden away. That got me as far as Dorset. I found some work as a maid at a small inn. I was lucky. My employers were good people. In time, I married their nephew, Arthur."

"Did something happen to Madame LeNoir as well? An accident of some sort when she was young?"

"Not that I know of. There were those in her family who had limited abilities with contacting the twilight world, but she didn't inherit these. She just told people she did. Her skills lay in mesmerism and deception."

"And she had no idea that you'd bound her soul to this place until after she had passed away?"

"Well, it wasn't to this place, but to me. Her soul is tethered to mine. She remained here because she knew I would return in time. That I would have to if I wanted my spirit made whole. But, no, she didn't know what I had done until her passing."

Trying to take everything in, I stare at Clara in the mirror. And the question that has been in the back of mind the whole time we've been speaking finally finds its way to my lips.

"Can you ... are you able to see my mother? Is there a way?"

Clara gives me a sad smile. "I'm sorry, no. You see me only because I'm bound here. I wish there was a way."

I knew it. Of course I knew it. I look away, wondering, as I always have, of what the point is. What's the point of me seeing all these leftover people if I can't see the one person I really need to see?

"Lolli?"

I look back into the mirror. "I don't know what you want me to do," I say. "Help you find the object? The one Madame LeNoir bound your soul to? The thing is, I don't see how I can do that. You're stronger than me. I can't do any of those things you're talking about — mess with people's souls — or anything like that. I can only see spirits. And you and Elsie would know far better than I do which items were here in your time and which ones have been brought in since. If you and Elsie haven't been able to find the object, how am I supposed to?" I take a step towards the door.

"It's not just the locating of the object. It needs to be destroyed. In the living world. It's only in hindsight that I realised this. I need someone in the living world who can help me and now that—"

"NO!" I stop her before she can go any further. I thought I could do this. I thought I could be brave and do the right thing. Help. But I can't. I can't. "No. Stop talking. Just stop. I don't know how to help you and I don't want to. You need to go away. Just go away!"

"Lolli?"

I look in the mirror to see not Clara, but Freya's reflection.

"What's the matter? I heard you shout."

I shake my head, trying to get a grip on myself. "Sorry, it's just ... my toe. I stubbed my toe. It really hurt, but it's okay now." I catch sight of myself in the mirror and can't meet my own gaze. I don't want to be this person I am. Always scared. Always afraid. Always saying no.

Freya breathes a sigh of relief and I can see she thought it was something else. "It's all right? You haven't broken it or anything?"

"It's okay now," I say, desperately trying to hold my tears in.

"Oh, good. Well, I was about to come and find you anyway. Britt's here with Suzie and a few of the others from Tiny Pieces. They've already started walking through, so I thought I'd slip you out while they're down in the kitchen now and you can meet them out front after they're done. Tanice says Jada will be here soon too."

"Okay." It's everything I can do to just squeeze that one word out when all I want to do is run from this place. Past Freya, down the stairs, out to the street and on and on forever.

"Oh, and did you find anything?" Freya asks.

I look over. What?

"On your walk-through, I mean. Anything we need to fix? To change?"

"Oh, no. I didn't see anything. I didn't see anything at all."

I follow Freya downstairs, trying to keep Madame LeNoir's energy at bay as I go. Speaking to Clara seems to have stirred her up and I keep my eyes on the stairs that lead upwards to the attic room as we head down, just in case. What I'd experienced with Clara had been exhausting. All I want to do is go back to the apartment and curl up in bed.

Instead, I opt for the next best thing — I grab my coat and go out and sit on the front steps. It's cold, but I don't care. It's good just to be by myself for a few minutes outside of the house, which is starting to feel like it's creeping inside of me — as if it's beginning to bind itself to *my* soul.

As I sit, I try to work through everything that Clara told me — everything she showed me. I can see her problem. She needs to find that object so she can make her soul whole again and be at peace once and for all. But I still don't see how I can help her. It's like I said — her gift is stronger than mine and if she and Elsie haven't been able to find that object in the house after so many years, what hope do I have?

"Hey, there." The door to the house opens and Britt appears.

I twist around to look up at her. "You can't have finished the tour yet. That was too quick."

She sits down beside me. "Yeah, well, sometimes I'm not so great at doing one thing for too long, you know?"

"Oh, okay. So what did you think?"

"It was good. I liked it. I went to some museums and an art gallery once when I was at school. I wasn't really into that. Bit boring. Lots of reading. But this ... yeah. It's really like walking into a painting, isn't it? Like being there in the past. I liked the kitchen the best. It was so cosy with the fire and the gingerbread men and the mince pies and all those plates and things. It feels like ... I don't know ... like how Christmas should be, I guess. With someone fussing about cooking for you and giving you warm drinks while people sing Christmas carols outside. I don't know if people really have Christmases like that anymore except on the TV, but it's nice to pretend. Are there other places around like this one?"

"I'm not sure. I think it's pretty unique. Freya's planning something similar, but different."

"Oh, yeah? Different how?"

"It's hard to explain, but it's like a bunch of crazy items that you just want to look at for ages. Weird stuff. Wonderful stuff. Both old and new."

"That sounds pretty good. When's she going to open it?"

"Someday. Oh!" I remember and reach into my pocket. "I have something for you."

"For me?"

"Sorry, it's not that exciting. It's just I was at the coffee shop on the corner this morning and they have a little noticeboard. This person was advertising dog walking and training and stuff. Like we were talking about with Suzie."

Britt is looking away down the street now. Like she wants to leave.

I get this feeling in my gut that I need to backtrack. I've got this all wrong. I think she thought I had a Christmas present for her or something. "It's just you were so good with those dogs. And their owners too."

Britt snorts. "Yeah, I don't think so. The dogs, maybe. People I'm not so good with."

"But you were! You knew exactly how to handle them and their dogs. Anyway, I thought maybe you could have some cards made. Or something like that."

Britt stares at the card for a moment. "I don't have a phone." She hands the card back.

"Britt, I didn't mean ..."

"Doesn't matter." She gets up and starts down the cobbled street, calling out as she goes. "But that card. It wasn't really something for me, was it? It was something for you. So you could feel good about yourself. Like you'd fixed me."

15

"**A**ren't you freezing sitting out here?" Jada stands above me.

"What?" I'd been completely caught up in my thoughts. I really thought picking up that business card had been the right thing to do for Britt. She'd been amazing with all those dogs and their owners. Why was she so angry with me? I didn't get it.

"Come on, let's go in." Jada reaches for the door. "Oh, hang on. Mum said there's people going through before the first open. Is that why you're out here?"

I nod. "They should be upstairs now."

"Let's go down to the kitchen then. You can't sit out here all afternoon."

To be honest, I'm not sure I care that it's cold. But Jada looks like she's going to pester me until I go inside with her, so I get up.

She opens the door just enough so we can slide inside.

"The audio won't reset then," she says.

I nod absentmindedly, following her.

It's as we get to the stairs that I realise my mistake.

Preoccupied by my argument with Britt (not to mention Clara), I've forgotten about Madame LeNoir. I haven't properly prepared myself for venturing inside the house.

Big mistake.

Huge mistake.

Now, as Jada continues down the hall, oblivious, I find I can follow no further. I am stuck to the spot with fear, my eyes on the stairs as I feel the thing — her — tumbling downwards in my direction. Hurtling towards me.

"Lolli?" I hear Jada's voice from what feels like streets away. "Lolli, what's the matter?"

I have to move.

Have to run.

Just like it had done years ago, my hand darts out for the wall. I'm drowning again. Ready to grasp at anything. Anything that might save me from going under.

"Elsie!" I call out, remembering. "Elsie!"

But Elsie can't save me this time.

"Lolli!" It's not Elsie, but Jada who appears at my side. "What's the matter? What's going on? Quick, come and sit down."

She pulls at me. Drags me down the hall somehow, just as the paint on the wall begins to pulse and bulge.

"Come on!" Jada links arms with me and helps me down the stairs.

The hearth. We have to get to the hearth.

The next thing I know, I am sitting in one of the carver chairs, the fire crackling away in front of me.

"What was that about?" Jada says, standing above me. "Are you all right?"

I stare up at her.

"Lolli?"

I exhale. "You wouldn't believe me if I told you."

There's a long pause.

"How do you know what I wouldn't believe?"

I look up at her.

Can I trust her? The question reminds me of the impossible one Britt asked me before about the business card. Is Jada trustworthy? Yes. Can I trust her? I'm not so sure.

"I'm waiting." She crosses her arms.

I guess it doesn't matter what I think. I'm going to have to tell her either way.

I tell Jada everything, from being uncomfortable with the house ever since I was a baby, to the first time I'd encountered Madame LeNoir when I was eight, right up to Elsie explaining why we can see spirits, asking me to help her and meeting Clara.

When I'm done, Jada sits back in her chair for a moment and stares at the ceiling.

"Mind. Blown," she says.

I give her some time.

Eventually, she pushes herself back up. "So Clara really did run away."

"Yes."

"And you're seriously not making this up? This

isn't one of those things where you make me believe you and then laugh at me for it?"

I open my mouth, but before I can speak, she holds up a hand. "Don't answer that. I saw you up there. You were ... waiting for that thing to come and get you, just like you said. I could see it on your face."

"I honestly was."

Another pause. "Do you think she could really hurt you?"

"I'm not sure. I think the big danger is she could make me hurt myself."

Jada nods. "I get it. Fall down the stairs. Run outside into traffic. Something like that."

"Yes."

We both look up at street level as the audio begins to play *The Holly and the Ivy*. It sounds as if there are carollers outside. But then the spell is broken as some sneakered feet appear on the pavement and we hear other voices.

"Everyone's outside," I say. "They've finished the tour."

"I'd better let Mum know we're down here." Jada whips her phone out of her pocket and begins to text.

She receives a reply and then slips the phone back in her pocket. Her brow furrows. "So. This object that Clara's searching for. What do you think it could be?"

I shrug. "Anything. It has to be something that was in the house at the time."

"I mean, the obvious thing is the locket. You said Madame LeNoir was holding it when the binding thing happened."

I nod.

"And there was such a big deal about the locket after Clara left. Remember? It's in Mum's book. The police were pretty interested in finding it. The maid said she saw it after Clara had run away. Just the once. Then no one ever saw it again. Except Madame LeNoir, I guess. She must have hidden it."

I shrug again. I really don't know. The object could be the locket. But it also could be anything in this place. Anything at all.

"And whatever it is has to be destroyed?"

"So Clara says."

Jada pulls a face. "Well, it had better be something insignificant. Because if I destroyed something here on purpose, Mum would destroy me. Well, unless it was that china goose. You know the one in the

Regency drawing room? She hates geese. She has this thing about them because one bit her once."

"I don't think it's the china goose."

Jada jumps up. "Hey, let's go through the house. Let's look. Together."

"I don't think that ..."

She crosses her arms. "Well, you're not going to find it sitting there, are you?"

Fair point.

"Okay," I say. "But just give me a moment." I close my eyes and attempt to push Madame LeNoir's energy far, far away. I imagine that door again. I close it tight. I do the same for Clara. I feel bad about it, but it's the easiest way.

When I open my eyes again, Jada is waiting.

"Let's go," she says.

With the adults still hanging about outside, Jada and I are free to wander silently from room to room without being questioned. Jada holds things up, points at things, gestures and I shrug, shrug, shrug.

I have nothing.

No clue.

No idea.

It's like I told Clara — if she and Elsie haven't been able to work this out, how am I supposed to? All the objects are just objects to me. I don't get any feelings from them. They're just ... things. They all feel the same.

We go through all the rooms on the ground floor — the dining room, the study, the Victorian parlour — then start on the rooms on the first floor.

The drawing room, bedchamber and dressing-room done, Jada goes to start up the next set of stairs to the attic room.

I grip onto the handrail tight, remembering being shoved up the stairs. The exhaustion. The hunger. Everything that Clara had felt.

"Jada, no. Not up there." I shake my head. "I can't."

Jada turns to look at me as if I'm mad. "Well, that's where it is then. *Obviously.*"

"What?" My fingernails slice into the wood harder. I want to go back downstairs. Now.

"Whatever it is you have to find. It's in there. She's protecting it. That's why she hides out up there. Why she rushes down the stairs at you, like you said. It's all about the attic room and always has been. Don't you see? She's been trying to keep you out of there ever since you were little."

She runs up a couple of stairs like it's nothing. Easy.

"Come on, we have to search the room. It won't take long. There's barely anything in there. Just an old bed."

"*Jada.*" There is more in there than the old iron-and-brass bed I'd seen in Clara's past. That much I know for sure. As if to prove it, inside me, I feel something begin to slam against the iron door I'd closed so firmly in my mind.

Whump. Whump. Whump.

I take a step backwards.

"I can't, Jada. I can't go up there."

She's at the top of the stairs now. "Maybe you can't, but I can. I'm going in."

16

I'm spineless.

Pathetic.

I want to climb those stairs. I want to follow Jada into the attic room. I want to help look for the object that has Clara's spirit bound to this place.

But I just can't bring myself to do it.

Instead, I stand there on the stairs, like the spineless, pathetic thing that I am and I wait.

It's not long before Jada reappears, but it feels like forever.

"Nothing," she says. "Just the bed. I checked under the mattress and for any splits or hiding spots. I can't find any hollow spots in the floor or the walls, either."

I hesitate. What she said before — about it being obvious the object was in the attic room — I know she's right.

It makes perfect sense.

Why else would Madame LeNoir protect that room so fiercely?

"It's got to be there," I say.

"I checked everywhere. Why don't you come and see for yourself?"

"No, I ..."

"There's nothing there. Just the bed."

I don't know what to say to her.

Jada's eyes narrow. "Look, is this all some sort of hoax? Are you just having a laugh?"

I shake my head. "See? This is why I didn't want to tell you. This is why I don't talk about what I feel every time I step into this house. Because it always ends up like this."

"Like what?"

"Like you telling me I'm a liar. *How do you know what I wouldn't believe?*" I mimic. "Yeah, well, I know exactly what you'd believe, okay? I know, because when I tell people what I told you, I usually end up at the psychologist. So you can believe what you like.

Or not. I don't care. But I'm telling the truth."

Jada's eyes narrow. She stares at me for a moment longer. And then she runs down the stairs, pushing past me, without saying another word.

I make Freya take me back to the apartment after that. I tell her I've got a headache and I guess I must look pretty bad, because she believes me. She even lets me stay at the apartment while she goes back for the first open that evening, just as it gets dark. And I'm not exactly lying. I do have a headache. I feel awful. I feel awful because I can't help Elsie. I can't help Clara. Britt hates me. And Jada thinks I've lied to her.

I lie on the couch and try to watch TV, but all I can seem to think about is all the people I've let down.

I doze on and off and try to forget.

Freya gets back just after 8 pm and makes us some scrambled eggs and toast.

"One of these nights, we are definitely going to Borough Market." She points her fork at me as we perch on the bar stools at the kitchen bench and eat.

"Okay." I don't have the energy to argue with anyone else today.

After we eat, I take a shower and then slink into bed.

Freya comes to say goodnight and starts picking up items off the floor. One of them she inspects with more interest than my dirty socks.

"Tanice told me you'd borrowed a copy," she says, placing Tanice's book on my bedside table. "I have to say I was surprised to hear it. Good surprised."

I shrug.

She sits down on the end of the bed. "So, tomorrow. There are five opens at the house — ten, twelve, two, four and six. Suzie offered to have you at Tiny Pieces for the day."

"Okay," I say, but then remember Britt. Still, I'd rather deal with her than with Jada, Madame LeNoir and Clara. And Elsie.

"I guessed you'd want to go and I thought Jada would too, but when Tanice asked her, she wasn't interested. Is there something going on? Did you two have a falling-out?"

"Not really," I lie.

"Is this about not wanting to go to Beebee's for Christmas Day?"

"No." To be honest, I'd completely forgotten about that.

"Hmmm ..." Freya gives me the eye. "Well, something's going on. Look, you can go to Tiny Pieces tomorrow, but it would be great if you could try to get along with Jada. We've got another two long days of opens after tomorrow."

"I know."

There is a long pause.

"All right then, have a good sleep. Hopefully you'll feel better in the morning."

I don't feel a whole lot better in the morning, because thoughts of the house and the spirits who reside in it bash and crash like bumper cars in my mind. I dream of the iron door. Of Madame LeNoir's face oozing its way out of the wall, of Clara appearing behind me in the dressing-room mirror.

Madame LeNoir and Clara. Clara and Madame LeNoir and Clara and Madame LeNoir and Clara and ...

Elsie.

"Elsie," I whisper as I wake up and look at the stark white ceiling.

I've been avoiding Elsie. I know I have. And that's not okay.

I have to see her today. I have to make all of this better somehow.

I owe her that much.

Anyway, it's like Freya said. Elsie always knows what to do. Or knows someone who will know what to do.

I'll go there. This afternoon. I'll go and try to fix it ... somehow.

Freya drops me off at Tiny Pieces. "Call me if you need anything!" she says, rushing off.

"Big day today," Suzie says, as we watch Freya make her way down the street. She closes the yellow door. "Right. We've got a few people coming in today. I know Roberta's definitely coming. And Lisa and Peta."

"But probably not Britt," I add.

"Ah, yes. I ran into Britt and she told me something

happened, though she didn't say much. Want to talk about it?" Suzie goes over to one of the tables and perches on a stool. She pulls out another one and pats it. I notice she doesn't insist on Santa hats.

I go on over and sit down. I tell her about the coffee shop and seeing the business cards for the person who was offering dog training, sitting and walking. How I'd thought of Britt and picked one up. And then how I'd given it to her, but it had come out all wrong and we'd argued.

"She'll probably never come back now. I've scared her off."

"Oh, dear. Well, that does happen around here, Lolli. People come and people go and that's okay."

"But it's my fault. I was too pushy."

"You know something? I don't think that was the problem at all."

"You don't?"

"No. I think it's something else entirely. You stood in that cafe and you thought about Britt and you cared. The thing is, some of the people who come here — lots of them, in fact — don't have people who think about them. Who care. And sometimes when people start to care, it scares them. It's a lot

of new emotions to deal with and change can be ...
confronting."

"Oh." I've just remembered something.

"What is it?"

"Just ... Freya sometimes talks about Clementine
being like that. That sometimes if someone was being
nice to her, or helping her, or things were going too
well, she'd wreck things, or stop them."

"Ah, I see. Yes, that can happen. Sometimes it's
easier to stick with what you know, even if what you
know doesn't make you particularly happy. So, when
we offer to help, like you did with Britt, you have to be
okay with the fact that sometimes people will accept
that help and sometimes they won't. Sometimes it
will take a couple tries before they're ready to accept
help. Does that make sense?"

I nod. It does.

"You know, this whole situation reminds me
of your mum so much. Because while Clementine
found it hard to accept help, she loved helping
other people. She had a kind heart. And I can see
that you're the same, Lolli. I think you did the right
thing by thinking of Britt when you saw that card.
What would be wrong is if you didn't care about

Britt anymore because she hadn't immediately gone out and done what you wanted. And I can see you don't feel that way."

"No." I remember something else. "That's what Freya's parents did, isn't it? They didn't want her to take me and when she did it anyway, they stopped talking to her."

"Ah. Freya told me you'd met with Robyn. She also told me you were open to seeing her again."

"Sort of. I felt bad for her. She was trying pretty hard. She just got it all wrong."

"Well, that was understanding of you. I guess we all get it wrong sometimes. Maybe she's changed her mind about a few things now that she's creating a new life for herself?"

"Maybe. I hope so."

"Gosh. That's all very deep for eight thirty in the morning, isn't it?" Suzie laughs. "You know what we need after all that?"

"What?"

"Sugar. And I just happen to know a place that does excellent sugar. I think eggnog chai and a Christmas doughnut are in order."

17

We pull on our coats and Suzie locks up the shop. "Come on, this way," she says.

I follow her past lots of little shops until we're in some sort of massive market with a high covered ceiling where people seem to be opening up their stalls for the day.

"This is Old Spitalfields Market. There's been a market here for over three hundred and fifty years."

Uh-oh. That's pretty old. Still, I guess everything in London is old. I'm probably lucky I haven't seen the spirit of a Roman soldier yet.

"Probably a few less bao buns and dumplings on offer three hundred and fifty years ago ..." Suzie adds.

"Poor them."

"I know. I'll take bao buns and dumplings over bunches of watercress and violets any day." Suzie grins. "We're going over there." She points out one of the plywood "kitchens", which are laid out in a row, with a central eating space that has tables and stools.

"I don't think it's open," I say.

"Ah, but we're special."

We approach the raw concrete counter. There's a glass cabinet where doughnuts of all shapes and sizes are being laid out. Custard-filled doughnuts, Nutella doughnuts, matcha doughnuts and then a whole bunch of Christmas offerings as well.

"Sorry, we're not . . ." a curly-haired young woman behind the counter starts to say as we approach. But then she double-takes. "Aunt Suzie!" She ducks under the counter and envelops her in a massive hug. "I was saying to Mum the other night that you're just around the corner and you never come!"

"I can't come too often. I like the doughnuts too much! Now, Margot, this is Lolli."

"Oh, hi, Lolli! I've heard lots about you."

"Hi."

"I hope you like doughnuts."

"Are there people who don't like doughnuts?"

"There shouldn't be! After all, we have gluten-free doughnuts, dairy-free doughnuts and we cater for lots of different sorts of allergies. So there are no excuses, really. What's your poison? Maybe a Christmas doughnut? Tomorrow's Christmas Eve, after all. Anyway, take a look, Lolli. Think hard. It's an important decision and one not to be taken lightly."

"Pick one out for me too," Suzie says.

As the pair catch up, I go over and begin to inspect the doughnuts. I decide we should definitely get two Christmas ones and opt for one decorated like a wreath for Suzie and one decorated like a Christmas bauble for me, with rows of sparkly cachous. I'm just about to turn around when something to my right catches my eye.

There's a spirit wandering around the market.

Quickly, I look away, in case she's noticed me looking at her.

Acting as if I'm looking at something else entirely, I turn again. It's a woman. She wears a long white shroud. She looks worried. Sort of ... as if she's waiting for someone.

"Decided, Lolli?" Margot asks.

I point out the two doughnuts.

"Nice choice. The bauble is my favourite. I love decorating those."

Margot sets us up at the kitchen's bench with two stools.

"Two doughnuts, two eggnog chais and a very Merry Christmas to you." She places two plates and two cups in front of us.

"Thanks, Margot," I say. "Merry Christmas."

"Yes, Merry Christmas to my favourite niece," Suzie says.

"She always says that," Margot tells me. "I'm her only niece."

"Be fair, I only say the Merry Christmas bit at Christmas."

Margot rolls her eyes at me. "I can't believe I give her sugar. It only makes her worse."

Margot leaves us to our doughnuts and drinks. The eggnog chai is super-yummy — all warm milky vanilla and cinnamony spice.

"Good, right?" Suzie says.

I nod. It really is. The doughnut is great too ... and all over my fingers. I lick them one at a time, not wanting to waste one bit.

"Margot's always loved baking," Suzie says. "Right from when she was little. And I've always encouraged her by offering to taste-test anything and everything she bakes."

"That's good of you."

"I do what I can."

As we chat, I keep sneaking glances at the spirit.

Usually, after noticing one, I wouldn't look back again. I'd go about my day and pretend like I never saw anything at all.

But today is different. I don't know why. Today, I can't stop looking at her as she roams the marketplace. And the weird thing is, the longer I look at her, the clearer she becomes.

Finally, I look too long and our gaze connects.

And in that moment, she knows.

She knows I've seen her.

She doesn't come over or anything. Just stares at me curiously.

Then she beckons me over.

My first instinct is to run. But I don't. Instead, I keep looking. She doesn't seem so scary. She just looks like she wants something.

"All done?" Margot asks.

I nod. "It was so good. Thanks again."

"You're most welcome. I'd say come back any time, but Freya probably wouldn't let me fill you up on doughnuts. So any time you're allowed. Now, quick question about Christmas Day," she turns to Suzie.

"Can I just run over and look at those T-shirts?" I ask Suzie.

She looks at where I'm pointing.

"Sure, but stay where we can see you."

"Okay." I run off. I won't have much time.

The stall owner is busy putting out her stock, but the table she's already set up is the perfect cover to get close to the spirit.

The spirit stares at me curiously, still looking concerned about something. And maybe a little confused.

I'm not sure what to say. I beckon her over like she'd beckoned me. After a while, she approaches. "Can I ... help you?" I try.

"You must be careful," she says. "Of the water. It's not the miasma. It's the water that's made us all sick. I heard a doctor talking about it in the hospital. It's not the miasma at all. It was too late for me, but we must warn the others."

It takes me a moment to work out what she's talking about. Sickness. Water. Miasma. I think she's talking about cholera. There would have been lots of people around here who'd become sick from contaminated water. Is that really why she's here? To deliver a message about dirty water?

"But ... it's all right. The water's clean now," I whisper.

"The water's clean?"

"Yes. It's definitely safe to drink. They fixed it. The water can't make anyone sick anymore. You don't need to worry about that at all and ..."

She's gone.

I blink. Turn.

She's really gone.

But ... no. It can't be that easy, can it? That's all I needed to do? Just put her mind at rest?

Was it really me who did that?

It had to be.

So why haven't I done this before?

What was I afraid of?

I stand there, staring at cute T-shirts for what feels like a very long time.

I mostly think about Clara. About how she'd

asked me to help her. About how I'd made up excuses. I wasn't as strong as her. I wasn't as gifted as her. How could I find the object she was looking for when she and Elsie hadn't been able to locate it?

I hadn't even tried.

Not really.

I'd just said I couldn't do it.

Because I was scared.

"Best head back," Suzie says, coming over. "Everyone will be in soon and I haven't set up properly yet."

I begin to follow her.

But, as we go, I have one last question.

"Suzie, what's a miasma?"

"Goodness, that's an old word. I believe it's like bad air — matter in the air that could make you sick. Why do you ask?"

"Oh, I just heard it somewhere, that's all."

We don our Santa hats and get down to work as soon as we return. Suzie gives me another piece of the pretty yellow glass with the gold vein running through it and I sit at one of the tables and get clipping. I don't say a word, caught up in my thoughts. I think Suzie senses something is wrong, because she keeps trying to get me to talk.

"You're probably wondering why we need so much of the yellow," she says at one point. "It's because it's the focus of the whole mosaic."

"Oh."

She pauses a moment and gets up from her stool. "I wasn't going to show you, but then I figured you might not be back for the unveiling. And I think you need to see what it is you've been working on." She brings over a sketch to my table. "This is the original design. The sun is the central piece. Maybe it reminds you of someone?"

I look at the sketchbook. It's a picture of a sun, with a woman's face in the middle. Rays emanate outwards, curling and swirling. It's beautiful.

I hate it.

"It doesn't remind me of anyone at all," I snap.

"Lolli …" Suzie says softly. She sits down beside me. "I know it's hard to talk about it."

I want to cover my ears with my hands. I don't want to talk about it. If I don't talk about it, it's not real.

But all the time, I know Suzie's right.

I can't ignore this any longer. I have to stop ignoring and looking the other way. I thought it would make things easier, but I actually think it's made everything worse. And still … still I have to try to make it all right somehow. I have to fix things. What had Elsie said? Acknowledge the fear and then do exactly what I knew I should do anyway. I think about Clara too, and what she'd said about her scars. That they reminded her that she was strong. Maybe, deep down, I was strong too, even if I didn't always feel strong. I take a deep breath and take off my Santa hat.

"Suzie, I need to go back to the house."

18

Suzie texts Freya and walks me back to the house. As we go, I tell her things she wants to hear. That the mosaic is going to look great. That I can't wait to see it. I don't want her to worry about me.

"I'll see you both soon." Suzie squeezes my shoulder and leaves me standing on the pavement with Freya outside the house. Freya's holding a white cardboard bakery box.

"I didn't think you'd be back so soon," Freya says. "The first viewing went really well. We're setting up for the second one now."

"What's that?" I nod at the box.

"Mince pies for the next viewing."

I know they serve the mince pies by the hearth. "I can take them down to the kitchen if you like."

"Would you? That would be helpful. Someone stumbled and knocked a figurine over in the parlour. I need to go and help Tanice clean it up. Wait. Offering to put out the mince pies doesn't mean *eating* the mince pies, does it?"

I roll my eyes. "I know not to eat the mince pies. Anyway, I just had a doughnut and an eggnog chai. Suzie's niece Margot has a stall in Old Spitalfields Market."

"That sounds pretty good."

"It was. It looked like they had pretty yummy food there. We should go to that one you've been talking about tonight."

"Borough Market? We should. We will. Definitely. It's a date."

"Okay." I wrestle the box off her. "Really. I won't eat them."

"What's the big rush with getting to the kitchen?"

"Um, warmth?" It's not like I can tell her the truth.

Finally she passes me the box. "Okay, just remember to wash your hands before you touch any food. I'll be down as soon as we've cleaned up the parlour."

Down in the kitchen, I wash my hands and carefully place the mince pies out on the cake stand that's waiting for them.

Then I turn to Elsie's chair.

"You've been avoiding me, Olivia," she says. "Again."

"I know. Sorry." I slink on over and sit down in the other carver chair. I can barely meet her eyes.

"Clara told me you don't want to help her. I have to say I'm disappointed, Lolli. I thought you could do this. I really did."

"You don't understand. I do want to help her ..." I'm already fighting to keep back my tears.

If Elsie notices this, she doesn't say anything. Her expression remains stern. "Then why did you tell her you couldn't?"

"You think it's because I'm scared," I say. "You think it's because I'm scared of Madame LeNoir, don't you?"

"Isn't it?"

"No! It's not about Madame LeNoir at all. Yes, I'm scared of her, but it's not about that."

An angry huff. "What is it then?"

"It's because I know how it works. I can feel it. I could feel it the moment I entered the house. If I find the object and destroy it like Clara wants, then she'll leave. And Madame LeNoir will disappear as well because her soul is bound to Clara's. That's all that's keeping her here."

"Yes. I know all this. Of course I do."

"So, don't you see? Don't you see why I don't want to help Clara? If I help her, it's not just Madame LeNoir who will go with her. *You'll* go too. You'll go and leave me all over again, Elsie." The horrible, ugly tears can be held back no longer.

I'd known it all along. Of course I had. It had happened only weeks after Elsie's visit to Singapore. The cancer had returned with a vengeance. Before Freya and I could make it to London, Elsie had slipped away. We'd flown to London for a few days — just to attend the big funeral at Christ Church Spitalfields. But that didn't mean I was going to admit she was gone. It hurt too much to do that.

So I didn't. I went back to Singapore and I pretended she was still alive. I told myself I'd see her at Christmas, like we'd agreed. And when we'd arrived and I'd seen her sitting in that chair by the hearth, I'd let myself keep right on pretending. I'd let myself believe I still had her. That she was still mine. Here, in the living world.

It was why I'd never been able to close Clara or Madame LeNoir's energies out. Not completely. Because if I wanted to see Elsie, I had to let them in too.

It was why I'd got so angry with Clara when she'd started talking about needing someone in the living world to destroy the object she was searching for. She'd been about to say Elsie couldn't do that for her anymore. So I'd stopped her. Refused to help. Run away.

And it was why I didn't want to admit it was Elsie's face that was pictured in the sun mosaic. The mosaic was obviously going to be a beautiful tribute to Elsie who was so important to so many people in Spitalfields.

I didn't want to admit to any of this because Elsie was my sun. My hearth. My safe, warm place. She was everything to me. I couldn't lose her again.

I just couldn't.

"Oh, Lolli ..." All of Elsie's anger has disappeared, her face soft.

"It's like you said in the ginger garden. I don't have anyone. It's only you and Freya. And if I let you go again, it's just Freya. And that's not enough, Elsie, it's not enough!"

"I know, sweetheart. I know it's not enough."

I sniff. "You tried to tell me that day, I know you did. But I didn't listen. You had things to say and I just brushed you away. Like I didn't care about you. But I did. Really, I did. I do."

"Oh, Lolli. Never for a moment did I think you didn't care. You simply weren't ready to listen. But you're ready now, I can see that."

I nod.

"We can fix this. You can fix it."

I pause. "You don't think it's too late? You think I can have more people?"

Elsie laughs that hearty laugh of hers that I've missed so much. "Sweet girl, I don't think it's too late. Lolli, the things you've had to deal with — your mum, your grandmother, Freya's parents — lots of adults can't deal with those sorts of things. You understanding all of this — understanding what I was trying to tell you in Singapore — I'm very proud of you."

"I'm sorry I didn't listen."

"It's all right, Lolli. You don't need to apologise. Anyway, maybe it's all happening as I planned? Remember I told you I wanted you to think about things and we'd talk about it at Christmastime? Well, look at us, sitting here, talking about it all."

I cough-hiccough-laugh. "This was your plan?"

"Hmm. Maybe not entirely. But it does prove what I already knew."

"What did you know?"

"That what we have — the two of us — is stronger than my old, sick body being here. It transcends that. Remember what I said about being connected to the past, to the present and to the future?"

I nod.

"Well, I can be connected to your future too. What you've learnt — about being open to people and experiences — think of that as a little piece of me that you can keep alive. You can treat that advice like the hearth here. Stoke it. Keep the flame bright. And I'll always be with you that way."

I nod. Listening now. *Really* listening. Like I wish I'd listened in the ginger garden.

"I really do want to help Clara. And maybe other spirits too. I helped one today."

"You did?"

I tell Elsie all about the lady in the market.

"Well, look at you."

"It was easier than I thought it would be. I mean, I don't think they would all be easy to help like that, but after I'd spoken to her, I couldn't really think why I hadn't done it before."

"For many reasons. But you can start now. That's the main thing."

I turn in my seat. "What about Clara? Can she come down here? Can I talk to her?"

"Oh, yes. She's been here the whole time. But she can only be seen as a reflection, remember?"

I look around the room. There's no mirror here. But then I spot something. I jump up and grab the big, shiny copper kettle and hold it up in front of me.

And there's Clara, standing behind me. She goes over to kneel beside Elsie's chair so I can see both of them at the same time.

"I'm sorry, Clara. I really am. I hope you understand."

"Of course I understand. I'm just happy you've come back. Elsie was worried about you. We both were."

A noise overhead sees all three of us look up.

"We have to hurry," I say. "Freya and Tanice will be down in a minute. So, tell me what I have to do to find this object. And when I've found it, I have to destroy it. Right?"

Elsie sits forward in her chair. "Yes. I'm worried about how much time we have. After Christmas, who knows what will happen? With you and Freya planning to return to Singapore, there's no saying what will happen to the house and its contents."

"You mean it will close?"

"I don't know. That's all up to Freya now the house is hers and I'm not sure what she's going to want to do. We had discussed Freya closing up here and doing a revamp for her cabinet of curiosities. But that would mean change, and change would mean items would be sold, or boxed up and stored. We'll just have to try our hardest to find this object with the time we have. Clara and I have been hoping your fresh eyes will work some magic."

"We've ransacked the house," Clara says. "Both in the living and twilight worlds. We've come to believe that whatever the object is, it's hidden."

I think of Jada's theory. "And you've tried the attic room?" I ask Elsie.

"Neither Clara nor I can go in there now because of Madame LeNoir's energy, but I could when I was in the living world. I searched and searched for a secret compartment, or a concealed space in the wall. Nothing."

I shake my head. I'm still sure Jada's right. "It has to be up there. It's the only thing that makes sense. Why else would she be so desperate to protect that space?"

"Well, it was her home," Clara says. "She spent years there as a virtual recluse."

"I know, but she guards it so fiercely. I honestly believe that's where the object is. Whatever it is. So that's where I'm going to try first."

19

"A re you sure you'll be all right up there?"
Freya sounds dubious. "It's not very nice.
And it's not heated."

I nod. "I'll be fine. I'll wear my coat. I just want
to have a poke around. I haven't been up there yet."

Freya pauses. Her mouth opens and shuts. "Well,
okay then. It's good that you seem to be losing your
fear of the house. I'm proud of you."

"Mmm ..." I make agreeing noises as I slip my
coat on. If only she knew my fear has spiked to new
levels now that I'm about to make the journey to the
attic. I head for the kitchen door before either Freya
changes her mind, or I chicken out.

"Jada should be here in about half an hour. I'll send her up when she arrives."

"Okay." Whatever I do up there, I'd better be quick about it. I'm not sure it would be a good idea for Jada to walk in unannounced. I don't know what Madame LeNoir is capable of. "See you soon," I say, still hovering in the doorway. I have to force myself not to run back over to Freya. To hug her. To cling on to her.

I don't want to go upstairs.

I don't want to do this.

But I'm going to do it anyway.

The first two flights of stairs are okay. I can feel Madame LeNoir's energy, like always, but she keeps her distance. It's almost like she's curious as to what I'm doing. I think she knows that something's changed. That something's different this time.

As I reach the final set of stairs — the ones that lead up to the attic room — my heart really starts to thump about in my chest. I close my eyes for a moment. Take a deep breath. I think of Elsie. Of Clara. They need me to do this. They believe I can do this.

I can do this.

Keeping my eyes closed, slowly, carefully, I open up those iron doors in my mind that I'd attempted to keep Madame LeNoir behind.

When I've done this, my eyes snap open again.

I feel the full force of her now. Waiting. Watching. Guarding.

Gulping down the sick feeling rising in my throat, I start up the stairs, gripping the handrail tight as I go. It takes forever and no time at all to reach the top. And when I get to the door, I don't hesitate. I kick it open wide with my foot.

She is everywhere and nowhere.

Small attic windows, half-obscured with time-worn wooden shutters, let in filtered winter light. The floorboards are wide and bare and the only items upon them are a dusty old travelling trunk and an uncomfortable-looking iron-and-brass bed with an ancient mattress. The walls may have been cream once, in Clara's time, but today are a grimy grey.

I understand now why Elsie decided to leave this room be. To not even use it as a storage room.

It is empty, but obviously occupied.

She is the room and the room is her.

"I know you're here," I call out to Madame LeNoir. "I can feel you."

There is no answer. No movement.

I go over and open the trunk. It's empty.

I lift the mattress and look underneath. Nothing. Check for slits down the side of the mattress and loose seams. Again, nothing.

There is still no movement in the room. I begin to check each wall for cracks, holes, secret compartments. I can't find any.

That done, I check the floorboards, one by one. They all seem firmly fixed.

I go over and stand in the middle of the small room. "So, are you coming out or not?" I try to sound like this is what I want, but the wobble in my voice gives me away. I clear my throat. "You don't scare me. Come out and talk to me properly. Stop lurking in the walls, spying on me and get out here."

At first there's nothing. But then there's a stillness. An airlessness. Even more so than before. Time slows. And then the wall directly in front of me, beside the window, begins to shift and move. With a ripple, it begins to push outwards. A face slowly swells.

Madame LeNoir.

I recoil as the mottled grey wall warps to reveal that pinched, downturned mouth, the deep-set eyes and the little round glasses. Those eyes stare at me, unblinking, seeing all.

I go to take a step back and then force myself not to. No. I have to stand my ground.

I can do this.

"Well?" I say.

The mouth twists into a smirk. "I thought you might never get here. So much running away like a skittish jack rabbit."

I can't let her get to me. "I'm here for the object."

"Oh? Which object might that be?"

"Don't pretend you don't know. I mean the object you bound Clara's soul to so she can't leave."

"Ah, that object. I suppose she's made you feel sorry for her with her pretty ways and darling curls. Don't forget she has trapped me here in this wretched place in exactly the same manner. I am in gaol just as much as she. And now she's caught your old friend up in it all too. She can't leave until Clara leaves. That was a mistake."

"No, it wasn't. Elsie knew what would happen. But she wanted to help anyway. It was her choice to offer to stay. To bind herself to Clara and help her find the object."

"Well, now she'll be helping forever."

"It doesn't have to be that way. If you tell me where the object is, I can destroy it and you can all be free."

The face thrusts forward. Not properly formed, it is like melted, dripping wax. "No!" she screeches, lips stretching horribly. "She will never leave this place! I took that girl in out of the goodness of my heart. I fed her. Clothed her. Made something of her. I made it possible that she could give readings to the Queen herself!"

I take a step closer. "You didn't take her in out of the goodness of your heart. You took Clara in so you could use her. And then you did just that. You might have bought her some clothes. But you also starved her. And you made her lie to the Queen. And to lots of other people too. People who were lonely and sad and missed their loved ones who'd died. And Clara didn't run away. You forced her to leave because of how you treated her. I saw what you did to her. Felt it. She was so weak. If she'd stayed here she would have died of starvation."

A sneer forms. "Think what you like of me. The girl owed me. And now she pays for it. Do you know what happened after she left? Everyone assumed I'd done away with her! And she did nothing about that. She just let them believe it was true. She ruined me. That stupid girl ruined me when she left that locket. The maid saw it and tattled and that was the end of it."

"But don't you see that none of that matters now? You can leave. You can leave and be happy. You can finally be free of each other."

"I'd rather stay and make her pay. It's as I said. She will never leave this place. I made sure of it. And I'll continue to make sure of it."

This isn't going well. She honestly doesn't seem to care if she's stuck here forever, so long as Clara is miserable. I think for a moment. "I know the object is up here." I try. I don't, of course, it's just a guess. A hunch. But it's worth a try. "Is it the locket? Is that what you bound her soul to? You were holding it in the vision she showed me."

The beady eyes stare at me. "Was I now?"

"You know you were."

Her cloudy eyes flick away. "And so what if I was? Go home, girl. Go home and leave us all be."

"No. I won't." There's something about how she doesn't want to discuss the locket. Something that makes me believe more than ever that it's the object I need to find. And if she'd hidden it away all those years ago, where else would she hide it, but the one place she spent almost all her time?

It has to be here.

It just has to be.

"Where's the locket?" I take my chances. "Where did you hide it?"

Keeping one eye on her, I begin to move about the room once more. I run my hands over every surface I can see. I must have missed something.

I open the trunk and feel the lining on the top and bottom. Check each wall again for the slightest bump, or crack.

The eyes watch me as I go.

"And what would you do, girl, if you found it?"

"I'd destroy it. That's what Clara says we have to do." I'm surprised she's asking this. Surely she knows that's our plan? She would have heard us talking.

She takes her time in responding, her gaze resting on something just behind me. When she sees me looking, her eyes dart away.

Ever so slowly, I turn. But there's nothing there. Nothing I could have missed. Just the blank wall and the bed, standing before it.

And then I see it.

I have missed something.

The bed has four posts on the corners, each topped with a brass knob.

And one of the knobs is ever so slightly shinier than the others.

I hesitate and then lunge for it. I grasp the knob and twist.

It loosens.

"No! Stop!" Madame LeNoir screeches, the wall throbbing. "Get away from there, girl. Get! Go!"

I keep twisting. The knob is stiff, but it turns. I grab it with both hands and force it.

It falls off and clatters to the floor.

Along with something else ...

A tarnished silver locket.

20

The wall heaves and surges as I run from the attic room, the locket clasped tightly in my hand.

"Give it to me, girl! Give it back!"

I ignore her and run.

I'm out the attic door in a second, bolting down the wooden steps at breakneck speed. I grab the newel post and throw myself around the corner. Jada is on the landing, her mouth open with surprise at all the noise I'm making.

All the noise I promised Freya I wouldn't make.

"Lolli, shhh!" she says. "There's a group in the dining room."

"I've got it!" I call out, as I pass her by. "I've got

the locket!" I can't stop to explain. There's no time. I've got to get to the hearth before Madame LeNoir catches me. Before she can stop me somehow.

"You what?" Jada says.

Another turn and I'm down the next set of stairs. I take them two at a time, jumping down the last three. I see the backs of two visitors entering the dining room and they turn to look at what all the noise is about.

Freya steps from a room and throws her hands up. "Lolli!" she mouths, her eyes wide.

"Sorry!" I mouth back, again not stopping to explain. I sprint as silently as I can along the hall.

I don't care about upsetting visitors.

All that matters is getting to the kitchen.

Getting to the hearth. Destroying the locket. Saving Elsie and Clara.

I'm down that last set of stairs in a heartbeat. As I cross the slate floor, I can hear footsteps thumping above me – Freya, Jada.

I snatch at an iron poker next to the hearth.

I throw the locket into the fire and ram the poker down into it.

One.

Two.

Three.

Over and over I stab at it, oblivious to anything else.

Over and over and over. Slam, slam, slam.

"Lolli!"

"Lolli! Stop!"

I hear my name as if from far away, but it isn't until the poker is wrenched from my hand that I'm able to pay any attention.

I watch silent, panting, as Freya pries the poker from my fingers. She steps forward and fishes about with it in the fire, pulling something out of the glowing coals.

She drops the item on the slate floor.

We all stare at it.

The locket is horribly warped and twisted, dented and bashed.

Freya gasps, seeming to recognise the piece of jewellery. "Oh, my." She drops onto her hands and knees to inspect the item more closely, Jada hovering behind her. "Oh. Oh, no." Her gaze lifts to meet mine. "The locket. Clara's locket! Lolli. Lolli, how could you?"

And that's when the laughing starts.

Freya can't hear it.

Jada can't hear it.

But I can hear it.

The terrible, evil cackle fills my head just as I begin to realise that I can still feel Elsie and Clara.

They are still here.

"You stupid girl." The cackling stops and Madame LeNoir's voice fills my head. "You walked right into my trap. And now *you'll* go. Swiftly ferried away to your foreign land once and for all. So, go now. Go and leave me in peace. It's as I told you so many times over. Clara will never leave this place. Never. Never. *Never.*"

What happens next is so awful I never want to think about it again, but I know it will keep me up night after night as I replay it in my head. Freya gets Jada to fetch Tanice. She has to be told the story twice before she'll believe what's happened. Tanice turns on Jada, thinking she's involved in the locating and destroying of the locket. Through rivers of tears,

I tell both Tanice and Freya time and time again that Jada had nothing to do with it. That it was all me.

Through my pleading, Madame LeNoir keeps laughing at me, lapping up every minute of the show. She couldn't be happier that I've played right into her hands. I wonder if this was her plan all along — right from the moment I stepped into the house — and she just took her time in executing it.

However long she's been planning this, her idea to get rid of me has worked perfectly. I doubt I'll ever be allowed to set foot in this place ever again. Freya won't let me. And after what's happened, Freya won't want to turn it into something new like her cabinet of curiosities. She won't want to have anything to do with it now I've made it a place full of bad memories for her. She'll probably want to sell it and everything in it. And both Clara and Elsie will be stuck here forever.

Stuck here with Madame LeNoir.

Tanice offers to take over the last viewing of the day so Freya can take me back to the apartment.

"That would probably be for the best," Freya says through gritted teeth. "I don't think Lolli should be here one minute longer."

We walk back to the apartment in silence. On the way, she begins texting someone. Suzie, I think.

When we get to the apartment, Freya lets me in. "Just go to your room for a bit while I calm down. And then we'll talk."

I do exactly as I'm told. I slink into my room and lie facedown on the bed. I don't even take my coat or shoes off. I don't think I have the energy.

In the lounge room, Freya makes a phone call. Every so often, I hear snippets of what she's saying. *I don't understand ... I thought she wasn't scared of the house anymore ... to destroy something so precious ... really concerned ... so unlike her ... think we should just go ...* Eventually she must move to another part of the room, because I can't hear her anymore.

I lie on the bed for what feels like hours before I get up the courage to creep out to the lounge room. Freya is sitting at the kitchen bench, just staring at it. When she notices me, she looks over. Her eyes are red.

"Hungry?" she says.

I shake my head.

"Me neither."

I remember how we were finally supposed to go

to Borough Market. I guess that's another thing I've wrecked.

Freya sighs, swivelling on her seat. "I don't know what to say, Lolli. I know you didn't want to come here. I know you're upset about Elsie. And that you've always had feelings about the house. But I didn't know you were this angry."

"I'm not angry."

"You seem angry. What you were doing with that poker — you were furious."

"That was different ... I ..." There's no way to explain. I can't make her understand. She won't understand. And, to be honest, I don't blame her. How could she possibly understand? Anything I told her would just sound like rantings from someone who'd lost their mind. Spirits that can only be seen as a reflection and faces in walls and hidden lockets with souls bound to them.

Or without souls bound to them, as it turns out.

Freya runs her hands through her hair. "Oh, I wish Elsie was here. She would know what to say. What to do."

I want to scream when she says this. To yell. Of course she would! I want to shout from the rooftops.

It was Elsie who asked me to destroy the locket! What I end up doing is shrugging. "You just don't understand."

"Then help me to understand. Try to explain. I'm listening."

I stare at Freya for a moment or two. Is there a way? Can there be a way? I guess I have to try.

I take a deep breath. "I thought something would happen. If I destroyed the locket."

"Wait. Like what? Like you thought I'd take you back to Singapore?"

I shake my head quickly. "No. Not that."

"Then what?"

"I thought . . ." I stop myself again. I can't. I'm going to sound insane. It will only lead to more trouble.

But Freya presses on. "Did you think that Elsie might come back? Something like that?"

Another shake of my head. "I can't. I can't say."

"Is someone asking you to keep secrets from me? To do things?"

"No!" Well, sort of. But not in the way that she means.

"And Jada really, truly didn't know?"

"She honestly didn't know I was up there." This is true.

We stare at each other, at an impasse.

When she sees we're clearly going nowhere, Freya crosses her arms.

"I wish you could tell me what's going on, Lolli, I really do. I'm not sure what to do now. I need to be at the house tomorrow for the Christmas Eve viewings and I don't think that's a good place for you to be."

"I can stay here. I won't do anything … weird. I promise."

Freya sighs. "I'd just told Tanice we'd go to her place for Christmas Day too. You and Jada were getting on so well. Now I'm not sure about that either."

"I'm sorry. I really am. I thought … I thought things would be different." But now I say this, I wonder if they really would have been? My plan had only ever been to find the object and destroy it. What did I think was going to happen afterwards? I suppose I'd hoped to destroy the locket in secret and that Freya would never find out and Clara and Elsie (and Madame LeNoir) would be released and it would all be over.

"I thought things would be different too," Freya replies.

21

I spend Christmas Eve in the apartment, reading Tanice's book over and over again. I search for anything I might have missed. Any hint of what object in the house Clara might be bound to.

I find nothing.

I still can't believe how I fell for Madame LeNoir's trap. Looking back, I see that it had all been far too easy. For a start, she'd allowed me to enter the attic room. She could have tried to stop me. But she didn't. That should have been my first clue that something was up. And then she'd let me have a big old hunt around. Made me think I'd outwitted her. That it was me who'd spotted the shiny bed knob. That I'd worked out her secret hiding place myself. Not only this, she hadn't really tried to stop me from twisting the bed knob off, had she? I can't remember her exact words, but it had been something along the lines of ... *oh, no. Stop. Don't. Give it back.* She hadn't even chased me down.

She was controlling everything the whole time.

And, like a fool, I hadn't noticed any of this, because I'd been so pleased with myself. Desperate to run straight to the hearth to destroy the locket.

Just like Madame LeNoir wanted.

The only thing in all of this that makes me feel slightly better is that I know Madame LeNoir thinks I'm a threat. Why else would she have wanted me to do something that would make Freya take me away once and for all? In life, she was so proud of that locket. I doubt she truly wanted to see it destroyed. But she was willing to give up her hoarding of it to get rid of me.

Why?

Because she was scared of me.

Madame LeNoir was — is — scared of me.

She knows I have the ability to find whatever it is that's holding Clara hostage.

In a way, she believes in me just as much as Elsie and Clara do.

I like the thought of this very much. Because it means releasing Clara and Elsie is a real possibility. Madame LeNoir knows I can do it.

I just have to work out *how*.

With renewed energy, I begin to brainstorm. I find some paper and a pen and begin to do a mind map like we've done at school, trying to get all my rambling thoughts out of my head and down on paper. Maybe the answer has been right under my nose the whole time. Maybe it's completely obvious. The mind map ends up a scribbled mess of headings and bubbles and off-shoots, but it feels good to untangle my thoughts from the snarled mess in my mind.

When I can't think of anything else to write, I lie down on the carpet and try something different – I do a walk-through of the house in my mind. Room by room I go, pretending I'm there, hoping that something might stand out. That a clue might be delivered to me.

Sadly, nothing does.

After this, I try Tanice's book again, concentrating on the photos this time. There are a few of Madame and Monsieur LeNoir with their spiritualist groups, posing inside the house. I look at those particularly closely, but I can't see anything unusual in them.

I hunt and hunt and hunt.

What's the object?

What could it be?

I spend all day on these questions and come up with a Big. Fat. Nothing.

I know the last viewing of the day is at 4 pm, so I'm surprised when Freya arrives back at the apartment just before 5 pm, laden with shopping bags.

"Tanice gave me an early mark," she says, dumping everything on the kitchen bench. "I realised I pretty much had nothing for Christmas Day. No presents. No food. I might have had a bit of a panic and she took pity on me."

"We can just go out tomorrow and find something to eat. We always find something."

Freya turns and begins to pull off her gloves. "Ah, about that. We're going to Tanice's for Christmas Day. She and Beebee are insisting."

I jump up. "What? Do we have to?" My stomach flip-flops at the thought of seeing Tanice again.

"Yes, we have to! It's very nice of Tanice and her family to include us."

"But ..." I can't help it. My eyes well up.

Freya comes over. "It'll be all right. Really, it will. Tanice is a good person. She's very worried about you. Anyway, let's cross that bridge when we come to it. Right now the bridge we need to cross is dinner. Which I haven't sorted. Oh! Hang on. Let me just check ..." She pulls out her phone and searches for something. "Well, there you go. We have another two hours before closing time. Come on, grab your coat. Scarf and gloves too. We'll be outside for a while."

"Where are we going?"

"We, Lolli girl, are finally going to Borough Market."

It's windy and cold outside and the moment we exit the revolving door of our building, we tug our beanies on and pull the hoods of our jackets right up.

"It's about a fifteen-minute walk across London Bridge. Should we get a cab?" Freya asks.

I've been cooped up all day. "Let's walk."

So we do. Rugged up in a scarf and a beanie and a hood, I don't get the most amazing view of the world outside, but what I do see is sparkly and bright. Christmas lights twinkle, reflected in the puddles some recent rain has left. People scurry by with bulging bags; having done their last-minute shopping, they're hurrying home. A man sells singed-black roasted chestnuts, cracks revealing their soft insides. A woman tends to some sweet-smelling candied peanuts that sizzle away as she stirs. I drink in all the movement and colour, surprised to find how alive the streets are. I think, sometimes, when you're not feeling so good inside yourself, you can start to believe that the rest of the world feels the same way. But away from the silent apartment, life is happening. Christmas is coming.

We've just passed the nut lady, when I see a man standing just behind a crowd of people at a bus stop.

A spirit.

Before he notices me, I avert my eyes.

I can't help you. I couldn't help Clara, or Elsie, or even Britt, in the living world. And I can't help you.

I don't look up again. I ignore the man. I ignore the lights. The decorations. The anticipation on people's faces. I just concentrate on my feet. I might have helped the spirit at the other market, but it was a fluke. I'd just got lucky.

Pulled along by the tide of people, we arrive faster than expected.

"Just in here." Freya guides me in. "We've got exactly an hour and a half because they pack up early tonight, so let's make it good."

Underneath the huge hanging wreaths, we start inspecting all the stalls — colourful fruit and vegetables, as bright as any bauble, cheeses stacked like presents under a Christmas tree. And then the ready-to-eat food — Iraqi and Cypriot, Korean and Taiwanese. It all looks so good.

"This place is amazing," I say.

"I'm pretty sure I could live here quite happily," Freya replies.

For a brief, fleeting moment, everything feels normal between us.

Unfortunately, it doesn't last.

Freya choses a spinach and feta gozleme and I get some soup and dumplings. We manage to find a table and perch on some stools.

But as we eat, it becomes more and more obvious that the mood at our table is as cold as the winter air. All around us, people laugh and chat and take selfies.

We don't take any selfies.

How could I? How could I?

How could I have damaged the locket?

The question echoes in Freya's green eyes.

How could you? How could you?

How could you have damaged the locket?

Every so often, when our gaze meets awkwardly, Freya gives me a "aren't we having such a great time!" fake smile.

It only makes me feel worse.

Things are so bad, we don't even get dessert. We leave behind the candy cane brownies, the gingerbread ice-cream, hot jam doughnuts and the steaming Nutella crepes. We just trudge on back to the apartment again.

We're about halfway across the bridge when Freya pulls over to one side and stops. She takes off a glove and holds her hand out.

"Is that ... snow?" she says, looking up.

That's when the icy rain starts to pelt down.

We run all the way back to the apartment.

By the time we get there, we're both soaked.

Which is okay, as it turns out, because this means I have an excuse to get straight into the shower.

And, in the shower, I can cry where Freya won't know.

22

J'm not expecting Christmas Day to be any better than Christmas Eve. When I open my eyes, the bedside clock tells me it's 8.45 am. Hours later than I've ever slept in on Christmas Day.

I force myself to get out of bed. I find Freya at the kitchen bench drinking coffee. She gives me three new books and a T-shirt I'd pointed out in a storefront window. I give her a bracelet she'd seen at a shop in Singapore months ago.

Then we sit about and look at each other.

"I'm sorry it's not much," she says. "I thought we might have a little more time to do things. Get out and about. Markets. Shops."

"That's okay." I just want the day to be over and done with. I'm dreading going to Tanice's. Having to spend the day trapped in a room full of people who know what I've done, but not why I've done it ... I can't think of anything worse.

I practically beg to walk to Tanice's, but Freya sees straight through me.

"No. We're not going to be late today. And anyway, I've got presents and food and things to carry. Here, take this." She hands me a large hessian carry bag.

"Oof. What's in it?"

"Plum pudding and rum butter and brandy butter and mince pies and cranberry shortbread."

Okay, so maybe it's worth carrying then.

Sadly, it doesn't take us long to get to Tanice's. The lift is working again at their apartment block, which means it's a quick ride to the top floor.

Just my luck.

Tanice herself opens the door.

"Merry Christmas, Freya! Merry Christmas, Lolli!"

"Merry Christmas," we chime.

"Come on in, come on in. Here, let me take your coats. You're the first here. My sisters are always late!"

As I peel my coat off, I take a deep breath, readying myself. I hand my coat to Tanice.

"Tanice, I'm sorry. Really, I am. About the locket."

Tanice's bright smile falters. "Ah, yes. Well, I'm sorry too. The thing is, we'd been hoping to find that locket for such a long time. But I know you've been through a hard year, Lolli. An upsetting year."

Beebee and Jada have been loitering during our exchange. Beebee moves forward.

"Chin up, buttercup," she says. "I know you must have your reasons."

Seriously, I almost start crying. I'd rather they were all angry with me. I'm not sure I can handle everyone being nice. My eyes begin to well up. Just as they're about to spill over, Jada speaks up.

"I keep telling you all. Madame LeNoir made her do it." There's something in her voice that tells me she's been saying this a lot.

Tanice throws her daughter a fierce look. "I said no more talk about ghosts, Jada. I made that very clear. I told you Lolli's always been concerned about ghosts in the house and now I'm worried that it's your talk that's led to the locket being ruined. So no more. Not one word. I think it's time we put it all behind us. We're looking into the locket being restored and that's that. What we have to do today is concentrate on having a lovely Christmas. Yes?"

I try to nod and smile, but I find it difficult. How am I going to have a lovely Christmas knowing that the minute it's over, Freya will surely change our flights and we'll be out of here. After that, I'm really not sure what will happen to the house. What if Elsie and Clara really are stuck in it forever with Madame LeNoir and her horrible cackly laugh.

Jada sighs. "Can we go to my room and use my new art set?"

"Yes. *But no ghost talk.*"

"I know! I know! Come on, Lolli." She stomps off down the hallway. I follow her, grateful to be leaving the adults behind.

When we get to her room, Jada closes the door behind us until it's left open only a crack. She goes over to her little desk and grabs a box before she sinks to the floor, cross-legged. "I thought we'd never get out of there," she whispers.

I go and sit down across from her.

"You and me both."

"Thanks for not telling them I knew about things," Jada says.

"Thanks for still talking to me after I yelled at you."

"That's okay. So, tell me exactly what happened. How did you find the locket? Where was it?"

I tell Jada everything. I tell her about Madame LeNoir. The bed knob. About destroying the locket. And how I'd then realised Elsie and Clara hadn't been released.

"She wanted me to find it," I say in a low voice. "Madame LeNoir, I mean. It was her plan. She knew Freya would take me home if I did something like that. And she was right."

"Wait. You're going home? Back to Singapore?"

"Well, that was always the plan, but now I think we'll go earlier. I don't think Freya's changed the flights yet, but I bet she's going to."

Jada thinks for a bit. "Making you wreck the locket was a pretty smart plan."

"Madame LeNoir's clever. Mean and clever. A bad combination."

"Her not wanting you around. It's kind of a good sign. Like she's worried about what you might do. What you might be able to do."

"Do you think so? I thought that too. Still, it doesn't matter now, does it? I can't see how I'm going to find the object that Clara's soul is bound to. There's no way Freya's going to let me go back to the house."

"I wish I could help. After you'd gone, I went through all the rooms, but I couldn't feel anything."

"I know. Thanks for trying."

Jada leans forward over her art set. "Even if you can't go to the house, I'll keep looking. Every time I'm there. Though I don't know if Mum will let me go back to the house anytime soon either."

"I'm sorry I dragged you into all this."

Jada shrugs. "Hey, that's what friends are for."

Friends. The words stops me in my tracks. We're friends? I guess we are.

I smile at Jada and she smiles back.

Friends. Elsie would like this. I know she would.

There's movement in the hallway.

"Quick." Jada opens the art set with lightning speed. "Draw something. Something happy. No ghosts or lockets or anything like that."

I laugh. "No ghost lockets. How about something cute and sweet. Like a rainbow. Or butterflies."

"Better make it both."

Lying in bed, I can barely believe Christmas Day turned out way better than I thought. No one was mad at me, or gave me funny looks. There were even a few times during lunch that I forgot about the locket and what I'd done altogether and was able to concentrate on eating lots of delicious things I'd never had before like gungo peas soup and sweet potato pudding.

None of this solves my problem, though — how am I going to help Clara and Elsie? I can't seem to go to sleep, however hard I try. For some reason, every time I close my eyes my mind keeps replaying the scene Clara had shown me. When I'd become her.

And even though I'm stuffed full of Jamaican Christmas dinner, I feel hungry and sick and weak as Madame LeNoir's hands flutter in front of my face.

Passing.

Passing.

Passing.

With a huge gasp, I sit straight up in bed.

The hands.

Madame LeNoir's hands.

Oh.

Oh.

OH.

How could I not have realised?

The answer really *has* been in front of my nose the whole time.

I jump out of bed, pull random clothes on over my pyjamas and burst into the living room.

The oven clock tells me it's 11.35 pm. Freya is just turning off the TV. She doesn't notice what I'm wearing initially because it's dark and she's busy collecting a few things from the coffee table.

"What are you doing up, Lolli? The airline called back. They managed to change our flights. We're headed home tomorrow night." Finally, she turns and sees me. "Why are you dressed?"

"Don't worry about any of that. We've got to go to the house."

"What?"

I run over to her. "You know how you said you wanted to understand? If we go now, I can show you. I can show you and it will all make sense." Oh, boy. Now I've said that, I really hope I can make that happen. I hope I can show her somehow. The thing is, I know I'm right. I've worked out Madame LeNoir's secret. I'm absolutely sure of it. But showing Freya? I just don't know if I can do it.

Freya frowns. "We can't go to the house. It's almost midnight. Even if we wanted to, it takes ages to light the candles. The fireplaces. You know it's not like a modern house."

"We only need to go to the kitchen. That's all."

"Lolli …" There's a warning note in Freya's voice.

"NO!" I take another step forward. "It's important, Freya. It's really, really important. And whatever you're thinking — that I'm crazy, or acting weird, or whatever, you just have to not think that for a minute and let me show you. I need to show you what's been going on. Just … please. Please, believe me about this."

Freya stares at me for a moment or two. She takes a deep breath. "Okay," she says. "Okay then, let's go."

I grimace. "There's just one more thing."

"And what's that?"

"I need Tanice and Jada to come too."

23

We get a cab and exit it directly outside the house in the dark, still night.

I don't visualise any iron doors to lock Madame LeNoir behind. I'm not scared of her anymore. And anyway, now everything seems so clear in my head, I wonder if it was her I was locking away after all. Maybe ... maybe it was a part of me.

Freya fumbles for her keys as her phone pings. "Tanice and Jada are on their way." She looks down at me in the dim light. "Oh, Lolli. This had better be good. I think we've put Tanice through a lot."

"It will be, I promise."

We start towards the door, both of us pausing as

Freya sticks the key in the lock.

We look up at exactly the same time.

"Oh my goodness," Freya says. "It's actually snowing."

She sounds surprised. But I'm not surprised at all.

Of course it's snowing.

It's going to be that kind of a perfect night.

Freya and I light the few candles we need to safely make our way to the kitchen. There, we light the fire. It doesn't take long before the small kitchen slowly starts to warm. In the meantime, I make sure every wick in the room is aglow, giving the space a snug, homey feel.

I've just finished lighting the last candle when I turn back to the hearth.

"Hello, Elsie," I whisper, running my hand over the back of her carver chair.

"Hello, lovely girl. I feel that you have something to tell me."

"I do."

"What did you say, Loll?" Freya says from across the room.

I beckon her over.

I really hope I can make this happen.

I have to make this happen.

Taking a deep breath, I move over to the mantel and adjust the brass kettle that's sitting upon it.

And there's Clara, in the reflection. She waves at me. "Hello, Lolli. I'm so happy to see you again."

I smile back at her, then close my eyes for a moment and concentrate.

Elsie? Clara? I have to show Freya. Please?

"Put your hand on my chair and hold Freya's hand," Elsie says.

I open my eyes again to find Freya by my side.

"What's going on?" Freya asks. "Lolli?"

I hold out my hand, which she takes, confusion on her face. I rest my other hand on the high back of Elsie's chair.

"Can you see? In Elsie's chair?" I say to Freya.

"See what?"

Oh, no.

"Freya," Elsie says. "Freya, can you see me?"

Freya gasps, dropping my hand. She turns to me, horrified. "Elsie! I can hear Elsie! How did you do that? It's not funny, Lolli."

I grab her hand. "I don't think you can let go. It won't work if you let go."

"What won't work? What are you doing? When did you record Elsie's voice? Did she put you up to this?"

"It's not a recording. Here, look in the kettle. The brass kettle on the mantel."

"Lolli, this is just ..." But Freya looks. Her eyes widen when she spots Clara's reflection and her head whips around to see a blank space. Back and forth, back and forth.

Her breath sucks in.

"Hello, Freya. I don't mean to frighten you," Clara says.

Once again, Freya lets go of my hand as both of hers rise to cover her mouth. "Lolli." Her voice is muffled by her hands. "Lolli!"

"I know," I say. "But you're going to have to keep it together. I don't think we have a lot of time." I can feel Madame LeNoir upstairs. Stirring.

But at least she has no idea why I'm here.

Not yet, anyway.

Freya's hand darts out to take mine again. She squeezes it hard as she peers into the kettle again. "So like the photo in Tanice's book. But it can't be."

"It is. It's Clara," I say.

There's a long pause.

"Clara?" Freya whispers.

"Yes," Clara answers.

"It can't be. It can't be. Oh, my. It's ... this is ... amazing. Incredible. Elsie?" Freya looks around the room. "Are you really here? I can't see you."

"I'm here, darling girl."

"But where are you? Why can't I see Elsie too?" Freya asks me.

"I don't know," I tell her. "I can see her. I've seen her the whole time we've been back. But I can only see Clara as a reflection. I bet you can guess where Elsie is, though."

Freya's gaze moves immediately to Elsie's chair.

"How did you know I'd be sitting here?" Elsie chuckles. "Was I really that lazy in life? It will have to be enough to listen to me. Though goodness knows, I've had a hard enough time of getting Lolli to do that."

Freya steadies herself, holding on to the mantel. "Oh, my heart. I can't ... is this ... this is all to do with the locket?"

I nod. "I'll have to explain everything later, but yes. It's about the locket. And Madame LeNoir."

"Wait. You can see Madame LeNoir too?"

"Sort of. Madame LeNoir I only see in the walls — as part of the house. I've always been able to feel her. That's why I've never liked coming here."

Freya's free hand rises to her cheek. "Oh, Lolli. I ... I had no idea. I'm so sorry." She gasps, her eyes widening. "It all makes so much sense now."

"What does?"

"That day. That day you came in here and had that terrible reaction. Elsie said, 'Get away from her, you old bat'. I asked her to explain what she meant so many times, but she always brushed it away. It finally makes sense. And all those times you tried to tell me about spirits when you were younger ... Oh, I'm so sorry, Lolli. I really am, I—"

"It's okay," I interrupt. "I didn't understand everything until this trip. Not properly. But Elsie helped me to understand and now I have to help to free her. And Clara."

"Elsie stayed to help me," Clara explains. "The truth is, I did run away. But before I ran, Madame LeNoir stole a piece of my soul and trapped me here. After I ran away, I was lucky to live a long and happy life, but I can't be happily at rest in the twilight until that piece of my soul is released. Elsie has been so kind to have helped me. And to risk remaining, bound to me in the twilight — I'm very grateful to her."

"Helping," Freya says. "It's what she does best."

"And now I have all the time in the world to do it in," Elsie says with a chuckle.

I can feel Madame LeNoir listening, gathering herself, her energy building. I have to be quick.

I'm right.

I'm sure I'm right.

I have to be right.

"Lolli?" Elsie says.

Clara moves forward.

I look at one of them, then the other. "I know," I whisper. "I know what to do. It's not like the locket — I thought I was right about it, but when I look back, it didn't feel right. This does. But just ... before I tell you ... I want you to know I'll miss you. I'll miss you both." I meet Clara's gaze. "I wish I'd had more time to get to know you, Clara. I wish I'd helped you earlier. I wish I'd let myself see you all those years ago. Maybe I would have been able to help you sooner?"

"It's all right." Clara comes closer still. "I wish we'd had more time together too, but I understand."

"And Elsie, I wish I'd listened to you. I wanted to listen — I had so many questions that day in the ginger garden — but I couldn't. I just couldn't."

"I know. But now you can. You know how to listen now. You know how to be open and unafraid."

I nod.

"And even if you can't see me, or hear me anymore, every time you sit here, by the hearth, you'll think of me and we'll always be together that way. And that will work well, because you're going to stay in London. You're going to keep this house that has been left to you both. You're going to turn it into something wonderful. Something new and exciting and full of curiosities. And you're going to live next door. And go to school with Jada. But first, before all that, you will free us. Because I know you can. I've always known it would be you since that moment I ran you down to this very spot and held you tight."

I nod. Yes. *Yes*.

Madame LeNoir leans in, waiting, listening. The walls have ears.

Literally.

I take a deep breath. "When I tell you, I think you'll have to go and you'll have to go fast. I'm not sure what Madame LeNoir's capable of. If there's a way of stopping you, she'll do it."

A bang upstairs makes us all jump.

"Oh! It's the front door. It's Tanice and Jada. Wait one second," Freya says.

I'm not sure I have that long. "Hurry," I tell her back as she dashes off.

"Would you mind if I came over to stand next to you?" Clara says.

"Of course not!" I beckon her over. "I'm sorry I told you not to move the first time we met. I didn't mean . . ."

"It is all rather disconcerting, I know." She comes over to stand right next to me and places a hand on Elsie's chair, right beside mine. In the kettle, our eyes meet and we smile at each other.

"Are you ready, Elsie?" Clara asks.

"I'm all set for my next adventure."

"Now, you have to be calm about this . . ." Freya enters the room, hustling Tanice and Jada along as she goes. She sounds so far from calm, I almost laugh. "Here, come over here. Come over and look in the kettle."

"In the kettle?" Tanice looks at Freya as if she's crazy. But she follows her across the room, peeling her gloves off as she goes.

"Don't forget, we have to hold hands. We have to be connected."

"Here. Tanice, you take my hand, Jada, you take your mum's hand. And I'll hold Lolli's. Then look in the kettle. Both of you."

The pair approach.

Tanice gives us a doubtful look. "I need to take Jada's hand. And yours. And look in the kettle. Just before midnight on Christmas Day. Okay."

"Just do it, Mum," Jada says, taking her mother's hand.

"I know it's weird. But trust us," Freya says.

"All right then." Tanice does what she's asked. "What am I looking ..." She gasps. Turns. Does the exact same thing both Freya and I had done the first time we'd seen Clara. Back and forth, back and forth. "Look, Jada! Look!"

Jada steps closer to the kettle. "Clara. It's Clara."

Tanice lets go. "Is this some sort of a trick?"

Freya shakes her head. "No. Though I don't blame you for thinking so."

Tanice looks at Freya, then me, sizing us up. Slowly, she reaches out for Freya's hand and peers into the kettle once more.

"Hello," Clara says, with a smile. "I've always wanted to meet you both properly."

"It really is Clara." Tanice's mouth is practically on the ground. "But ... how? Why?"

"Don't forget me!" Elsie pipes up.

Tanice reels back once more. "Oh my goodness. Elsie. Elsie too?" She scours the room. "It can't be! It's not possible! Where are you? Where is she?"

"In her chair, of course," Jada says.

"You can see her?" I ask.

"No, I just knew she would be."

There's another bang from upstairs. And it's not the front door this time. Slowly, surely, Madame LeNoir has gathered herself from all corners of the house. Pulled herself from every crevice and nook. I ready myself. "I have to do this," I say. "Now."

"We're ready, my lovely," Elsie says, looking up at me from her chair.

"Clara?" I move my gaze to the kettle. She nods at me encouragingly.

Everyone else holds tight, ready to hear what I have to say.

As does Madame LeNoir, hovering above, like a fierce, dark storm cloud.

I begin.

"Clara, there is no object. Madame LeNoir only made you believe there was. That scene that you showed me, in the attic room. She mesmerised you. She made you believe you were bound to an object in this place.

But you weren't. The clues were right there all the time. You told me yourself you didn't think Madame LeNoir had the ability to capture a piece of your soul. But you knew she had the ability to mesmerise. And to deceive. When she told you she'd bound a piece of your soul to an object, that was a lie. But it was true when she said you'd never find the object. You couldn't, because it didn't exist. She'd set you an impossible task. And it's that task that has kept you prisoner here all this time – that never-ending search. Your soul was always whole, Clara. It's always been up to you to leave. I think that now you know the truth, you'll be able to pass into the twilight. And if you go, Elsie and Madame LeNoir will go with you."

In the kettle's bright reflection, Clara's eyes stare back at me, shocked. She looks as if she's just awoken from a horrible dream.

"Clara?"

She shakes her head from side to side, her curls bobbing, her hands rising to cup her mouth.

"I know it's hard to believe, but I'm sure it's true. I just can't believe I didn't see it sooner. I mean, you even showed me that scene and I didn't realise. It's just that I believed it because you believed it –

you were so convinced that your soul was torn in two. And I knew that it was possible to bind one soul to another because you'd done it yourself with Madame LeNoir and Elsie."

"You're right," she finally whispers. "You're right. It is true. But how could I not have known? How could I not have realised? I knew Madame LeNoir had no such abilities. Why did I ever believe her?"

"Because she mesmerised you. You can't blame yourself for that."

"But I wasted so much of Elsie's time. Your time. Oh, what a fool I've been." Clara's face falls into her hands. "I'm so sorry. I'm so, so sorry, Elsie."

But Elsie doesn't look like she's sorry. Elsie is beaming. "I told you," she says to me. "I told you you could do this, Lolli, and you did."

Bang. Bang.

Crash.

The attic door.

I turn to Clara. "It's all right, Clara. We understand. What's important now is that you go. Go!" I implore. "Before it's too late. Madame LeNoir's anger has made her stronger over the years. She might be capable of more than we know."

It happens just like that time I'd stood at the bottom of the stairs. Madame LeNoir charges. Angry and hateful she comes barrelling down. Growing, doubling, pulsing, rolling. Once again, I am glued to the spot, the air drawn from my lungs, my head tight.

She is coming for me.

For all of us.

But this time I'm not scared.

This time I won't cower.

Creak, crack, the house shifts and groans.

Crash, something falls to the floor.

"Let go, Clara! Let go!" I yell into the kettle.

Elsie's hand darts up to take Clara's and her eyes, unblinking, meet mine.

For what I know will be the very last time in this world.

The house begins to shake, the porcelain on the sideboard rattling like chattering teeth.

She is coming. Hurtling downwards. Incensed.

She has lost at her own game and she knows it.

"We love you, Elsie," Freya says. "Go well, Clara."

My eyes never leave Elsie's. *Say hello,* I beg her silently. *Say hello to my mother. To Clementine.*

Of course, she says. *Of course.*

We'll be all right, I tell her. *Freya and me. We'll be all right.*

I never doubted it for a moment, precious girl, she replies.

I glance at Clara. Silently, she nods her thanks. I nod back. We don't need to say anything. Everything is going to be as it should be. As it should always have been.

The kitchen door slams.

Boom.

A final jolt of the blue-and-white porcelain.

And the house stills.

It's over.

Done.

Elsie's chair is empty. I focus on the brass kettle. But I already know. I can feel it. They are gone. All three of them are gone – Clara, Elsie and Madame LeNoir.

They're gone.

Really gone.

But the strange thing is, while I find my face is wet with tears, I'm not sad.

The house is empty.

They are free.

And it never felt so good to have lost something.

In the silence, the remaining four of us look at each other. And then we begin to laugh crazy, nervous laughter as everyone drops hands.

"The house," Freya says, looking up, down and all around. "It feels so *different*."

"Lighter somehow," Jada says.

"Free," Tanice agrees. She shakes her head in wonder. "But I can't believe it! If I hadn't seen it with my own eyes ..."

We laugh again, not knowing where to start. What to say.

"It was just ... it was crazy, Lolli. Amazing!" Jada jumps up and down. "I saw a ghost! A real ghost! And I heard Elsie. I can't even."

Freya simply can't stop laughing. And crying. And laughing. She stops. Wipes her eyes. And then starts crying again.

The four of us hug and laugh and cry and one thing is for certain ... there's no way any of us are going to sleep tonight.

It's Beebee who finally gets us to pull ourselves together, because Tanice's phone pings.

"Beebee's wondering what on earth we could possibly be doing out on the streets at one thirty in the morning," she reads her text.

"Better not tell her," Jada says. "Beebee doesn't like anything to do with duppy."

"Jamaican ghosts," Tanice explains. "She'd worry. She wouldn't believe they could be friendly."

"Well, thankfully the non-friendly one has now disappeared," Freya says.

"It's a pity Elsie had to go with her," Jada says. "It would have been nice to have her around. Sitting in her chair. Hanging out."

I shake my head. "No. That would have been for us. Not her. She's happy now. And so is Clara. I just know it. Hopefully Madame LeNoir too."

"I'm not sure Madame LeNoir knows how to be happy," Tanice says.

"Maybe you don't need to know how, in the twilight world," I say. "Maybe you just *are*."

"I hope you're right," Freya says. "I think everyone deserves that. Maybe even Madame LeNoir." She sighs. "Come on then. We don't want to worry Beebee.

We'll walk you back to your apartment and get a cab from there."

The four of us snuff out the candles and close up the house, which now feels strangely like … just a house. A shell. Old wooden walls and rooms with possibilities.

Outside, I look up and see that the snow has stopped falling. But there's enough that the world has become white and fresh and clean. And, in the dead of night, the white blanket that's been left on every surface is unmarked.

Everyone has a million questions about spirits. I explain as best I can, including Elsie's theory about portals. All the way to Tanice and Jada's apartment, we talk about spirits and the house and make tiny piles of snow wherever we can. It quickly turns to slush, but we don't care. Tonight we have no cares. Everything is new again.

"It's true what Elsie said. We're going to move back to London," I announce.

"Freya's going to change the house and make her cabinet of curiosities. And I'm going to go to school with Jada."

Tanice smiles. "The house is ready for a change. I'm looking forward to helping out, especially as

I've seen Freya's collection. It's amazing. That scene that Elsie set up with the mole and the tea trolley … I laughed so hard when I saw it the first time."

"I know," Freya replies. "It's so Elsie. Oh, I'm missing her all over again."

Tanice reaches over to touch Freya's arm. "We all are. But this will be so good for you both. A fresh start."

"Yes, a fresh start," Freya replies, taking my hand. "Starting tonight."

"This morning," Jada corrects, making us all laugh.

"We're really going to do it." I look up at Freya. "We're going to move. We're going to open up the cabinet of curiosities."

"I think you might be right." She squeezes my hand.

One.

Two.

Three.

And you know something?

I am right.

Because that's exactly what we do.

Epilogue

The spring sun streaming down warm on the back of my neck, I reach out and brush my fingers over the sparkling pieces of mosaic. I can even find some of the pieces I clipped myself – the pretty yellow glass with the gold vein running through it. The finished piece is just like Suzie had shown me that day in her sketchbook – a sun, with a woman's face in the middle.

Elsie's face.

I remember Suzie had asked me, at the time. "Maybe it reminds you of someone?" she'd said.

Back then, I didn't want to admit that it did. I couldn't think about Elsie being gone from this world. It hurt too much. But now I see her in all her glory. She is the central piece of the large mosaic and the sun's rays — Elsie's rays — curl and swirl along the wall, reaching out to touch everyone.

It's a beautiful tribute.

Freya comes to stand beside me. "It really is gorgeous, isn't it?"

I nod. "I love it. So much."

"Are you nervous?" She swivels me around by my shoulders.

"A bit."

"Well, that's only normal. You know, I read some poll a while ago in a newspaper. Apparently public speaking comes out as people's number-one fear. Then heights and things like bugs. Those things I expected. But I was surprised to learn people are more scared of clowns than ghosts."

"What? Are you serious? Clowns are *way* scarier than ghosts."

Freya thinks about this for a moment. "I didn't used to think so, but now that I've met some nice ghosts, care of you, I'll go along with that. I guess the important thing to remember is that everyone here knew Elsie and they'll all totally be behind what you have to say. Which I'm sure is wonderful."

"I hope so." Freya had offered to help me write my speech, or to at least read over it, but I told her it was something I wanted to write by myself. I wanted it to be a surprise. Now, of course, I'm doubting every sentence on the piece of paper clutched in my sweaty hand.

"Of course it's wonderful. And look, they're all waiting to listen to you."

Freya swivels me around again so that I can see some of the people who have gathered. I immediately see Beebee and Tanice. Jada waves furiously at me, grinning.

"Yeah, thanks. Now I'm nervous. But too late. It looks like it's time." Suzie is beckoning me over.

Freya and I make our way to stand beside Suzie, up front of the small crowd that's gathered in a park near the house for the mosaic opening. I've already had my photo taken with some of the Tiny Pieces crew for the local paper, including Britt and Alfie. I was so happy when Britt came back to Tiny Pieces and I know now to give her the space she needs. Funnily enough, another dog – Toby – had made it into the photo today as well. Britt's looking after him while his owner is away visiting her daughter for a week.

She's walking someone else's dog regularly too, but says she isn't ready for business cards yet. We've agreed she'll let me know when it's time and we'll design them together.

I take my place beside Suzie. Freya goes to stand beside her mother, who is wearing crazily inappropriate heels for a park. We've seen Robyn once since that day she dropped by our apartment unannounced. We went out for high tea at a fancy hotel, because Freya said it was the place her mother would be least likely to make a scene. There were a few awkward moments, but we mostly managed to fill them with more tea and ribbon sandwiches. It was — I'm not sure what to call it. A start? I guess that's as good a word as any.

Suzie introduces a woman who is apparently some kind of famous comedian. She grew up around here and has agreed to officially open the mosaic. "I'd rather it was just us talking, but famous people mean more photographs and, hopefully, funding," Suzie had told me. I vaguely listen in to what the comedian has to say. I think she's funny, because people laugh, but all I can think about is what *I'm* about to say and the five million ways I could possibly get it wrong and everyone will laugh at me for all the wrong reasons.

Well, that and Elsie, of course.

I think about her too.

A lot.

Finally, it's my turn.

Suzie introduces me, lowering the microphone.

And I begin.

"Elsie really was like the sun," I say, my gaze moving over to the mosaic. "She gave light and warmth to us all, her rays reaching out to touch everyone and nourish them ... whether they liked it or not."

There's a chuckle or two at this. I'm sure, like me, there were plenty of times Elsie gave her opinion or help when it was decidedly not wanted. Needed, sure, but not wanted.

"For a while, after she'd gone, I panicked. I thought that was it. I thought that everything she'd helped to nurture and flourish inside me would wither and die. That the soil beneath my feet would crumble. But then I looked down and I saw that Elsie had this covered. Because Elsie had made sure that my roots were strong. She'd also checked that there were lots of other strong roots surrounding me. And in case you don't get it yet, the soil is Spitalfields and we have to look after it. And each other."

Now everyone really laughs.

Okay, they get it.

"I think, sometimes, it's scary. To be like Elsie. It feels like too much effort to reach out. To care. To think about other people. To join in. To show up. Elsie had a lot to say about all of this before she died. She was worried about me. That I didn't – wouldn't – couldn't – connect with other people. She kept poking me about it. Over and over. And you know what? I hated it. I ignored her. I didn't listen. And then … well, when I was finally ready to listen, it was too late. She was gone. Of course, Elsie being Elsie, she wasn't going to let a little thing like death stop her. She still managed to get through. She just made me work it out myself. She made me promise to come back to Spitalfields. And she finally got me to understand that while it might feel safe to keep myself to myself – that it might feel easier and smarter – what it actually meant was that I was alone. Turns out it's not much fun being alone.

"I've been trying to look at lots of things differently because of Elsie. When I saw the whole mosaic for the first time, sure, I thought it was beautiful. And I knew how much work had gone into it. But the longer I looked at it, the more I saw past its beauty. I began to realise that Elsie would want me to see the mosaic in a completely different way. She wouldn't want me to take in just the surface — the lovely sun, the glorious colours, not even her face, which I miss so much. No. What she'd want me to really notice is what lies beneath all that. What she'd want me to take away from the mosaic is something else entirely ... that really the mosaic only looks the way it does because of what makes it possible in the first place. And that's the cement that's holding it together. That cement? That's us. All of us. It might be grey and not as pretty as the glass that lies on top of it, but the cement is what really matters. Because without the cement, there's nothing — just tiny pieces. Scattered, tiny pieces. It's only because of the cement that something beautiful forms. Something more. Something truly beautiful."

Everything is quiet. Too quiet.

Oh, no. They hated it.

Slowly, I lift my gaze from the page.

Everyone is staring at me, silent and still.

My eyes find Freya in the crowd. She isn't moving either, but it looks like tears are sliding down her cheeks.

"That's ... um ... that's it. All I wanted to say. I think it's time for cake now and I know some of you feel as strongly about cake as I do, so ..." I go to scuttle away, but Suzie moves into action and catches me, pulling me into her side.

It's like everyone wakes up then. There's a roar of laughter. I hear the word "cake" mentioned a few times. People look at each other. And then they all start clapping. Really, really loudly. Freya claps so loudly I think her hands will hurt later.

And somehow I know, somewhere, Elsie and Clara and Clementine are clapping too.

Author's Note

Several years ago, I had a magical Christmas in a wintry London. My family and I booked an incredible four-bedroom houseboat called The Harpy, right next to Tower Bridge and stayed there for a week on the Thames, mostly gaping at the view. During that visit, a friend had told me to book tickets for the Christmas installation at Dennis Severs' house in nearby Spitalfields. I didn't really know what to expect. When I looked it up, it seemed to be a sort of "not museum" place, a mishmash of time periods and ideas. When I read reviews about the house, they were mixed. Some people adored it. Others loathed it.

When I turned up at the black front door of 18 Folgate Street, I have to admit I was a little worried.

I needn't have been.

As Dennis Severs himself said, "You either see it, or you don't". And, oh, I saw it.

From the wonderful, warm, welcoming kitchen with its translucent, shining jellies and jaunty string of gingerbread men, to the inviting Victorian parlour crammed full of Christmas splendour, I drank it in.

And I knew, knew, knew, I would have to write about this place.

The House in Spitalfields that appears in The Ghost Locket is not Dennis Severs' House. It is different in many ways. But in many ways it is also similar. I would love to encourage everyone to go and experience this wonderful place for themselves.

Finally, I would like to note that Tiny Pieces is a fictional organisation, born out of some beautiful mosaics I viewed in London that were produced by the Hackney Mosaic Project.

Acknowledgements

Novels are like jigsaw puzzles in many ways, and I've not yet met an author who doesn't need some help putting the puzzle pieces together. Thanks to all who contributed along the way. To all at Walker Books Australia, who always seem to understand my strange little stories and help to turn them into what I actually meant to say. And an especially big thank you to Linsay Knight for her continued support over eleven books – it's been such a pleasure working with you. To Rovina Cai for yet another brilliant cover. To my family who read early on (as per usual, the finished product does not at all resemble the version I gave you). Thanks also to my agent Annabel Barker. And to Allison Tait and Megan Daley for our continued larks at *Your Kid's Next Read*.

About the Author

Allison Rushby, the daughter of an author, was raised on a wholesome and steady diet of classic English literature. Some of her favourite books, re-read countless dog-eared times include Rumer Godden's *The Dolls' House*, Frances Hodgson Burnett's *The Secret Garden*, Dodie Smith's *I Capture the Castle* and Noel Streatfeild's Shoes series. She has always been a fan of cities with long, winding histories, wild, overgrown cemeteries, red brick Victorian museums, foxes and ivy. She prefers to write with a cup of Darjeeling tea by her side, a dog at her feet and a cat curled up in her lap. Her work includes *When This Bell Rings*, which was a Notable in the CBCA Awards, *The Mulberry Tree*, which was shortlisted in the West Australia Young Readers' Book Award, *The Turnkey of Highgate Cemetery*, which was awarded Best Children's Crime Novel in the Davitt Awards and *The Seven Keys*, which was longlisted in the Davitt Awards.

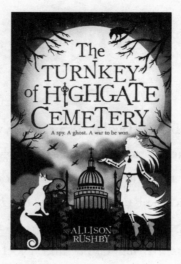

Twelve-year-old ghost-girl Flossie Birdwhistle is the Turnkey at London's Highgate Cemetery, where she cares for all the buried souls and keeps them at rest.

During the Blitz bombings of World War II even the dead are unsettled, and Flossie encounters the ghost of a German soldier spying amongst the wreckage. What *is* the magical object he carries, and *how* is he moving between the wartime worlds of the living and the dead?

A sinister supernatural plot is afoot, and courageous Flossie must fight for her cemetery and her country.

"Cleverly weaves a supernatural plot into a page-turning mystery with a strong heroine at its centre."
BOOKS & PUBLISHING